G000069554

CIMA

Managerial Paper P5

INTEGRATED MANAGEMENT

For exams in 2009

Practice & Revision Kit

In this January 2009 new edition

- We discuss the **best strategies** for revising and taking your CIMA exams
- We show you how to be well prepared for the **2009 exams**
- We give you **lots of great guidance** on tackling questions
- We show you how you can **build your own exams**
- We provide you with **three** mock exams including the **November 2008 exam**

BPP's **i-Pass** product also supports this paper.

BPP LEARNING MEDIA

First edition 2005
Fifth edition January 2009

ISBN 9780 7517 6549 6
(previous ISBN 9780 7517 5189 5)

British Library Cataloguing-in-Publication Data
A catalogue record for this book
is available from the British Library

Published by

BPP Learning Media Ltd
BPP House, Aldine Place
London W12 8AA

www.bpp.com/learningmedia

Printed in the United Kingdom

Your learning materials, published by BPP Learning Media Ltd, are printed on paper sourced from sustainable, managed forests.

We are grateful to the Chartered Institute of Management Accountants for permission to reproduce past examination questions. The answers to past examination questions have been prepared by BPP Learning Media Ltd.

Contents

Page

Question index

The headings in this checklist/index indicate the main topics of questions, but questions often cover several different topics.

BPP LEARNING MEDIA

	Marks	Time allocation Mins	Page number	
			Question	Answer

Part B: Project Management

Part C: Strategic Management

Planning your question practice

Our guidance from page xxvii shows you how to organise your question practice, either by attempting questions from each syllabus area or by **building your own exams** – tackling questions as a series of practice exams.

Extra guidance

You can find additional guidance on a number of questions in this kit on BPP's website: www.bpp.com/cima/extra-question-guidance

Topic index

Listed below are the key Paper P5 syllabus topics and the numbers of the questions in this Kit covering those topics.

If you need to concentrate your practice and revision on certain topics or if you want to attempt all available questions that refer to a particular subject, you will find this index useful.

Note that Section A questions are not included in this index.

Syllabus topic	Question numbers
Resource-based view	72, 78
Risk	39, 79
Scientific Management	19
Stakeholders	47, 58, 77, Mock 2 Q2, Mock 2 Q6
Strategic analysis	53, 60, 61, 62, 65, 69, 70, 78
Strategic theory	56, 57, 59, 67, 68, 76, 77, Mock 1 Q7
Stress management	14
SWOT	61
Time management	6, 21, 75
Tools for project managers	33, 35, 36, 38, 74, Mock 2 Q5
Transaction cost view (Williamson, Coase)	71
Tuckman	24
Value chain	72
Work Breakdown Structure	48, 74

Using your BPP Learning Media Practice and Revision Kit

Tackling revision and the exam

You can significantly improve your chances of passing by tackling revision and the exam in the right ways. Our advice is based on recent feedback from CIMA examiners. You may be surprised to know that much examiner advice is the same whatever the exam, and the reasons why many students fail don't vary much between subjects and exam levels.

- We look at the dos and don'ts of revising for, and taking, CIMA exams. Making the most of your revision time can make a big, big difference to how well-prepared you are for the exam
- We focus on Paper P5; we discuss revising the syllabus, what to do (and what not to do) in the exam, how to approach different types of question and ways of obtaining easy marks

Selecting questions

We provide signposts to help you plan your revision.

- A full **question index**
- A **topic index** listing all the questions that cover key topics, so that you can locate the questions that provide practice on these topics, and see the different ways in which they might be examined
- A **BPP question plan** highlighting the most important questions and explaining why you should attempt them
- **Build your own exams**, showing you how you can practise questions in a series of exams

Making the most of question practice

At BPP we realise that you need more than just questions and model answers to get the most from your question practice.

- Our **Top tips** provide essential advice on tackling questions, presenting answers and the key points that answers need to include
- We show you how you can pick up **Easy marks** on questions, as we know that picking up all readily available marks often can make the difference between passing and failing
- We summarise **Examiner's comments** to show you how students who sat the exam coped with the questions
- We refer to the **BPP 2008 Study Text** for detailed coverage of the topics covered in each question

Attempting mock exams

There are three mock exams that provide practice at coping with the pressures of the exam day. We strongly recommend that you attempt them under exam conditions. **Mock exams 1 and 2** reflect the question styles and syllabus coverage of the exam; **Mock exam 3** is the actual November 2008 exam. To help you get the most out of doing these exams, we not only provide help with each answer, but also guidance on how you should have approached the whole exam.

How to revise

☑ Plan your revision

At the start of your revision period, you should draw up a **timetable** to plan how long you will spend on each subject and how you will revise each area. You need to consider the total time you have available and also the time that will be required to revise for other exams you're taking.

☑ Practise Practise Practise

The **more exam-standard questions** you do, the **more likely you are to pass** the exam. Practising full questions will mean that you'll get used to the time pressure of the exam. When the time is up, you should note where you've got to and then try to complete the question, giving yourself practice everything that the question tests.

☑ Revise enough

Make sure that your revision covers the breadth of the syllabus, as in most papers most topics could be examined in a compulsory question. However it is true that some topics are **key** – they often appear in compulsory questions or are a particular interest of the examiner – and you need to spend sufficient time revising these. Make sure you know the **basics** – the fundamental calculations, proformas and report layouts.

☑ Deal with your difficulties

Difficult areas are topics you find dull and pointless, or subjects that you found problematic when you were studying them. You mustn't become negative about these topics; instead you should build up your knowledge by reading the **Passcards** and using the **Quick quiz** questions in the Study Text to test yourself. When practising questions in the Kit, go back to the Text if you're struggling.

☑ Learn from your mistakes

Having completed a question you must try to look at your answer critically. Always read the **Top tips** guidance in the answers; it's there to help you. Look at **Easy marks** to see how you could have quickly gained credit on the questions that you've done. As you go through the Kit, it's worth noting any traps you've fallen into, and key points in the **Top tips** or **Examiner's comments** sections, and referring to these notes in the days before the exam. Aim to learn at least one new point from each question you attempt, a technical point perhaps or a point on style or approach.

☑ Read the examiners' guidance

We refer throughout this Kit to **Examiner's comments**; these are available on CIMA's website. As well as highlighting weaknesses, examiners' reports often provide clues to future questions, as many examiners will quickly test again areas where problems have arisen. CIMA's website also contains articles that are relevant to this paper, which you should read.

☑ Complete all three mock exams

You should attempt the **Mock exams** at the end of the Kit under **strict exam conditions** to gain experience of selecting questions, managing your time and producing answers.

How NOT to revise

☒ Revise selectively

Examiners are well aware that some students try to forecast the contents of exams, and only revise those areas that they think will be examined. Examiners try to prevent this by doing the unexpected, for example setting the same topic in successive sittings or setting topics in compulsory questions that have previously only been examined in optional questions. Remember you have little choice of questions in most CIMA exams.

☒ Spend all the revision period reading

You cannot pass the exam just by learning the contents of Passcards, Course Notes or Study Texts. You have to develop your **application skills** by practising questions.

☒ Audit the answers

This means reading the answers and guidance without having attempted the questions. Auditing the answers gives you **false reassurance** that you would have tackled the questions in the best way and made the points that our answers do. The feedback we give in our answers will mean more to you if you've attempted the questions and thought through the issues.

☒ Practise some types of question, but not others

Although you may find the numerical parts of certain papers challenging, you shouldn't just practise calculations. These papers will also contain written elements, and you therefore need to spend time practising written question parts as well.

☒ Get bogged down

Don't spend a lot of time worrying about all the minute detail of certain topic areas, and leave yourself insufficient time to cover the rest of the syllabus. Remember that a key skill in the exam is the ability to **concentrate on what's important** and this applies to your revision as well.

☒ Overdo studying

Studying for too long without interruption will mean your studying becomes less effective. A five minute break each hour will help. You should also make sure that you are leading a **healthy lifestyle** (proper meals, good sleep and some times when you're not studying).

How to PASS your exams

☑ Prepare for the day

Make sure you set at least one alarm (or get an alarm call), and allow plenty of time to get to the exam hall. You should have your route planned in advance and should listen on the radio for potential travel problems. You should check the night before to see that you have pens, pencils, erasers, watch, calculator with spare batteries, also exam documentation and evidence of identity.

☑ Select the right questions

You should select the optional questions you feel you can answer **best**, basing your selection on the topics covered, the requirements of the question, how easy it will be to apply the requirements and the availability of easy marks.

☑ Plan your three hours

You need to make sure that you will be answering the correct number of questions, and that you spend the right length of time on each question – this will be determined by the number of marks available. Each mark carries with it a **time allocation** of **1.8 minutes**. A 25 mark question therefore should be selected, completed and checked in 45 minutes. With some papers, it's better to do certain types of question first or last.

☑ Read the questions carefully

To score well, you must follow the requirements of the question, understanding what aspects of the subject area are being covered, and the tasks you will have to carry out. Make sure you are aware of what the **question verbs require**; CIMA provides a table of verbs used together with their meaning as part of the question paper (see p xxv in this Kit). The requirements will also determine what information and examples you should provide. Reading the question scenarios carefully will help you decide what **issues** to discuss, what **techniques** to use, **information** and **examples** to include and how to **organise** your answer.

☑ Plan your answers

Five minutes of planning plus twenty-five minutes of writing is certain to earn you more marks than thirty minutes of writing. Consider when you're planning how your answer should be **structured**, what the **format** should be and **how long** each part should take.

Confirm before you start writing that your plan makes **sense**, covers **all relevant points** and does not include **irrelevant material.**

☑ Show evidence of judgement

Remember that examiners aren't just looking for a display of knowledge; they want to see how well you can **apply** the knowledge you have. Evidence of application and judgement will include writing answers that only contain **relevant** material, using the material in scenarios to **support** what you say, **criticising** the **limitations** and **assumptions** of the techniques you've used and making **reasonable recommendations** that follow from your discussion.

☑ Stay until the end of the exam

Use any spare time to **check and recheck** your script. This includes checking you have filled out the candidate details correctly, you have labelled question parts and workings clearly, you have used headers and underlining effectively and spelling, grammar and arithmetic are correct.

How to FAIL your exams

☒ Don't do enough questions

If you don't attempt sufficient questions on the paper, you are making it harder for yourself to pass the questions that you do attempt. If for example you don't do a 20 mark question, then you will have to score 50 marks out of 80 marks on the rest of the paper, and therefore have to obtain 63% of the marks on the questions you do attempt. Failing to attempt all of the paper is symptomatic of poor time management, poor question selection or failure to revise the whole syllabus.

☒ Include irrelevant material

Markers are given detailed mark guides and will not give credit for irrelevant content. Therefore you should **NOT** braindump into your answer all you know about a broad subject area; the markers will only give credit for what is **relevant**, and you will also be showing that you lack the ability to **judge what's important.** Similarly forcing irrelevant theory into every answer won't gain you marks, nor will providing uncalled for features such as situation analyses, executive summaries and background information.

☒ Fail to use the details in the scenario

General answers or reproductions of old answers that don't refer to what is in the scenario in **this** question won't score enough marks to pass.

☒ Copy out the scenario details

Examiners see **selective** use of the right information as a key skill. If you copy out chunks of the scenario that aren't relevant to the question, or don't use the information to support your own judgements, you won't achieve good marks.

☒ Don't do what the question asks

Failing to provide all the examiner asks for will limit the marks you score. The question part may include two requirements and you should answer **both**, not just the first one. If the requirements specify you should present your work in a certain format (memo, report) there will be marks for doing so, and you will not obtain these marks if you do not use the format specified. You will also decrease your chances by not providing an answer with enough **depth** – producing a single line bullet point list when the examiner asks for a discussion.

☒ Present your work poorly

Markers will only be able to give you credit if they can read your writing. There are also plenty of other things as well that will make it more difficult for markers to reward you. Examples include:

- Not using black or blue ink
- Not showing clearly which question you're attempting
- Scattering question parts from the same question throughout your answer booklet
- Not showing clearly workings or the results of your calculations

Paragraphs that are too long or which lack headers also won't help markers and hence won't help you.

Revising P5

General comments

The objective test in Section A of the paper gives the examiner the chance to test a large proportion of the syllabus in every exam. This means that you will need to revise **all areas of the syllabus**. During your studying, you will have covered the whole syllabus as you worked through the Study Text. The next step is to start your revision.

Bear in mind that any area of the syllabus can be tested in **any section of the paper**. Again, this means that you must have enough knowledge of all areas of the syllabus. **Therefore question spotting is difficult and not advised.** The nature of the paper suggests that the examiner will draw widely upon all of its relevant aspects.

The examiner commented in her report on the May 2008 exam that good candidates had 'appeared to be very well prepared. They demonstrated a firm grasp of the theory, had read the scenarios and questions very carefully, had planned their answers before starting to write and then applied the relevant theory, taking full account of the scenario context in their answers.'

Our analysis of the examiner's comments on past exams, together with our experience of preparing students for this type of exam, suggest that to pass Paper P5 you will need to develop a number of **key skills**. Think about what the examiner said in her report as you read through our key skills guidance. We list these skills here.

1. **Planning** your answer to ensure **relevance** and **completeness**. When you sketch your answer plan, think about **what** the examiner wants and how you will answer this. Then make short notes covering the points you will put in your answer.

2. Understanding and applying **the CIMA active verbs**. The most common learning verbs in P5 are **explain**, **evaluate** and **analyse**. You need to understand what these mean and practice answering questions which use them. Refer to 'What the examiner means' to ensure you are clear on their exact meaning. Look at answers to questions in the kit and see how these are structured. In particular **do not stick to bullet points** and **be prepared to comment and explain**.

3. **Knowledge of the syllabus** is essential for all sections of the exam.

   You may have a good memory or just be lucky in exams! It is more than likely, however, at this stage in your exam career that you use mindmaps, mnemonics or some other memory aid to help you learn.

4. Knowing **how** and **when** to **use theory** in your answer. You may know a lot of theory but you also need to make sure you only **apply** it if this is relevant to the question.

5. Producing an answer that is more than a general analysis, ie is **tailored** to the particular organisation in the exam question.

   Answers at this level must contain a balance of practical and theoretical points as well as relate to the particular organisation and its specific issues.

Question practice

Your revision time should be spent learning the material and practising questions. Use our advice on **key skills** to extract the maximum benefit from question practice.

It is vital to practise all three types of question. Section A style questions are easier to practise when your time is limited, and you may feel that Section C questions are important as they are worth 25 marks each. Make sure, however, that you don't neglect Section B question practice. These are compulsory and you can't guess the answers.

Page xxvii gives you a **question plan** and you must attempt all of the boxed questions to give yourself a good chance of passing the exam.

If you find that you are struggling in the early stages of your revision with some questions, then don't be afraid to look at the answers and use them as a revision tool. You can then go back to the Passcards or Study Text and highlight the areas that you need to revise further. In the later stages of revision and when you are attempting the mock exams, you should avoid looking at the answers. The **mock exams** in particular should be attempted **under exam conditions** to give you a fair idea of how well you are progressing.

Develop time management skills

Examiners have routinely identified time management as being a problem. It is particularly important, therefore, that you practise all types of question, only allowing yourself the time you will be given in the exam.

Develop business awareness

Candidates with good business awareness can score well in a number of areas.

- Reading articles in CIMA's *Financial Management* magazine and the business press will help you understand the practical application of many of the theories covered throughout the syllabus.
- Being aware of the work of different departments in your own organisation (or others you know about) will help you discuss the practical management issues involved in running a business.

This kind of awareness will not only give you ideas on which to model your solutions to the business/management problems passed in exam scenarios. It will also help you to think practically and realistically about the solutions you propose – which is what real-world management is all about.

Develop your exam technique

Another good reason to practise past and exam-style questions is to get into good habits for the exam, in terms of:

- How to make best use of your reading time
- How to ensure that you obey the examiner's instructions
- How to analyse the precise requirements of each question – and stick to them in your answers

We will give some guidance on tackling each of the P5 question types, a bit further on.

Passing the P5 exam

Displaying the right qualities

The examiner will expect you to display the following qualities.

Qualities required	
Depth of knowledge	Make sure that you write enough to show your depth of knowledge. One line bullet points don't generate sufficient depth.
Application skills	You must be able to **apply** relevant theories, models and frameworks to the scenario given. This means that you will need to use your knowledge to find solutions. It will not be enough to quote a standard solution and state, for example, 'Porter's five forces are relevant here'. You will need to look at the scenario and say **why** they are relevant for that particular company.
Requirements focus	You must focus on the question requirements rather than writing down everything you know about a particular topic. This is known as brain dumping! You must ask yourself if you can relate what you are saying to the scenario in some way. If you can, it is worth doing.
Good planning	Prepare answer plans for all parts of Section C questions before you start answering them. This will ensure the answer is relevant and there is no duplication between different parts. There are several ways of planning. You can make notes on the exam paper and number them in the order you are going to write about them. You can use mind maps. You can also try brainstorming. This is writing down key words and how they relate to the scenario.

Avoiding weaknesses

There have now been eight sittings of P5 and so the examiner has commented on weaknesses that occur in many students' answers at every sitting.

Try to avoid these pitfalls:

- **Inadequate preparation**. Make sure you have covered all areas of the syllabus and practised all types of questions.
- **Lack of theoretical knowledge**. Again, this means having adequate knowledge of all areas of the syllabus.
- **Lack of depth of knowledge**. As mentioned above, make sure you explain fully what you mean, to demonstrate your depth of knowledge.
- **Repetition of scenario material**. The examiner wants to you discuss items in the scenario but doesn't want chunks of the scenario to be copied onto the answer paper.
- **Lack of time management**. It is important to stick to the time limit for each question. Move onto the next question when the time is up.
- **Focusing on to a single word in the question**. Make sure you satisfy the full question requirement. Don't just read the work 'appraisal' for example, and write all you know about appraisals.
- **Quoting theories that aren't relevant to the scenario**. You won't score any marks for discussing a theory which is not relevant to the scenario.
- **Lack of application**. The examiner wants you to apply the issues being examined to the scenario in the question.

Using the reading time

During the 20 minutes reading time you are allowed to write on the exam paper but not in your exam answer book.

We recommend that you spend the reading time:

- Answering as many as possible of the objective test questions
- Planning answers to longer Section B questions
- Selecting which Section C question you will do and jotting down ideas for answering these

The examiner however, has said that the reading time should be used to analyse the question requirement carefully; look at the whole question and break down the question requirement.

Choosing which questions to answer first

There are no strict rules on which questions you should answer first. It is probably a good idea to start with the objective test questions and then do Section B because all of these are compulsory. **You must stick to the time plan of 1.8 minutes per mark**. This means you should have finished Section A and B half way through the exam time. You could do Section C questions first if you prefer essay style questions but again, make sure you stick to the time plan.

Approach to questions

Most Section B and Section C questions will involve a scenario. Many students find these difficult to deal with. If you have this problem, try the approach outlined below.

Step 1 Read the requirements first to identify the knowledge areas being tested and see if there are links between them. This helps with focusing on what's important in the scenario. Ensure you can define technical terms used so that you know what the question is about.

Step 2 Identify the action verbs in the requirement because this conveys the level of skill you need to exhibit (eg define, illustrate, evaluate require quite different skills see what the examiner means list on page 30).

Step 3 Identify the parts to the question. For example a requirement with 'and' implies two parts to the question that may be linked.

Step 4 Check mark allocation of each section. This shows you the depth anticipated and helps allocate time

Step 5 Read scenario/preamble and put key points under headings related to requirements (eg by marginal notes, highlighting or jotting down on page).

Step 6 Scribble a plan answer (just a few words jotted untidily under the key requirements not a summary that someone else could write the answer from. Perhaps a brainstorm or spider diagram/mindmap).

Step 7 Write answer.

Discussion questions

Remember that **depth of discussion** is also important. Discussions will often consist of paragraphs containing 2-3 sentences. Each paragraph should:

- **Make a point**
- **Explain the point** (you must demonstrate **why** the point is important)
- **Illustrate the point** (with material or analysis from the scenario, perhaps an example from real-life)

Gaining the easy marks

There are likely to be easier marks available for stating the risks you've spotted in the scenario, also for defining key topics in general terms when the question doesn't require you to link these definitions in with the scenario. The examiner has stated that on some papers you may see an essay question that doesn't link into a scenario and this type of question may well be easier than other scenario-linked questions on that paper.

Often the easier marks will be in the first part(s) of the question. If they are in subsequent parts, we would not recommend that you do these parts first, as question requirements and hence answers will generally have a logical flow to them. However you must give yourself enough time on these parts, and not get bogged down in the more difficult question parts.

There will also be some easy marks available for answering using an appropriate format, for example a report.

Tackling multiple choice questions

The MCQs in your exam will contain four possible answers. You have to **choose the option that best answers the question**. The three incorrect options are called distracters. There is a skill in answering MCQs quickly and correctly. By practising MCQs you can develop this skill, giving yourself a better chance of passing the exam.

You may wish to follow the approach outlined below, or you may prefer to adapt it.

Step 1 Skim read all the MCQs and identify which appear to be the easier questions and which questions you will not need a calculator to answer.

Step 2 Remember that the examiner will not expect you to spend an equal amount of time on each MCQ; some can be answered instantly but others will take time to work out.

Step 3 Attempt each question. **The questions** identified in Step 1 are questions which you should be able to answer during the 20 minutes reading time. Read the question thoroughly. You may prefer to work out the answer before looking at the options, or you may prefer to look at the options at the beginning. Adopt the method that works best for you.

You may find that you recognise a question when you sit the exam. Be aware that the detail and/or requirement may be different. If the question seems familiar, read the requirement and options carefully – do not assume that it is identical.

Step 4 Read the four options and see if one matches your own answer. Be careful with numerical questions, as the distracters are designed to match answers that incorporate **common errors**. Check that your calculation is correct. Have you followed the requirement exactly? Have you included every stage of the calculation?

Step 5 You may find that none of the options matches your answer.

- Re-read the question to ensure that you understand it and are answering the requirement
- Eliminate any obviously wrong answers
- Consider which of the remaining answers is the most likely to be correct and select that option
- In questions with non-numerical answer options, choose the answer that is closest to your preferred answer

Step 6 If you are still unsure, make a note and continue to the next question. Likewise if you are nowhere near working out which option is correct, leave the question and come back to it later.

Step 7 Revisit unanswered questions. When you come back to a question after a break, you often find you can answer it correctly straightaway. If you are still unsure, have a guess. You are not penalised for incorrect answers, so **never leave a question unanswered!**

Step 8 **Rule off answers** to each MCQ in the answer booklet.

Tackling objective test questions

What is an objective test question?

An objective test (**OT**) question is made up of some form of **stimulus**, usually a question, and a **requirement** to do something.

- **MCQs.** Read through the information on page xviii about MCQs and how to tackle them.
- **True or false**. You will be asked if a statement is true or false.
- **Data entry**. This type of OT requires you to provide figures such as the answer to a calculation, words to fill in a blank, single word answers to questions, or to identify numbers and words to complete a format.
- **Word-limited answers**. You may be asked to state, define or explain things in no more than a certain number of words or within a single line in the answer booklet.
- **Multiple response.** These questions provide you with a number of options and you have to identify those that fulfil certain criteria.

OT questions in your exam

Section A of your exam will contain different types of OT questions. It is not certain how many questions in your exam will be MCQs and how many will be other types of OT, nor what types of OT you will encounter in your exam. Practising all the different types of OTs that this Kit provides will prepare you well for whatever questions come up in your exam.

Dealing with OT questions

Again you may wish to follow the approach we suggest, or you may be prepared to adapt it.

Step 1 Work out **how long** you should allocate to each OT, taking into account the marks allocated to it. Remember that you will not be expected to spend an equal amount of time on each one; some can be answered instantly but others will take time to work out.

Step 2 **Jot down answers, workings or ideas** for as many OTs as possible on the question paper during the 20 minutes reading time.

Step 3 **Attempt each question**. Read the question thoroughly, and note in particular what the question says about the **format** of your answer and whether there are any **restrictions** placed on it (for example the number of words you can use).

You may find that you recognise a question when you sit the exam. Be aware that the detail and/or requirement may be different. If the question seems familiar read the requirement and options carefully – do not assume that it is identical.

Step 4 Read any options you are given and select which ones are appropriate. Check that your calculations are correct. Have you followed the requirement exactly? Have you included every stage of the calculation?

Step 5 You may find that you are unsure of the answer.

- Re-read the question to ensure that you understand it and are answering the requirement
- Eliminate any obviously wrong options if you are given a number of options from which to choose

Step 6 If you are still unsure, **continue to the next question**.

Step 7 Revisit questions you are uncertain about. When you come back to a question after a break you often find you are able to answer it correctly straightaway. If you are still unsure have a guess. You are not penalised for incorrect answers, so **never leave a question unanswered!**

Step 8 Make sure you show your **workings** clearly on calculation OTs, as you may gain some credit for workings even if your final answer is incorrect.

Step 9 Rule off answers to each OT in the answer booklet

Exam information

Format of the paper

		Number of marks
Section A:	Up to 10 multiple choice and other objective test questions, 2-4 marks each	20
Section B:	3 compulsory questions, 10 marks each	30
Section C:	2 out of 3 questions, 25 marks each	50
		100

Time allowed: 3 hours

Question weighting will reflect syllabus weighting.

Section A will always contain some multiple choice questions but will not consist solely of multiple choice questions. Further guidance on objective test questions and multiple choice questions is included on pages xviii to xx.

Section B may include a short scenario that could relate to several of the questions.

Section C questions are likely to be scenario-based and include sub questions. The examiner has said that there is unlikely to be a single 25 mark requirement in Section C.

November 2008

Section A

1 9 multiple choice and objective test questions

Section B

2 Scientific Management
3 Projects and progress reports
4 Mintzberg's structural configurations

Section C

5 Social and environmental responsibility
6 Strategic models
7 Stakeholders and conflict

This paper is Mock exam 3 in this Kit.

May 2008

		Questions in this Kit
Section A		
1	7 multiple choice and objective test questions	86
Section B		
2	Levels of strategy	65
3	Communication	18
4	Project completion	42
Section C		
5	Models evaluating strategy, cultural differences	73
6	Group formation and problems in groups	29
7	Entrepreneurship and innovation	30

Examiner's comments. Performance was similar to recent sittings. High scoring scripts displayed a firm grasp of the theory, had read the questions and scenarios carefully, planned the answers before writing and applied the relevant theory taking full account of the scenario context in the answer.

November 2007

		Questions in this Kit
Section A		
1	9 multiple choice and objective test questions	85
Section B		
2	Organisational culture	64
3	Health and safety	17
4	Project feasibility	41
Section C		
5	Project management and control	49
6	Strategy, resource based view, value chain	72
7	Leadership styles, mentoring	28

Examiner's comments. The overall performance was similar to recent exams but with rather more candidates attaining very high scores. Question 1 and 4 were well done. Question 6 was the least popular and few competent answers were provided for this question.

May 2007

		Questions in this Kit
Section A		
1	9 multiple choice and objective test questions	84
Section B		
2	Strategic planning	62
3	Project stages	40
4	Corporate governance and ethics	63
Section C		
5	Performance and appraisal systems	26
6	Organisational structure	27
7	Project planning and tools	48

Examiner's comments. The overall performance was better than recent exams. Candidates scored reasonably well on questions 1, 3 and 4. However, many candidates still fail to read questions thoroughly and this showed in answers to questions 2, 3, 6(b) and 7(a).

November 2006

		Questions in this Kit
Section A		
1	9 multiple choice and objective test questions	83
Section B		
2	Sources of power	16
3	Project risk management	39
4	Undertaking a corporate appraisal	61
Section C		
5	Project management, software and stakeholders	47
6	Transaction cost analysis and achieving flexibility through structure	71
7	Team working, leadership and conflict	25

Examiner's comments. Overall, performance has fallen since May 2005 when the first paper was set. General weaknesses were evident in both **theoretical knowledge** and in its **application**. Candidates often didn't read questions properly and so didn't answer the question set. This particularly applied to Question 5. Questions 2, 3 and 4 were, overall, quite well answered. Candidates often struggled with Question 6 unless they knew about Transaction Cost Theory. Question 7 was reasonable. Question 5 was poorly answered.

May 2006

		Questions in this Kit
Section A		
1	8 multiple choice and objective test questions	82
Section B		
2	Time management	6
3	Matrix structure	7
4	CSFs and core competences	54
Section C		
5	Five forces and Hofstede	68
6	Nature of projects; project lifecycle	46
7	Negotiation; researching staff attitudes	22

Examiner's comments. Candidates' performance was similar to that at recent sittings. A significant number of students had problems with question 1.7, question 4 and question 5.

Questions in Section C require students to develop their answer more fully, beyond just description. To ensure success, candidates therefore need to revise the breadth of the syllabus and practise applying models to real world situations.

November 2005

		Questions in this Kit
Section A		
1	8 multiple choice and objective test questions	81
Section B		
2	Mission and objectives	55
3	Project management methodology	37
4	Disciplinary procedure	12
Section C		
5	Leadership style and project management skills	44
6	Approaches to strategy	67
7	Meetings; project closure	45

Examiner's comments. There were general weaknesses in both candidates' theoretical knowledge and their ability to apply that knowledge, with too many coming to the examination inadequately prepared. This was particularly noticeable in:

- Question 2, the nature of strategic objectives
- Question 3, the concept of a project methodology/approach
- Question 5(a), style theories of leadership
- Question 6(b), differences in approaches to strategy
- Question 7(b), differences between project closure, post completion review and project audit

May 2005

Section A		*Questions in this Kit*
1	8 multiple choice and objective test questions	various
Section B		
2	Stress management	14
3	Social responsibility vs shareholder value	59
4	Network diagram and discussion	38
Section C		
5	Organisation structure; encouraging creativity and innovation	23
6	Project planning activities; roles of project sponsor and project manager	43
7	Nature and sources of departmental conflict; factors in building a successful cross-functional project team.	24

Examiner's comments. Common errors included failure to read the question with sufficient care and failure to answer all parts of the question. Most candidates did quite well on Section A, less well on Section B and least well of all on Section C.

A common weakness was a liking for repeating elements of the scenario as an answer. A further problem was a lack of ability in summarisation of key points.

Pilot paper

Section A		*Questions in this Kit*
1	8 multiple choice and objective test questions	80
Section B		
Split scenario: project management and strategy		
2	Benefits of work breakdown structure	74
3	Time management	75
4	Environment analysis	76
Section C		
Strategic management scenario		
5	Strategic approach; stakeholders	77
6	Resource-based strategy; international cultural differences	78
7	Project risks; negotiation	79

What the examiner means

The table below has been prepared by CIMA to help you interpret exam questions. The examiner for P5 has said that, 'analyse', 'advise' and 'recommend' are key verbs for this exam.

Learning objective	Verbs used	Definition	Examples in the Kit
1 Knowledge What you are expected to know	• List • State • Define	• Make a list of • Express, fully or clearly, the details of/facts of • Give the exact meaning of	2.8 2.2 –
2 Comprehension What you are expected to understand	• Describe • Distinguish • Explain • Identify • Illustrate	• Communicate the key features of • Highlight the differences between • Make clear or intelligible/state the meaning of • Recognise, establish or select after consideration • Use an example to describe or explain something	9 55 6 9 55
3 Application How you are expected to apply your knowledge	• Apply • Calculate/compute • Demonstrate • Prepare • Reconcile • Solve • Tabulate	• To put to practical use • To ascertain or reckon mathematically • To prove the certainty or to exhibit by practical means • To make or get ready for use • To make or prove consistent/ compatible • Find an answer to • Arrange in a table	73 83 72 76 – – –
4 Analysis How you are expected to analyse the detail of what you have learned	• Analyse • Categorise • Compare and contrast • Construct • Discuss • Interpret • Produce	• Examine in detail the structure of • Place into a defined class or division • Show the similarities and/or differences between • To build up or complete • To examine in detail by argument • To translate into intelligible or familiar terms • To create or bring into existence	5 – 67 36 14 – 15
5 Evaluation How you are expected to use your learning to evaluate, make decisions or recommendations	• Advise • Evaluate • Recommend	• To counsel, inform or notify • To appraise or assess the value of • To advise on a course of action	20 27 27

Exam update

There are no technical updates for *CIMA P5* but always remember to consult the CIMA website for articles written on management. These come out regularly and the latest article on Performance Management was published in June 2008.

Useful websites

The websites below provide additional sources of information of relevance to your studies for *Management Accounting – Decision Management.*

- BPP — www.bpp.com/learningmedia

  For details of other BPP material for your CIMA studies
- CIMA — www.cimaglobal.com

  The official CIMA website
- *Financial Times* — www.ft.com
- *The Economist* — www.economist.com
- *Wall Street Journal* — www.wsj.com

Using your BPP products

This Kit gives you the question practice and guidance you need in the exam. Our other products can also help you pass:

- **Learning to Learn Accountancy** gives further valuable advice on revision
- **Passcards** provide you with clear topic summaries and exam tips
- **Success CDs** help you revise on the move
- **i-Pass CDs** offer tests of knowledge against the clock
- **Learn Online** is an e-learning resource delivered via the Internet, offering comprehensive tutor support and featuring areas such as study, practice, email service, revision and useful resources

You can purchase these products by visiting www.bpp.com/mybpp.

Planning your question practice

We have already stressed that question practice should be right at the centre of your revision. Whilst you will spend some time looking at your notes and the Paper P5 Passcards, you should spend the majority of your revision time practising questions.

We recommend two ways in which you can practise questions.

- Use **BPP Learning Media's question plan** to work systematically through the syllabus and attempt key and other questions on a section-by-section basis
- **Build your own exams** – attempt the questions as a series of practice exams

These ways are suggestions and simply following them is no guarantee of success. You or your college may prefer an alternative but equally valid approach.

BPP's question plan

The plan below requires you to devote a **minimum of 35 hours** to revision of Paper P5. Any time you can spend over and above this should only increase your chances of success.

Step 1 **Review your notes** and the chapter summaries in the Paper P5 **Passcards** for each section of the syllabus.

Step 2 **Answer the key questions** for that section. These questions have boxes round the question number in the table below and you should answer them in full. Even if you are short of time you must attempt these questions if you want to pass the exam. You should complete your answers without referring to our solutions.

Step 3 **Attempt the other questions** in that section. For some questions we have suggested that you prepare **answer plans or do the calculations** rather than full solutions. Planning an answer means that you should spend about 40% of the time allowance for the questions brainstorming the question and drawing up a list of points to be included in the answer.

Step 4 **Attempt Mock exams 1, 2 and 3** under strict exam conditions.

Syllabus section	2009 Passcards chapters	Questions in this Kit	Comments	Done ☑
Management of relationships	1-6	1-4	Answer all of these objective test questions.	☐
Management and leadership	1	13	You need a good understanding of what general management is about and this basic question is good test of that.	☐
		11	This is a good question for getting to grips with the reality of managing people. Prepare a full answer.	☐
		19	Do an answer plan only. This is an important topic.	☐
		16	Power is a feature of all organisations. Try this short question from the November 2006 exam, which covers this topic.	☐ ☐
		28	This longer question from the November 2007 exam is a good test of your knowledge of leadership. It looks at styles of leadership and then asks you to describe a particular theory and apply it. Mentoring is the third aspect you need to consider.	
Organisation structure	2	23(a)	Prepare a full answer to part (a) Organisation structure is fundamental to the management of organisations. This is a basic question, which you should be able to answer with ease.	☐
		7	You must be aware of modern trends. Do an answer in note form for this question.	☐
		5	Answer this question in full.	☐
		27	This is a fairly detailed question from the May 2007 exam looking at organisational structures and the most appropriate structure to suit an organisation's circumstances.	☐
		30	An interesting longer question from the May 2008 exam which covered aspects of entrepreneurship and links this to creativity, culture, management and organisational structure.	☐
Control systems	3	26	This question from the May 2007 exam looks at performance and appraisal. You need to think about organisational culture and theories of motivation too.	☐
		17	Health and safety policy is covered in this short question. This has not been tested much but is useful to know in practice!	☐
Groups and teams	4	9 10	Group and teams are related topics and of significant interest to the manager. Answer these two questions in full. Our suggested answers were prepared in eighteen minutes each and give you a good idea of how much you need to write to earn a pass.	☐
		25	This question from the November 2006 exam covers teams and motivation in detail.	☐

Syllabus section	2009 Passcards chapters	Questions in this Kit	Comments	Done ☑
		29	A good longer question which covers group formation and potential problems in teams. The examiner set this in May 2008.	☐
Conflict and discipline	5	Mock 2 q4	A good test of your knowledge of disciplinary procedures and also why discipline is a good idea.	☐
		12	Discipline is important in any organisation. It is also one of the functions that in the real world is hedged about legal provisions. You cannot make it up as you go along, either in the exam or at work.	☐
Management skills	6	24	This is from the May 2005 exam and deals with some important syllabus topics. Thus you will need to discuss conflict and then go on to write about teams and team building.	☐
		6	This short question is a good test of your knowledge of time management techniques.	☐
		21	Some of the topics that fall under this heading are essentially practical ones and questions about them should be answered in a practical fashion. Note, however, that this does not mean that 'common sense' is all you need to do so! You will also need background knowledge.	☐
		15	Prepare an answer plan for this question.	☐
		22	Negotiation is a key management skill. Attempt this longer May 2006 question and test your knowledge of negotiation and information gathering.	☐
		14	This question from the May 2005 exam is typical of the short questions that the examiner sets testing a particular topic.	☐
Project management	7, 8	31, 32	Answer all of these objective test questions.	☐
	7	34	A short question that covers PRINCE2 or similar framework for thinking about issues surrounding projects.	☐
		37	Prepare a full answer on this short November 2005 question. Remember to apply whatever methodology you recommend to the company.	☐
		39	This November 2006 question brings together two topics within project management. These are project management and risk management. Make sure you understand how these are linked.	☐
		40	This May 2007 question tests your understanding of project management. Use the information in the question to illustrate your points.	☐
		43	This May 2005 question gives good general coverage of the nature of project management and the roles of those involved in projects.	☐

Syllabus section	2009 Passcards chapters	Questions in this Kit	Comments	Done ☑
		44	This November 2005 question encompasses different areas of the syllabus. So remember to refer to leadership style as well as project management.	☐
		45	A short question from the November 2005 exam looking at project management and project closure.	☐
		46	A nice question from the May 2006 exam examining projects and their stages in depth.	☐
		Mock 1 q4	A good test of your knowledge of PRINCE2, which is a key project management method.	☐
		Mock 2 q5	This question runs through critical path analysis, Gantt charts and the project lifecycle.	☐
		49	This longer question in the November 2007 exam tests the responsibilities of project managers, the purpose of project control and controls used over the stages of the project.	☐
Project management tools and techniques	8	33, 35	Two short questions testing network analysis. Use these to practise your skills at drawing the network diagrams.	☐
		36	Prepare a full answer to this question testing critical path analysis.	☐
		38	You need to be able to draw a basic network quickly and accurately. The logic of dependencies and interactions must be carefully analysed and the critical path arithmetic completed. Prepare a full answer.	☐
		47	A question from the November 2006 exam covering a specialist area, project management software. Remember to make clear points about stakeholders too in part (b).	☐
		48	This May 2007 question tests project planning and project tools in some detail. Attempt it once you are confident with your knowledge of these topics.	☐
Strategic management	9-12	50, 51	Answer all these objective test questions.	☐
	9-12	70	Prepare a full answer to this question, which ranges widely across aspects of competences, entry barriers and environmental analysis.	
Approaching strategy	9	56	Theories about how business strategy is prepared are fairly unlikely topics for questions: they are essential background knowledge, however. On the other hand, you must be prepared to think about the practical interaction of theory and business problems. This question is a good example of that interaction. Prepare a note form answer.	☐
		67	Use this November 2005 question to test your knowledge of different approaches to strategy.	☐
		62	This short May 2007 question tests when it is appropriate to use the formal approach to strategic planning.	☐

Syllabus section	2009 Passcards chapters	Questions in this Kit	Comments	Done ☑
		57	This short question tests your knowledge of the theory of strategy formation.	☐
		71	A question from the November 2006 exam that examines transaction cost theory and then tests another area of the syllabus with the shamrock organisation or flexible firm model. The examiner does set questions like this so be prepared to be tested on more than one area in a longer question.	☐
		72	This November 2007 question tests your knowledge across Part A of the syllabus. So think about strategic approaches but also tools that are used in strategic analysis.	☐
Goals of the organisation	10	54	Make sure you understand what Critical Success Factors are and how these affect strategy when answering this May 2006 exam question.	☐
		55	Prepare a full answer to this question from November 2005 which tests mission and objectives.	☐
		59	Ethics, corporate social responsibility and corporate governance are likely to feature regularly in the exam as a matter of policy. Governments and professional bodies all over the west are very concerned about recent ethical failures and are doing everything they can to promote higher standards. This includes setting questions about ethics and corporate governance in your exam. Answer this question in full.	☐
		63	This shorter question from the May 2007 exam wants you to show your knowledge of corporate governance. Answer it in full.	☐
		52	Prepare an answer plan for this question.	☐
		66	Answer this question in full. The work you did for question 52 will help you with part (b).	☐
Organisational culture	11	53	Prepare a full answer to this question. This question should give you a good workout on the basics of culture.	☐
		60	Another question that looks at culture. You could use one of the models in the Study Text to frame your answer.	☐
Strategic and management tools	12	69	This is a gentle introduction to the use of strategic ideas. Most examination questions built around strategic models are likely to require you to decide which model to use. Prepare a full answer to this question.	☐
		68	A longer question from May 2006, which requires you to apply Porter's model. You need to think across the syllabus here too as the question asks about Hofstede which relates to culture and leadership.	☐

Syllabus section	2009 Passcards chapters	Questions in this Kit	Comments	Done ☑
		61	Corporate appraisal is a specific strategic tool. Try this ten-mark question from November 2006, which tests this topic.	☐
		73	This longer question in the May 2008 exam covers topics across the syllabus. It will test your knowledge of strategic models. Part b looks at cultural factors so you need to cover more than one area of the syllabus.	☐
Various	8	74	These six questions formed Part B of the Pilot Paper. They differ from the May 2005 exam questions in that they form two sets of linked case study questions. We do not know if the examiner will use this technique again, but you should attempt full answers to these questions so as to be prepared if he does. They are also good, wide-ranging questions in their own right.	☐
	6	75		☐
	12	76		☐
	10, 12	77		☐
	1, 9	78		☐
	6	79		☐

Build your own exams

Having revised your notes and the BPP Passcards, you can attempt the questions in the Kit as a series of practice exams. You can organise the questions in the following ways:

- Either you can attempt complete old papers; recent papers are listed below.

	P5								
	Pilot paper		May'05	Nov'05	May'06	Nov'06	May'07	Nov '07	May'08
Section A									
1	80		See page xxiv	81	82	83	84	85	86
Section B									
2	74		14	55	6	16	40	17	18
3	75		38	37	7	39	62	41	42
4	76		59	12	54	61	63	64	65
Section C									
5	77		23	44	68	25	26	28	29
6	78		43	67	46	47	27	49	30
7	79		24	45	22	71	48	72	73

- Or you can make up practice exams, either yourself or using the mock exams that we have listed below.

	Practice exams					
	1	2	3	4	5	6
Section A						
1	1.1-1.3 31.1-31.3 50.1-50.2, 51.4	1.4-1.6 31.4-31.5 50.3-50.4, 80.8	1.7-1.9 31.6 50.5-50.6 51.8	2.1-2.3 32.1-32.3 50.7-50.8, 51.7	2.4-2.6 32.4-32.6 50.9, 81.5	2.7-2.9 32.6-32.7 51.8
Section B						
2	13	11	14	9	10	6
3	56	12	37	38	38	7
4	36	57	59	55	75	74
Section C						
5	29	24	23	22	77	44
6	43	44	49	30	45	78
7	71	46	73	73	69	79

- Whichever practice exams you use, you must attempt **Mock exams 1, 2 and 3** at the end of your revision.

Questions

Extra guidance

Remember you can find additional guidance on a number of questions in this kit on BPP's website: www.bpp.com/cima/extra-question-guidance

MANAGEMENT OF RELATIONSHIPS

Questions 1 to 30 cover the management of relationships, the subject of Part A of the BPP Study Text for Paper P5.

Section A questions: Management of relationships

1 Objective test questions **36 mins**

1.1 *Handy* suggests that managers are frequently required to resolve managerial dilemmas. Which of the following is not one of the dilemmas he discussed?

A Trust – control dilemma
B Dilemma of time horizons
C Authority – accountability dilemma
D Dilemma of the cultures **(2 marks)**

1.2 A chartered management accountant working as head of internal audit reports to the audit committee of the group board that the finance director of a certain SBU has falsified the end of year stock valuation. The report is an example of:

A Whistle blowing
B Compliance based ethics
C Social responsibility
D Professional ethics **(2 marks)**

1.3 Which of the following is not a component of *Mintzberg's* model of the organisation?

A Technostructure
B Operating core
C Ideology
D Administration staff **(2 marks)**

1.4 *William Ouchi* identified three types of control within organisations. Which of the following is not one of them?

A Clan
B Contingency
C Bureaucratic
D Market **(2 marks)**

1.5 Double loop control exists when there is:

A Comparison of results with plan and standards of performance
B Incorporation of feedback in the control system
C Ability to modify the plan and standards of performance in the light of achievement
D Comparison of extrapolated future results with original plan. **(2 marks)**

1.6 *Burns and Stalker* identified two organisational types. What were they?

A Machine bureaucracy and professional bureaucracy
B Social and technical
C Mechanistic and organic
D Functional and matrix **(2 marks)**

1.7 Which of the following would be a valid objective for an appraisal scheme?

A Provide the manager with an opportunity for friendly one-to-one interaction with staff

B Generate documentary evidence of positive management techniques for potential future use at employment tribunals.

C Strengthen the performance of organisational systems by identifying the weaknesses of those who operate them

D Establish the level of an individual's performance against standard for the purpose of adjusting bonuses **(2 marks)**

1.8 Identify the term that completes this statement from the list below.

'The .... is extrovert, dominant and passionate about the task.'

(Finisher, plant, monitor-valuator, resource-investigator, shaper, implementer) **(2 marks)**

1.9 Identify the terms that complete this table from the list below.

Configuration	Co-ordination mechanism	Key part
Machine bureaucracy		
Adhocracy		

(Direct supervision, support staff, standardised outputs, standardised work processes, operating core, middle line, technostructure, standardised skills, mutual adjustment, strategic apex) **(4 marks)**

(Total = 20 marks)

---

2 Objective test questions **36 mins**

2.1 Which author(s) analysed the spectrum of management styles into (1) exploitative authoritative, (2) benevolent authoritative, (3) consultative, (4) participative?

A Rensis Linkert
B Frederick Herzberg
C Tannenbaum and Schmidt
D Huneryager and Heckman **(2 marks)**

2.2 State which ONE of the following represents the four phases of negotiation: **5/05**

A Preparation, opening, bargaining, closing
B Opening, bargaining, decision, closing
C Preparation, bargaining, negotiating, closing
D Opening, negotiating, decision, closing **(2 marks)**

2.3 Which ONE of the following organisational forms is best suited to a project which requires integration from a number of different functions? **5/05**

A Functional
B Network
C Divisional
D Matrix **(2 marks)**

2.4 What were the stages in team development identified by *Tuckman*?

A Givens, processes, leadership, outcomes
B Forming, storming, norming, performing
C Argument, competition, conflict, consensus
D Forming, norming, storming, performing **(2 marks)**

2.5 Under UK employment law, what is unfair dismissal?

A Resignation by the employee provoked by the employer's breaches of the terms of the contract of employment
B Dismissal within the terms of the contract of employment but for a legally unacceptable reason
C Dismissal that breaches the terms of the contract of employment
D Dismissal without notice **(2 marks)**

2.6 What is indirect discrimination?

A A group of people is treated less favourably than other groups
B Conditions are imposed with which a substantial proportion of a particular group cannot comply
C Preference is given to a particular group of people
D Women are not allowed to return to part-time work after maternity leave, having previously worked full-time **(2 marks)**

2.7 Which of the following is characteristic of a team but not of a group?

A Sense of identity
B Loyalty
C Leadership
D Work organisation **(2 marks)**

2.8 The Ashridge College research identified four management styles. List three of the four styles.

(3 marks)

2.9 Blake and Mouton developed the managerial grid to provide a framework for applying effective management. Draw the managerial grid labelling the horizontal axis and vertical axis and identify on the grid where the team management style is located. 5/05

Note: graph paper is not required.

(3 marks)

(Total = 20 marks)

3 Objective test questions **36 mins**

3.1 Typically, vary large bureaucratic organisations will present problems of management that differ from those of small organisations. Which of the following is not a problem you would expect to find in a large bureaucratic organisation?

A Poor record of innovation
B Tendency towards slow collective decision-making
C Workforce alienation
D None of the above **(2 marks)**

3.2 Mission is sometimes defined in terms of four elements: purpose; strategy; policies and standards of behaviour; and values. Which of the following would not constitute an example of 'policies and standards of behaviour, for an international parcels carrier?

A Staff at all levels are expected to behave in an ethical fashion
B When deliveries are delayed, the customer is to be informed promptly
C The company values its employees highly and will reward loyalty with loyalty
D Operations will not be subcontracted; the company will retain control over consignments at all times **(2 marks)**

3.3 Responsibility for safety in the workplace is with:

A The employer
B The employee
C Both of the above
D Neither of the above **(2 marks)**

3.4 The management theories known as the 'human relations' school is most closely associated with which author?

A Peter Drucker
B Henry Mintzberg
C Elton Mayo
D Rensis Likert **(2 marks)**

3.5 An employee who exposes the ethical misconduct of others in an organisation is known as a(n):

A Ombudsman
B Whistleblower
C Stakeholder
D Monitor **(2 marks)**

3.6 Which of the following organisational structures violate the 'unity of command' principle as stated by *Henry Fayol*?

A Functional
B Matrix
C Geographical
D Divisional **(2 marks)**

3.7 If a manager justifies an instruction to a subordinate by saying, 'because I am your superior', she is relying on which one of the following power bases?

A Referent
B Reward
C Legitimate
D Expert **(2 marks)**

3.8 Problems of managing complex work and providing a progressive career structure are associated with:

A Wide span of control
B Tall organisations
C Decentralisation
D All of the above **(2 marks)**

3.9 Which of the following is not a characteristic of *Burns and Stalkers'* organic (or organismic) organisation?

A Doing the job takes priority over serving the interests of the organisation.
B Commitment to the concern's mission is more highly valued than loyalty as such.
C Knowledge and experience of the way the organisation does things is less highly valued than general knowledge and expertise.
D Job descriptions and responsibility are carefully defined. **(2 marks)**

3.10 *Hofstede* identified four dimensions of difference in national managerial cultures. Which of the following is not one of them?

A 'Masculinity'
B Uncertainty avoidance
C Power distance
D Independence – centralisation **(2 marks)**

(Total = 20 marks)

4 Objective test questions **36 mins**

4.1 In the analysis of power in organisations, what is the term that is used to describe the power exerted by managers by virtue of the positions they hold?

A Legitimate power
B Expert power
C Resource power
D Personal power **(2 marks)**

4.2 Hydra Ltd has three product managers each responsible for the development and marketing of one of the product groups manufactured in its single factory. The finance director has provided each product manager with a part-qualified management accountant for four mornings each week to assist with budgets and costs. Is this an example of:

A Project management
B Matrix structure
C Functional departmentation
D Complex organisational form **(2 marks)**

4.3 John Adair's action centred model of leadership identified three sets of needs that require the leader's attention. Which of the following is not one of those sets of needs?

A Group needs
B Individual needs
C Task needs
D Functional needs **(2 marks)**

4.4 In the typical hierarchical organisation, the requirement of a lower-level manager to answer to a higher-level manager in the chain of command is referred to as

A Authority
B Empowerment
C Accountability
D Super ordination **(2 marks)**

4.5 The division of an organisation into various departments such as purchasing, manufacturing, marketing, finance, research and development results in what kind of organisational structure?

A Network
B Functional
C Product
D Matrix **(2 marks)**

4.6 An effective appraisal system involves

A Assessing the personality of the appraisee.
B A one-sided process by the manager.
C Advising on the faults of the appraisee.
D A participative, problem-solving process between the manager and appraisee. **(2 marks)**

4.7 Recent developments toward greater employee involvement, flexible working and flatter organisational structures have placed greater emphasis on which ONE of the following styles of management?

A Exploitative authoritative
B Autocratic
C Participative
D Benevolent authoritative **(2 marks)**

4.8 Research on group effectiveness has concluded that the most consistently successful groups

A are those in which all members are innovative
B comprise a range of roles undertaken by various members
C are those in which all members are very intelligent
D comprise a range of roles all undertaken by a few members of the group **(2 marks)**

4.9 Any claim that unethical behaviour is in an organisation's best interest is an attempt to

A follow the principle of procedural justice
B do the right thing for society
C rationalise the unethical conduct
D look after the interests of oneself **(2 marks)**

4.10 According to *FW Taylor*, which ONE of the following is a characteristic of scientific management?

A Work specialisation
B Group working
C Socio-technical system
D The informal system **(2 marks)**

(Total = 20 marks)

Section B questions: Management of relationships

5 Dr Strong **18 mins**

The C Pharmaceutical Company is in a state of crisis. The development of new drugs and treatments on which the vary survival of the organisation depends has slowed dramatically in recent years. An investigation into the operation of the organisation's research and development (R&D) unit has revealed that the slow rate of innovation has much to do with the way the department has been managed.

The head of the unit, Dr Strong, regards it as his duty not to exceed the unit's budget allocation and has introduced strict controls to avoid this happening. Members of the R&D unit are set clear targets with time limits and expected to be working in the laboratory or office on a 9-5 basis every working day. This system of control is not to the liking of research staff and several of the most innovative members have left. The morale of the remaining staff is very low and further resignations are expected.

Required

Analyse why the problems in the R&D unit of the C Pharmaceutical Company might have developed. Recommend what actions could be taken to encourage creativity and innovation. **(10 marks)**

6 L Company (5/06) **18 mins**

M is a member of the finance department of L Company. She joined the company two years ago on its management development programme and is currently studying for the CIMA examinations.

A keen and enthusiastic member of staff, M likes to get involved in different aspects of work and is always volunteering to be involved on various committees. She is always ready to chat to her colleagues who pass by her desk and is known as the social events organiser for the department. M likes to be seen to be helping other people and is an expert on the internet, spending a significant amount of her time searching out different websites.

However, at her appraisal interview a few weeks ago, M was surprised that her manager, P, raised concerns over the fact that she often appeared to be rushing her work to meet deadlines, and that it had been noted that she often arrived at meetings late. P also made the observation that whilst M's reports are always carefully researched and very well presented, much of the information is not relevant to the tasks that she has been given. P suggested that M needs to improve on how she manages her time.

Required

Explain how time management techniques could help M become more efficient and effective in her work.
(10 marks)

7 H Company (5/06) **18 mins**

H Company designs and manufactures sports equipment and is currently positioned as the market leader in the industry. However, whilst operating in a growth market there are new competitors entering the market with innovative new product offerings. The Marketing Director is aware that to retain market leader position the company must improve its practices involved with New Product Development (NPD), and the time taken to get from the product idea to launch needs to be much quicker.

The company has a functional structure with the Marketing Director heading up the marketing function and the R&D Director heading up the function responsible for research and product development. In addition there are separate functions for Production, Human Resources, Finance, Sales and IT.

The Marketing Director feels that the functional structure is impeding the company's NPD. Having recently read an article on organising for NPD, he is proposing that the best way to manage the process is to adopt a project management approach. This will involve introducing a matrix structure and the use of cross functional teams.

However, at a recent meeting of the functional heads, the Research and Development Director said that, in his experience, the potential difficulties in using a matrix structure for project management offset the benefits.

Required

Describe the advantages and disadvantages for H Company of using a matrix structure in project management work for New Product Development (NPD). **(10 marks)**

8 Icebergs **18 mins**

Organisations have been compared to icebergs, with the formal aspects being the visible part and the informal and cultural aspects being the much larger hidden part.

Required

Explain the nature of informal organisation and detail its disadvantages and advantages for a business. **(10 marks)**

The following data are given for questions 9 and 10 below

The T Aerospace Company is in the early stages of planning the development of its latest commercial jet, the 007. The aircraft industry is a fiercely competitive one, dominated by a few large global players who operate at the forefront of technology. In this industry, competitors quickly copy any advance in technology or new management technique that might provide them with a competitive edge. Some of the T Aerospace Company's competitors have adopted team working as a means of speeding up their development and production processes.

The T Aerospace Company is thus considering the adoption of team working in its operations, but some of the traditionalists in the company are doubtful. They are concerned that the benefits of work specialisation will be lost. Some of the managers have had negative experiences with team working and so have strong reservations about the proposed changes.

9 Aerospace team 1 **18 mins**

Required

(a) Describe briefly the essential features of a team. **(4 marks)**

(b) Identify the benefits that the T Aerospace Company can expect to gain from the adoption of team working. **(6 marks)**

(Total = 10 marks)

10 Aerospace team 2 **18 mins**

Required

Describe the difficulties that the company is likely to encounter in the management of its teams and recommend how it might overcome these. **(10 marks)**

11 Joan Timmins **18 mins**

Before taking up her position as head of the finance department of the SOFT Corporation, Joan Timmins had enjoyed a career in the army where she had attained the rank of major. The military style of command had suited Joan's personality. She is by nature an assertive kind of individual, so giving orders is something that comes naturally to her.

The start of her new post of head of finance has not been easy. She has found that her previous style of management has not been well received by her new staff. Her enthusiasm for improving the way things are done in the department is not matched by that of her staff. In fact, if anything, an air of resentment seems to exist in the department. More generally, she is finding it difficult to adjust to the whole way of operating in the SOFT Corporation. In her view, so much time seems to be spent in meetings and in consultation generally that she wonders how the organisation manages to compete the in the market place as successfully as it does.

Required

Using any appropriate theory of management style, explain why Joan Timmins is experiencing the difficulties described in her new post, and recommend the kind of management style which might be more appropriate.

(10 marks)

12 S and C (11/05) — 18 mins

S has recently been appointed as the Finance Department Manager in Z Company. During the first month in her new role she has observed that one member of staff, C, is underperforming. C is frequently arriving late to work with no explanation and he is taking extended lunch breaks without permission. He is also making errors and refuses to do certain tasks which are part of his role. One of his colleagues has spoken to S confidentially, saying that C's poor performance in his work is having an adverse impact on the rest of the team. It is apparent that the problems have been going on for some time but the previous manager had preferred to ignore them. S has decided that she must now take action on what appears to be a disciplinary case, but is unclear on how to deal with the situation.

Required

Explain to S the stages involved in taking disciplinary action against C. **(10 marks)**

13 Functions — 18 mins

Drury has argued that the primary objective of management accounting is to provide management with information for decision-making. In order to be aware of the information needs of management, we must first understand the management functions that accounting serves. *Drucker*, following *Fayol,* has suggested that management consists of the functions of planning, controlling, organising, communicating and motivating.

Required

Describe *any two* of the functions of management, using appropriate examples from an organisation with which you are familiar. **(10 marks)**

14 Stress management (5/05) — 18 mins

T, the HR manager of X Investment Bank is keen to develop and introduce policies that will enhance the relationship between managers and their subordinates. Having recently attended a conference on workplace stress, T has recommended that the Bank should introduce a stress management programme. He feels that the introduction of such a programme would not only minimise the harmful impact that stress can have on organisational performance, but could also improve working relationships.

Required

Discuss the measures that T could introduce as part of the proposed stress management programme to minimise stress related problems. **(10 marks)**

15 PB Company 18 mins

Background and Introduction

The PB company sells an Internet security product called OneR. This product guarantees the security of electronic transmissions over the Internet by providing an easy-to-use encryption system.

PB has been in business for 6 years, and now has an annual turnover of $45 million. The company's clients include many government departments as well as 11 of the top 100 companies in the country in which it operates.

Sales systems

Sales are generated by potential customers visiting the company's website and reading about the product, or by referral from existing customers. An initial enquiry to PB results in a sales representative booking an appointment with the potential customer to demonstrate the OneR product. The demonstration normally lasts a whole day due to the complexity in setting up OneR to run on different computer configurations. However, most demonstrations result in sales.

A significant minority of demonstrations fail because the hardware configuration at the potential customer cannot run the OneR product, or where the OneR system cannot be configured to run on the operating system on the computer.

The effectiveness of sales representatives is monitored on whether on not they have achieved their sales targets for each month. Under-achieving the target results in representatives being encouraged to do better next month, although the sales target remains the same. Selling more than the target results in a small bonus for that representative, with the target being increased to encourage the representative to sell even more of the product.

Amendments to sales system

The Board of PB are investigating the possibility of amending the method of selling the OneR product. Most companies already have an Internet connection, so it is possible to download a version of the OneR product from the Internet. Rather than visit the client's premises, sales representatives can then provide e-mail and telephone support to help the customers install and try out the product for themselves. The main benefits to PB are a decrease in travelling time and expenses of sales representatives, and representatives being able to complete two demonstrations each day rather than one.

Sales representatives have reacted poorly to this suggestion with fear of job losses, decreased commission and loss of other benefits such as company cars all being given as reasons not to change the existing system. Although all representatives appear to share these views, the representatives who joined the company only 4 months ago appear to be the most vocal opponents of the move. Other representatives appear to want to know more about the proposals and so are reserving their judgement.

To try and resolve this issue, the Managing Director of PB has organised a meeting with the sales representatives for next Saturday morning to discuss the situation and try and resolve the problems. Saturday was chosen for the meeting because it is a non-working day and so it will minimise the disruption to clients and loss of commission to the sales representatives.

The MD has recognised that holding a meeting may produce additional conflict between the sales representatives and the senior management of the company; however, he is keen to go ahead. He has asked you, as a recently qualified Management Accountant, to use your extensive study skills to assist him in preparing for the meeting.

Required

Produce briefing notes for the Managing Director which provide an outline agenda for the meeting with reasons for the different subjects on the agenda. **(10 marks)**

16 Power (11/06) — 18 mins

G, the senior partner of L, a medium sized accountancy firm, has worked for L for over twenty years and has a sound knowledge and understanding of the different activities of the firm's business. Over the years, G has become known for his fairness in how he manages staff. He is also well liked and respected for his enthusiastic approach. He always has time to encourage and mentor younger members of staff.

The firm has recently invested in new technology which will improve the effectiveness of its office systems, but will mean the roles and responsibilities of the support staff will change. G, has taken on the unenviable role of leading the project to introduce the technology and new working practices. He knows that the project will be met with resistance from some members of staff and he will need to draw on various sources of power to ensure the changes are successfully implemented.

Required

Describe the different sources of power that G has and which will help him in introducing the changes.

(10 marks)

17 Health and safety policy (11/07) — 18 mins

Whilst Z Company has a policy and a code of conduct on health and safety, the results from a recent survey suggest that many senior managers are not aware of their responsibilities for health and safety in the workplace.

The Board has nominated H, the finance director, to deliver a seminar to help senior managers appreciate the importance of health and safety at work. He is currently considering what he should include in the seminar.

Required

Explain the key areas that H should cover in the health and safety seminar. **(10 marks)**

18 Communication (5/08) — 18 mins

P is the project manager responsible for managing the relocation of H Company's head office to new premises. He thought all was going well with the project and is very surprised when he learns that various project stakeholders are complaining about his poor communication skills.

Some of the complaints made relate to the complex messages he sends and his use of very technical language associated with the project. Whilst he feels he is keeping the project team members up to date, they feel they are overloaded with e-mails covering lots of different issues, not all of which are relevant to them.

Required

Explain to P what he could do to ensure that his communications with stakeholders about the relocation project are more effective. **(10 marks)**

Section C questions: Management of relationships

19 *Preparation question: Scientific management* 45 mins

Telephone call centres have grown rapidly in recent years. In the USA, they employ 3% of the working population and already account for one in a hundred of the working population in the UK.

These call centres are often part of an after-sales service which provides customer support but many also operate to sell goods and services via the telephone. The operators, mainly young people, are carefully selected for their voice characteristics, telephone manner and computer keyboard skills. Training is provided in the carefully detailed procedures that have been found to be most efficient and effective in providing the service.

The use of modern technology in these centres provides the ultimate means for work measurement; almost every aspect of the telephone operators' work can be, and is, measured. Supervisors in these centres can monitor the calls of each operator for speed of response and the duration of each call. Time away from the workstation is easily tracked and recorded. The quality of the operators' performance can be, and is, constantly monitored by weekly customer 'call backs'. The means for controlling the workforce is thus complete.

Performance-related payment is common in these centres and provides the main means of maintaining employee performance. The rapid and continuing growth of these centres is testimony to the fact that they provide a profitable business opportunity for investors but the working conditions in these centres raise questions about whether they are also such a great opportunity for workers.

The design of the work in telephone call centres appears to owe much to scientific management.

Required

(a) What is scientific management and why does the design of jobs in telephone call centres appear to owe so much to this approach to management? **(13 marks)**

(b) Scientific management has been much criticised. What are these criticisms and to what extent do they apply to the design of jobs in telephone call centres? **(12 marks)**

(Total = 25 marks)

20 *Preparation question: Performance appraisal* 45 mins

The performance appraisal process is now well established in large organisations.

Required

(a) Describe briefly the most common objectives of a performance appraisal system. **(10 marks)**

(b) Explain why appraisal systems are often less effective in practice than they might be, and advise what management can do to try and ensure their effectiveness. **(15 marks)**

(Total = 25 marks)

21 Workload 45 mins

Laura Lee switched off the light and prepared to lock up the accounts office. This was the third time this week she had worked after seven o'clock in the evening and the eighth occasion this month. She had thought that her workload would drop after the busy first few weeks following her appointment as financial accountant at ZX Systems Limited but if anything the workload was increasing.

As financial accountant she was responsible for nine staff in the sales, purchase and nominal ledger sections, two staff from the cashiers office and three payroll administration staff. All 14 staff were classified as accounts assistants under the company's job description scheme. In addition Laura carried specific responsibility for the monthly financial reports, VAT operations and the preparation to first draft stage of the company's annual accounts. Laura reported directly to the chief accountant who, from time to time, gave her special projects.

As she saw the situation, her work pressure problems fell into three distinct groups.

- The constant stream of queries and questions from the accounts assistants who seemed unable or unwilling to use any initiative in problem solving
- The need to meet the tight timetables on monthly, quarterly and annual reporting
- The special jobs and projects received from the chief accountant, always with an 'urgent sticker' attached

Eventually one aspect of her work would suffer. She could not keep up her present rate of work for much longer without some sign that the workload would reduce to a more reasonable level.

Required

(a) Discuss ways in which Laura Lee can manage better the job pressures she is experiencing. **(15 marks)**

(b) Delegation can assist in such situations but needs to be effectively managed. Explain how Laura Lee might achieve this. **(10 marks)**

(Total = 25 marks)

22 D Company (5/06) 45 mins

D Company is a manufacturer of electrical components, supplying the car industry. As a result of the downturn in the demand for its products and in response to difficult operating conditions in its existing market, the company is currently going through a major restructuring. It is anticipated that the restructuring plan will involve the consolidation of some business activities which will result in a number of staff having to move to different areas of the company. This could mean re-location to different sites, and other staff being made redundant.

While employee relations have in the past been good, the management of the company is aware that employees and their trade unions which represent their interests will be resistant to the changes that need to be made. The first stages of change will require skilful negotiation between the management and unions on a range of issues relating to the movement of staff jobs, the proposed job losses and, specifically, the criteria for redundancy and the redundancy package.

The company recognises the potential impact of the changes on staff morale and intends to implement a programme of research amongst staff to gain feedback on the way the change process is managed.

Required

(a) Discuss the role of negotiation in the management of change in D Company, making reference to the different stages involved in the negotiation process. **(13 marks)**

(b) Identify the methods that could be used to collect information on staff attitudes towards the changes, explaining for each method the issues that need to be considered when planning the research. **(12 marks)**

(Total = 25 marks)

23 Structure and innovation (5/05) **45 mins**

A is the Chief Executive Officer (CEO), of L Company, which manufactures and sells electrical appliances such as vacuum cleaners, washing machines and dish-washers. She founded the company fifteen years ago, along with W who provided the financial backing for the business. Whilst A is the CEO, her main interest is inventing new product designs. The company's competitive advantage has, in the past, been achieved through innovative technological and design features that have been difficult for other companies to copy. This has allowed the company to charge premium prices for its products.

Over the years the company has grown significantly, and it now employs over 1,000 staff. It has diversified into producing televisions and media equipment and has more recently moved into the PC market. The company has manufacturing plants around the world, but the headquarters remains in country G.

When the company was first established it was very much based on an entrepreneurial structure with no formal control systems in place. Staff joined the company because it provided an exciting and creative environment in which to work. Teamworking and lateral communications to solve problems were encouraged. Everyone was on first name terms and the company invested in the development of staff.

However, over time the company has changed to a functional structure and bureaucratic and rigid control mechanisms have been put in place. In recent months sales have slowed down. A is concerned that the company may have lost its ability to be creative and innovative, as well as its entrepreneurial spirit. This could mean disaster in the future.

Required

(a) (i) Compare and contrast an entrepreneurial structure and a functional structure. **(7 marks)**

(ii) Advise A why a functional structure may no longer be appropriate for L Company **(6 marks)**

(b) Discuss the different approaches that could be used to encourage creativity and innovation in L Company. **(12 marks)**

(Total = 25 marks)

24 Departmental conflict (5/05) **45 mins**

V is the Chief Executive of M Company, a manufacturer of prepared frozen foods. The company is facing difficult business conditions with strong competition from supermarket own brand products and consumer demand for variety and new products as their tastes change.

However, V is aware of the problems the company has encountered when undertaking new product development (NPD) in the past. Whilst collaboration is essential, instead there have been disagreements and arguments between the various departments.

The marketers complain that the Research and Development (R&D) department is very slow in responding to their proposals for new recipes and the whole process of R&D takes too long. The production department has protested that R&D does not consider the implications for the production process when coming up with new recipes and product packaging. The sales team is frustrated by the length of time the whole NPD process takes. The lack of new products puts it at a disadvantage when negotiating with retailers to sell M Company products.

The Finance department is concerned that the investment in NPD does not provide adequate returns, and both the marketing and R&D departments are always over budget. However, other departments see Finance as controlling and sanctioning spend rather than supporting new product development.

V knows that to remain competitive, changes need to be made to the NPD process in the company. He has decided to establish a cross-functional team to work on a new range of ready prepared frozen foods to appeal to the luxury end of the market.

Required

(a) Analyse the nature and sources of conflict between the different departments in M Company. **(10 marks)**

(b) Describe the factors that V should consider in building a successful cross-functional project team. **(15 marks)**

(Total = 25 marks)

25 Sales targets (11/06) 45 mins

The Direct Sales and Customer Contact Centre (the Centre) of A Insurance Company deals with vehicle, home and contents insurance products. B, who has been the manager of the Centre for the last three years, has a participative leadership style, involving staff in key decisions about the Centre. Initially she was very successful in achieving high staff morale as evidenced in the results of annual staff surveys for the first two years of her appointment. The Centre scored consistently higher on dimensions such as job satisfaction, communication and co-operation when compared with other parts of the company.

However, twelve months ago B was responsible for introducing a sales target system which involved allocating staff to teams as part of a restructuring programme. Each team is set targets and the results are published on a monthly basis in a league table. The team that is top of the league receives a cash bonus.

B is concerned that the restructuring has had an adverse effect on the performance of the Centre. She is particularly concerned that the results of the most recent staff survey show that communication and co-operation between teams have fallen dramatically. She has also observed animosity between the team leaders. Absenteeism has increase significantly, particularly in team Y. As part of her review of the issues facing the Centre, she has noted the following:

- Team X is always at the top of the league and, as a result, receives the cash bonus. The team leader of X is highly motivated and team spirit is high. Team members are constantly coming up with ideas on how to increase sales. The team seems to be very cohesive group and team members regularly organise social events for themselves.
- Team Y never succeeds in meeting its targets. The team leader does not seem bothered by this, and appears more interested in working out how much longer he needs to work before he can retire. Team members have complained to B about the team leader, and two members have resigned. There is a personality clash between the team leader and another member of the team who is viewed by the rest of the team as the 'unofficial' leader.
- Team Z, whilst achieving its targets, is always behind Team X. The team members are an extremely tight knit group, but have become very insular and are no longer responsive to the work needs of other members of staff in the Centre. They appear to have their own agenda.

The restructure of the Centre into teams and the sales target system was dictated by Head Office. Nevertheless, B is determined to take action to resolve the problems she currently faces.

Required

(a) Discuss the benefits and problems of introducing sales teams and the sales target system in the 'the Centre' of A Insurance Company. **(13 marks)**

(b) Explain the strategies that could be used by B to minimise the problems caused by introducing sales teams and the sales target system in order to improve performance in 'the Centre'. **(12 marks)**

(Total = 25 marks)

26 Performance and appraisal (5/07) 45 mins

B Local Council is responsible for providing public services, serving the local community. A new Chief Executive has recently been appointed with the explicit brief of improving the performance of the Council, which is currently in the spotlight for being inefficient and not focused enough on the needs of the local residents.

Over the last three months the Chief Executive has undertaken a review and is not impressed with what he has found. He has identified a number of weaknesses and problem areas which need to be remedied. The culture of the Local Council needs to change radically to become a more performance oriented one.

The initial findings from the review suggest that B Local Council is typified by a very bureaucratic culture, where power is determined by position and status. The managers in the Council defend their territory and are unwilling to share information and cooperate with other departments. Staff are only allowed to undertake the specific activities included in their job description. Many say they have had no training and that opportunities for career progression are limited. They receive no feedback on their performance but work under close supervision in what appears to be a 'them and us' culture between management and staff.

The review also identifies that morale is low. Staff feel they are not encouraged to participate in decision making and any ideas they have are stifled as a result of the chain of command. A significant number of staff have told the new Chief Executive that if they could get another job, they would leave the Council. Discussions with the HR Manager reveal that both absenteeism and staff turnover are high, despite competitive salaries and other excellent working conditions and benefits such as free car parking, a subsidised canteen and sports facilities.

The Chief Executive has identified a number of significant changes that need to be made to improve the performance of B Local Council. He is surprised that there is currently no staff performance appraisal in place and is keen that an effective system should be designed and implemented.

Required

(a) Analyse the problems in B Local Council, and discuss what the Chief Executive could do to improve performance. You should include reference to appropriate theories to support your analysis. **(13 marks)**

(b) Explain the key issues that should be considered in the design and the implementation of an effective staff performance appraisal system for B Local Council. **(12 marks)**

(Total = 25 marks)

27 Organisational structure (5/07) 45 mins

C Company operates in the leisure and entertainment industry. The company has achieved significant growth over the last five years through the acquisition of bars, restaurants, coffee shops and, more recently, roadside hotels. The company is organised on a functional basis and the senior management team has maintained tight control over the operations of the different business areas, making decisions centrally.

Despite its successes in making acquisitions, a number of key performance indicators are concerning the Board. It has recently undertaken a benchmarking study and discovered that the costs of the company are significantly higher than other operators in the industry. Decision making takes longer and the company is slower than its competitors to respond to new trends in the industry. It is also difficult to determine the revenue contributions of the different business activities.

Complaints have been made by managers working in the bars, restaurants, coffee shops and hotels that they need to be much more responsive to the needs of their customers but they have no authority to make decisions. Any suggestions they make have to go up the hierarchy, and so take far too much time. They also feel that the senior managers in Head Office are too removed from the business activities, each of which has different needs and priorities.

The Board is undertaking a major review of the strategy and organisational structure of the company. The HR Director is insistent that the problems facing the company are not so much to do with the strategic direction, but more about the unsuitable structure and mechanistic design. She believes that the functional structure is no longer appropriate. Her proposal is that the structure should change and that a more organic organisational design with decentralisation would help to improve performance.

Required

(a) Explain the purpose of organisational structure and explain why it is an important concept for C Company. **(10 marks)**

(b) Evaluate the extent to which the HR Director's proposal will help to resolve the problems facing C Company and recommend what would be an appropriate organisational structure. **(15 marks)**

(Total = 25 marks)

28 Leadership (11/07) **45 mins**

J has worked for P Accountancy and Consultancy firm for over fifteen years. For the last five years she was the team leader for client support. J has a vast amount of experience and her overall outlook to work is positive. She takes a keen interest in the performance of individual members of her team, holding regular team meetings and encouraging her staff to contribute their ideas and to participate in target setting and decision making. The team always achieves its targets.

Six months ago, J gained a well deserved promotion which meant moving to another department. Her replacement is T, who has just completed his professional accountancy qualifications and has recently joined P Accountancy and Consultancy. This is his first leadership role and he is keen to impress his departmental manager. T feels that J's approach had been too soft. His view is that too much time had been spent in meetings and consultation and that staff would have been better just 'getting on with their work' since it is his job to make all the decisions.

T expects people to respect his position and authority without question. All his communications are sent by email or memo and he does not see the point of holding team meetings. He has recently introduced new performance targets without consultation. Most of the team feel the targets set are unreasonable. T has little time for people who need support in performing their role. Morale within the team is at an all time low and absenteeism has increased. Some staff are now looking to move out of the client support department.

T's line manager, F, is aware that T is very ambitious and hopes to progress in the firm. When T was recruited he was identified as having the potential to move quickly up the career ladder within P Accountancy and Consultancy. F feels that T might benefit from the mentoring system operated by the firm. However, F is also aware that there are problems in the client support department since T took over as team leader. He feels that T needs training to help him become more effective in his leadership role.

Required

(a) Explain the different approaches to leadership demonstrated by J and T, making reference to leadership theories. **(12 marks)**

(b) Describe how the concept of action-centred leadership would help in identifying the training T needs to become a more effective leader. **(7 marks)**

(c) Explain how a mentoring system could help T. **(6 marks)**

(Total = 25 marks)

29 Groups (5/08) **45 mins**

T works for J Company which designs and manufactures children's toys. She has recently been appointed as the project manager of a project to design a new range of educational toys for children aged 3 – 6 years. She is currently thinking about the issues that will face her in delivering the objectives of the project. She is confident that she has a good understanding of what needs to happen at the various stages of the project lifecycle and has strong technical skills which will help her in using some of the project management tools and techniques.

T realises that this will not be enough to ensure successful project outcomes and knows that it will be important to have a good project team. However, she is also concerned that people working in teams can sometimes be problematic, particularly since the project team will be made up of people from different parts of the organisation, who have not worked together before. The team members will come from finance, marketing, production, IT and sales.

Required

(a) Describe the stages of group formation, as suggested by researchers, that T's project team should pass through if it is to become effective in performing the project task. **(10 marks)**

(b) Explain the potential problems that could hinder the effectiveness of T's project team and explain how they might be overcome. **(15 marks)**

(Total = 25 marks)

30 Entrepreneurs (5/08) **45 mins**

E Company, established over ten years ago, designs interactive games software. Up until two years ago it was very successful, performing well in the market place and returning high dividends to its shareholders. However, in recent years, E Company has lost significant market share. The Board decided to employ a consultant to try to help it determine what it needs to do to re-establish the company as market leader.

The findings from the consultant's initial investigation reported that as the company has grown, bureaucratic controls have been put in place which are stifling the creativity and innovation needed to be at the forefront of games software design and to compete in the current competitive conditions.

Employees no longer feel inclined to contribute new ideas because of the lengthy decision making processes needed to gain approval. In addition, they are unwilling to try out new ways of working because now, when things go wrong, they are blamed for making mistakes. Rather than adopting an open and flexible approach, managers conform to E Company rules. This has led to the organisation failing to exploit potential new ventures because they are considered to have too great a risk. People are rewarded for achieving their personal objectives but this often means that they are not encouraged to think beyond the boundaries of their current activities.

In making her recommendations to the Board, the consultant has suggested that the company needs to encourage greater entrepreneurial spirit within the organisation and reduce the barriers to creativity and innovation.

Required

(a) Explain the characteristics / qualities that people who exhibit an entrepreneurial spirit have, which might make it difficult for them to work in the environment of E Company. **(10 marks)**

(b) Explain what could be done to encourage greater creativity and innovation in E Company. **(15 marks)**

(Total = 25 marks)

PROJECT MANAGEMENT

Questions 31 to 49 cover project management, the subject of Part B of the BPP Study Text for Paper P5.

Section A questions: Project management

31 Objective test questions — 36 mins

31.1 Identify which ONE of the following best describes the scope of a project? 5/05

- A A statement a client needs
- B The extent of work needed to produce the project's deliverables
- C The specification of resources required
- D The sequence of activities

(2 marks)

31.2 In the PRINCE2 system of project management, what is the name of the process that controls work done by specialist teams by agreeing what work is to be done and ensuring it is carried out to the proper standard?

- A Managing product delivery
- B Configuration management
- C Directing a project
- D Managing stage boundaries

(2 marks)

31.3 Identify three missing words (using a, b and c) to complete the diagram of the five process areas of project management proposed by the Project Management Institute. 5/05

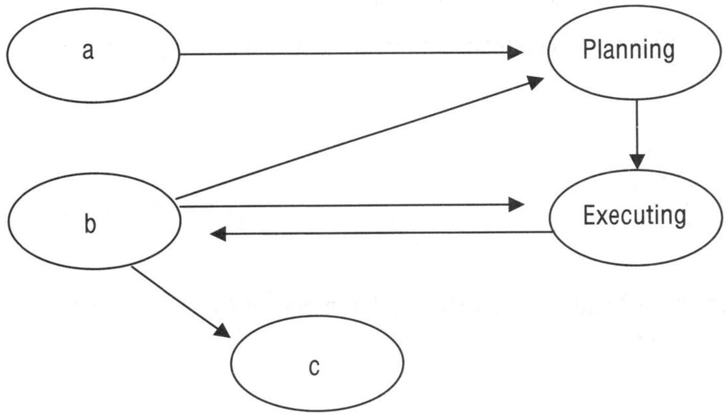

(3 marks)

31.4 List **three** types of feasibility study that might be undertaken as part of project planning. 5/05

(3 marks)

The following data is to be used to answer questions 31.5 and 31.6 below

A company is about to undertake a project about which the following data is available.

Activity	*Preceded by activity*	*Duration* Days	*Workers required*
A	–	3	6
B	–	5	3
C	B	2	4
D	A	1	4
E	A	6	5
F	D	3	6
G	C, E	3	3

31.5 What is the duration of the critical path for this project? **(4 marks)**

31.6 What is the minimum number of staff that will be required on day 6 of the project, assuming the critical path is not extended? **(6 marks)**

(Total = 20 marks)

32 Objective test questions — 36 mins

32.1 Project W is a severely time-constrained research project and must be completed to high quality standards. The project staff all have academic qualifications and a wealth of relevant experience. They are divided into four specialist teams, each working on separate, complex problems. Each team is headed by an expert in the relevant field. The project manager has good experience of the general theoretical background to the work being done but ceased to be involved in practical research some years ago.

Using the Ashridge classification, which management style would you expect to be least useful to the project manager?

A Tells
B Sells
C Consults
D Joins **(2 marks)**

32.2 The project 7S model and the McKinsey 7S model differ in only one particular. Which of the following is not part of the project 7S model?

A Strategy
B Stakeholders
C Systems
D Specialisation **(2 marks)**

32.3 What is the role of the project sponsor?

A Provides and is accountable for the resources invested in the project
B Communicates the project vision within the organisation
C Takes responsibility for delivering the project on time
D Represents the interests of the project board **(2 marks)**

32.4 Which of the following is not a feature of the PRINCE2 project management system?

A A project is driven by its business case
B The system may be used for projects of any size
C The system focuses on the technical processes of project management
D A clear management structure is defined **(2 marks)**

32.5 In *Maylor's* 4D model of the project lifecycle, the components of the delivery stage are:

A Planning, execution, handover, review
B Startup, execution, completion, handover
C Planning, startup, execution, completion
D Startup, planning, execution, completion **(2 marks)**

The following data is to be used to answer questions 32.6 and 32.7 below

Activity	*Immediately preceding activity*	*Duration (weeks)*
A	–	5
B	–	4
C	A	2
D	B	1
E	B	5
F	B	5
G	C, D	4
H	F	3
I	F	2

32.6 What is the duration of the critical path for this project? **(5 marks)**

32.7 What is the free float on activity D? **(5 marks)**

(Total = 20 marks)

Section B questions: Project management

33 Project network **18 mins**

The following tasks, estimates and precedences have been agreed in a project.

Task ID	Task description	Estimate (in days)	Precedences
A	Write project initiation document	3	
B	Research Site One	4	A
C	Research Site Two	2	A
D	Document requirements – Site One	6	B
E	Document requirements – Site Two	5	C
F	Define non-functional requirements	2	A
G	Define agreed requirements	3	D, E, F
H	Write invitation to tender	4	G

Required

(a) Construct a project network for this project. **(6 marks)**

(b) Which activities are on the critical path of the project? **(1 mark)**

(c) What is the estimated elapsed duration of the project? **(1 mark)**

What would the effect be on the elapsed duration of the project if:

(d) Task C overran by two days? **(1 mark)**

(e) Task B overran by one day? **(1 mark)**

(Total = 10 marks)

The following data are given for questions 34 and 35

You work for a firm of management accountants that specialises in implementing information systems. The latest assignment is to implement new systems at a small chain of ten shops managed by FRS Co and to integrate these into the systems of a multinational retail organisation (MRO Inc) that has recently acquired them. FRS Co sells a range of wines, spirits and groceries.

Draft implementation plans

The information systems department of MRO Inc had drawn up an outline timetable for the introduction of the new system to FRS Co.

The first draft of this follows.

Task	*Description*	*Planned duration (weeks)*	*Preceding activities*
A	Communication – inform staff at each FRS shop and indicate how it will affect them	1	–
B	Carry out systems audit at each FRS shop	2	A
C	Agree detailed implementation plan with board of directors	1	B
D	Order and receive hardware requirements	4	C
E	Install hardware at all FRS shops	4	D
F	Install software at all FRS shops	2	D
G	Arrange training at premises of MRO Inc	3	D
H	Test systems at all FRS shops	4	E and F
I	Implement changeover at all shops	10	G and H

34 FRS 1 **18 mins**

Required

Describe the major issues to be considered in managing the project to implement the new system at FRS Co.
(10 marks)

35 FRS 2 **18 mins**

Required

Produce a critical path analysis of the draft implementation plan suggested by the IS department manager. (This should identify the critical path and the total elapsed time.) **(10 marks)**

36 Critical path analysis **18 mins**

The following activities, time estimates and precedences have been identified for the selection, purchase and implementation of a software package.

Activity		*Precedence*	*Estimate (days)*
A	Define Project Initiation Document	–	5
B	Define requirements	A	8
C	Define training plan	B	3
D	Issue Invitation to Tender	B	3
E	Select Supplier	D	2
F	Install hardware and software	E	5
G	Training course	C,F	3
H	Enter master file data	G	5
I	Convert operational data	F	9
J	Parallel running	H,I	10

Required

Construct a network diagram for this project. Identify the critical path. **(10 marks)**

37 R Company (11/05) **18 mins**

R Company, a manufacturer and retailer of fashion clothes, has invested in a new technology system to improve the logistics of the movement of clothes between its warehouses and chain of 250 retail outlets. Ensuring that the outlets have the right supply of clothes is a critical success factor for the company. However, the warehousing inventory control and logistics project set up to develop and deliver the new system has experienced numerous problems. The project ended up being well over budget and was also late in delivering the system. Now, only three months after the new system has been installed, it is apparent that the project has not delivered its objective. Instead, the company is facing a crisis with many store managers complaining that they are not receiving the correct inventory. Even worse, some stores are out of stock of key ranges, whereas the warehouses are full of clothing.

A meeting between the project team and project sponsor has ended up with everyone blaming each other, saying it was not their responsibility. It is clear that they did not use a project management methodology and did not have adequate project control systems in place so that the problems that have now transpired could have been identified and rectified earlier in the project lifecycle.

Required

Recommend to R Company a project management methodology/approach, explaining how it could have helped to prevent the failures of the warehousing, inventory control and logistics project. **(10 marks)**

38 Conference network (5/05) **18 mins**

R has taken on the responsibility for organising the annual conference for the local Society of Management Accountants. Remembering the project management techniques she came across when studying for her professional qualification, R has decided that critical path analysis may be helpful in planning the conference.

As a start, R has drawn up a list of the activities she must complete in preparation for the conference, she has identified the dependency between the different activities and the time she thinks each will take.

Activity		*Dependency*	*Time (weeks)*
Determine conference theme	A	–	3
Research alternative venues	B	–	6
Identify and book guest speakers	C	A	4
Book venue	D	B	2
Print conference papers	E	C	8
Print and send out invitations	F	D	4
Confirm final arrangements with venue and deliver documents	G	E, F	2

Required

Using the information from the scenario, construct a network diagram and explain how information from this could be useful to R in planning the conference. **(10 marks)**

39 Risk (11/06) **18 mins**

It is often claimed that all project management is risk management since risk is an inherent and inevitable characteristic of most projects. The aim of the project manager is to combat the various hazards to which a project may be exposed.

Required

Explain the concept of risk and the ways in which risk can be managed in a project. **(10 marks)**

40 Project initiation stage (5/07) **18 mins**

A number of volunteers were so moved by news coverage reporting on the difficulties facing earthquake victims in F country that they organised a sponsored walk to raise funds for the appeal. Two of the volunteers visited some of the worst hit areas and this prompted them to set up their on charity. Their first major project is to rebuild and provide equipment for a school in one of the villages that has been devastated by the disaster. They hope to have the school up and running in twelve months' time.

A number of people have been enlisted to help with the project, including some local businesses as well as family and friends. The volunteers realise this will be a more complex project than organising a sponsored walk and therefore will require a much more professional approach to ensure that they achieve their objectives. They have limited experience of managing projects and are trying to determine the purpose of the different phases and activities. P, one of the volunteers, has been given the task of finding out about the first stage, initiating the project, and specifically, how to put together a project initiation document.

Required

To help P, describe what is involved in the initiation stage of a project and explain what should be included in the project initiation document for the school project. **(10 marks)**

41 Project feasibility (11/07) 18 mins

S Company operates in the leisure industry and already has a number of different business interests including ice skating rinks and an outdoor artificial ski slope. At the last Board meeting, a suggestion was put forward to convert the 'dry' ski slope into an indoor Snow Dome to compete with rival companies who have successfully introduced similar facilities in other parts of the country, and which customers of S Company are now travelling to use.

Such a development for S Company would involve using the latest snow making technology to create real snow in a controlled environment. This would provide a better experience for customers than the 'dry' ski slope, which currently uses plastic matting in place of the snow.

A project team has been set up to develop the idea. Having set out the scope for the Snow Dome project, the project team is now at the stage of investigating the feasibility.

Required

Explain the purpose of a project feasibility study, making reference to the different types of feasibility that should be considered for the Snow Dome project. **(10 marks)**

42 Project completion (5/08) 18 mins

S has been working on a major IT project for his client, X Hotel chain. The project brief was to design and implement a customer reservation system, which would enable customers to book on-line for rooms at any of X's hotels worldwide. When commissioning the project, the hotel chain required that the new system should be ready to coincide with the launch of its new flagship hotel opening in six months' time.

The project is now in the final stage of its lifecycle and the customer reservation system is ready to 'go live'. S is from an IT background and this is his first time in the role of project manager. He is finding the whole process of finishing off the final details of the project tedious, and is keen to get started with the next project that he is due to manage.

Required

Explain to S why project completion is an important activity and explain what is involved during this stage of the project management lifecycle. **(10 marks)**

Section C questions: Project management

43 Project planning and roles (5/05) 45 mins

S Company is a major retailer selling mobile phones. In recent years the Company has opened new outlets and taken on more support staff at the head office. As a result the Company has outgrown its existing headquarters and so the decision has been taken to relocate to a larger purpose-built building.

Although the building work is complete, there are a number of different initiatives associated with the relocation. These include making sure that the premises are ready to move into on time and within budget and setting up a customer service contact team to support the retail outlets dealing with customer enquiries and complaints. In addition, an upgraded office IT support system is to be designed and must be ready for installation in the new premises.

P, the head of facilities management, has decided to establish a project team to ensure that all of the activities associated with the move to the new premises are co-ordinated and within budget. She has the formal role of project sponsor working on behalf of the Board and has appointed D to manage the project.

Required

(a) Identify and explain the activities that D would need to undertake in the planning phase of the project for re-location. **(15 marks)**

(b) Compare and contrast the roles of P, as the project sponsor and D, as the project manager. **(10 marks)**

(Total = 25 marks)

44 X Company (11/05) 45 mins

X Company is a global consultancy company specialising in organisational change and restructuring. The service offered to clients usually involves the formation of teams to carry out change projects in companies. The teams are drawn from different areas of X Company, based around different specialisms.

T, the HR Director, is concerned that the methods of recruitment and selection for new consultants has emphasised the skills associated with particular specialisms, for example marketing expertise, technology or financial technical skills. He feels that insufficient attention has been given to the skills of the project manager which are essential to the success of the company's project based work.

As a result, he has recently introduced a new recruitment and selection system, which includes a specification of the skills the company should be looking for in future project managers. One of the selection tests he has devised will involve candidates in delivering a presentation which explains why they may need to use different styles of leadership during a project and provides examples of the other key skills that they feel a project manager should possess.

Y recently applied for a job in X Company, specialising in finance, and whilst confident that he has the financial expertise required, he is less certain about the project manager skills he might need. He is pleased that he has been short listed for interview and is researching what he might include in his presentation. As part of this he has asked you to help him to understand the key skills of an effective project manager.

Required

(a) Explain to Y how an understanding of leadership style theories could help him to be more effective as a project manager. **(10 marks)**

(b) Describe the other project manager skills, besides leadership skills, that Y should include in his presentation, explaining why they are important. **(15 marks)**

(Total = 25 marks)

45 Z Company (11/05) — 45 mins

T has just returned to his job in the Finance Department of Z Company, having spent the last six months as a member of a project team working on the development of an Educational Visitor Centre for the company.

Reflecting on his experiences whilst working on the project, he feels that most of his time was spent in meetings that did not achieve anything, but rather wasted his time. He also feels that the final stages of the project were not dealt with effectively, with the project members going back to their functional jobs without any discussion or feedback on the project performance and outcomes.

He has now been asked to take on the role of project manager for a new project and is determined that he will improve the experience for his project team.

Required

(a) Discuss the problems that may be associated with project meetings. Make recommendations on the methods T could use to ensure the meetings he arranges as project manager, are effective. **(15 marks)**

(b) Evaluate the contribution of the various activities that should be carried out as part of project closure, the post completion review and audit of the project. **(10 marks)**

(Total = 25 marks)

46 C Hospital (5/06) — 45 mins

The main agenda item at the meeting of the Executive Board of C Hospital is to discuss the new pay and reward system. The hospital needs to make changes to the existing pay systems to respond to government requirements to reform reward systems as part of its pay modernisation agenda. The aim is to harmonise the payments systems for different categories of workers in the hospital on to one pay scale. This will mean that there is one pay scale for all employees of the hospital including nurses, physiotherapists, radiographers, technicians and support staff (ie cleaners, porters, and kitchen staff). The rationale for the new system is to achieve greater flexibility, to assist in recruitment and retention of staff and to reward people for their contribution to the achievement of hospital targets.

The hospital has twelve months in which to design and implement the new system in order to meet the government target of May 20X7. There is a huge amount of work that will need to be undertaken to deliver the new system, and a number of different stakeholders to satisfy.

At the meeting of the Board there was some discussion concerning who should be responsible for undertaking all tasks and activities associated with the development of the new system. The Human Resource (HR) director proposed that a project manager should be appointed and a project team set up. Whilst he would expect some members of his HR team to be part of the team, he is adamant that although his staff are responsible for administering the current payroll system and dealing with staff enquires about pay and rewards, designing a new pay system should not form part of the 'business as usual' work for the HR department.

Required

(a) Describe the attributes of the proposed project in C Hospital that distinguish it from 'business as usual' work. **(10 marks)**

(b) Produce an outline of the different stages in the project to design and implement a new pay and reward system for C Hospital. **(15 marks)**

(Total = 25 marks)

47 Project Management Software (11/06) **45 mins**

As part of M University's ambitious strategy for growth, investment is being made in the development of a student village.

The finance director of M University has been appointed as the project manager and is in the early stages of setting up the project. This will be a complex project involving the construction of new buildings to provide for the growth in student numbers, including living accommodation for students, teaching rooms, a state-of-the-art business and conference facility aimed at attracting corporate clients to work with the University, and sports and recreation facilities. The build will be a collaborative venture funded by the University and investment from two local businesses.

The regional authority currently owns the land that the University wants to acquire to build the student village. The authority, the members of which are directly elected by local residents makes the decision on whether to accept or reject planning proposals made. It was recently reported in the local paper that the local residents are unhappy about the proposal.

The development will mean that staff from two University departments will be relocated to the new site which is two miles away from the main campus. In the first open meeting held by the finance director to communicate the proposals he was net with a hostile reaction from staff, with most of them being very unhappy about moving to the new site.

The finance director knows that this will be a complex project to manage and that project management software will be essential in making his job objective achievable. He is also aware that the project has a number of different stakeholders that he must consider in putting together the project plan.

Required

(a) Discuss how project management software might help the finance director and his team successfully carry out the project. **(15 marks)**

(b) Using examples, explain why the finance director should consider the interest of the different stakeholders in the student village project. **(10 marks)**

(Total = 25 marks)

48 Project planning (5/07) **45 mins**

Over the years, D, an entrepreneur, has had a number of business successes in the retail sector. She is keen to move on to bigger things and has identified an opportunity to develop a Shopping Centre.

Having secured the interest of several potential investors, identified a suitable site, had an architect draw up plans and received planning permission, D is eager that construction work on the Shopping Centre should start as soon as possible. She appointed G, who has an impressive record of managing successful projects, to be project manager. However, D is already interfering in the management of the project and is in conflict with G. She is frustrated by the time G seems to need in the planning phase, and is irritated by his insistence on formalising the project management process. D is now putting pressure on G to miss out elements in the first stages of planning the project, and to get started on the construction work for the Shopping Centre.

Required

(a) Explain the potential problems that the Shopping Centre project could face without good project planning. **(10 marks)**

(b) Explain the contribution of different project management tools and techniques that could help G in planning the project. **(15 marks)**

(Total = 25 marks)

49 Project management (11/07) **45 mins**

X is the project manager responsible for the implementation of the new customer information database in Y Company. He was selected to take on the role of project manager because of his strong technical capability.

The project represents an important development and financial investment for Y Company. A number of different business areas in the company have interests in the project and are dependent on the new customer information database going live on the due date.

Unfortunately, the project is not going well and the project steering committee wants answers from X. He feels he is under pressure to keep on schedule but lacks the support of his project team, who keep complaining that they do not know what they are supposed to be doing. It would appear that some members of the project team are not completing tasks on time and are not providing the information needed to progress with the system development. At the same time, the project sponsor is pushing X to make short cuts to make sure the system goes live on time.

X feels that many of the problems he faces are due to lack of project controls.

Required

(a) Explain the responsibilities of X in his role as project manager **(12 marks)**

(b) (i) Discuss the purpose of project control. **(4 marks)**

(ii) Explain the controls that should be set up for the customer information database project in order to help X manage the various stages of the project. **(9 marks)**

(Total = 25 marks)

STRATEGIC MANAGEMENT

Questions 50 to 73 cover strategic management, the subject of Part C of the BPP Study Text for Paper P5.

Section A questions: Strategic management

50 Objective test questions **36 mins**

50.1 Which of the following is least likely to be characteristic of a strategic decision?

A Matches the organisation's activities to its environment
B Sets the organisation's overall long term direction
C Determines the organisation's choice of accounting software
D Has important implications for organisational change **(2 marks)**

50.2 Which of the following is an aspect of an organisation's environment?

A A history of labour disputes
B A declining share price, which limits the organisation's ability to raise new capital
C Pressure from the production director to adopt a demanding trade association-approved testing system
D Acceptance of a government-promoted commitment to reduce atmospheric pollution **(2 marks)**

50.3 What is business strategy concerned with?

A What business the organisation should be in
B How the organisation approaches a particular market
C Decisions of strategic importance at operational level
D Decision of strategic scope **(2 marks)**

50.4 What is the difference between (a) a deliberate strategy and (b) a realised strategy?

A (b) is one type of (a)
B (a) is the result of detailed planning while (b) emerges from a pattern of behaviour
C (a) is one type of (b)
D (a) is the result of detailed planning while (b) derives from logical incrementalism **(2 marks)**

50.5 With which of the phrases below, associated with assessing the processes the organisation must excel at, are the names *Kaplan and Norton* associated?

A Goal congruence
B Internal business perspective
C Critical success factors
D System goals **(2 marks)**

50.6 Bargaining, satisficing and sequential attention are all methods of dealing with what?

A Goal conflict
B Stakeholders
C Ideological goals
D Goal congruence **(2 marks)**

50.7 Which of the following are connected stakeholders, as opposed to internal or external stakeholders?

A A company's work force
B A company's local municipal authority
C A company's management
D A company's suppliers **(2 marks)**

50.8 Which of the following does not feature in the McKinsey 7S model?

A Style
B Shared objectives
C Skills
D Staff **(2 marks)**

50.9 In a multi-divisional organisation producing a range of products for different markets, business strategy is primarily concerned with:

A Setting the direction for the organisation.
B The competitiveness of a particular division.
C The efficiency of production, marketing and other functions.
D Alignment of strategy with other organisations. **(2 marks)**

50.10 The external stakeholders of an organisation include

A Pressure groups, government, community.
B Employees, Board of Directors, middle management.
C Government, Board of Directors, suppliers.
D Community, management, government. **(2 marks)**

(Total = 20 marks)

51 Objective test questions 36 mins

51.1 Identify which ONE of the following perspectives of strategic management is defined by Mintzberg as 'patterns or consistencies realised despite, or in the absence of, intentions'? 5/05

A Rational
B Local Incrementalism
C Emergent
D Positioning **(2 marks)**

51.2 The logical incrementalist approach to strategy resembles the rational model in that it

A Is similarly dependent on detailed medium-term forecasting
B Depends on managerial activity
C Emphasises the possession of core comptences
D Can deal with a wide range of strategic possibilities **(2 marks)**

51.3 *Mintzberg* suggests that systems goals can subvert mission. Which of the following is likely to be a system goal rather than an element of mission?

A Performance standards
B Purpose
C Values
D Growth **(2 marks)**

51.4 Porter's work on industry competition suggests that the strength of market entry depends on the existence of barriers to entry against the entrant. Identify **three** factors that create barriers to entering an industry.

5/05

(3 marks)

51.5 Say whether the statement below is true or false.

'The organismic (or organic) organisation described by *Burns and Stalker* appears to have much in common with the task-oriented organisation described by *Harrison*. **(1 mark)**

51.6 The Boston Consulting Group matrix classifies companies in terms of two business variables. What are they? **(2 marks)**

51.7 *Michael Porter* identifies five competitive forces in the task environment. State four of them *other than current competitor rivalry.* **(4 marks)**

51.8 Identify the terms that complete this statement from the list below.

'*Mendelow* proposed classifying stakeholders in terms of their level of .... and ....

(shareholding, authority, interest, turnover, power influence, profitability) **(2 marks)**

51.9 Which of the following is described as a primary activity in *Porter's* value chain?

A Procurement
B Human resource management
C Service
D Technology development

(2 marks)

(Total = 20 marks)

Section B questions: Strategic management

52 Professional ethics **18 mins**

Required

Recommend the steps that both professional accountancy bodies and organisations more generally can take to ensure that their members take seriously the ethical principles included in their organisations' codes of conduct.
(10 marks)

53 Fast food culture **18 mins**

A very successful multinational fast food company (FFC) from country S has just opened a small group of restaurants in country C, but a range of problems has affected the new venture. Customers have complained about the menus, the seating arrangements and the music that is played. Local residents have protested about the architecture of restaurant buildings, and the restaurant employees have complained about the style and practices of the managers from country S who run the business.

Required

Using your knowledge of national and corporate cultures, explain why FFC is experiencing the problems noted in the scenario. **(10 marks)**

54 T Venture (5/06) **18 mins**

T is seeking investment funds for his new venture to open a chain of fast-food restaurants. Despite the competition in this sector, having undertaken market research amongst his target market, T is convinced that he can succeed with his fast-food concept.

He is currently in the process of putting together a business plan which will outline his strategy to enter the market place. Having recently attended a seminar on what to include in a business plan, T remembers that he will need to determine what the critical success factors (CSFs) for his business are, but he is confused about how these differ from core competences.

Required

(a) Explain why T needs to determine the CSFs as part of the development of his strategy and how they differ from core competences. **(6 marks)**

(b) Identify what the CSFs might be for T's chain of fast food restaurants. **(4 marks)**

(Total = 10 marks)

55 N Airline (11/05) **18 mins**

N Airline operates in the short haul flight industry. Unlike many of its competitors who are constantly seeking to reduce costs, often at the expense of customer service, the foundation of N's business strategy is based on providing a superior quality of service. Its mission is to be market leader, providing unrivalled customer service, in flight comfort and reliability in the short haul airline industry. N Airlines views its customers as central to strategic developments, and values its staff in building success.

Required

(a) Distinguish between the concepts of mission and objectives. **(4 marks)**

(b) Using examples, illustrate how the mission for N Airline could be translated into strategic objectives. **(6 marks)**

(Total = 10 marks)

The following data are given for questions 56 and 57 below

The E Company consists of automobile engine, marine engine and aerospace engine businesses. It has built its global reputation for engine design and quality on its engineering capability. Though the marine engine business has not been performing well for some time, the E Company has dominated the supply of engines for the luxury end of the automobile market for years. Unfortunately for the E Company, however, the market in luxury automobiles is changing. Exchange rate movements and increased production costs have made the E Company less competitive and its rivals are rapidly catching up in terms of engine quality and design. As a result, the latest annual report shows turnover down, margins reduced and the company barely breaking even.

You have just attended a strategy meeting at the E Company in which:

- Manager A argued that the automobile engine business strategy was wrong;
- Manager B claimed that the major problem had been the failure to properly implement functional strategies;
- Manager C said that more attention should be paid to the threats and opportunities of the external environment so that the E Company could position itself more realistically; and
- Manager D claimed that the company should really be seeking to develop further its core engineering competence if it was going to regain its competitiveness in the market place

After the meeting, a junior manager who had been in attendance asks you to explain what his senior colleagues had been talking about.

56 Engines 1 — 18 mins

Required

Explain the differences between corporate level strategy, business level strategy and functional level strategy in E Company. **(10 marks)**

57 Engines 2 — 18 mins

Required

For the benefit of the junior manager, explain the theoretical perspective on strategy formation adopted by manager C and manager D. **(10 marks)**

58 Screen — 18 mins

Screen was established in 1960 as a charitable trust to promote and increase public awareness of the cinema as an entertainment and cultural medium. Screen is managed through a part-time board of governors drawn from the film industry, from government nominees and from the membership of the Screen Institute. Screen has five major activity areas or operational divisions each of which has its own manager. These are as follows.

- The multi-screen Film Theatre (FT) which provides performances for the general public of new releases, classic films and minority interest films.
- The Museum of the Cinema (MoC) which provides a permanent exhibition of the history and development of the film industry.

- The Globe restaurant, bars and cafeteria, which are open to cinema goers and to the general public.
- The Film Archive Unit (FAU), which is concerned with the transfer of old film archive material to video as a means of long-term preservation.
- The Screen Institute (SFI), membership of which is open to members of the public by annual subscription. Members receive preferential bookings to events, seat discounts and a free copy of CiniCentre's monthly magazine, 'Film Fan'. The magazine and associated publishing activities also form part of the responsibilities of the film institute.

Screen is partly funded by government grant and partly funded from its own commercial activities. However, as a part of government policy to reduce the contribution to the arts, the grant to Screen will, over the next three years, be reduced by 20%.

The board of governors were directed by the government to bring in an external CEO as a result of a series of management problems, which have attracted considerable adverse publicity.

- A failure to stay within government financial guidelines of not operating an annual financial deficit.
- Press criticism about the loss of archive film due to the failure to speed up the transfer to video tape.
- Further press criticism on the recent imposition of an admission charge to the Museum of the Cinema.
- Reports of poor quality service and expensive food in the Globe restaurants.
- Persistent labour relations problems with the public sector staff trade union, which represents almost all the non-managerial museum, film theatre, clerical and catering staff.
- Complaints from the CFI membership that the film season has concentrated too much on popular income earning mainstream films with a subsequent fall in the number of showings of classic and non-English language films.

Required

Identify four different Screen stakeholder groups, indicating for each, its potential power and influence and its likely expectations. **(10 marks)**

59 Social responsibility (5/05) 18 mins

Many organisations now include explicit reference to their commitment to act in a socially responsible manner in their mission statement. This then forms an integral part of organisational strategies and policies. However, some shareholders see social responsibility as conflicting with their main interest in the company which is that of creating maximum shareholder wealth.

Required

Explain the main arguments for and against the view that socially responsible business decisions can achieve sustainable competitive performance and improve shareholder value. **(10 marks)**

60 Company J 1 18 mins

In order to avoid payment of the tariffs imposed on imports by a Western country, W, a Japanese automobile company, J, has decided to produce its cars within W. Company J intends to staff the car plant initially with its own Japanese managers and supervisors and to use Japanese working practices. Production-line and other employees will be recruited from the country in which it is located.

Required

Explain the factors that can influence the culture of an organisation. Discuss why Company J's new plant may develop a different culture to other Western plants. **(10 marks)**

61 Corporate appraisal (11/06) **18 mins**

T is the CEO of S Company, a manufacturer of hair and body care products. Over the years the company has been market leader in its field, achieved through being at the forefront of product innovation. S company has invested heavily in research and development, which has enabled it to be the first in the market to introduce new variants of the product range. However, this has meant that the cost of operations has spiralled leading to an increase in the price of the company's products.

Up until last year, the company had been very successful in increasing its market share. However, the most recent key performance indicators show that sales are down. It would seem that supermarket 'own brand products' are stealing market share and T is worried about the future ability of the company to meet its objectives for continued growth. T has decided to undertaken a strategic review, the first stage of which will involve conducting a corporate appraisal.

Required

Explain what would be involved in undertaking a corporate appraisal, demonstrating how the information could be used to help T in his review. **(10 marks)**

62 Strategic planning (5/07) **18 mins**

T is the owner manager of a small business that designs and produces high quality garden furniture. The business started out as a hobby using T's creative design and carpentry talents, and he has been surprised by his success. Over the last year the business has experienced unplanned growth and by chance T has just won a contract to supply a local chain of DIY stores.

The local Chamber of Commerce has recently sent him an invitation to attend a number of seminars entitled 'Formal Strategic Planning for Small Businesses'. However, T is doubtful that the content of the seminars will be of any relevance to him and feels he cannot afford time away from his business. His view is that it is best to let the strategies and developments for his business emerge.

Required

Explain the reasons why T is right to be doubtful about the relevance of formal strategic planning for his business. **(10 marks)**

63 Corporate governance and ethics (5/07) **18 mins**

M is Chairman and Managing Director of Y Company which he started 15 years ago, specialising in the manufacture of hospital uniforms. The company has been very successful and, through a series of acquisitions, has diversified into the manufacture of a range of corporate and other uniforms, employing 3,500 people. M is a major force in the company. His management style is very autocratic and he is unwilling to involve others in decisions about the future strategic direction of the company. Recently, M announced to the Board that he is intending that Y Company becomes listed on the stock exchange.

D, the Finance Director of the company has become increasingly concerned about the decisions being made by M and the fact that he has put pressure on her to participate in some questionable accounting practices. She has had to cover up M's substantial remuneration package, which M has awarded to himself. D is also aware that M has accepted bribes from foreign suppliers and of insider dealing relating to a number of the acquisitions. There is a lack of appropriate control systems and accountability in the company.

D has discussed her concerns with other members of the Board, all of whom work for Y Company, including the Marketing Director, Production Director and HR Director. However, they seem willing to overlook the wrongdoings of M and never challenge the decisions made by him. The opportunity to do so is limited since the Board meets on an irregular and infrequent basis.

At the last Board meeting M set out his plans to close the existing factories and move operations to L country where he has been in secret negotiations with representatives of the government. The main objective is to benefit from low cost labour, since the country has very little employment legislation to protect workers and has a poor human rights record.

Required

Explain the corporate governance and ethical issues facing Y Company. **(10 marks)**

64 Role culture (11/07) 18 mins

Up until two years ago, E Company enjoyed a monopoly position in the energy industry. However, a change in government policy has meant that new competition has been encouraged to move into the industry, with E Company losing its monopoly. The Company now finds itself facing severe difficulties.

E Company has developed a strong culture over the years which can be typified as a role culture. This is now acting as a barrier to the organisation's ability to change, to become more flexible and to be able to respond more quickly to changes in the environment and initiatives by its competitors.

E Company is falling behind its competitors when it comes to innovations in energy services. Developments in new services require staff to work together across functional boundaries. However, this is unheard of in E Company, where people fiercely protect their functional specialism and will only work on the tasks specified in their job descriptions.

Required

(a) Discuss why a role culture may no longer be appropriate for E Company. **(5 marks)**

(b) Recommend, with reasons, the type of culture to which the company now needs to move. **(5 marks)**

(Total = 10 marks)

65 Levels of strategy (5/08) 18 mins

V plc operates in the leisure and entertainment industry. It has a range of different ventures worldwide including fitness centres, casinos, cinemas and sports bars, each of which operates as a separate business.

Required

Distinguish between the different levels at which strategy should exist in V plc. **(10 marks)**

Section C questions: Strategic management

66 Key influences **45 mins**

The discovery of heavily overstated profits in some of the largest US corporations in 2002 undermined investor confidence in company accounts and called into question the integrity of senior managers, their professional staff and the presumed independence of external auditors.

Required

(a) Describe the *key influences* on the ethical conduct of senior management of business corporations, their professional staff and those involved with auditing their accounts **(12 marks)**

(b) Explain what both businesses and professional bodies can do to influence the ethical behaviour of their organisational members. **(13 marks)**

(Total = 25 marks)

67 F Company (11/05) **45 mins**

F Company is a medium sized business that manufactures electrical kitchen appliances including food processors, toasters, juicers and coffee makers. In the last twelve months the company has lost market share to its competitors and has underperformed on most of its key performance indicators. Its future survival is threatened as new entrants are stealing market share and the customers are demanding new product and design features.

G, the company's management accountant, suggests that F Company's difficulties are because it has been too complacent, not responding to changing environmental conditions and not having undertaken any formal strategic planning. He is also concerned that different areas of the company appear to be pursuing conflicting objectives.

To help the company develop a sustainable competitive advantage, G proposes that a more formal top down approach to developing business strategy should be adopted. He is also of the view that greater emphasis should be placed on understanding the external environment.

However, at a recent meeting where G outlined the benefits that a more formal approach to planning would bring, he was surprised that P, the HR director, disagreed. P argued that the dynamic environment that F Company operates in means that the formal approach is a waste of management time. She suggested that the company should assess how sustainable competitive advantage can be achieved through using its unique combination of resources, skills and capabilities.

Required

(a) Explain the benefits and drawbacks associated with F Company adopting a top down approach to the formulation of business strategy. **(12 marks)**

(b) Compare and contrast the different views held by G and P on how F Company can gain competitive advantage. **(13 marks)**

(Total = 25 marks)

68 X Company (5/06) **45 mins**

X Company is a manufacturer of non alcoholic soft drinks and has a well established position and brand recognition in country Z. The potential for future growth in country Z is, however, limited, with the market reaching saturation. One option for expansion is to move into new markets in other countries offering its existing product range.

The business development team is evaluating this option and is currently working on proposals to sell the company's range of drinks in country Y. One possible strategy to achieve market entry that the team is investigating is through a joint venture with a company that is already established in country Y, and is in the drinks distribution business.

The Board of X Company has given the business development team the task of undertaking a feasibility study to explore the viability of the proposed strategy. As part of the feasibility study there needs to be some assessment of industry competition and the attractiveness of the market in country Y. The feasibility study also needs to assess the cultural compatibility of the ways of doing business in country Y compared to how X Company currently operates in country Z.

Required

(a) Advise the business development team on how Porter's five forces model could be used to assess industry competition in country Y. **(15 marks)**

(b) Discuss how Hofstede's research could be used to assess the compatibility of X Company's strategy with the culture of country Y. **(10 marks)**

(Total = 25 marks)

69 Imperial Traders plc — 45 mins

Imperial Traders plc was established in 1785 and its head office has always been in London. Currently, most of its business takes place in and around the 'Pacific Rim', ie in Japan, Korea, Malaysia and Australia.

Required

(a) Explain what a position audit is and describe the benefits to Imperial Traders plc of conducting such an audit in respect of a possible move of the head office from London to a Pacific Rim country. **(10 marks)**

(b) Discuss the effects of a relocation to a Pacific Rim country on the various aspects considered by the position audit. **(10 marks)**

(c) Describe briefly the cultural differences that Imperial Traders plc may encounter in its new domicile. **(5 marks)**

(Total = 25 marks)

70 Bowland Carpets — 45 mins

Bowland Carpets is a major producer of carpets within the UK. The company was taken over by its present parent company, Universal Carpet Inc, in 1993. Universal Carpet is a giant, vertically integrated carpet manufacturing and retailing business, based within the USA but with interests all over the world.

Bowland Carpets operates within the UK in various market segments, including the high value contract and industrial carpeting area – hotels and office blocks etc – and in the domestic (household) market. Within the latter the choice is reasonably wide ranging from luxury carpets down to the cheaper products. Industrial and contract carpets contribute 25% of Bowland Carpets' total annual turnover which is currently $80 million. During the late 1980s the turnover of the company was growing at 8% per annum, but since 1992 sales have dropped by 5% per annum in real terms.

Bowland Carpets has traditionally been known as a producer of high quality carpets, but at competitive prices. It has a powerful brand name, and it has been able to protect this by producing the cheaper, lower quality products under a secondary brand name. It has also maintained a good relationship with the many carpet distributors throughout the UK, particularly the mainstream retail organisations.

The recent decline in carpet sales, partly recession induced, has worried the US parent company. It has recognised that the increasing concentration within the European carpet manufacturing sector has led to aggressive competition within a low growth industry. It does not believe that overseas sales growth by Bowland Carpets is an attractive proposition as this would compete with other Universal Carpet companies. It does, however, consider that vertical integration into retailing (as already practised within the USA) is a serious option. This would give the UK company increased control over its sales and reduce its exposure to competition. The president of the parent company has asked Jeremy Smiles, managing director of Bowland Carpets, to address this issue and provide guidance to the US board of directors. Funding does not appear to be a major issue at this time as the parent company has large cash reserves on its balance sheet.

Required

Acting in the capacity of Jeremy Smiles, you are required to outline the various issues which might be of significance for the management of the parent company. Your answer should cover the following.

(a) Discuss the extent to which the distinctive competences of Bowland Carpets conform with the key success factors required for the proposed strategy change? **(10 marks)**

(b) Identify the main entry barriers prevalent in the carpet retailing sector. **(7 marks)**

(c) In an external environmental analysis concerning the proposed strategy shift, what are likely to be the key external influences which could impact upon the Bowland Carpets decision? **(8 marks)**

(Total = 25 marks)

71 Transaction cost theory (11/06) 45 mins

N Company is a manufacturer and retailer of electrical goods such as cameras, PCs, TVs and hi-fi equipment. The company has its head office , four manufacturing plants and a chain of 350 retail outlets in K country. It also has a call centre, which is on the same site as its head office, to deal with customer queries and provide service support for PCs. Following the appointment of a new CEO, the senior management of N company is evaluating options for its future strategic development. The company faces a challenging time with the growth and increased strength of competition in the sector.

N Company has previously had excellent employee relations and staff have enjoyed superior reward and recognition packages. However, the arrival of D, the new CEO, had unsettled staff. They have heard that D is proposing a major restructure aimed at improving efficiency and controlling costs. They understand that this will mean some of the manufacturing plants will be closed and more emphasis placed on selling cheaper 'bought-in' products. In addition, certain activities related to the facilities management of the company such as catering, cleaning and store maintenance are likely to be outsourced. It also seems that the senior management is investigating the possibility of moving the call centre to another country where operating costs are lower.

D has been heard to say that to compete effectively the company needs to be more flexible, and that he will be using the ideas of the 'flexible firm' model and the 'shamrock organisation' as the basis to create greater flexibility and adaptability in N Company.

Required

(a) Use transaction cost theory to analyse the restructure strategy D is proposing in N Company. **(13 marks)**

(b) With reference to **either** the 'flexible firm' model **or** 'shamrock organisation' discuss how N Company might achieve greater flexibility. **(12 marks)**

(Total = 25 marks)

72 Resource based view (11/07) 45 mins

C Chocolate Company makes and supplies high quality hand made chocolate products. Since the launch of its internet business, it has experienced huge success and is currently enjoying its position as market leader and has built up a strong brand.

The owner of the business attributes much of the success to a combination of factors, including the unique recipes and the skills of staff associated with hand made chocolates and the procurement of high quality cocoa beans. The company's marketing capability and use of IT in developing the company's website has enabled it to track and quickly spot trends in changes to consumer buying patterns. It is clear from the company's research information, that to prosper in the industry, constant product innovation is critical in building and maintaining the customer relationship. The flexible approach to new product development allows the company to quickly come up with new chocolate products.

Required

(a) Explain the extent to which C Chocolate Company is adopting this strategic approach to gain competitive advantage, making reference to the principles of the Resource Based View. **(13 marks)**

(b) Demonstrate how the value chain framework would assist C Chocolate Company in understanding its internal position. **(12 marks)**

(Total = 25 marks)

73 Strategic models (5/08) 45 mins

W Company is a fashion retailer which designs and sells its own brand of women's clothes through its chain of shops in F country. However, it is facing tough operating conditions in its home market where strong competition means there is little opportunity for future growth. The Board has taken the strategic decision that expansion can only be achieved through market development abroad.

Initial research has identified L country as offering the potential to be a possible suitable location for W Company to develop a new market. Further information now needs to be collected on the external environment and competition in L country in order to help evaluate the viability of the strategy being proposed.

If the outcomes from the research are positive, W Company intends to find an existing retail chain in L country that it can acquire, rather than set up a new operation through internal development. A senior management team will be sent from W Company to manage the operations in L country. However, the Board is aware that this could create challenges for the managers if there are cultural differences between the two countries.

Required

(a) Apply appropriate strategic management models/frameworks to explain the key external environmental and competitive factors on which information should be collected to help W Company evaluate its proposed strategy to move into L country. **(13 marks)**

(b) Discuss, with reference to appropriate theory, why the management team from W Company will need to take account of cultural differences when managing the new operation in L country. **(12 marks)**

(Total = 25 marks)

CASE STUDY QUESTIONS (Pilot Paper)

Questions 74 to 79 originally appeared in the P5 pilot paper. They differ in style from the rest of the questions in this kit in that they are in the form of extended case studies. We have therefore included them in this separate section.

House Project – Part 1

E, a management accountant, and three of her colleagues have decided to venture into the buy-to-rent market. Recently, they set up a company, Enterprise Associates, and purchased a house in which they would each hold a share. E inherited some money and holds a 50% share. The other 50% is divided equally between the three other partners. E, however, will take on much of the responsibility for the company's first venture and she has been given a free hand to develop the property as she thinks fit.

The house purchased by the colleagues is 150 years old and has been poorly maintained. The interior fixtures, fittings and décor are also old fashioned. A survey of the house also reveals that the electric wiring and water piping do not conform to modern standards and that the walls are subject to rising damp. Without extensive repairs and renovation the house would be almost impossible to rent.

With interest rates at an all time low and the demand for rented accommodation at a very high level, E has decided, in consultation with her partners, to renovate the house before offering it for rent.

The easiest option for E would be to employ a builder to carry out all the renovations at an agreed price. After obtaining a number of estimates, however, she decides that she and her husband can carry out some of the basic repairs and manage the decorating themselves at a considerable saving.

E realises that this will make considerable demands on her time and that careful planning will be necessary to fit the work on the house with her demanding job as a management accountant, as well as fulfil her family obligations. Conscious of the need to maintain the quality of her work, E has decided, with the agreement of her employer, to work part-time for the duration of the house project, but she recognises that even with this change she will have to manage her time very carefully.

On this basis, E has agreed with her partners in Enterprise Associates a profit sharing ratio of 70:10:10:10 with all expenses for materials and specialist labour shared equally between the four.

As well as being methodical and hard working, E has developed a number of practical skills over the years while improving the family home. Hence many of the decorating tasks are familiar to her. If E has a weakness, it is that she enjoys conversation and meeting people and often takes more time than is necessary to conduct business and social transactions.

The damp proofing, writing and plumbing will need to be carried out by skilled specialists but E already has contacts with an electrician and a plumber (fitter of water pipes) and they, in turn have contacts with other specialists in the building trade such as carpenters (wood workers) and plasterers (who specialise in covering walls with a skimming of plaster).

Although she has no experience of house renovation on this scale, E has a rough idea of the sequence in which the various jobs – damp proofing, plumbing and so on – will need to be carried out and has received advice from a builder on the estimated time that each job will take to complete. She has also contacted the various skilled specialists for estimates of the cost for each job.

This information is most timely for E because she has just had a firm offer from a prospective tenant, J, to rent the house, provided he and his family could move into the house in three months' time. E, knowing the family, and confident that they would be good tenants, has agreed that she will have the property ready for them in three months and available for rent at an agreed price.

While E naturally wishes to keep costs to a minimum, she also requires that the renovation meets quality standards acceptable to customers who wish to rent property.

74 Enterprise Associates 1 — 18 mins

Required

Explain to E the benefits of using a Work Breakdown Structure in the planning of the project. **(10 marks)**

75 Enterprise Associates 2 — 18 mins

The management of time is going to be a major issue for E.

Required

Identify the key factors that will have a bearing on E's use of time and explain what action she can take to make the best use of time. **(10 marks)**

House project – Part 2: four years later

The renovation of Enterprise Associates' first house went well and the house is still rented by the original family. Four years have now gone by and since then much has changed. Not only has E retired from her position as a management accountant; as Enterprise Associates' Chief Executive Officer she has helped the company to grow very rapidly.

Encouraged by the initial success, by a buoyant housing market, and by low interest rates, E has negotiated a series of bank loans to buy up other old houses in the locality and Enterprise Associates has renovated these and rented them at market rates.

Unfortunately for Enterprise Associates and others in the buy-to-rent business, however, conditions in the housing market have changed since the company rented its first property. Many more people have entered the buy-to-rent property sector, interest rates have increased and are forecast to rise sharply in the next year. This will probably reduce the demand for new houses to some extent, and will also deter some would-be entrepreneurs, who might have borrowed funds to enter the buy-to-rent market.

The central government has acted to increase the amount of building land available and this, in turn, has resulted in a shortage of supply of builders, plumbers, plasterers, electricians and others in the building trades. There is also some evidence from market research that householders have an increasing preference for new houses. Also, in the town in which Enterprise Associates conducts it business, the local government has plans for compulsory purchase and demolition of some of the older properties as part of a new road building programme.

Faced with these changing circumstances, E is not sure what Enterprise Associates' future strategy should be. She feels the need for a better understanding of the changes that are affecting the buy-to-rent market and has asked you, a management consultant, to provide Enterprise Associates with an analysis of the buy-to-rent industry.

76 Enterprise Associates 3 — 18 mins

Required

Prepare a report for Enterprise Associates which:

(a) briefly explains Porter's Five Forces model;

(b) discusses the main opportunities and threats in the buy-to-rent industry. **(10 marks)**

Read the following scenario and answer TWO questions ONLY – 25 marks each

The WAM Organisation is one of the most successful supermarket chains in its own country. Its reputation for innovation is unparalleled in its own country with the successful launch of its personal finance, telecom, and internet shopping services.

The WAM Organisation customer focus and its ability to provide value for money through efficient operations and the use of the latest technology has enabled it to gain the largest share of the market.

Following a careful process of internal and external analysis, the senior management of WAM Organisation has concluded that the domestic market for its goods and services has reached saturation point and that the only opportunity for significant growth lies in venturing abroad.

Acting partly on the advice of the central government's Overseas Advisory Board, and using its own research team, WAM Organisation's management has decided to locate its first overseas supermarket in country Y. The location selected is in the suburbs of a growing city, where groceries, clothing and the other non-food products that WAM Organisation intends to supply are currently provided by a large number of small shops.

The new overseas outlet will be staffed initially by managers from WAM Organisation's home country, but other staff will be recruited and trained in country Y. The company has also made it clear that its human resource policy is to provide management opportunities to local people once the business in country Y is established.

The manager for the overall project is Ms D from WAM Organisation's Business Development division, while the project manager for the construction of the buildings, roads and car park that will make up the supermarket outlet is Mr G from the WAM Organisation's Property and Estates division.

The land on which the supermarket outlet will be built has been purchased and following a series of tough negotiations with state and local government officials, planning permission has been granted. Vigorous protest, however, has come from the City's Civic Society, local residents and shopkeepers who are located near to the proposed development.

The Civic Society is concerned about the detrimental impact on the local environment. Residents are concerned about the potential increase in traffic and the danger it poses to the children in the local school. The shopkeepers are fearful about the impact of the new supermarket on their future business prospects.

The media, including television, radio and newspapers, have publicised the fears of the local residents and shopkeepers and these two groups, together with the City's Civic Society, have formed a coalition to attempt to prevent the development.

77 WAM Organisation 1 — 45 mins

Required

(a) Explain the approach to strategy formulation and the content of the WAM Organisation's strategy. **(10 marks)**

(b) Identify the secondary stakeholders in the WAM Organisation's supermarket project and explain how the project team should manage these stakeholders. **(15 marks)**

(Total = 25 marks)

78 WAM Organisation 2 — 45 mins

Required

(a) Prepare a report for the directors of a major investment bank which explains the resource-based approach to strategic management and analyses the resources/core competences that appear to give the WAM Organisation competitive advantage. **(15 marks)**

(b) Using your knowledge of research findings on international cultural differences, explain why WAM Organisation's management might encounter some problems with managing local staff in Country Y.

(10 marks)

(Total = 25 marks)

79 WAM Organisation 3 — 45 mins

Required

(a) Identify the major risks associated with the WAM Organisation's development project. **(15 marks)**

(b) Discuss the general negotiating strategy and principles that would be required by WAM Organisation's managers in order to gain planning permission to site their new supermarket outlet in Country Y.

(10 marks)

(Total = 25 marks)

Mixed objective test questions

80 Pilot paper **36 mins**

80.1 In a multi-divisional organisation producing a range of products for different markets, the business level strategy of each unit or division is mainly concerned with

A Setting the direction for the organisation
B The competitiveness of a particular division
C The efficiency of production, marketing and other functions
D Alignment of strategy with other organisations **(2 marks)**

80.2 In the typical hierarchical organisation, the requirement of a lower-level manager to answer to a higher-level manager in the chain of command is referred to as

A Authority
B Empowerment
C Accountability
D Super ordination **(2 marks)**

80.3 Recent developments towards greater employee involvement, flexible working and flatter organisational structures have placed greater emphasis on which ONE of the following styles of management?

A Exploitative authoritative
B Autocratic
C Participative
D Benevolent authoritative **(2 marks)**

80.4 Research on group effectiveness has concluded that the most consistently successful groups

A Are those in which all members are innovative
B Comprise a range of roles undertaken by various members
C Are those in which all members are very intelligent
D Comprise a range of roles all undertaken by a few members of the group **(2 marks)**

80.5 When designing an organisational structure, or reviewing the effectiveness of an existing structure, the first thing that must be clarified is

A Informal organisational relationships
B Objectives of the organisation
C Size of organisation
D Division of labour **(2 marks)**

The following data is to be used to answer questions 80.6, 80.7 and 80.8 below

Blake plc is a large multi-national designer and manufacturer of specialist road vehicles. Blake plc's products include fire engines, breakdown trucks, rescue vehicles and ambulances. Customer organisations, that are often government-owned, order Blake plc's products in small quantities. Each 'batch' of products is deigned and built by Blake plc to meet a unique customer specification.

Blake plc has been approached by The Armana Airports Authority (AAA) to provide four rescue trucks to carry emergency equipment and personnel at a large provincial airport. This contract must be completed (that is, the trucks delivered to AAA) within 16 weeks of today's date. This is essential, as the trucks currently used by AAA have been deemed unsuitable by the Armana Government Airport Inspectorate (AGAI).

Blake plc has just submitted a proposal to AAA, following an invitation to tender received two weeks ago. The project manager at Blake plc, for the AAA project, is Annie Li. Annie has a meeting scheduled for later today with the Director of Procurement at AAA, Charles Crowe. This is Annie's first meeting with Charles. Annie is aware that Charles is likely to ask for several modifications to the design of the trucks proposed by Blake plc, and that this will have a 'knock-on' effect on other aspects of Blake plc's proposal. Annie is concerned about the impact of any changes on Blake plc's ability to deliver the trucks in 16 weeks.

The normal programme for a project of this scale at Blake plc is as follows.

Activity		*Duration (weeks)*	*Depends on*
A	Prepare proposal	2	–
B	Negotiate with customer	6	A
C	Modify and finalise design	4	B
D	Build chassis	3	C
E	Build bodyshell	4	C
F	Paint bodyshell	1	E
G	Assemble, fit out and finish	2	D, F
H	Write manuals	3	C
I	Print manuals	1	H
J	Test	1	G, I
K	Inspect and deliver	1	J

80.6 Based on the normal programme for a project such as this, what is the project elapsed time, from beginning to end?

A 18 weeks
B 19 weeks
C 21 weeks
D 28 weeks **(4 marks)**

80.7 Assuming that the durations and dependencies of activities (C) to (K) in the programme cannot be changed, how long can Annie spend negotiating with Charles (Activity B), yet still deliver the vehicles in 16 weeks?

A 1 week
B 3 weeks
C 6 weeks
D The vehicles cannot be delivered in 16 weeks **(3 marks)**

80.8 Identify three stakeholders in the project, each of whom is specifically mentioned in the scenario, *other than Annie and Charles.* **(3 marks)**

(Total = 20 marks)

81 November 2005 examination — 36 mins

81.1 Identify which ONE of the following strategies should be used to deal with stakeholders who have high power but low interest:

A Keep informed
B Minimal effort
C Keep satisfied
D Key player **(2 marks)**

81.2 The cultural dimension that describes a cultural value where individuals are expected to take care of themselves is referred to by Hofstede as:

A Individualism
B Collectivism
C Power distance
D Masculinity

(2 marks)

81.3 According to transaction cost theory, the mechanisms that organisations have to choose between to control their resources and carry out their operations are:

A Markets or structures
B Hierarchies or markets
C Structures or culture
D Hierarchies or culture

(2 marks)

81.4 Which ONE of the following is a part of the 'identification of need' phase of the project life cycle:

A The Completion Report
B The Milestone Review
C Project scheduling
D The project initiation document

(2 marks)

81.5 List **three** benefits of mentoring. **(3 marks)**

81.6 Identify the missing words needed to complete the rational model of strategic management. Record your answers by making reference to the corresponding letters **A, B, C** and **D**.

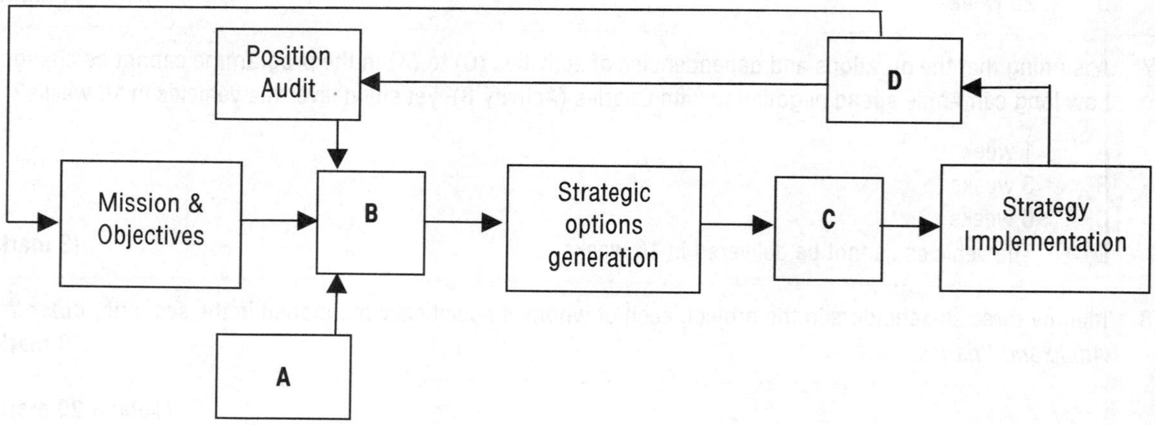

(4 marks)

81.7 Complete the gaps to determine the four stages in the project lifecycle.

(1) Identification of a need; (2)____________(3) Implementation; (4)______________________________________. **(2 marks)**

81.8 Briefly explain the interests of a 'project owner'. **(3 marks)**

(Total = 20 marks)

82 May 2006 examination **36 mins**

82.1 Corporate appraisal involves

A evaluating strategic options
B communicating the mission
C identifying strengths and weaknesses
D implementing strategy **(2 marks)**

82.2 A project management maturity model is used to

A control the project
B identify opportunities for continuous improvement
C determine project risk
D assess the feasibility of a project **(2 marks)**

82.3 Which of the following can be used to describe the homogeneity of objectives and thinking in group work?

A The Abilene Paradox
B Risky shift
C Group polarisation
D Groupthink **(2 marks)**

82.4 Which of the following project stakeholders is the person who provides the resources for a project?

A Project sponsor
B Project manager
C Project owner
D Project customer **(2 marks)**

82.5 Identify **four** benefits of corporate governance. **(4 marks)**

82.6 In **one** sentence, explain the purpose of Work Breakdown Structure. **(2 marks)**

82.7 Draw the framework that can be used to classify the different ways of managing conflict, labelling the axes. Use the framework to show where the two approaches, collaborating and avoiding, should be located. **(4 marks)**

82.8 Identify **two** ways in which project risk can be classified. **(2 marks)**

(Total = 20 marks)

83 November 2006 examination **36 mins**

83.1 Which one of the following are three elements of the 7S model proposed by McKinsey?

A Staff, support, sponsor
B Systems, style, support
C Structure, style, status
D Style, systems, structure **(2 marks)**

83.2 At what level of control are staff performance appraisal systems used?

A Operational
B Tactical
C Corporate
D Strategic **(2 marks)**

83.3 The Deal and Kennedy cultural typology that is characterised as having high risk, long decision cycles and slow feedback is:

A Work hard/play hard
B Bet your company
C Tough guy macho
D Process **(2 marks)**

83.4 Which one of Mintzberg's configurations emphasises standardised skills as the coordination mechanism, has the operating core as the dominant force and operates best in a complex but stable environment?

A Adhocracy
B Machine bureaucracy
C Professional bureaucracy
D Divisional form **(2 marks)**

83.5 Identify the approach to strategy which proposes that competitive advantage is achieved from the organisation's unique assets or competences.

(2 marks)

83.6 Describe **two** of the situational factors Fiedler uses as the basis of his contingency model of leadership.

(4 marks)

The following data are for sub-questions 83.7, 83.8 and 83.9

R is the operations director of P paper mill. He is in the process of putting together a project plan for the introduction of a new mill that will enable the company to produce a high quality paper product demanded by customers. The sales director has asked for R to advise him on when he should start the sales campaign for the new paper product.

Activity	*Preceding activity*	*Activity duration in weeks*
A	-	8
B	-	10
C	-	6
D	A	8
E	B, C	9
F	C	14
G*	D, E	14
H	F, G	6

*G = sales campaign

83.7 Using the information, identify the critical path for the introduction of the new mill. **(2 marks)**

83.8 Calculate the overall expected duration of the project **(2 marks)**

83.9 Identify the earliest event time for the sales campaign activity. **(2 marks)**

(Total = 20 marks)

84 May 2007 examination 36 mins

84.1 The scope and amount of discretion given to a person to make decisions by virtue of the position he/she holds in the organisation is referred to as

A Accountability
B Responsibility
C Delegation
D Authority **(2 marks)**

84.2 Which ONE of the following provides a common understanding of a project for all its stakeholders by defining the project's overall boundaries?

A Project lifecycle
B Project milestones
C Project scope
D Project schedule **(2 marks)**

84.3 Which ONE of the following leads to high buyer power?

A High capital requirements
B Low switching costs
C Economies of scale
D Limited substitute products **(2 marks)**

84.4 Which ONE of the following is the term used in project management to assess how achievable various project options are?

A Feasibility analysis
B Risk analysis
C Contingency analysis
D Resource analysis **(2 marks)**

84.5 Explain briefly the characteristics of the positioning view of strategy. **(3 marks)**

84.6 An organisation is experiencing conflict up and down the hierarchy, between the executive team in head office and regional offices. What type of conflict is this? **(2 marks)**

84.7 Name the technique used in network analysis that allows the uncertainty about the times of each activity to be considered. **(2 marks)**

84.8 In critical path analysis what is the spare time for an activity called? **(2 marks)**

84.9 Identify each of the different team roles, as defined by Belbin, from the following descriptions.

(i) Imaginative and very good at coming up with original ideas and suggestions.
(ii) Gives attention to detail and is concerned with meeting deadlines.
(iii) Supports other members of the team and helps to promote harmony.

(3 marks)

(Total = 20 marks)

---

85 November 2007 examination — 36 mins

85.1 Which ONE of the following types of flexibility is described as the ability to redeploy employees to different tasks through multi-skilling?

A Numerical flexibility
B Organisational flexibility
C Temporal flexibility
D Functional flexibility **(2 marks)**

85.2 At which stage of group formation and development does establishing standards and agreeing ways of working occur?

A Storming
B Performing
C Norming
D Forming **(2 marks)**

85.3 At what stage in the project lifecycle is the scope of a project determined?

A Planning
B Initiation
C Growth
D Control **(2 marks)**

85.4 Decisions about acquisitions, mergers and sell-offs occur at which one of the following levels?

A Functional level
B Corporate level
C Business level
D Competitive level **(2 marks)**

85.5 Explain briefly what the *critical path* is in relation to a project. **(2 marks)**

85.6 Strategy, style, structure and systems are all Ss in the McKinsey 7 S framework. Identify the **three** missing Ss needed to complete the model. **(3 marks)**

85.7 Mintzberg's organisational configuration is made up of the strategic apex, operating core and which three other components. **(3 marks)**

85.8 Identify, in the correct order, the **four** main stages in the negotiation process. **(4 marks)**

(Total = 20 marks)

86 May 2008 examination — 36 mins

86.1 In the hierarchy of objectives, what kind of objective is 'increase earnings per share'?

A Tactical
B Secondary
C Primary
D Operational **(2 marks)**

86.2 Which ONE of the following refers to power which is derived from the personal qualities of the individual and the desire of followers to be like that person?

A Expert power
B Referent power
C Reward power
D Coercive power **(2 marks)**

86.3 Which ONE of the following perspectives of strategy is where an organisation avoids radical strategies but instead takes small steps based on what has been done before and worked in the past?

A Ecological
B Positioning
C Bounded rationality
D Logical incrementalism **(2 marks)**

86.4 Which ONE of the following is the term used in project management where the potential for risk cannot be removed, but analysis has enabled the identification of alternative ways to lower risk exposure?

A Containment
B Transference
C Absorption
D Reduction **(2 marks)**

86.5 Distinguish between the terms 'span of control' and 'scalar chain'. **(4 marks)**

86.6 Identify FOUR characteristics that distinguish a project from 'business as usual'. **(4 marks)**

86.7 Identify the reason why diagrams (i) and (ii) shown below do not conform to the accepted conventions of network analysis. (You should provide a different reason for each diagram.) **(4 marks)**

(i)

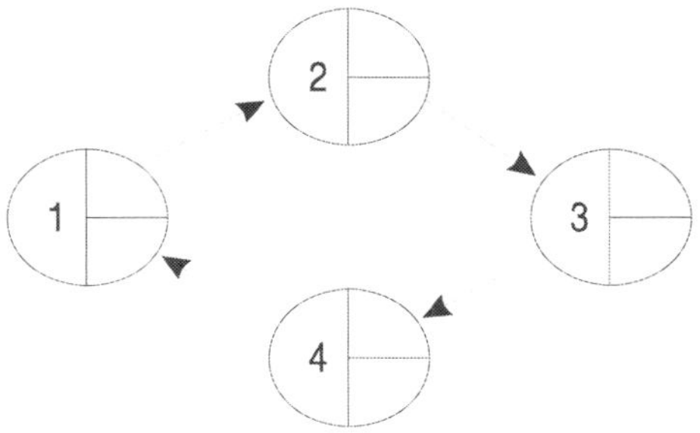

(ii)

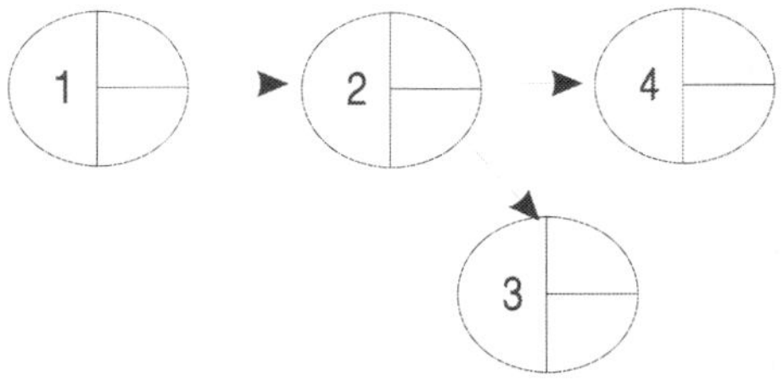

(Total = 20 marks)

Answers

Extra guidance

Remember you can find additional guidance on a number of questions in this kit on BPP's website: www.bpp.com/cima/extra-question-guidance

1 Objective test questions

Top tips. If you got a bit stuck here, look back at the introduction and advice on how to tackle these types of questions.

1.1 C Fact

1.2 B Whistle blowing is informing the public of wrongdoing. Social responsibility is the modification of profit seeking behaviour to support socially desirable objectives. Professional ethics are what the financial director has breached. Internal audit is an example of the mechanisms that support a compliance-based approach to ethical behaviour.

1.3 D *Mintzberg* uses the term 'support staff'. 'Ideology', while not a **structural** component, is part of Mintzberg's model.

1.4 B Fact

1.5 C A and B are part of single loop control. D is an element of feedforward control.

1.6 C A is two of Mintzberg's configurations; B is two of the organisational sub-systems described by *Trist and Bamforth;* D is two other widely encountered forms of organisation structure.

1.7 D While a link between appraisal and reward is played down in many organisations, there is no doubt that it is a valid objective for an appraisal scheme. The other options are uses that may be made of an appraisal scheme, but they would not be described as objectives. Friendly interaction must not preclude hard talk where it is needed Documentation may ultimately be used in court but its generation is not what an appraisal scheme is about; and systems that cannot accommodate individual failings are not themselves robust enough.

1.8 The **shaper** is extrovert, dominant and passionate about the task.

1.9

Configuration	Co-ordination mechanism	Key part
Machine bureaucracy	**Standardised work processes**	**Technostructure**
Adhocracy	**Mutual adjustment**	**Support staff**

2 Objective test questions

2.1 A Fact

2.2 A B and D are incorrect because they include the term *decision.* It is more useful to think of reaching agreement, since the point of negotiation is that neither side is in a position to take and enforce a final decision. C is wrong because it includes both bargaining and negotiation as distinct phases: negotiation is the name of the overall process. Also, C makes no mention of *opening*, the phase in which detailed initial positions are established and without which bargaining is not possible.

2.3 D This is a low-level question concerning basic knowledge. It could actually be the topic of endless debate over real world examples, so do not look too deeply into it.

2.4 B Fact

2.5 B A is constructive dismissal. D is wrongful dismissal, C is summary dismissal and may be unfair, wrongful, both or neither.

2.6 B A is direct discrimination, C is positive discrimination, D may be an example of direct discrimination.

2.7 D Many groups exist outside the work environment. Note that 'team' in the sense of a group organised to play a game is a special usage in this context.

2.8 Tells
Sells
Consults
Joins

2.9 This is a very basic piece of knowledge. It is difficult to see why it was worth three marks, especially as the Examiner's answer did not include the numbered scales on the axes. Presumably there was one mark for each of the axes and one for positioning the team management style correctly.

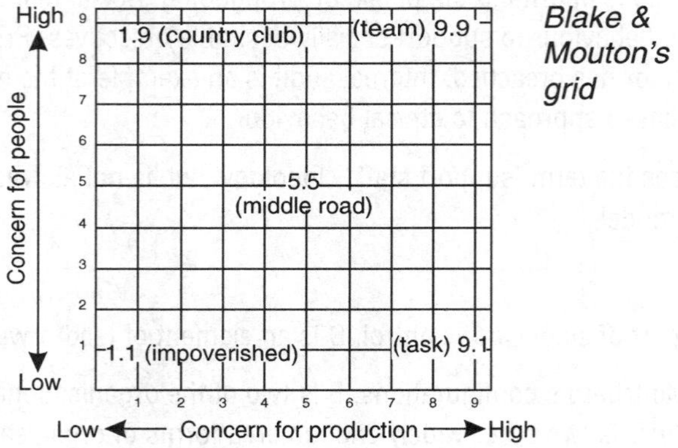

3 Objective test questions

3.1 D A, B and C are all problems typical of large organisations and less common in small ones.

3.2 C This is not an easy question. Option A might possibly be regarded as a statement of values, but it is more obviously a standard of behaviour. Option B is clearly an operational policy. Option C is undoubtedly a statement of cultural aspiration: it is designed for the long term and deals with relationships between the company and its employees. Option D could be seen as an element of strategy: it could, for instance, be exploited as a unique selling proposition and an element that differentiates the company from its competitors. However, it is best regarded as a policy. The best answer, therefore, is C, the element of culture.

3.3 C While primary responsibility may lie with the employer, the employee is responsible for such things as operating machinery in a safe fashion (after suitable training).

3.4 C *Elton Mayo* is regarded as one of the main theorists of human relations.

3.5 B The relevant learning outcome is: explain the purpose and principles of good corporate governance.

3.6 B The relevant learning outcome is: evaluate different organisation structures.

3.7 C The relevant learning outcome is: explain the concepts of power, bureaucracy, authority, responsibility, leadership and delegation.

3.8 A A wide span of control implies a flat organisation with few layers of management and, indeed, few managers. Career progression is constrained by the lack of posts to be filled and the management of complex work is hampered by the need for work to be largely unsupervised. The contrary of all this is true of tall organisations, which in themselves imply fairly narrow spans of control. Decentralisation may be associated with a range of degrees of flatness or tallness, but implies the existence of a larger number of management posts than would be the case in an equivalent centralised organisation.

3.9 B The organic organisation is the antithesis of bureaucracy. Procedures, internal rules and hierarchical control are minimised. Innovative ways of working, wide general knowledge, co-operative endeavour and supporting the overall mission are highly valued. Options A, C and D are all typical of the mechanistic approach.

3.10 D The fourth dimension is individualism – collectivism

4 Objective test questions

4.1 A Legitimate power is also called position power. Expert power accrues to recognised expertise; resource power derives from control over scarce resources; personal power lies in the manager's personality.

4.2 B This question requires some discussion. Project management exists when a team is assembled to pursue an identifiable project. It is likely to include specialists from more than one functional area, such as finance and marketing, as here, but there is no project mentioned in the question, so A is inappropriate. Functional departmentation seems to exist at Hydra Ltd, to at least some extent, since the Finance Director is in a position to divert the employment of finance specialists and presumably utilises the services of the management accountants when they are not working for the product managers. However, the narrative clearly indicates a strong element of cross functional organisation. 'Complex organisational form' is a phrase normally used to indicate a degree of boundary-spanning organisation as in, for instance, partnerships, alliances and consortia. There is no mention of this in the narrative. B would appear to be the best option.

4.3 D Adair's model is connected with his concept of **functional leadership**, which emphasises what leaders *do* rather than what they *are*.

4.4 C **Authority** in a hierarchical organisation derives largely from the position held: this is **position power** or **legitimate power**. Subordinate managers are **accountable** to their superiors for the way in which they use their authority. **Empowerment** is a process rather than an attribute: it occurs when enhanced authority is granted to those who previously had little or none in order reduce the need for managerial oversight. **Super ordination** simply means being placed higher in any given hierarchy and is not a term commonly used of managers.

4.5 B **Networks** are usually taken to be groups of suppliers and customers that co-operate on non-core competence matters in order to share benefits. A **functional** structure divides the organisation up by reference to type of work done. A matrix organisation superimposes one hierarchy on another, usually adding a product/market or project based structure to a functional structure.

4.6 D This is another poor question since, before we can call something effective, we need to know what it is supposed to achieve. Option D is a description of a currently fashionable approach to appraisal but all three other options are features of well-established appraisal systems that meet the requirements of certain organisations. For example, some appraisal systems have the **assessment of suitability for promotion** as a major purpose. Options A and B would be entirely appropriate for such a system.

4.7 C The wording of the question is almost a definition of the participative style.

4.8 B *Belbin's* is the best-known work on this topic.

4.9 C 'Procedural justice' *may* be a reference to the need for 'due process' when administering justice, but knowing the way the Examiner's mind works, it is probably just a term he has invented to confuse you. Option B is obviously nonsensical, while option D may be true, but only if the person making the claim is the organisation's PR spin doctor.

4.10 A *Taylor* was concerned with making the individual worker more efficient. Group working as a subject of study and theory is a post-Scientific management idea. It can be traced back to the work of *Mayo's* team at *Hawthorne*, which laid the basis for the human relations approach and first described the informal organisation. Socio-technical systems is a work-group related idea developed by *Trist and Bamforth* in their study of developments in the UK coal-mining industry after World War II.

5 Dr Strong

Text references. Chapter 2.

Top tips. This question invites a very wide-ranging answer. Note that it is only worth ten marks and do not let your enthusiasm run away with you! Make sure you understand and apply the CIMA active verbs in the requirement. You must **analyse** and **recommend** in your answer. There are lots of points to make, but you must try even harder than usual to be concise. Note that a mention of *Burns and Stalker* and the organic-mechanistic spectrum is almost mandatory: their book was called *The Management of Innovation*, after all.

Easy marks. The characteristics of the organic organisation may well be worth up to half of the total available marks.

Why C Company's problems may have developed

System of management

Dr Strong's system of management clearly does not support the innovatory science that the C Pharmaceutical Company depends on for its commercial success. Dr Strong's system, with its strict financial and personnel discipline, clearly **constrains the creativity** of the R&D unit's scientists.

Mechanistic or bureaucratic system in place

It is widely accepted that a management system based on rules, procedures and routine (that is to say, a **bureaucratic** system) is unsuited to dealing with new problems and rapid developments. *Burns and Stalker* called such a system a **mechanistic** system and contrasted it with an **organic** (or **organismic**) system. The latter emphasises interactive teamwork, collaborative problem solving, respect for individual expertise at all levels and commitment to the overall task. This is likely to be very effective in contexts such as R&D.

However, such an approach is not a licence for random, unstructured activity more or less directed at a vague objective. There is still a need for **control of resources and effort**. In an organic system this is achieved largely by cultural means. There is a network structure of control, with decisions and plans being made after consultation with all parties concerned. The bureaucratic idea of power flowing down from the top of the hierarchy is largely abandoned: prestige and influence can exist anywhere and tend to revolve around expertise.

Actions to encourage creativity and innovation

Replacing Dr Strong

It is probably impossible for Dr Strong to preside over such a system, because of his commitment to the more formal current methods. **He may have to go**. However, scientists generally will find a more collegiate approach familiar and easy to operate. If it is necessary to replace Dr Strong, an important criterion for the selection of a replacement will be experience of operating a more organic system of management.

Teamwork and collaboration

It would then be appropriate to **encourage teamwork and collaboration** within the R&D unit by employing suitable HRM policies. For example, recruitment should emphasise commitment to those ideals, appraisal should be based on actual work done rather than procedures adhered to and remuneration should be include an element of reward for team success. However, none of this should be done at the expense of individual creativity.

Innovation can be encouraged in other ways

(a) Leaders must create a **vision and a climate of support** that takes a long-term view of R&D. Suitable targets should be set to cover both short and long-term timescales.

(b) **Risk** must be accepted. Not all programmes may come to fruition, but there must be no recriminations for failure not caused by incompetence.

(c) A careful watch should be kept on what is going on in the **wider pharmaceutical development world**. This is not so that so that ideas can be copied, but so that R&D staff can learn from others and are stimulated into speculation and experiment. It is also appropriate to keep abreast of emerging requirements for new products.

6 L Company

Text references. Chapter 6.

Top tips. This is a straightforward practical question on time management requiring a number of **key skills**. So you need a **knowledge** of time management techniques and the ability to **relate these** techniques to the circumstances set out in the question. Look at the guidance in the front pages on discussion questions to help you here.

Easy marks. Use an approach that can be replicated for many questions: set the scene by setting out what time management **involves**, its **purpose**, its **importance** and its key **principles**. Then apply the principles to the particular circumstances in the question.

Introduction

Time is a scarce resource. Time management is the process of allocating time to tasks in the most effective manner such that we make the best use of the time available to us.

M's difficulty in meeting deadlines and her tendency to arrive late at meetings suggest that she is not managing her time effectively. In particular, her tendency to provide irrelevant information suggests that she is failing to prioritise appropriately with the result that time is being wasted on unproductive activities.

Practical steps and key tasks

To improve her time management M should take a number of practical steps. She should first identify her objectives and the key tasks which are most relevant to achieving them – sorting out what she must do, from what she could do, and from what she would like to do.

M should then assess her key tasks for relative importance and amount of time required. Routine non-essential tasks should be delegated – or done away with if possible. Routine key tasks should be organised as standard procedures and systems. Non-routine key tasks will have to be carefully scheduled as they arise, according to their urgency and importance. An up-to-date diary with a carry forward system to follow-up action will be helpful.

Short and long term plans

With these procedures in place M should plan each day. A task list of things to be done each day will be a start, but a simple task list gives no idea of the priority of each task. The daily list should include the most important tasks as well as urgent but less important tasks.

M should also produce a longer-term plan. This should highlight the important elements of the information that she is required to research so that sufficient time is spent on them on a daily basis. A longer term plan could also help her cope with more complicated jobs, by breaking them down into a number of stages. In addition, long-term planning would help M anticipate busy periods so that backlogs of routine work are cleared during quieter times.

Prioritising

As noted above, key to M's success will be her ability to prioritise her work successfully. When assessing the relative importance of her tasks she should determine whether they satisfy at least one of three conditions:

(a) It adds value to the finance department's output.
(b) It comes from a source deserving high priority, such as a customer or a senior manager.
(c) The potential consequences of failure are long-term, difficult to reverse, far reaching and costly.

Urgent and important

Another technique she should employ is to distinguish between tasks which are important, as defined above, and those which are urgent, which may have a deadline but are of less importance. M could pursue the following approach:

(a) Tasks both urgent and important would be dealt with immediately, and given a fair amount of time.

(b) Tasks not urgent but still important will become urgent as her deadline looms closer. Some of these tasks can be delegated.

(c) Tasks urgent but not important should be delegated by M, if possible, or she should seek to have them removed from her job.

(d) Tasks neither urgent nor important should be delegated or binned.

Summary

The establishment of these procedures and use of these techniques should create an ongoing discipline that helps M to counter her natural inclination to give very freely of her time when she cannot afford to do so.

7 H Company

Text references. Chapter 2.

Top tips. Another straightforward question, seeking the advantages and disadvantages of an important type of organisation design that is covered in detail in the Text. The key here, as ever, is to be able to **apply** the principles underlying matrix structure to the particular circumstances of this Company where rapid new product development is of crucial importance. Refer back to the key skills approach in the introduction. So **plan** your answer, correctly **understand** and apply the verbs in the question, use any theoretical knowledge appropriately and tailor this to the circumstances of H Company.

It is a good idea to start your answer with a brief definition of what a matrix structure is. Writing about the features of a matrix structure will help you think about advantages and disadvantages too.

Easy marks. The easy marks in this question are for setting out the features of a matrix structure. Explaining the potential benefits and drawbacks in relation to project management work will be more difficult.

Introduction

The marketing director of H Company has identified the need to pursue a project management approach in order to get products to market more quickly. This will involve introducing a matrix structure and the use of cross functional project teams to design and develop new sports equipment products.

A matrix structure involves the establishment of a dual command arrangement and can be thought of as a reaction against the classical form of bureaucracy where there is unity of command and an individual should have only one boss. **A matrix structure is often appropriate for multi-product companies such as H Company where co-ordination of a variety of operating units and project based work is of particular importance.**
In practical terms this will involve each project team member reporting to both a project manager and to a functional head.

The **advantages of a matrix structure** in project management work for NPD could include the following.

(a) **It offers greater flexibility** which will be important given the competitive nature of this growth market and the need to respond swiftly to changing circumstances. This applies both to people, as H Company's project members adapt more quickly to a new challenge or new task, and develop an attitude which is geared to accepting change; and to task and structure, as the matrix may be short-term (dependent on the length of the project) or readily amended (eg a new project manager can be introduced by superimposing his tasks on those of the existing functional managers). This flexibility should facilitate efficient operations in the fast moving sports equipment market.

(b) **It should improve communication** within H Company.

(c) **Dual authority gives H Company multiple orientation** so that **functional specialists do not get wrapped up in their own concerns** to the detriment of the need to work together in order to get products to market quickly.

(d) It provides a **structure for allocating responsibility** for timely product delivery to project managers.

(e) It provides for **inter-disciplinary co-operation** within H company and a mixing of skills and expertise which should be of benefit to employees.

Disadvantages of a matrix structure

(a) **Dual authority threatens a conflict between the project managers and the functional heads** at H Company. It will be important to ensure that the authority of superiors does not overlap and that areas of authority are clearly defined. A subordinate must know to which superior he is responsible for each aspect of his duties.

(b) **One individual reporting to both a project manager and a functional head** is **more likely to suffer role stress at work.**

(c) It **could increase costs** since the project managers are additional jobs which were not previously required in H Company's functional departmentation.

It may be difficult for the management of H Company to accept a matrix structure. It is possible for example that a functional manager may feel threatened that a project manager will usurp his authority.

8 Icebergs

Text references. Chapters 1 and 2.

Top tips.

- Managers make a major contribution to the informal organisation. *Mintzberg* mentions that managers have many contacts outside the chain of command.
- The informal organisation is key in internal politics. The formal organisation by contrast may be mock bureaucracy.
- A lighthearted survey in the Financial Times suggested that smokers, who congregate outside office buildings where smoking is prohibited, are becoming an informal organisation – the tobacco leaf, perhaps, has replaced the grapevine.
- Do not confuse 'informal organisation' with 'organic organisation' as described by *Burns and Stalker*. Even the most rigid bureaucracy has a network of informal links.

Easy marks. The subversive potential of the informal organisation is obvious to anyone who has ever worked in any but the smallest ones.

The **informal organisation** develops within an organisation as a means of communication, often stemming from the **social contacts** within the organisation. It utilises communications and cultural structures which are different from those provided by the formal organisation. If the formal structure does not provide adequate or flexible enough means for employees to get the job done, they will find ways of circumventing it and develop the informal structure.

Informal organisations develop through the social activities that employees carry out together, The informal groups created which then form part of the informal communications network in the organisation. Often peer groups, such as people who joined at the same time, constitute much of the informal organisation. The informal organisation is likely to **span the various levels and boundaries** of the organisation, extending to customers and suppliers, creating a network of contacts.

Disadvantages

(a) **Sub-optimal behaviour** can emerge if the informal organisation creates a culture or way of operating that is not beneficial to the organisation as a whole. This could occur throughout the organisation or as the result of an informal group operating in a part of the organisation.

(b) **Resistance to management actions** could also cause considerable disruption to operations if the informal organisation encourages resistance.

(c) **Influence** can be exerted by informal groups which could undermine management direction.

(d) It is **hard to control**.

(e) It is a **source of rumour** and misinformation.

Advantages

(a) It is a good way of **disseminating information**. It can jump levels of hierarchy. Speeding up the communications process in this way may not be possible through the formal structure.

(b) Although the managers should not use the informal network to manage the organisation, it is useful to be able to tap into the informal network to **keep close to what the employees, colleagues or rivals really think** about an issue.

(c) Humans are social animals and therefore the informal contact can act as a **morale booster**, enabling people to get matters of their chest without fear of retribution.

9 Aerospace team 1

Text references. Chapter 4

Top tips. Remember to use your key skills when answering a question. Thus a definition is a good way to start a question like this, to show that you understand the **key terms**. This is especially helpful (a) if the question seems ambiguous, in order to help the examiner to see how you have interpreted the question, and (b) to focus your thoughts on the specific topic key words in the question. Look at the advice in the front pages on how to approach answering written questions and follow the seven-step plan therein.

Easy marks. This should be straightforward in its theoretical aspects. For part (b), you should be able to take the 'advantages of team working' and *apply* them to the specifics of the aerospace company: hints are given in the scenario.

(a) **Essential features of a team**

A team is a 'small number of people with complementary skills who are committed to a common purpose, performance goals and approach for which they hold themselves mutually accountable'.
A team has the following four essential features.

Common goals or purpose

Team members have common goals, aims, and purposes resulting in higher levels of goal congruence, or 'unity of direction'.

Complementary skills and defined roles

Belbin's research suggests that certain roles must be present and balanced in a team in order for it to function effectively. This includes both task or 'content' roles and 'process' roles, concerned with the functioning and maintenance of the team (leader, ideas person, co-ordinator and so on).

Good communication

In order to add multiple efforts together for positive (as opposed to negative synergy), co-ordination is required. In a team, this comes through multi-directional, open information and knowledge exchange.

Cohesiveness and sense of identity

Handy defined a group as 'a collection of people who perceive themselves to be a group'. Members of an effective team are bound to each other by a sense of belonging, and a shared set of interests and behavioural norms (which develop with membership). The greater the sense of this, the greater the loyalty and interaction amongst the group.

(b) **Benefits of team working for T Aerospace**

The benefits that T-Aerospace can expect to see from the adoption of team working may include the following.

More and faster innovation

As the company will be **drawing together different workers with different backgrounds and expertise** it is likely that **working together these multidisciplinary teams will be able to provide new engineering solutions** that working alone they would not have achieved. For example if an electrician works with an interior designer it may be that the new application of electronics is found in some of the interior design of a new aircraft.

This advantage is likely to be particularly important to T-Aerospace as we are told that their 'new technology... might provide them with a competitive edge'.

Given the relative importance of innovation in the aerospace industry as noted in the previous point **a second major advantage the company may gain would be faster innovation from team working.** This appears to be likely given that we are told that this is a benefit gained by some of the company's competitors after adopting team working practices.

Increased staff loyalty

If the company successfully adopts team working practices it can expect its staff to show more loyalty. In addition to the employees having loyalty to the company it is likely that they will also start to owe loyalty to other team members as friendships and personal relationships evolve. The **positive impact of this for T-Aerospace may include lower staff turnover and increased morale**, which should both lead to higher productivity in the longer term.

Multi-skilled staff

As mentioned earlier, if staff work in teams drawn from different backgrounds it is inevitable that there will be some knowledge and skills transfer. If for example an electrician works closely with a computer engineer they are both likely to learn from each other giving them broader skills set and enabling them to be able to perform a wider range of tasks. **The benefit for the company is that it now has a more flexible, highly skilled workforce.**

10 Aerospace team 2

Text references. Chapter 4.

Top tips. You should be able to see that this question is simply the 'flip side' of Question 9: the potential **difficulties** of team working (or managing teams), as opposed to its potential **advantages**. This should help to keep you focused. Don't overlook the second requirement: to recommend ways of overcoming the problems you identify.

Easy marks. There are plenty of theoretical points on 'potential barriers to effective team-working', which you could apply to the case study: potential for intra-team conflict, excessive cohesion and group think, risky decision-making, the need for co-ordination and so on. However, we have taken a different, more applied approach (to show you how it can be done), thinking systematically through the details given in the case study and *relating* them to team work issues. Note that we have also been systematic in identifying the problem and then immediately recommending solutions – to be sure that we earn all the marks available.

Difficulties that T-Aerospace may encounter, and how to resolve them

Resistance from managers

Some of the existing management teams have had negative experiences of team working in the past, as such they are likely to resist any move to implement new working procedures.

The best way to overcome this is likely to involve consultation with these managers. If we could find out what caused their negative experiences in the past and take their views on board when implementing our new system this will help allay their fears as well as possibly getting them to 'buy into' the process.

Lack of team working skills

Team working will require additional and new skills for our existing workforce. If they have previously worked as individuals they are unlikely to be able to immediately work as effectively in teams, causing short-term falls in productivity.

A solution to this problem may well to be to provide teamwork training courses, or to recruit and selection staff with a team working background. It would also be necessary to make senior management aware of the likely impact on productivity, thus ensuring realistic budgets and targets are set during the transitional phase.

Resistance to change

It is well known that people do not like change, and that this intolerance increases with age. A change in working practices will involve physiological, physiological, and circumstantial change for the majority of the workforce, in the form of new working hours, colleagues, shift patterns etc. This could result in staff resistance to change, industrial action if the workforce is unionised, or falls in morale and productivity.

Staff resistance is best overcome by using experts in change management. Appointing an experienced change manager, 'champion of change', will ensure that appropriate levels of communication, counselling, consultation, and coercion are used when necessary. This should help minimise any passive or active resistance to change.

Concern over loss of work specialisation

It appears that the company has a culture that values 'experts', being employees who have highly developed, but narrow skill sets. In an industry where expertise, accuracy, and reliability are crucial a loss of skills will adversely affect the companies abilities to maintain quality and innovate. Again this perception amongst staff over loss of skills could cause a lowering of staff morale or increase staff turnover.

This concern could be allayed by again consulting with staff and management. It is likely that the company will continue to employ people because of their high degrees of specialisation and provide training to support this. However if it can be explained and demonstrated that these skills will be enhanced, rather than degraded by team working then the workforce may see the changes in a more positive light.

Co-ordination of the workforce

The company is likely to move towards a matrix structure in order to create multi-disciplinary teams. This is turn is likely to make it harder to control and co-ordinate its workforce. Additionally this could make the staff a more difficult resource to drive efficiently.

The company may need to invest in new human resource software in order to be able to track and allocate its staff efficiently. A new layer of management may also be required, as a matrix structure requires each team member to report into a project manager as well as their line manager.

11 Joan Timmins

Text references. Chapter 1.

Top tips. This is a simple question about management style that could be answered by reference to any of the style spectrum models. **Remember your key skills here**: the key here is to pick a **good theory** to **apply** to Joan's situation.

Candidates often have difficulty applying their theoretical knowledge in papers that require written answers. To help overcome this difficulty, we print the application points in this answer in *italic*. Note that we also continue to use italic for technical references and to indicate a particular emphasis on some words.

For some other handy tips on how to answer scenario questions refer back to the guidance in 'Approach to questions' in the front pages.

Easy marks. It would be possible to score close to 50% on this question by setting out an appropriate theory of leadership style and identifying two things: where Joan Timmins style lies on the model, and where her subordinates' expectations lie. You should bring any personal experience you may have to bear in questions like this.

Theories of Management styles

Style is a difficult factor to measure or define. Most of the early theories were based on the different uses made of authority. Some of the leadership theories present two basic choices – a task centred leader on the one hand and an employee-centred one on the other. *Likert's* theory offers four choices and the managerial grid offers five. *Huneryager and Heckman* identified four different management styles.

(a) **Dictatorial style** – where the leader forces subordinates to work by threatening punishment and penalties.

(b) **Autocratic style** – where decision-making is centralised in the hands of the leader, who does not encourage participation by subordinates.

(c) **Democratic style** – where decision-making is decentralised, and shared by subordinates in participative group action.

(d) **Laissez-faire style** – where subordinates are given little or no direction at all, and are allowed to establish their own objectives and make all their own decisions.

Application of theory to Joan Timmins

The style of a manager is essentially how he or she operates, but it is a function of many factors – one of which is culture. *Joan Timmins has moved from a military position, with its authoritarian style of leadership, to her current position as Head of the Finance department of the SOFT corporation and is finding that the style of management she is used to is not going down well in the new environment. Her style is still authoritarian. All decisions are taken by her, with little or no discussion with the subordinates, and possibly not even with fellow members of the top management team. Unfortunately for Joan, this style is causing resentment.* What generally happens in this type of situation is that the work gets done, but productivity is both very low and quality indifferent, or it requires a high level of overheads to ensure that there is any output at all.

It is obvious that her new team expect a different, more participative style of leadership. Recommendations should be made to Joan to adopt a participative or democratic style of management.

At SOFT, the leaders share their decision-making activities with their subordinates as much as possible while not compromising their ultimate responsibility or authority. Much decision making, therefore, is done using discussion and consultation, either on a formal or informal basis. This approach permits effective delegation and is thus highly motivational. There must always be scope for individuality of working, and hence idea generation, if a business is to succeed and continue to be successful. The democratic process creates the environment for this to grow. *Likert* is the leading advocate of this general approach, linking together worker satisfaction and high company effectiveness as resulting from a democratic management approach.

12 S and C

Text references. Chapter 5.

Top tips. You need a good **knowledge** of the appropriate area of employment law to answer this question: there is an unspoken assumption that a proper answer will reflect modern attitudes to the relationship between employer and employee.

Our answer is based on UK law and procedure, which can be taken as representative of the situation in the EU generally. You could use another legal system as a basis for an answer if you were more familiar with it.

Easy marks. Employment law is complex and it would not be appropriate to approach this question looking for easy marks.

Disciplinary action is undertaken to improve future behaviour. It has considerable potential for creating serious disputes, so managers should always act consistently and in accordance with their organisation's established procedures. All disciplinary incidents should be **thoroughly investigated** and a written record kept by the manager concerned.

Stage – informal advice/coaching or counselling

Many minor cases of poor performance or misconduct are best dealt with by informal advice, coaching or counselling. S should certainly start by taking this course of action, using the medium of an **informal interview**. C should be informed that his behaviour has caused concern and be asked to account for it. This should focus his mind and reveal if there are any extenuating circumstances, such as illness or a family crisis. In the absence of such circumstances, C should be informed firmly that an improvement is required. A record should be made of the interview.

Stage – formal disciplinary procedures

Should there be no improvement, it may be necessary to deal with C through more formal disciplinary procedures. In the UK, such procedures are governed by the **ACAS code of practice**, which among other things, provides for full investigation, a right to be accompanied at any disciplinary proceeding and a right of appeal against sanctions. S, as a newly appointed manager should take advice from HRM professionals within Z Company.

The next stage would be the issue of a warning. This could be oral or written.

(a) An **oral warning** should include the reason for issuing it; notice that it constitutes the first stage of the disciplinary procedure; and details of the right of appeal. A note of the warning should be kept on file but disregarded after a specified period, such as six months.

(b) A **first written warning** is appropriate in more serious cases. It should inform the employee of the improvement required and state that a **final written warning** may be considered if there is no satisfactory improvement. A copy of a first written warning should be kept on file but disregarded after a specified period, such as twelve months.

(c) A first written warning may also be appropriate if there has not been satisfactory improvement after an oral warning.

In the case of C, an oral warning is probably appropriate, as the disciplinary offences are fairly minor.

If the first warning is still current and there is no improvement, S may have to consider disciplinary sanction. Any sanction must be preceded by a **final written warning**.

The ultimate disciplinary sanction is dismissal. This is only appropriate for the most serious breaches of discipline. Demotion and suspension without pay are less drastic alternatives, but they must be provided for in the contract of employment.

Background material

In the UK, any imposition of disciplinary sanction must be in accordance with the statutory procedure introduced on 1 October 2004. This has three steps.

Step 1 S writes to C stating why disciplinary action is being taken and inviting him to meeting to discuss the matter. C has the right to be accompanied by an advisor at the meeting.

Step 2 At the meeting, S must explain the problem and allow C to respond. C must decide what is to be done and, after the meeting, explain her decision and inform C that he has the right to appeal to a different and preferably senior manager.

Step 3 C may appeal and has the right to be accompanied by an adviser at the appeal meeting.

13 Functions

Text references. Chapter 1.

Top tips. The requirement to illustrate your answer with examples from an organisation with which you are familiar is unusual, though by no means unique to this question. What are you to do if you are unable to give examples from an organisation with which you are familiar? Invent some. We have used an entirely imaginary organisation. Look back at our advice in the front pages under ' Develop business awareness' which will give you some help here.

Candidates often have difficulty applying their theoretical knowledge in papers that require written answers. To help overcome this difficulty, we print the application points in this answer in *italic*. Note that we also continue to use italic for technical references and to indicate a particular emphasis on some words.

Easy marks. You are given the functions of management in the question requirement: do not be tempted to invent two of your own! **We deal with all five for completeness.**

We cannot do better than to combine and paraphrase the descriptions of these activities provided by *Drucker* and *Fayol*. We illustrate them with examples from the practice of Albert-Delameter Ltd (ADL), a large privately owned machine tool manufacturer specialising in the manufacture of sophisticated spline-shaft broaching machines.

Planning consists of the selection of objectives and the strategies, policies, programmes and procedures for achieving them. Drucker emphasise that targets must be quantified. *ADL do not have a mission statement in the commonly accepted sense but the Chairman regards it as the role of the company to make a decent profit by manufacturing machines of good workmanlike quality for the general engineering industry. Spline-shaft broaching machines are rather specialised machine tools, so ADL works closely with its customers to modify existing designs and create new ones to satisfy their requirements. Manufacture is planned for up to one year ahead, as the lead time for a new batch of machines can be several months, and is carried out by a works planning cell whose supervisor reports to the works manager.*

Organising, according to Fayol involves establishing a structure of **tasks** to be performed to achieve the organisation's goals, grouping these tasks into **jobs** for individuals, creating **groups of jobs** to create departments, delegating **authority** to carry out the jobs and providing systems of **information**. Organising therefore inherently includes the design of the organisation. *ADL is a hybrid organisation. Its fundamental structure is functional, but superimposed on this is a project organisation for the introduction of new products. These normally appear in response to customer requirements and project teams including representatives of sales, costing, design and production engineering are set up as required.*

Additional material

Communicating is not specifically defined as a management function in this sense by either Fayol or Drucker. However, Fayol speaks of **commanding** and **co-ordinating**. By commanding, he means **giving instructions** to subordinates to carry out tasks over which the manager has authority for decisions and responsibility for performance. By co-ordinating he means **harmonising the activities** of individuals and groups within the organisation. Drucker speaks of managers communicating **targets** and providing the **information people need** to do their work. *The CEO of ADL has made it his business to ensure that people throughout the organisation are aware of what is going on by means of quarterly face-to-face briefings. There are usually two or three sessions each quarter to ensure maximum attendance. The briefings are held in the works canteen. They rarely last more than half an hour and include a summary of achievements, problems and future prospects.*

For Fayol, **controlling** means measuring the activities of individuals and groups, to ensure that their performance is in accordance with plans. Deviations from plan are identified and corrected. This is a simple description of a cybernetic or feedback control system. *ADL uses a normal system of budgetary control for its continuing operations. The production engineering and works planning staff are able to make accurate forecasts of cost because of their training and experience; the works manager and his assistants use these estimates in a flexible way to control costs.*

Drucker, writing much later than Fayol differs from him in his awareness of the human resource management role of managers. He regards it as fundamental that managers both **motivate** and **develop** their employees. The manager 'brings out what is in them or he stifles them. He strengthens their integrity or he corrupts them'. *ADL's HR manager refined the company's payment scheme to give greater emphasis to individual achievement. The company operates a single-status pay scheme, with all employees receiving a monthly salary. There was already a company-wide bonus scheme in existence, with payment based on annual profits. This has been modified so that managers can recommend individuals for extra bonuses for good performance. In addition to this and the communication programme outlined above, the company also ensures that its managers are trained in the skills of people management, using* Adair's **contingency based scheme**. *Newly appointed managers are sent off-site for two days to HR consultants who provide appropriate training.*

14 Stress management

Text references. Chapter 6.

Top tips. The scenario is very brief but, even so, the marking scheme requires answers to refer to it in order to score well. This is a **practical** question so you need to provide **practical** advice and not lots of theory. Notice how our opening paragraph explains how stress can harm the running of an organisation and how it can be unrelated to work.

Easy marks. Stress is regularly mentioned in the business press and many organisations have undertaken stress management programmes. You should have been able to mention two or three measures that could be taken from your general knowledge.

Examiner's comments. There was some failure to read the question carefully and to discuss the consequences of stress rather than how the problems it presents could be overcome.

Introduction

People who are over-stressed are likely to display a range of symptoms that can **prejudice the efficient running of the organisation**. These can include deterioration in personal relationships, absenteeism, irrational behaviour and impaired work performance. In an organisation such as a bank, with its emphasis on correct procedure, such effects can be particularly significant. Work itself and workplace relationships can be significant sources of stress, though they are not the only ones: domestic concerns can be equally significant. Whatever its origin, stress is a problem that managers must be prepared to manage.

Stress management measures

(i) **Promote understanding of stress in the organisation and stress management programme**

Part of the problem is that many high achievers cope well with stress. Such people tend to do well and be promoted and, as a result, **it is common for managers to be unaware of the significance of stress** in their organisations or to underestimate its importance. The first step for T to take would be to **promote understanding among managers of its significance**. This could be combined with an acknowledgement of the problem of stress to the workforce at all levels through the launch of a **stress management programme**. The aim should be to encourage the staff of X Investment Bank to accept the existence of stress as a problem and, in the case of those affected by it and their managers, to take positive steps to deal with it.

(ii) **Stress audit**

T should take a proactive stance and attempt to establish the incidence and effects of stress within the organisation. Such a **stress audit** might be undertaken through a programme of interviews or by means of confidential questionnaires, possibly involving external consultants to ensure confidentiality. It is **unlikely that the appraisal system** would be a suitable mechanism for such an investigation, though managers should certainly be encouraged to use every opportunity to establish the incidence of stress within the Bank.

Workplace stress may be induced by aspects of the job content or the physical work environment and by the formal and informal social aspects of the employment. There are not likely to be any major stress-inducing aspects of the **work environment** in a bank compared with, say, a foundry, but job content or social factors may be significant.

(iii) **Dealing with stress**

When T has a better idea of the extent to which stress is a problem in the Bank, he might then take steps to deal with it. These might have two aspects: first, removing or reducing as many as possible of the **factors that produce stress**; and second, **ameliorating the effect** of any remaining factors.

In a bank, the need for accuracy, judgement and caution may clash with the drive for expansion and profit, for example, producing stress in the managers responsible for **reconciling these conflicting objectives**.

Similarly, unsympathetic superiors and irritating colleagues, themselves stressed by the demands of their roles, can exist in almost any job.

It is unlikely that all stress-inducing factors can be removed from any work and it may be that some degree of stress is an important **spur to high performance**. However, employers must take care that they do not allow stress to have adverse effects on their employees' health. **Counselling programmes** are becoming common: they are a good way to both monitor the incidence of stress and to provide some amelioration where it is required.

15 PB Company

Text references. Chapter 6.

Top tips. Note the way we have chosen to lay out our answer to this question. This is not the only possibility – you could also set out the agenda and append notes below it – but this has the advantage of dealing with one thing at a time.

Easy marks. Any meeting other than the most informal ones is likely to include simple predictable items such as the minutes of the last meeting. Most of the items in the left hand column of our table are entirely predictable and between them might produce as many as three marks.

Outline Agenda and banking notes for Saturday's meeting

Agenda Item	Reason for inclusion
Open the meeting and welcome representatives	Important because representatives will have given up part of their weekend to attend. Need to recognise this and try and decrease the amount of hostility for being at the meeting.
Apologies for absence	Some representatives may have wanted to attend, but can't for various reasons. These names should be recorded to show they do have an interest in the proceedings.
Minutes of last meeting	As this is a one-off meeting, there is no need to have the minutes or similar formalities.
Agree items for discussion	The main item for discussion will be the proposed change to working conditions. It is important to confirm this and also produce a longer list of other grievances. If other problems are recognised then these can be left for later discussion and not 'get in the way' of the main issue.
Discuss the proposed change in providing demonstrations to potential customers.	It is important to obtain a detailed list of objections; only then can specific actions be taken to overcome those objections. Record comments on a flip chart so representatives can see what is being discussed.
Agree action plans	For each specific problem area, try and agree an action, although some actions may be very limited where company policy cannot be changed. State trying to be helpful but some items become difficult, if not impossible, to change.
Discuss other issues.	Any other problem areas can be discussed, if there is time.
Confirm dates for action plans	Agree dates when minutes and then actions resulting from the meeting will be distributed to all attendees.
Close the meeting	With thanks for attending and being willing to discuss views openly.

16 Power

Text references. Power and influence is covered in Chapter 1.

Top tips. 'Describe' is a low level question requirement, testing your comprehension rather than analytical ability. **Remember the advice on key skills in the introduction**. So make sure you are clear what the examiner means by a verb by referring back to the ' What the examiner means' table in the front pages.

Nevertheless it is very important to think first about the position that G is in, and then **apply** the types of power identified in Chapter 1 of the Study Text. Ask yourself which types of power are likely to be used by G. It may even be helpful to think about the power exercised by senior management in similar circumstances within your own company, if this is relevant. The marking guide gives up to two marks for each source of power, full marks required candidates to apply these to G.

Easy marks. The easy marks come from your knowledge of power and your descriptions of the different types of power.

Examiner's comments. The question requires candidates to explain the different **sources** of power in G. A helpful structure for explaining this is *French* and *Raven's* classification of the sources of power. Good answers will draw on the scenario in the question to give examples illustrating the different sources of power and how they would bring about change. Overall, candidates appear to have answered this topic well. Weaker candidates could not write about the types of power.

Power is the ability to do something, or get others to do it. The following types of power have been identified, some of which apply to G's position. The power he chooses to wield will be far-reaching within the organisation.

Physical power is the power of superior force. It is generally absent from most commercial organisations and certainly does not apply to G's position within L. Similarly, **negative power** will not apply to G as it is related to disruptive and negative attitudes and behaviour.

Resource power is the control over resources which are valued by others. G, as the senior partner, is likely to have the resource power to grant any necessary promotion or pay increases to staff affected by the proposed changes (this is also called **reward power**). He will also have the power to set up new working methods, by controlling the resources that are required to operate them (such as giving approval for investment in new IT systems for data storage, for example).

Position power or **legitimate power** is the power associated with a particular job in an organisation, and equates to **authority**. Senior managers enjoy position power, taking major decisions and setting constraints over others. G as the senior partner (and head of the project to introduce the new technology and working practices) has the right to organise the new working conditions. He may need to resort to this type of power to 'persuade' staff members who are strongly opposed to the changes. He may do this by establishing rules and procedures that he enforces.

Expert power is power based upon expertise; his staff will acknowledge that G has this, since he has worked for L for over 20 years. He has sound knowledge of the firm, and all areas of its business. He has become a trusted leader, and any staff who may be concerned about the proposed changes could be 'won over' by the fact that it is G himself who is championing them.

Referent power lies in the personal qualities of an individual. G is well liked and respected by the staff of L, and is seen as fair and open. He is likely to be capable of influencing staff in an informal way, gaining their support for the changes on a personal level, in almost the same way that expert power works: staff trust and like him both for his personality and his experience within the company. This is power operating at a more informal level. It is effective because senior managers such as G will always depend upon the co-operation given and decisions made by subordinates, and it is preferable that such support be willingly given.

17 Health and safety policy

Text references. Chapter 3 covers health and safety policy.

Top tips. You must emphasise that good health and safety is a **statutory** requirement and not just best practice. So a health and safety policy must comply with legislation. There are benefits too in an enhanced corporate image and good ethical practice. Remember that the company already has a health and safety policy so the question is not about putting one in place but about reminding management of their **responsibilities** in this area. Our suggested answer has only considered the viewpoint of the **employer** where senior management are representatives, though in fact senior management are also employees.

Easy marks. You can gain a few marks from listing employer responsibilities under the legislation.

Examiner's comments. This question was answered moderately well. Some candidates tended to give specific examples of health and safety rather than key areas that should be covered.

Key areas that H should cover in the health and safety seminar

H needs to cover the following areas in his seminar.

(a) **Legal requirements**

The main legislation dealing with health and safety in the UK dates back to the **Health and Safety at Work Act (HSWA)(1974)**. Secondary legislation is covered in several **regulations** covering topics such as manual handling, VDU, health and hygiene and consultation on health and safety matters.

Both employers and employees have responsibilities under the legislation. These require them to ensure that the systems, environment, equipment and conduct in the workplace are such as to minimise the risk to health and safety of employees and visitors alike.

Specifically, **employers** have the following responsibilities under the **HSWA**.

(i) To provide **safe systems** (work practices)
(ii) To provide a **safe and healthy work environment** (well-lit, warm, ventilated, hygienic and so on)
(iii) To maintain all **plant and equipment** to a necessary standard of safety
(iv) To **support safe working practices** with information, instruction, training and supervision
(v) To consult with **safety representatives** appointed by a recognised trade union
(vi) To appoint a **safety committee** to monitor safety policy, if asked to do so
(vii) To **communicate safety policy** and measures to all staff, clearly and in writing

The regulations impose additional duties on the employer, including to carry out risk assessments, to introduce controls to reduce risks, provide health and safety training, provide information to employees on health and safety and to employ competent health and safety advisors.

Where regulations cover specific areas such as VDU safety and manual handling, the employer must also make sure that appropriate **assessments** of the relevant operations are undertaken. Thus in the case of manual handling, the employer must ensure an assessment is made of all manual handling operations and take steps to reduce or eliminate the risks. Where VDU usage is concerned, the employer must arrange for adequate breaks, arrangement of the workstation and training and consultation to improve work practices.

(b) **Corporate image and cost to the organisation**

A business' **corporate image and reputation** as an employer may suffer if its health and safety record is poor. This would discourage potential employees and even customers. A **poor safety record** can lead to fines, lost productivity and the cost of hiring replacement workers.

(c) **Ethical practice**

Employees have a right to be protected from needless pain and suffering and employers have a **moral obligation** to ensure this right is upheld.

18 Communication

Text references. Chapter 6 has a good section on communication.

Top tips. Do not be fooled into thinking this is a question about project management! You need to use your knowledge of communication to explain to P how he could make communication more effective. We have included a little preamble explaining how communication is used in project teams which sets the context for the answer. Start by thinking about the possible barriers to effective communication that may impede P's success. Refer to information in the brief scenario to back up your argument. The examiner uses a visual model of communication in her suggested answer which we suggest you consult on the CIMA website as this is a good summary of the process of communication. The examiner awarded a mark for each aspect of this model giving a maximum of ten marks. For instance, there would be a mark for use of appropriate language, medium selected as appropriate to the message and explanation of noise.

Easy marks. There are clues in the scenario such as 'complex', 'technical' and 'overloaded' which tell you where P's communication is ineffective.

Examiner's comments. Weak answers developed in terms of stakeholder mapping to identify stakeholder power and interest but failed to extend this to advise P on how he could ensure his communications with stakeholders could be more effective.

In an organisational context communication has a variety of purposes. Among these is providing information to support managerial decision-making and to co-ordinate the plans and activities of different units and functions. Project teams usually communicate laterally and the project manager needs to use communication to co-ordinate the work of several stakeholders who are individuals and possibly departments with a stake in the project.

There are certain general problems in communication that can arise. Based on the information in the scenario, relevant problems would include **distortion** whereby the meaning of a message is lost between sender and receiver. **Misunderstanding** is also arising due to lack of clarity or technical jargon. It also appears that **overload** is an issue whereby the recipients of the information are being given too much information to digest in the time available. Certainly senior management would not be able to read detailed information and it would have to be edited for them. Timing may also be an issue here if information is being sent which has no immediate use. It is safe to say that there are also **poor communication skills** between P as sender and his audience although it is unclear whether this is two-sided as the team have made the complaints but are unlikely to admit any fault in their part.

Given the problems identified there are several suggestions to make communication more effective:

Give P training and guidance in communication skills including how to consider the information needs of the recipients of his messages, listening to them and acting on their feedback. **P needs to encourage feedback** as this is an important part of the communication process. **P also needs clear objectives about what he wants to achieve as a project manager** and this should frame his approach to communication. This would help P overcome problems with using inappropriate language unsuited to his audience, in his case, technical jargon.

It may be that P is uncomfortable with face to face communication. In this case, P could be given training on how to run meetings and make presentations. This would include looking at his non-verbal skills and giving him advice on how to make these cues consistent with the message he communicates verbally. In this way, he would also enhance personal interaction between the project team members, spread important information to all members at the same time and build relationships in a way that is not possible with remote ways of communicating.

Establish suitable communication channels and mechanisms that are suitable to all recipients. So the project group could agree to meet to update themselves if this was more suitable or agree the timing and form of regular email updates to avoid the danger of becoming overloaded with information (or 'noise'). The most appropriate medium for updating the team depends on factors such as complexity (face to face is often better here), urgency (email is best here), permanency (any written form) and cost effectiveness. P needs to anticipate the reaction of those receiving the message so that any bad news is probably better communicated face to face.

19 *Preparation question: Scientific management*

Text references. Chapter 1.

Top tips. This is not an exam standard question. The answer should be used for revision purposes. Make sure that you remember to **apply** your explanations to the call centre as required in the question.

(a) **Scientific Management and call centre design**

Scientific Management

Scientific Management was concerned with the rational organisation of work as a means of increasing productivity. The emphasis was on the problem of obtaining increased productivity from individual workers through the technical structuring of the work organisation and the provision of monetary incentives as a motivator for higher levels of output.

Taylor considered that all work processes could be analysed into discrete tasks and that it was possible to find the 'one best way' to perform each task. Each job was broken down into component parts, each part timed and the parts rearranged into the most efficient way of working.

Taylor believed that a scientific approach to management could make work more profitable for all concerned. Workers could be controlled, not only by giving orders and maintaining discipline, but also by removing from them any decisions about the way their work was carried out. **By division of labour and by dictating precise stages and methods for every aspect of work performance, management could optimise work processes.** The application of techniques to decide what should be done and how, using workers who are both properly trained and willing to maximise output, should result in maximum productivity. Obtaining the highest possible wages through working in the most efficient and productive way would motivate workers.

The legacy of Taylor lives on. Time study, motion study, standardised tools and materials, methods simplification, careful selection and training, rigorous measurement, payment by results, management by exception, production control, endless and expensive experiments, even benchmarking (although it wasn't called that back then), have all been left to modern management by Taylor and his disciples.

Call centre design

The design of jobs in telephone call centres appears to owe quite a lot to scientific management.

(i) The operators are carefully selected for their voice characteristics, telephone manner and computer keyboard skills.

(ii) Unskilled operators are trained to be most efficient and effective in providing the service.

(iii) Operators cannot make decisions on how to carry out their work.

(iv) The use of modern technology provides the means for measuring almost every aspect of the telephone operators' work.

(v) The work is closely supervised with time away from the workstation easily tracked and recorded and the quality of the operators' performance constantly monitored by weekly customer 'call backs'.

(vi) Quantitative and qualitative measures of performance can be used to re-programme work practices and ensure yet more efficiency and effectiveness.

(vii) Performance-related pay provides the motivation to work harder.

(b) **Criticisms of scientific management**

There are a number of valid criticisms of Taylor's approach.

(i) It put **the planning and control of workplace activities exclusively in the hands of the management.** This reduces the workers' role to that of a rigid adherence to methods and procedures over which they have no discretion.

(ii) **It led to the fragmentation of work on account of its emphasis on the analysis and organisation of individual tasks or operations.**

(iii) **It generated a 'carrot and stick' approach to** the motivation of employees by relating pay to be geared tightly to output.

(iv) **It ruled out any realistic bargaining about wage rates** since every job was measured, timed and rated by management.

Perhaps the key idea of scientific management and the one that has drawn the most criticism was the concept of 'task allocation'. The criticism of this approach is that it omits the worker's own contribution to the design of work and, thereby, alienates the worker from the job. It is seen as leaving no scope for the individual worker to excel or think. Workers also find the work repetitive, boring and requiring little skill.

Repetitive jobs can cause strain-induced injuries while boredom can lead to accidents and low quality output.

Most of these criticisms can be applied to the work in telephone call centres. The operator's response follows carefully detailed procedures. Performance (and probably pay) is measured by the number of calls taken per operator per hour and there are no opportunities for job enrichment, enlargement or rotation to ease the boredom.

Whilst it is true that organisations the world over have benefited from, and are continuing to use, techniques that have their origins in scientific management, in the West there is a reaction against the basic philosophy. A better educated workforce allows for the re-integration of task components and the exercise of discretion and judgement at the operator level.

20 *Preparation question: Performance appraisal*

Text references. Chapter 3.

Top tips. All exam standard questions may require you to apply your knowledge of appraisals to a given scenario.

(a) **Objectives of performance appraisal**

The general purpose of any assessment or appraisal is to improve the efficiency of the organisation by ensuring that the individual employees are performing to the best of their ability and developing their potential for improvement. Performance appraisal may be defined as 'the regular and systematic review of performance and the assessment of potential with the aim of producing action programmes to develop both work and individuals.'

The common objectives of a formal performance appraisal system include the following:

(i) **To enable a picture to be drawn up of the human 'stock' of an organisation** – its strengths and weaknesses, enabling more effective personnel planning.

(ii) **To monitor the undertaking's initial selection procedures** against the subsequent performance of recruits, relative to the organisation's expectations.

(iii) **To establish what the individual has to do in a job** in order that the objectives for the section or department are realised.

(iv) **To assess an individual's current level of job performance.** This can be used both as a base line against which performance can be measured in future and as a means of deciding how the individual has improved since the last performance appraisal. It allows managers and subordinates to plan personnel and job objectives in the light of performance.

(v) **To identify weaknesses in an individual's performance** and identify training needs. Actual performance is compared with pre-defined objectives; shortcomings in performance are then used as indicators of the training required to achieve improvements. Training needs may arise for reasons other than the capabilities of individuals, such as new demands made by changing legislation, new technology and so on. Once training has taken place, performance appraisal enables some evaluation of training effectiveness.

(vi) **To assess the level of reward payable for an individual's efforts**, eg, in merit payment systems. It represents an opportunity to provide positive feedback to employees on their performance and to set new targets and challenges for the coming period along with the a reminder of possible rewards.

(vii) **To assess potential**. At the organisational level this permits career and succession planning. At the individual level it permits superior and subordinate to assess the most effective development plans for the subordinate.

(b) **Problems with appraisal in practice**

There are various problems with appraisal in practice.

(i) They **tend to reinforce hierarchical, formal relationships** between managers and their staff, with a 'judgemental'/critical aspect, and are perhaps unsuitable to organisations where the relationship between management and their subordinates is fluid or participatory. This can lead to suspicion and defensiveness on the part of both appraiser and appraisee.

(ii) They **focus on the lowest level of performance feedback** (individual behaviour or results), largely ignoring the organisational and systems context of that performance. Attention may not be given to problem-solving in regard to technology, procedures, leadership or other factors impacting on the individuals' (or teams') performance.

(iii) They are **highly dependent on individual managers**, who:

(1) May not understand the value of the process, or put sufficient effort and time into it

(2) May be insufficiently skilled in feedback-giving and coaching to be able to give constructive criticism, encourage employee acceptance or support problem-solving

(3) May have personal bias in relation to individuals or issues

(iv) They are **highly dependent on the quality and reliability of assessment criteria** and methods used. Variations in the consistency of reporting standards can be (or be perceived to be) unjust. There are many potential sources of rating errors including, for example, inadequate definition of ratings; excessively rigid ratings (not allowing for qualification or elaboration for accuracy); criteria that are irrelevant to the job; or bias on the part of the appraiser.

(v) **They tend to concentrate too much on feedback on past performance** and especially (subjectively) on the recent past, rather than on improvement/development needs and opportunities.

(vi) There is **not always potential to link positive performance or performance gains directly to rewards** – and if this is the expectation, it can lead to disappointment and frustration. On the other hand, a direct link between appraisal and reward can add pressure to the process, turning 'learning opportunities' into 'penalties'.

What can be done to improve the effectiveness of appraisal

In some organisations the problems associated with performance appraisal have been recognised and management have taken steps taken to limit their detrimental effect.

(i) **Competence- and results-based frameworks** have been introduced that focus on the performance rather than on the qualities of the appraisee. This can increase the objectivity of the appraisal.

(ii) **Multiple sources** of assessment and feedback can be used, to involve people in the process, extend the range and relevance of feedback provided – and to reduce the likelihood of personal bias. Approaches such as 360-degree feedback embrace a range of options, for example, including self-appraisal, peer appraisal, upward appraisal and customer appraisal.

(iii) A **performance management** approach can be adopted, whereby there is joint improvement/development and performance target setting and *on-going* monitoring, feedback and adjustment – as well as a retrospective end-of-period review. This can reduce the backward-looking and 'judgemental' aspects of appraisal, and separate reward-linked review from on-going feedback for improvement.

(iv) A **constructive, co-operative orientation** can be adopted by managers implementing appraisal. Maier, for example, advises a 'problem-solving' approach to appraisal interviewing, in which the appraiser adopts a coaching/facilitating role to help the employee diagnose work problems and articulate work/improvement ambitions, and to develop action plans. This can reduce the one-directional, judgemental perception of appraisal.

21 Workload

Text references. Chapter 1 deals with delegation. Chapter 6 deals with time management.

Top tips. This is a very practical question, as questions on this topic tend to be. There is little theory to consider and it is appropriate to plunge straight into sensible recommendations.

Easy marks. Laura's actions to improve her own time management are standard and should be easy to note down if you have done even a little preparation for this topic.

(a) **How Laura can better manage her workload**

In situations such as this, it is easy to take a one-sided view and either blame Laura entirely for being overworked, or blame her employers for over-working her. In practice, both are probably to blame.

If Laura appears willing to work long hours, then her employers will, inevitably, take this for granted. However, the ability to 'manage the boss' is an important facet of surviving in organisations and Laura should manage her boss and her time more effectively.

Laura's own approach to time management needs to be analysed, perhaps with the help of a mentor, coach or counsellor.

(i) **Laura allows herself tends to be a victim of events.** She allows events such as interruptions from assistants to happen 'to' her. She does not shape what goes on.

(ii) **Laura is perhaps not suited to the job**. Laura does not appear to enjoy the HRM aspects of the job. If she embraced these more forcefully, she might save time in the end, by matching the development of her staff with a reduction in her workload.

(iii) **Laura is not using her staff profitably**. Laura could make their jobs more interesting, give them more responsibility and save herself time.

(iv) **Urgency and importance**. Laura perhaps does not ask the chief accountant whether the ad hoc projects are as urgent as she thinks they are. They may not need to take priority over other things.

The firm's approach to Laura also needs to be reviewed. The firm does not make it easy for Laura to prioritise her time. When she is doing monthly and quarterly accounts, she should not be interrupted with ad hoc projects. The chief accountant should act as a filtering mechanism for these.

Actions Laura should take in order to manage her time better include the following.

(i) As a first step, she should **keep a time diary** over a typical month. Although time consuming in itself, this should enable her to see where particular problems lie. Interruptions are disruptive not only because of the time they take, but also because they interrupt Laura's train of thought and make her work more difficult to complete. Interruption is one of the essential characteristics of a manager's job (according to Mintzberg) – but Laura's job is not solely managerial, as it has a technical aspect.

(ii) **Once she has reviewed the results of her time diary, she can then plan her time better.** This means reviewing the extent to which she is available to her assistants (eg to discuss queries, which might all be dealt with together), the importance of deadlines and so on.

(iii) She can increase **delegation** – some of the assistants should be suitable candidates, especially if the delegated tasks can be part of their training.

(iv) She can institute a **closed door policy** on occasions to let her get on with her technical tasks.

(v) **She should set her team deadlines** and allocate their work so that it ties in easily with her own; in other words she should ensure that, for month-end and quarterly reporting, she is undisturbed and that they are working on other things. She needs to establish a routine for the department.

(vi) She should arrange a **meeting with the chief accountant** to **agree priorities**. In the case of ad hoc assignments given to her when she is busy, she should learn to say 'no' on occasions. This means educating her boss into giving adequate notice and details – not the easiest things to do, but necessary nonetheless. The boss can also let her know how long a project will take. He may have no idea as to the complexity of some of the tasks he has asked her to do. Some of the ad hoc tasks can be given to one of her juniors.

(vii) She should learn to distinguish **between urgency and importance**. Importance can be assessed in relation to her own mission in the organisation. Monthly and quarterly financial reporting is **always important** and always **urgent** at the month end. Ad hoc projects may appear urgent, if the person requesting it would like an answer tomorrow, but Laura might have to say 'no' – unless of course it is the managing director.

(viii) Eventually, she might want to **restructure her job** – but the firm may not take kindly to requests for this nature.

(b) **Effectively managed delegation**

By delegating authority to subordinates, Laura takes on the extra tasks of calling her subordinates to account for their decisions and performance, and also of co-ordinating the efforts of different subordinates. This is why delegation must be effectively managed if it is to be helpful rather than dysfunctional for Laura.

Effective delegation can be achieved as follows.

(i) The **expected task outcomes and performance levels** should be clearly specified, ideally in the form of SMART objectives. Laura should ensure that all subordinates fully understand and accept (and are capable of achieving) these outcomes .

(ii) **Tasks should be formally assigned** to the subordinates, who should agree to do them: this way, the delegation will be unambiguous and each party knows what its role is.

(iii) **Resources, information and authority should be allocated** to the subordinates to enable them to carry out their tasks at the expected level of performance. This will be particularly important for the accounts assistants, who currently seem unable or unwilling to use initiative: they need to be assured that they have the authority – and may perhaps need coaching in problem-solving skills before they are sufficiently confident to take more initiative.

(iv) **Responsibility should be exacted** from the subordinate for results obtained (because ultimate responsibility remains with Laura).

(v) The **subordinates' ability and experience must be borne in mind** when allocating tasks and responsibilities: Laura will need to investigate the cause of the accounts assistants' current inability (or unwillingness) to take the initiative. More able or experienced team members may be appointed to supervise or coach less confident members: delegating not only workload, but also team building and development in a way which might improve team cohesion and morale – as well as making the best of available resources.

(vi) **Frequent contact must be maintained** between Laura and her team, in order to review the progress made and resolve any problems – particularly given the importance of the tasks. However, delegation will not improve Laura's time management problems – nor the abilities and satisfaction of her team – if she 'micro-manages' or over-supervises. Having given clear guidelines and resources, she should be able to 'back off' and foster subordinate initiative – with the understanding that she is available (on a 'reporting by exception' basis) if any queries or problems arise.

By such effective delegation, Laura can cover two aspects of her job at once. Not only can she make her own life easier, but she can contribute to the development of her assistants. She is responsible for their professional development: delegating tasks to them, with appropriate supervision, satisfies this requirement.

22 D Company

Text references. Chapter 6.

Top tips. The opening paragraph of the answer could usefully have included a definition of negotiation and an explanation of its uses – setting up discussion of the particular nature of change management (conflicting interests of stakeholders) which requires negotiation. Remember to keep a balance between writing all you know about negotiation and **applying** this to D Company. **The examiner is keen on practical application of theory**.

If you are uncertain how to start your answer refer back to the advice on 'Approach to questions' in the front pages.

Easy marks. Easy marks were achievable by setting out the four phases in the main stages of a negotiation (as required by the question) and summarising the key features of each stage. However, you also had to explain *why* these features were relevant in the specific context of change management.

(a) **Role of negotiation in managing change**

Negotiation is a process whereby two parties come together to confer with a view to concluding a jointly acceptable agreement. This is conducted through a process of both **purposeful persuasion** (persuading the other party of the merits of one's case or position) and **constructive compromise** (being willing to move closer toward the other party's position).

This is a particularly helpful process for **change management** in any situation, as it:

(i) Recognises that stakeholders in the change (eg management, employees and trade unions) will have **differing and potentially conflicting interests** in the situation

(ii) Recognises that stakeholder interests should be **taken into account** in developing a solution and change plan, whether because they have immediate power in the situation (eg the authority of managers to impose solutions, the power of employees to resist) or because there is a key need to preserve constructive working relationships for the future. Most employee (as opposed to commercial) negotiations recognise this need, and seek at worst an acceptable compromise and at best a 'win-win' solution which can be committed to by both parties

(iii) Recognises that there may genuinely be **common ground** which can be built on, and other view points which can be taken into account, in order to develop **better solutions** which genuinely benefit both parties: a 'win win' solution to the need for change.

Restructuring in D company

D company is going through a major restructuring that could mean re-location of staff to different sites and other staff being made redundant. The company is aware that employees and their trade unions will be resistant and has recognised the potential impact of the changes on staff morale. In these circumstances, negotiation may be the only way for the company to achieve its objectives. **Non-negotiatory approaches** such as coercion (imposed solution) or information/persuasion (selling an already-decided change plan) **may at best result in compliance** (often with underlying resistance) and at worst in a costly and damaging campaign of industrial protest.

In order **to secure commitment and genuine co-operation**, and to preserve on-going employee relations, D Company should specifically **pursue an integrative, rather than distributive or 'zero-sum'**, approach to negotiation, aiming to work constructively towards mutually acceptable solutions.

The role of the four phases of negotiation

The negotiations between D Company and the trade unions, if they follow the conventional pattern, will fall into four phases.

(i) In the **preparatory phase**, appropriate arrangements should be made, as for any other meeting. These should include the establishment of an agenda, which may itself be the subject of negotiation, and the provision of a suitable meeting room.

If D Company and the unions are realistic, they will have established in their own minds not only their **ideal** outcomes, but also a **minimum acceptable** outcome. If the acceptable outcomes overlap, it should be relatively easy to reach a **mutually acceptable** result. If they do not, the task becomes much harder.

(ii) In the **opening phase** the company and the unions should both state their positions clearly and realistically. The opposing position should be challenged on its merits; it is important to leave the opponent with room for manoeuvre. If C Company adopts an integrative approach, it may wish to use this phase specifically to indicate its desire to consult employees and to develop mutually acceptable solutions – rather than engage in adversarial tactics. In this case, all concerns and needs can be frankly put on the table for discussion.

(iii) The **bargaining phase** is a process of argument and persuasion. The key role of this phase is to create incentives for change. For instance, by offering counter-arguments and incentives, to create movement (eg by persuasively putting an alternative perspective or proposal) and to begin to 'refreeze' the newly agreed position (eg by rewarding it with concessions in return, or proceeding to joint problem-solving and implementation planning).

(iv) The **closing phase** of a negotiation is similar to closing a sale. The key roles of this stage will be:

(1) To provide final incentives for each party to move towards the other, in order to create a win-win or compromise solution that both parties will be able to live with.

(2) To emphasise the movement that has taken place, in order to enable both parties to feel that their concerns and needs have been met, and to emphasise the desire to continue a positive working relationship on implementation of the agreement.

(3) To clearly state, ratify and circulate the final agreed position, in order to ensure that both parties are clear on the outcome, without risk of further misunderstanding or post-negotiation conflict.

(b) **Collecting information on staff attitudes**

Top tips. This was an example of a question where a little thought and imagination could have produced a common sense answer that could command a worthwhile number of marks.

Easy marks. The methods (meetings/interviews/survey) by which information could be collected from staff were not difficult to identify and many of the associated issues (who/when/where etc) could also be surmised.

A number of methods could be used to collect information on staff attitudes towards the changes arising from the proposed restructuring. Meetings could be held with staff at both departmental and company wide levels. A more structured approach could also be pursued via one to one interviews and a staff attitude survey. Given the potential sensitivity of this situation management should consult with staff representatives at an early stage.

Meetings

Departmental and company wide meetings are an **effective** and **rapid** means for management to explain the background to, and need for, the proposed changes but offer limited opportunity to gather **feedback** from employees. The employees however may well feel reluctant to air their views in public or may feel that their views are unlikely to be taken into account. Such meetings can however be an appropriate means of **initiating** the collection of information since they can be used to explain the importance which management attaches to gathering the views of staff and to set out how their views are to be gathered.

Interviews

One to one interviews, if conducted effectively, are more likely to provide insights into the underlying views of staff towards the changes but are relatively costly and time consuming to organise. Such an approach should however ensure a **high response rate**. A key decision will be to decide who should conduct the interviews. Use of an **external organisation** may encourage greater frankness on the part of employees and help to demonstrate that the company is genuinely concerned to identify staff concerns. The **quality** of staff used, whether internal or external, will be important in helping to convince staff of the genuineness of management's intentions in relation to their welfare. Similarly, the decision as to which staff should be interviewed will be important. Ideally all staff should have the opportunity of an interview. Frequently however this will not be practicable and a **representative sample** of staff should be identified.

Interview procedure

A detailed record should be kept of each interview and the interview should be carefully structured to ensure that the **topics covered adequately address all the key issues as perceived by management**. The interviewee must be given ample opportunity however to raise issues and concerns that have not been covered by the interviewer. The results of these interviews may be to highlight concerns of which management was unaware and to give less weight than management had envisaged to other 'obvious' concerns.

Staff attitude survey

A staff attitude survey offers the opportunity to gather a **comprehensive** and **quantifiable** understanding of staff views, particularly if the survey is carried out on an anonymous basis. If time is an issue the use of an **external agency** experienced in this field may be of particular benefit in terms of the design of the questionnaire and the ability to process and tabulate the results. This tabulation should provide management with a clear and quantified picture of the nature and depth of the key **employee concerns** and their views of management's plans to accommodate these concerns.

Summary

If D Company has the time and resources available it may judge that the best approach is to conduct company wide and departmental meetings combined with one to one interviews and a staff attitude survey, thereby gathering both qualitative and quantitative data.

23 Structure and innovation

Text references. Chapter 2.

Top tips. Notice the breakdown of marks in this question. Part (a)(i) is worth only seven marks and part (a)(ii) only six. There is a very great deal that could be said on the topics introduced but there is not much time in which to say it. The mark allocation is an indication of the depth and extent of the answers the Examiner wants and also of the amount of time you have available for your answers. Do not get carried away!

Understanding and applying CIMA active verbs is key here. Perhaps the most difficult element of part (a)(i) is the requirement to '**compare and contrast**'. This term means 'show the similarities and/or differences between', so something more than descriptions of the two structures is needed. Using words and phrases' such as 'like', 'unlike', 'by contrast', 'similarly' and 'in comparison' can help you to satisfy this requirement. You would be well advised to start with the entrepreneurial structure, since this is the simpler of the two, and then go onto combine a description of the functional structure with comments on how it differs.

In part (b) you need to combine practical advice with how this may help the company. By all means quote theories such as Kanter as part of your suggested answer.

Easy marks. The easy marks, as is often the case, are available in part (a) and particularly in part (a)(i): the simple structure and functional structure are perhaps the simplest types of organisation and the ones that most people are most familiar with.

It is reasonable to use *Mintzberg's* terminology as this is widely understood.

Examiner's comments. In part (a)(ii), there was a tendency to be prescriptive about future changes rather than to explain what the current problem was.

(a) (i) **Entrepreneurial v functional structures**

An entrepreneurial structure is very simple, with a **small strategic apex** (often consisting of a single owner-manager) and an informal system of control. It is suited to new, small organisations in which the founder knows all the details of what has to be done and runs everything by **personal supervision**. While there may be specialist members such as accountants and designers, coordination is centralised and there is no **middle line** or **technostructure**. In *Harrison's* terms, this is organisation falls into the **power** type.

By contrast, a functional structure is more commonly found in **larger organisations** dealing with **greater complexity**. This complexity makes personal supervision by a single person, or even a small group, impossible and **managers with specialist expertise** have to be employed. Specialised technical expertise forms the basis for departmentation and hierarchy, since **expert supervisors are needed** and **delegation** is only possible if subordinates themselves possess a degree of technical competence. **Communication and control** are vertical, rather than fluid and free as in the simple structure and there may be little contact between departments. Technostructure and support staff emerge. There is a tendency to formalise work and the organisation displays a **role culture**.

(ii) **Why the functional structure may no longer be appropriate for L Company**

L Company is part of an industry that is constantly introducing new products and ideas; continuing technical innovation and a high degree of enterprise are essential if it is to survive and prosper. *Burns and Stalker* described both L Company's earlier informal and creative approach to business and its current rather bureaucratic methods in their book *The Management of Innovation,* calling them **organismic** (or organic) and **mechanistic** styles respectively. They had no doubt that the organismic style was best suited to a rapidly changing technical environment.

The mechanistic style, rooted in procedure and functional structures tends to be slow to change because of its **focus on specialist responsibilities**. It does not have sufficient people taking a broad view of what is going on and what should be done and it tends to become slow in its responses because of **poor cross-functional communication and decision-making**. Innovation depends to some extent on the **free exchange of ideas and responses** between people of differing backgrounds and specialities: functional organisation tends to inhibit this and may actually reduce cross-functional co-operation and increase conflict.

(b) **Approaches to encouraging creativity and innovation**

Top tips. There is a very large number of things that can be discussed in this part of the question. We have tried to give reasonably full coverage in our answer: for the twelve marks available, a good discussion of four points should suffice. Remember to **tailor** your response to L Company rather than making a series of general points.

Easy marks. The fact that you have spent some time discussing structural matters in part (a) does not disqualify you from proposing structural changes in part (b).

Examiner's comments. We constantly reiterate the importance of making your answers relevant to the question scenario: in his comments on this part of the question, the Examiner stated clearly that a pass mark would only be awarded if suggestions were explained in terms of how they could make a difference at L Company.

As discussed above, L Company's current organisational approach may well be inhibiting creativity. A should review the existing structure and methods used to see if suitable changes could be made. The aim would be to encourage cross-functional communication; devolve power and responsibility; and reduce formality of structure and procedure where appropriate.

An overall **matrix structure** might be considered as a way to enhance customer focus and encourage cross-functional liaison. However, L Company's range of products is now quite diverse and a better approach might be **divisionalisation**. While there is plenty of scope for innovation in basic products such as kettles and vacuum cleaners, it is likely that the main managerial emphasis would be on cost-effective manufacturing. PCs and media equipment, on the other hand, would probably require much greater investment in new product development if market opportunities were to be seized. A policy of devolving responsibility on a product line basis should be considered, divisions being set up to design, manufacture and market compatible groups of products. **Team working** and **matrix approaches may then be useful within divisions**.

Control systems should be examined alongside the structure of the organisation. Any organisation will have areas, such as financial reporting compliance, that must be subject to strict control; however, if creativity is to be encouraged, such control should be restricted to the areas where it is necessary and a **looser approach** used elsewhere. **Cultural forms of control** should be developed, perhaps based on devolved budgets and performance measurement in terms of results rather than procedures. A **balanced scorecard** approach, with its emphasis on customer service and innovation and learning, may be useful.

Linked to culture is **management style.** A should satisfy herself that individual contributions are not being stifled by an over-authoritarian style of management. Creativity generally thrives best when there is a degree of empowerment and participation in the development of the organisation.

Rosabeth Moss Kanter's general prescriptions for encouraging organisational creativity provide a good summary of what can be done.

Accept change

Encourage new ideas

Permit interaction and communication

Tolerate failure

Reward creative behaviour

24 Departmental conflict

Text references. Chapter 4 contains material on teams, Chapter 5 covers conflict and Chapter 6 includes information of managing disputes and negotiation.

Top tips. This question is a real test of your ability to produce an answer that is more than just a general analysis. You must be able to make points that apply to the specific circumstances of M Company. Note the word 'nature' in the requirement for part (a). The Examiner is actually using the word with a specific meaning. He is asking you to put conflict that is taking place into some sort of classification of type or category. As you will see in our answer we classify the problems at M Company as **horizontal conflict**.

Easy marks. There are few easy marks in this requirement. You would glean a mark or two for pointing out the different attitudes of the departments, but this would not count as a full analysis since both **goal incompatibility** and **cognitive and emotional orientation** are involved.

Examiner's comments. Perhaps unsurprisingly, many candidates found it difficult to provide the detailed analysis required and merely repeated the detail of the scenario.

(a) **The nature and sources of conflict at M Company**

M Company is suffering the effects of **horizontal conflict**: that is, the conflicts are arising between groups and individuals that do not have a hierarchical relationship and are of more or less equal status in the company.

The various disputes have occurred for several reasons.

Operative goal incompatibility: the primary goals of the various departments involved, rather than supporting the overall objective of successful NPD, are themselves effectively incompatible. For example, the apparent slowness of the R&D department may reflect a goal of high technical excellence, while the anxiety of the sales department and the frustration of the marketers may, in turn, reflect goals of continuing growth and good customer relations.

Emotional and cognitive orientation: People working in different functions tend to have rather different personal priorities, interests, attitudes and values. For example, the perception of the finance department as unhelpful controllers of resources may say more about the attitudes prevailing in the other departments than the actual nature of the finance department's motivation.

Task interdependence: it is necessary for all the departments to cooperate closely if successful NPD is to take place, since information, in particular, must flow effectively back and forth between them. Any lack of co-operation from any department, perhaps rooted in one of the other causes of conflict mentioned here, is likely to produce significant frustration and further conflict as a result. This may be behind some of the production department's complaints about lack of co-operation from the R&D people.

Work pressure: M Company is facing difficult business conditions, which is likely to produce stress effects all responsible members of staff, both because of awareness of the need for improved performance and as a result of pressure from above. Conflict is a possible symptom of this stress.

(b) **Factors in building a cross-functional project team**

Easy marks. As with any question on teams, when thinking about this requirement, your mind should instantly make an agile leap to the work of *Tuckman* and that of *Belbin*. In fact, the Examiner's marking scheme indicates that discussing these two topics could almost take you to a pass mark. Naturally, you would not overlook the fact that the leader is part of the team and a consideration of management style would provide the remaining marks required.

Examiner's comments. Answers were generally good, confirming our impression that this is a friendly, manageable question. However, some candidates missed the point of the wording of the requirement and discussed project management rather than building a team.

The task of developing a new team might be considered under three headings: the individuals needed, the functioning of the group, and the leadership of the team.

The individuals

V must ensure that the members of the new project, between them, possess the skills, experience and aptitudes necessary to develop successfully his new range of luxury foods. Past disputes mean that perhaps the most important personal quality the team members will require a **commitment to working productively together**. They must retain their orientation towards the role of their own departments, but they must supplement that with a willingness to understand the needs and priorities of their colleagues. The emphasis must be on a judicious **balance of departmental concerns** in order to **support the overall goal**.

Belbin suggests that the effective functioning of a team depends, at least in part, on the ability of the members to play a range of important team roles. These roles are co-ordinator, shaper, implementer, monitor-evaluator, resource investigator, team worker, specialist and finisher.

Top tip. The Examiner's own suggested solution does not include an explanation of these roles: we think that it would be appropriate for you to include such an explanation if you wished to do so.

The group

New teams develop and mature over time, finding ways to operate and relate. The leader can build the team by controlling and accelerating this process. The development process was described by *Tuckman* as taking place in four stages.

(i) **Forming** is the process of bringing the group together and beginning to work out its aims, structure and processes. The 'getting to know each other' process should be encouraged here since team members come from different functions and may not even know each other. The team members are likely to be wary of one another and social relationships will be unformed.

(ii) **Storming** is a period of open conflict between members about objectives, methods and relationships during which priorities and roles emerge. It should lead to a robust basis for co-operation in the future.

(iii) **Norming** is a period of settling down with the development of group norms about work requirements and methods and social expectations. The leader may need to encourage 'overarching' norms and goals in order to overcome inter-functional differences.

(iv) **Performing** productive work follows as the final phase, when the team is ready to collaborate on efficient task performance.

Leadership

Leadership style will be important. The project team will include experienced professionals with their own competences and expectations. An autocratic style is unlikely to be the most productive when working with such people. In *Hersey and Blanchard's* terms the **maturity** of the team is high, therefore a low degree of directive behaviour on the part of the leader will be appropriate. **Participation in decision-making** and a high degree of **delegation** will be important. In addition, it will help maximise the potential synergy of cross-functional working by drawing on the various stakeholders and areas of expertise.

The complexity of the task and the need for a wide range of co-ordinated inputs will make **communication** very important. Providing for this will be a major leadership role. V must, in the first place, ensure that he communicates effectively with his team himself. He must provide clear objectives and decisions, brief future activity and plans clearly and give feedback on progress. He must also ensure that the team members communicate effectively with each other. No doubt much important communication will be **verbal, face-to-face and informal**, but there should also be **meetings** held at suitable intervals to ensure that important matters are not overlooked and there is general understanding of work and progress.

25 Sales targets

Text references. Teamworking is covered in Chapter 4.

Top tips. This question brings teambuilding and teamworking theory into a realistic commercial setting and demonstrates how teams can either work very well or not at all. A key theme that seems to stand out from the question wording is the lack of control that the team members now have over their working environment – from a happy and participative group there is now a disjointed series of insular teams that seem to have forgotten all about overall organisational objectives in the pursuit of non-participative sales targets. The problems with the new structure are evident and wide-ranging. It is important in part (b) to provide **practical** advice not waffley theory. In part (a), the examiner suggested up to six marks for the benefits of sales teams and seven marks for the problems of sales teams. In part (b), there were **up to two marks each** available for each strategy listed.

The examiner's comments on this question show the importance of understanding and applying the CIMA active verbs. Students failed to **discuss** or **explain** in their answers.

Easy marks. For part (b), as there are twelve marks on offer so make sure that you come up with at least six suggestions.

Examiner's comments. In part (a), most candidates were able to pick out the pros and cons of teamworking. However these were not always applied to the scenario given. In part (b), candidates needed to write more about than just the balance of roles identified by *Belbin* when discussing teams. In both parts, common errors included missing out key points or not 'discussing' or 'explaining' as required.

(a) **Benefits and problems of introducing sales teams and the sales target system**

The introduction of the sales target system in the A Insurance Company would have had the achievement of organisational sales growth targets as its main aim. It is not stated how the targets were set, but unless the teams were allowed to set their own targets, and measure their own progress, it is likely that the targets could be resented when they are not achieved.

Incentive schemes such as the one described are a common **motivational** technique. Given that 'the Centre' had been achieving such good results in the past, it was probably never anticipated that the restructuring that has taken place could have such a negative impact on working relationships, morale and productivity.

Benefits

Organising work groups into teams is a common form of work organisation, and a powerful motivator for performance. Teams combine the skills of different individuals, and fear of 'letting the side down' can be a powerful motivator. Effective teams could bring the following benefits to 'the Centre'.

(i) Loyalty and hard work is encouraged
(ii) Skills and information are shared
(iii) New ideas can be tested
(iv) Individuals are encouraged to participate
(v) Goodwill, trust and respect can be built up
(vi) Targets may be regularly exceeded

Problems

These benefits do seem to have occurred in Team X, the most successful team. The success becomes self-generating. Unfortunately, teamworking of this kind is rarely an unqualified success and Teams Y and Z are struggling in different ways. Some obvious problems can be identified.

(i) **Conflict** and personality problems can arise, as has happened in Team Y. Informal networks come to the fore, which may work against overall organisational objectives.

(ii) The **rigid nature** of the new team-based structure has meant that Team Z has abandoned the rest of 'the Centre'.

(iii) Differences of opinion are always likely to occur.

(iv) Group consensus (groupthink) can stifle thought and close the team off from the rest of the organisation. This appears to have happened to Team Z.

When teams rather than individuals are rewarded, it is easy for unmotivated or otherwise undeserving individuals to get by with little effort. There is no direct evidence from the scenario that this is the case with some members of Team X, but if it were then it would add more fuel to the resentments and difficulties faced by the other teams. As the reward is in the form of cash, it is very easy for unsuccessful teams to feel resentful and become increasingly alienated. When this happens, inter-group conflict is likely to arise.

(b) **Strategies that could be used to minimise problems**

Assuming that B cannot disband the team structure, here are some ideas for B to consider on how to manage the current situation, minimise its problems and improve morale in 'the Centre'.

Participation in target setting

This would have the effect of gaining the 'buy-in' of team members to the targets, and encourage them to see the targets as achievable.

Split teams by product

It may be desirable, if the product portfolio allows it, to give each team its own product (one team for vehicle, one for home and one for contents insurance) and, rather then having them compete directly, reward them on percentage improvement each month or quarter. Because the products may all be bought by one customer, it would encourage cross-team co-operation to reward all teams when overall sales are increased.

Different incentives

It may be time to remove the cash incentive, and replace it with a reward that is a little less emotive and less likely to cause resentment. It may be worthwhile to replace it with a 'team of the month' trophy or similar prize. A 'suggestion box' system, independent of team membership, should be set up to reward individual ideas.

Mix up the teams

This is going to be needed to shake up some of the cliques and insularity that have been formed and which are proving to be a barrier to proper co-operation. B may need to refer to *Belbin's* roles to ensure that teams have a good mix of people. The current leader of Team Y needs to be replaced.

Regular meetings of all team members

These will encourage cooperation between the teams, reinforce organisational objectives and provide a mechanism for conflicts and disagreements to be aired and resolved. Informal networks can be given an outlet, and valuable insights gained by management as to future staffing of the teams. Social events involving all teams should be encouraged.

Counselling and discipline

The leader of Team Y is not performing in his role and this is affecting his team members adversely. This needs to be sorted out by way of counselling or some sort of disciplinary procedure as it is affecting his team.

Team leader briefings

These should be held regularly with B, so that team leaders can keep their members up to date, and be made to feel that they are part of the decision making process. This should reduce any potential for animosity between them as they should be reminded that they are all working for the same organisation.

26 Performance and appraisal

Text references. Performance management is covered in Chapter 3.

Top tips. In part (a) you need to choose a theory that describes performance. This is a key skill: **knowing how and when to use theory in your answer**. The examiner uses Herzberg which is a good basis for discussing individual motivation and therefore performance but you could also discuss the role of structure and leadership styles. The suggested mark allocation would be up to eight marks for identifying problems using the theory and another eight marks for suggestions on how to improve performance.

You need to explain the **reasons** for introducing a performance appraisal system in part (b) and then **how** this would be implemented. This needs to be in the context of the council so you must write about the issues that apply to the scenario and not abstractly. Suggested marks would be one mark each per valid point made.

Easy marks. A brief explanation of whatever theory(s) you choose should earn you a couple of marks.

Examiner's comments. Some students scored well in part(a) but weaker answers didn't refer to the scenario. Part(b) was disappointing and was often answered in general terms rather than addressing the specific requirements.

(a) **Problems in the council and what the chief executive could do to improve performance**

Problems in the Council

The council has several problems which are clear from the scenario. These are primarily based on **structure** and the **culture** of the organisation and are interrelated. Thus some problems arise from the **bureaucratic culture** which links power to position and status. This may be related to the leadership style of managers which is defensive and territorial. The absence of a **staff appraisal system** means that there is no clear link between performance and reward or the development needs of employees.

Herzberg's theory

It is useful to analyse these problems using a tool such as **Herzberg's theory of hygienes and motivators**. **Hygienes** are factors at work that can be dissatisfying and demotivating and must be dealt with before **motivation** is possible. If dissatisfaction exists then performance will suffer. **Motivators** are factors that are motivational. Hygiene factors are usually related to the conditions of work whereas motivators are embedded in the job itself and include achievement, recognition or even advancement.

Hygiene factors in the council relate to supervision, salary, interpersonal relations and physical working conditions. Some of these are satisfied such as competitive salary and some excellent working conditions. Others are clearly not and these include the nature of supervision which has generated a 'them and us' culture. Management need to move away from an autocratic style to something more inclusive and democratic. Once the reasons for dissatisfaction are dealt with then motivation can be considered.

Motivators in the council relate to factors in the job and therefore include recognition and opportunities for progression. The council doesn't have an appraisal scheme and this is likely to affect the employees' perception of being rewarded appropriately for the work they do. There will therefore also be no forum to discuss individual progression. Employees have no training and limited career opportunities. They are effectively expected to work to the job and no more. This is a feature of **bureaucratic cultures** where duties are clearly prescribed and carried out uniformly whoever performs the particular task. The **bureaucratic structure** will impede career progression too as power is based on status rather than performance.

What the Chief Executive could do to improve performance

The Chief Executive can take steps to remedy these problems. Thus he can introduce an **appraisal scheme** that relates reward to performance. **This is also an opportunity to create the link between the council's own objectives and the performance of its employees by setting individual targets that tie into organisational goals.** It will also get rid of the 'work to rule' aspects of individual jobs by rewarding those who go beyond the limits of their role. However the chief executive needs to introduce a scheme that has been vetted by the employees or else there is little likelihood of it being accepted and deemed valid by them.

Employees could be offered **job rotation** to gain new skills and keep them from getting stale. **Job design** is another way of expanding the opportunities in jobs by making roles more flexible and challenging. Employees are empowered by having more responsibility and involvement in decision-making. **Recognition schemes** can also work where employees are given rewards for success or improved performance. These may include public recognition and financial rewards.

He can also dismantle aspects of the bureaucratic culture such as the layers of command to make the organisational structure flatter and more flexible. This **may take time to do**, and feed through to a change in culture. Therefore the chief executive needs to ensure all of those affected are aware this is not a 'quick fix' approach to the problems in the council.

(b) **Key issues to consider in the design and implementation of an effective staff performance appraisal system**

Performance appraisal is the systematic review and assessment of an employee's **performance, potential** and **development** or improvement needs. Its aim is to improve the **efficiency** of the organisation by ensuring that employees are performing at their best and developing their potential. Therefore B Local council must consider how a staff appraisal system will simultaneously benefit the organisation and its employees. It must be clear to all parties that the **appraisal system is based on performance** though performance can also be linked to rewards

The design of an **effective** appraisal system will ensure that all involved understand how appraisal is designed to **benefit both the employee and the organisation**. The design of an effective appraisal system should be **fair and objective** as perceived by all parties involved. A **good scheme** only appraises people on those things they can influence. The appraisers and appraisees should both understand the **purpose** of an appraisal. This suggests that the council should try to involve a selection of employees in the design of the system so that they understand from the implementation of the scheme what its aims are. The Chief executive should also make sure that **senior management are committed to the introduction of the appraisal system** so that staff can see that the system is being taken seriously throughout the organisation. Finally the appraisers and appraisees should be **trained** in how to use the appraisal system and assessment techniques.

The **appraisal process** should strive to be as **objective** as possible. So there must be a **consistent approach** to appraisal throughout the council. An effective appraisal system must be **relevant, fair** and **objective** to minimise bias or personality differences during the appraisal process. Ideally there should be a **clear link** between the organisation's key objectives and the performance measures used.

Performance appraisal should be part of a **continuous process of performance management**. This allows goals and targets to be timely, relevant and suited to the overall aims of the council. How appraisal fits into the organisation's aims should be made clear to all participants in the appraisal process. Staff should be given time to prepare and the appraisals should be given sufficient time to be meaningful.

The process must also be seen as a **participative** and **problem solving** activity where employees can **develop** rather than merely a means of controlling them. So the council must make sure that all outcomes are agreed and documented and any required actions are followed up.

27 Organisational structure

Text references. Organisation structures are covered in Chapter 2.

Top tips. In part(a), you should be able to explain the purpose of organisational structure using information straight out of Chapter 2. Make sure that you state clearly the **relationship between structure and strategy** and consider how this relationship is two-way. Refer directly to the information in the question to explain why the existing functional structure may not be suitable for the organisation. The suggested marking scheme gives up to six marks for putting down the purposes of an organisational structure and five marks for why it is important to the company.

Part (b) requires you to **evaluate** the HR Director's proposal. So don't just agree with her recommendations but craft an argument stating whether you think that the organic structure would be suitable for C Company. Take note of the key words '**mechanistic**' and '**organic**'. These refer to Burns and Stalker's classification of organisations. Remember to comment too on the features of a **decentralised** organisation and whether these would suit C Company. Finally you need to **recommend** an organisational structure that would suit C's circumstances based on your discussion in part(b). There were up to six marks each for an evaluation of an organic organisational design, an evaluation of decentralisation and finally recommending an appropriate organisational structure.

Make sure you produce an answer that is more than a general analysis. The examiner complained that many candidates failed to answer part (b) properly and didn't **tailor** their findings to C Company.

Easy marks. Explaining the purpose of organisational structure as there is plenty of material straight out of the Study Text that you can use to answer this part.

Examiner's comments. Part(a) saw mediocre answers in general. Many candidates failed to explain the purpose of organisational structure or its importance to the company. Many answers to part (b) suggested that candidates had failed to read the question thoroughly and so answers neglected to recommend an appropriate structure for the company.

(a) **Purpose of organisational structure and why is it important for C Company.**

C Company has a **functional structure** which groups together people who do similar tasks.

Organisation structure is formed by the grouping of people into departments or sections and the allocation of responsibility and authority. In its simplest form, as a horizontal structure it consists of work groups organised according to the **span of control** and the work to be done. There are several reasons why an organisational structure is useful. These include

(i) **Linking individuals** in an established network of relationships so that **authority, responsibility** and communications can be controlled. The **vertical hierarchy** of the organisation is known as the **scalar chain.** This principle states that authority should flow down the organisation in accordance with a clear chain of command.

(ii) **Allocating the tasks** required to fulfil organisational objectives by giving these to suitable individuals and groups.

(iii) **Giving appropriate authority** to individuals and groups to perform their allocated tasks.

(iv) **Co-ordinating** the objectives and activities of separate units to achieve overall aims without repetition or gaps arising.

(v) Ensuring the **flow** of work, information and other resources throughout the organisation.

However the primary function of organisational structure is to enable the successful implementation of strategy. Thus organisations will often develop their structure as they grow becoming more formal.

Nonetheless, this relationship between **strategy and structure** is not as simple as it appears. Structure is influenced by factors other than the organisation's strategy. Furthermore, strategy can also be affected by structure. **So a strategy is often selected on the basis of the resources and processes available.**

Structure can help or hinder the achievement of organisational objectives. The HR Director believes that the 'unsuitable structure and mechanistic design' are causing the problems experienced by the company.

A functional structure does have weaknesses. Broadly, the structure creates rigidity through the lack of communication horizontally between individuals and an overemphasis on structure and processes at the expense of customers, outputs and the 'big picture'. **Conflict may arise** between individuals as **communication is poor and morale goes down. New opportunities are lost as staff do not have the authority to act independently**. Costs rise due to duplication of effort and possibly overstaffing. These weaknesses are manifest in C Company by the inability to make decisions at lower levels resulting in poor responsiveness to customer needs. **There is also a slow hierarchy of decision-making**. Management are felt to be too removed from the actual business. The company are unable to clearly identify revenue from the different outlets.

(b) **How the HR Director's proposal will help resolve C Company's problems and recommend an appropriate organisation structure**

The HR Director believes that the company's problems arise out of an unsuitable structure and **mechanistic** design. She believes that the present **functional** structure should be changed to one that is more **organic** and **decentralised**.

Mechanistic organisations are stable, efficient and suitable for slow-changing operating environments. **Organic organisations** are flexible, adaptive and suitable for dynamic operating environments. These classifications were drawn up by **Burns and Stalker** when considering which type of organisations were suited to different environments. Organisations often combine features of both and these are really the two ends of a spectrum of types.

C Company has seen significant growth in recent years. Staff have complained of a lack of responsiveness to customer requirements. The current mechanistic structure is clearly unable to respond to the changes happening in C's environment. This is because mechanistic structures are slow in making decisions, slow to change and restricted in their channels of communication.

An **organic organisation** is not hierarchical, and people are given recognition for their knowledge and expertise wherever they are in the organisation. Communication can be across functions as well as along vertical chains of command. Leadership involves participation, information and advice rather than leading by command. So the structure is more flexible, open and responsive to local operating requirements. Decisions are made by those with the relevant knowledge, often the 'front line' staff. As staff are more involved in decision-making there should be a positive effect on **motivation**. This clearly applies to C as staff lack motivation and would benefit from being able to exercise decisions.

Decentralisation is the process of delegating decision-making authority from the centre to the constituent parts of the organisation and their managers. It offers greater flexibility in decision- making. It also allows senior management to concentrate on strategic decisions as other decisions are now delegated to an appropriate level.

Centralisation is a feature of **mechanistic** organisations where decisions are made by senior management using their overall viewpoint to balance the interests of different functions. In C Company, decentralisation would allow the divisions a greater degree of autonomy and independence. Being able to make localised decisions would also speed up decision-making as managers would not have to refer decisions up to senior management. Once again **motivation** should be improved as staff are **empowered** to have more control over decisions and respond to their customers faster and directly.

The HR Director's proposals advise rejecting the functional structure in favour of one that is more flexible and decentralised. A **divisional** structure has decentralised decision-making where business units have

responsibility for their own budgets. Each division must have properly delegated authority and be held **accountable** for activities under its control.

If C Company adopts a divisional structure the divisions or **business units** could be the bars, restaurants, coffee shops and hotels where managers meet customers directly. Managers would run their divisions with minimum guidance from senior management. Decisions would be made more quickly. Managers could communicate across divisions with other managers pooling expertise. Managers would be assessed on their areas of responsibility and financial performance would be clearly identified.

As C finds itself in a dynamic environment where frontline staff need to respond quickly to customer needs an organic organisational model would be better suited to C's environment.

28 Leadership

Text references. Chapter 1 includes useful material to help answer parts (a) and (b) of this question and Chapter 6 for part (c).

Top tips. In part(a) we have introduced our **explanation** by drawing on definitions of leadership. This is purely to illustrate that leadership is a dynamic and interactive process. We have quoted sources though you don't need to and certainly don't do this incorrectly!

You should be able to contrast the differing approaches to leadership using **style theories**. Make sure you do use the correct names of theorists when you come to explain the various style theories. *Tannenbaum and Schmidt* and *Blake and Mouton* are mentioned in the syllabus specifically and have been tested in the past. So it would be a good idea to mention these somewhere as they are relevant! Aim for around six points for each theory which should get you your twelve marks.

Part (b)requires you to **describe** *Adair*'s model of leadership which is action-centred. This is a different approach to leadership than style theories so the emphasis is on action rather than recommending an ideal style.

Look at around two marks each for identifying the needs of the group and of the individual. Aim for two marks for an explanation of *Adair's* model and one for identifying T's training needs.

In part (c) **explain** what mentoring is and then use this to draw out what needs T has and how mentoring can help him.

Easy marks. Much of this question asks for explanations so you should be able to get a few marks from writing about the style theories and mentoring. As ever, application is somewhat harder!

Examiner's comments. Weaker answers showed a lack of knowledge and/or application to the scenario. Again, in part (b), some candidates did not go on to apply the theory of action centred leadership to T's circumstances.

(a) **Different approaches to leadership shown by J and T**

One definition of **leadership** is the activity of influencing people to strive **willingly** for group objectives. Other definitions develop this thread such that **leadership** is contrasted with **management**. **Leaders** have followers but **managers** have subordinates *(Yukl)*. **Managers** maintain the current position whilst **leaders** introduce new ideas *(Zaleznik)*.

J and T have different styles of leadership, which can be **explained** using **style theories** of leadership.

Style theories of leadership

These mainly measure leadership style on a continuum of the task/ performance and relationships/people. *Tannenbaum and Schmidt* classify leadership along a continuum of behaviours from **authoritarian** with an orientation to the task to **democratic** with an orientation toward relationships. The more democratic the style the more **freedom** subordinates have to make decisions. J tended toward democratic and relationship-oriented leadership. She showed interest in individual performance, encouraged participation in target setting and decision making and held regular meetings.

In contrast, T does not hold team meetings, expects people to get on with their work, has introduced performance targets without consultation and expects people to respect his position and authority without question. His leadership style would be nearer **authoritarian** and **task-oriented**.

Tannenbaum and Schmidt's model

Tannenbaum and Schmidt in their model describe four management styles which are **tells, sells, consults and joins.** Their study found that staff preferred the consults style overall but in practice, staff valued consistency in management style above a particular style. In terms of this model, T has a **tells** style of management. In this style, the leader makes all the decisions and issues instructions which must be obeyed without question. It is useful when management need to make **quick decisions** or work is **routine**. However it does not **encourage opinions** or **communication** or **initiative** by subordinates, all of which may be vital to **decision making**.

Using the model, J had a **joins** style of leadership. Here leaders and followers make decisions on the basis of consensus. This style can engender **high motivation** and **commitment** from employees as well as drawing on their **knowledge** and **experience**. There are drawbacks too which include the **time taken to** reach consensus and that the authority of the leader may become **undermined**.

Blake and Mouton's model

Blake and Mouton observe there are **two basic dimensions of leadership which are concern for production and concern for people.** Leaders could exhibit various combinations of these two dimensions, which are best expressed on a grid with high/low degrees of concern for production and people. So a manager could have a low concern for people and for production which they termed '**impoverished**'. In contrast, a manager could be both highly concerned for his staff and highly productive/inclined toward production. This type is known as a 'team' type. The model assumes that the team type is the desirable model for effective leadership.

Using this grid, J would be somewhere near the **team type** with a high concern for people but also getting her team to achieve their targets. T is nearer the **task type** which shows a high concern for production with a low concern for people. The grid is used to suggest **management training** and **development needs** or a **balance of types** in a team. However it must be used **cautiously** as it only suggests a manager's preferred style rather than an in-depth analysis of their style. It is also **simplistic** to assume that the team type of leader is ideal in all situations as in some routine environments compliance is all that is required.

(b) **How action centred leadership would help identify T's training needs for leadership**

Adair's model

Adair's model of action centred leadership is a **contingency model** because it sees leadership in the context of the needs of each of the task, the group and the individual roles, which will all, differ depending on particular circumstances. **Thus there is no one ideal type of leadership**. The depends on the overall situation which then dictates the **relative priority** assigned to each set of needs. Effective leadership requires a **mix** of the three roles and this can be **dynamic**, changing as circumstances change.

This model is a more **fluid analysis** of effective leadership than the style theories explained earlier. So there is no ideal style that T could be directed toward. He would however need to recognise that leadership changes as the three roles change. This suggests that **T would need training in being flexible and in being able to identify and act on the relative priorities of the task, the group and the individual.**

Applying this model

T could consider some ways of satisfying the needs of the individual, group and task at the same time. At any point one of these three roles is most important. So if the group had an imminent deadline or emergency work request the task would have to take priority.

The **task dimension** could be assisted by involving the group in roles including diagnosing and making decisions.

At other times the other two roles would take precedence. It is clear given the current low morale in the team that T should focus on group maintenance and encourage the team.

He will also need to consider the needs of the individuals in the team especially setting goals and going feedback and recognition.

(c) **Explain how a mentoring system could help T**

Mentoring is a long-term relationship designed to support learning and career development. It has the following advantages for T as the person being mentored:

(i) Advice in drawing up self-development programmes or learning contracts

(ii) General help with learning programmes

(iii) **Advice on dealing with administrative, technical and people problems**. T's staff are experiencing low morale and some want to leave. T clearly needs advice on stemming the flow of disaffected staff, and addressing low morale.

(iv) **Information on 'the way things are done around here'** (corporate culture and management style). No specific corporate culture is identified but the staff prefer the open collaborative approach taken by J to the more authoritarian approach by T. This is perhaps the culture that they identify with and one that works better for productivity too. T may need to recognise that this culture suits relationships and productivity better than his approach and learn to work within it.

(v) **Coaching in specific skills**. T may benefit from training using the **action centred approach** discussed earlier. Other training in skills that enable him to be more collaborative and also maintain productivity could be useful too.

(vi) **Guidance in tackling projects** (ie helping protégés to help themselves). This would suit T well as he appears to be proactive and focuses on tasks, albeit at the expense of team relationships.

29 Groups

Text references. Chapter 4 covers group formation and Chapters 4 and 5 include useful material on managing team conflict to help answer part (b) on project teams.

Top tips. In part (a) you will need to refer to Tuckman's model of group development found in the Study Text. When you encounter a question on groups that includes **hesitancy, conflict or role negotiation** in a new project team these are often clues that Tuckman's model is relevant.

Set your answer out using the stages of the model and remember to link these to the details in the scenario given. There are only ten marks in total for this part so keep your points brief and aim for two or so marks for each stage described.

Part (b) then requires you to use the scenario and any reasonable comment to draw up a list of potential problems and the ways in which these may be overcome. Again, keep your answers brief as you have fifteen marks to write about problems and their solutions. If you do mention a problem make sure you mention a matching solution too! We have done this by listing the problems and referring to solutions alongside them. We suggest a mark for each problem and another mark for each solution.

Easy marks. You should be able to get around a mark for each correct stage, listed in the correct order, in Tuckman's model.

Examiner's comments. Some candidates mixed up the stages of group formation. Weaker candidates focused on general project management issues rather than project team effectiveness.

(a) **Stages of group formation to become an effective group**

A team develops in consecutive stages which Tuckman named forming, storming, norming and performing. Two additional stages added by later researchers are dorming and mourning/adjourning. Team development can be aided by active team building measures which often involve outward bound courses and/or active team exercises guided by managers or trainers.

T will need to use teambuilding techniques to guide the new team through these stages and get it working effectively.

Forming. At this stage the team is just coming together and members will want to assert their personalities in the group. A leader may not have been appointed yet. At this stage the team will want to establish behaviours, roles and relationships. Normally, it is also likely that team objectives are unclear and norms have not yet been established. **However T's team is a project team and so the objectives will be clear albeit possibly open to some modification**. The project team come from a variety of backgrounds and have not worked together before so this stage of the group may take some time.

Storming. This stage may involve more or less open conflict between team members. Objectives may be amended, norms and procedures established and a sense of realism established for team goals and working. **The team come from different backgrounds and so some conflict in roles is likely**. This is the stage at which the original objectives of the project to design the toys will be refined given the input of the team set up to carry them out.

Norming. The team begins to settle down and agrees how to share work. Individuals agree their requirements for working in the team and what is expected of them as outputs. Any conflicts from the storming stage need to be resolved. Norms and procedures may evolve which enable methodical working to be introduced and maintained**. The project team will begin to establish cohesion and the members brought together with specialist skills will start to use these.**

Performing. The team sets to work to execute its task. There are no longer difficulties of growth and development. **The project would be up and running by now and the individuals should be bringing their separate skills into the project and the team be working effectively.**

(b) **Problems that could hinder the effectiveness of the project team and how these might be overcome**

The project team come from a range of backgrounds in the organisation and have not worked together before. They are working on a project that may be critical and the pressure that this brings may accentuate any differences already existing. Potential problems include:

Unclear objectives for the project. If the group has not satisfactorily discussed what the objectives are these may remain unclear. Slippages may start to happen and quality begin to suffer. T may need to brief the team formally on the objectives and make sure all members are clear on what these are and agree with them. These may need to be reinforced from time to time.

Differing opinions on how work should be carried out. The group may not have reached agreement on how work should be undertaken and waste time arguing over the detail of how tasks should be performed. Again T as project leader must get the group to go through the work that needs to be done and agree how tasks will be successfully completed.

Team members from different backgrounds with different views. The team come from many different functions in the organisation and may have distinct values and views on how the team should carry out the project. This is a particular difficulty with functional specialists such as production and finance staff. T will need to make sure team members admit their differences and work through these to some agreement so that the team can start to operate as a coherent whole. The ownership of the project and team objectives must be stressed.

Lack of clarity of roles. Functional specialists may believe that they know why they have been drafted into the project team. However their project role may be broader than expected or they may have other skills that are useful in the project. Thus T will have to brief them on the roles expected of each member at the start of the project so that they are clear about what they are doing.

Lack of balance of roles. If Belbin's team roles are used as a template for a balanced team, the team may not have all of the roles needed to operate well. There is no need for nine team members to fulfil the nine roles so long as team members between them occupy the roles. T can do much here to articulate roles and ensure a balanced mix of team roles if necessary by drafting in suitable members and removing duplication. However this must be done within reason as other, especially functional, roles may take precedence.

Groupthink or conformity in decision making. Where teams are very cohesive they may focus energy on maintaining group relationships rather than on the task. Outside influences can be rejected if these contradict the group's own ideas and any dissent may be squashed. This groupthink is a problem as it can lead to risky and unreliable decisions being made by the group. If this occurs in the project team then T should encourage the team to actively seek outside ideas and feedback as well as consciously evaluate conflicting evidence and opinions.

Too many meetings getting in the way of work. There is always a danger of project teams receiving too much information and attending too many meetings at the expense of actual work being done. T should set clear agendas for meetings and set dates for meetings to catch up on work done rather than just for the sake of having a meeting.

Poor leadership style. T has good technical skills but may fall short in her ability to lead the project team. This can arise for a variety of reasons including poor communication skills to lack of control over the team and its outputs. If poor leadership becomes apparent, T will need to admit to any shortfall in her style and adopt an appropriate management style. Possible approaches include running and planning meetings, frequent and appropriate communication.

This can come about through coaching or mentoring by more experienced managers, team exercises to work though problems including intervention by coaches or simply adopting better communication techniques in meetings.

30 Entrepreneurs

Text references. Chapter 2 covers ideas on entrepreneurship under innovation.

Top tips. In part (a) you should be able to pick out the key features of E company that would inhibit entrepreneurs, from the scenario. Then you should comment on each in the context of entrepreneurial qualities. Use *Moss Kanter* or similar as your starting point for discussing entrepreneurial qualities.

We suggest a mark for each point made and remember there are ten marks for this part so aim for around half a page.

Part (b) wants you to take the information in the scenario and make suggestions on how creativity and innovation may be encouraged. Think widely so mention organisational structures, *Moss Kanter's* ideas on encouraging **innovation**, the style of management and organisational culture in general. Again aim for a mark for each point made. There are fifteen marks available here so you may need to write around a page.

Easy marks. Use the characteristics of E Company to get you thinking about entrepreneurs. How would they cope in E Company and if not why not?

Examiner's comments. A significant number of candidates were unable to identify entrepreneurial qualities or described **structures** rather than **individuals**. Another weakness was in the failure to explain specifically how greater creativity and innovation could be achieved.

(a) **Characteristics and qualities of people who have an entrepreneurial spirit which may hinder their working in E company's environment**

Entrepreneurs are typically people who **take risks and expect rewards** when they set up businesses. They flourish in fast-moving competitive situations where decisions must be made quickly and creativity and flexibility are important qualities. In terms of the growth of the firm, they are best suited to the growth stage of a start up before structures become fixed. Entrepreneurs like to do things their own way.

Thus they show the following qualities that might make it difficult for them to work in E company:

They encourage new ideas. However E company has lengthy decision making processes to gain approval and this is off-putting to employees who want to contribute new ideas.

They tolerate failure and take risks. But E company has a 'blame culture' when things go wrong which makes employees unwilling to try new ways of working. The organisation fails to exploit potential new ventures because they are considered too great a risk.

They reward creative behaviour. Bureaucratic controls have been put in place that stifle creativity and innovation which are essential to the creative software development business. E company is losing market share because these core skills are being discouraged.

They encourage interaction and communication. However they can be tactless as they feel they can do the job better than anyone else. E company has a bureaucratic structure which discourages openness and people tend to hide behind their formal role. This would frustrate entrepreneurs.

They encourage open and flexible behaviour. They break the rules and challenge convention. E company doesn't encourage this rather it expects managers to conform to company rules.

(b) **Explain what could be done to encourage greater creativity and innovation in E company**

E Company wants to recapture the success it enjoyed up until recently in the interactive games market. This was largely due to innovation and creativity being encouraged within the company. However the company has moved beyond the growth phase where this occurred spontaneously. New systems and procedures have formalised the way in which the organisation operates. Decisions take far longer and mistakes are blamed.

Any remedies would need to take into account the structure of the organisation, management style, recruitment and the prevailing culture.

Moss Kanter writes on ways in which organisations can become more creative. This includes **introducing polices that accept change, encourage new ideas, permit interaction and communication, tolerate failure and reward creative behaviour**. Thus the organisation needs to change its culture to one where these policies are accepted. This would require endorsement at the highest level to ensure managers and employees accept these policies.

These policies would also need to be put in place alongside **structural changes** to replace the bureaucratic structure in place with one that frees up individuals to interact and take risks more freely. **An organic structure** would allow greater freedoms as control takes place through a shared corporate culture and values. Commitment is greater in an organic organisation and expertise is valued over hierarchical position. [***The examiner mentions Mintzberg's adhocracy too***]

Management style would also need to allow more **delegation** and participation in decision-making. Initiatives should be encouraged and failure not blamed so readily. These changes would have to be reflected in **appraisal mechanisms** whereby some freedom to experiment and make mistakes is recognised. Initiative should be recognised and rewarded say by using a staff suggestion scheme. **Recruitment** should be tailored toward individuals who bring in the necessary traits of innovation and creativity where they work in the software design area.

The organisation could also look at the prevailing culture which is a role culture [based on *Harrison]* showing characteristics of a classical bureaucracy. It **seems that a task culture would suit the organisation better** as this is directed at outputs and values team working get the job done.

Finally the organisation could consider pursuing its new strategy of innovation through a **new venture** which carries out new activities. This would be a separate division with explicit remit to experiment and be creative. Features include using task forces and teams form across the organisation to work on projects, strict project evaluation procedures, and autonomy to foster innovation.

31 Objective test questions

31.1 B A statement of client needs would form an important input into the project charter (project brief, initiation document). The specification of resources required and the sequence of activities would form part of the overall project plan

31.2 A Configuration management is a *component* rather than a *process:* it controls the processes by which projects evolve. Directing a project is the responsibility of the project board and consists of the higher aspects of control and decision-making. Managing stage boundaries ensures that one stage of a project is properly completed before the next one begins.

31.3 The answers are a: *initiating*; b: *controlling*; c: *closing.* The Examiner noted that acceptable alternatives included *defining* for a; *monitoring* or *reviewing* for b; and *completion* for c.

31.4 It is important to realise that in this question, the Examiner did not intend to imply that feasibility studies could be carried on in three distinct ways, which is what you might have understood by his use of the word 'type'. He was actually asking you to list three *topics* that might be the subject of feasibility studies. The list of such topics is quite long and includes those below. The three most important ones are listed first.

Technology
Finance
Environment and sustainability
Social
Politics
Marketing

31.5 B **12 days are needed for the critical path A-E-G.**

Activity-on-node style

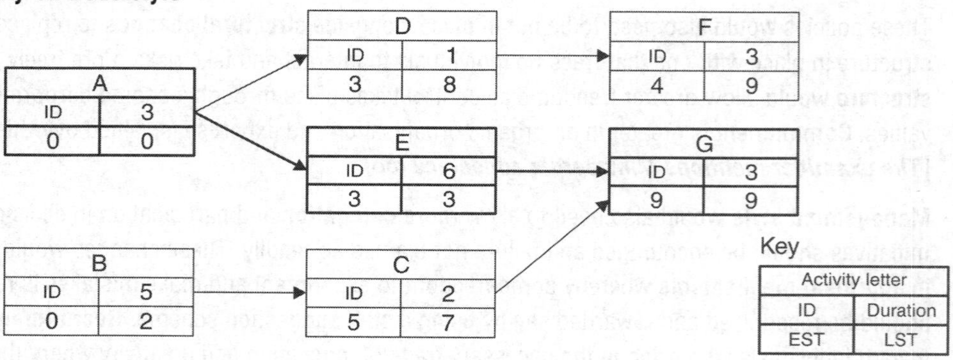

Activity-on-line style

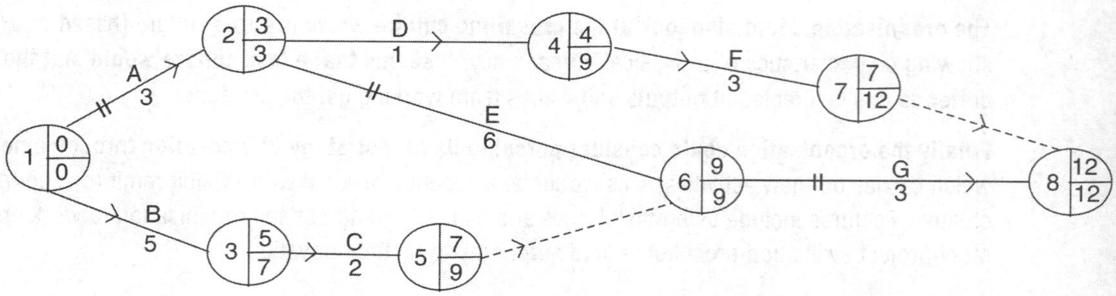

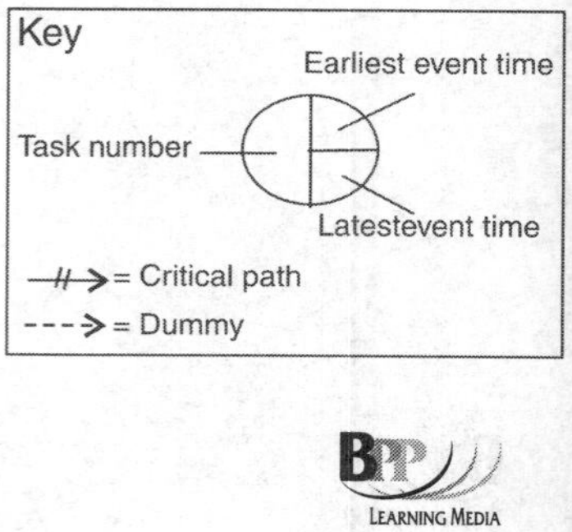

Duration of critical path is 12 days

31.6 A The dependencies given mean that the activities can be thought of as forming three main strands as shown in the Gantt chart below. Two of these strands can be manipulated to reduce the staff requirement on day 6 to the five people needed for activity E.

(a) Activity B is started on day 1 and is therefore complete by the end of day 5

(b) Activity C, which depends on activity B, is not started until day 8. This allows it to be completed by the end of day 9 so that activity G is not delayed.

(c) Activity D can be undertaken on any day from day 4 to day 9 inclusive. We show it happening on day 4.

The disadvantage of this manipulation is to produce a requirement for thirteen staff on day 9.

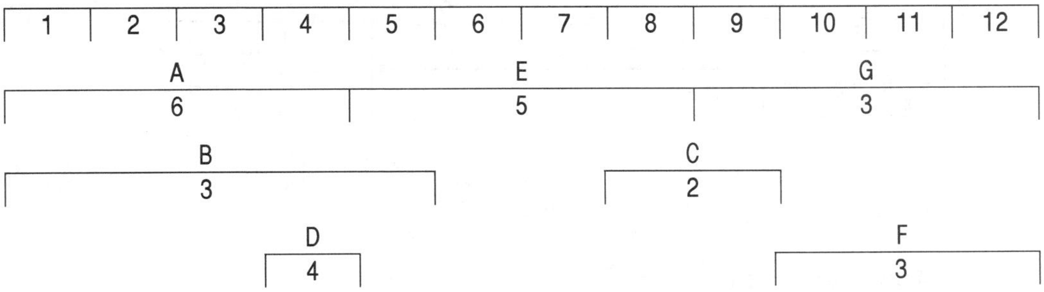

Total

1	2	3	4	5	6	7	8	9	10	11	12
9	9	9	12	8	5	5	7	7	6	6	6

Answer 5 workers

32 Objective test questions

32.1 A This is a tricky question. The characteristics of the project staff are such that a **consultative** or even **democratic** style might be recommended. However, the time and quality constraints mean that the project manager is likely to have to exercise firm control on occasion. This would probably be best done in a **persuasive** style. The conclusion is that the **autocratic** style will probably be of least use.

32.2 D Specialisation appears in neither the project 7S nor the McKinsey 7S model.

32.3 A Communicating the project vision within the organisation is the role of the project sponsor; the project manager is responsible for delivering the project on time; the project board represents the interests of the project sponsor.

32.4 C The system focuses on products rather than processes.

32.5 B Fact.

32.6 12 weeks are needed for the critical path B-F-H.

Use either the activity-on-node style or activity-on-line style to plot the correct path.

Activity-on-node style

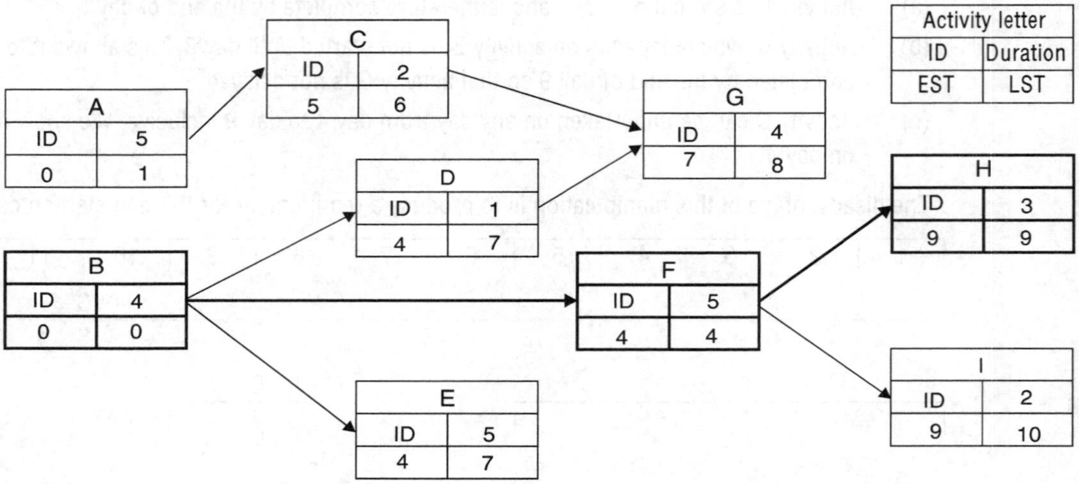

Activity-on-line style

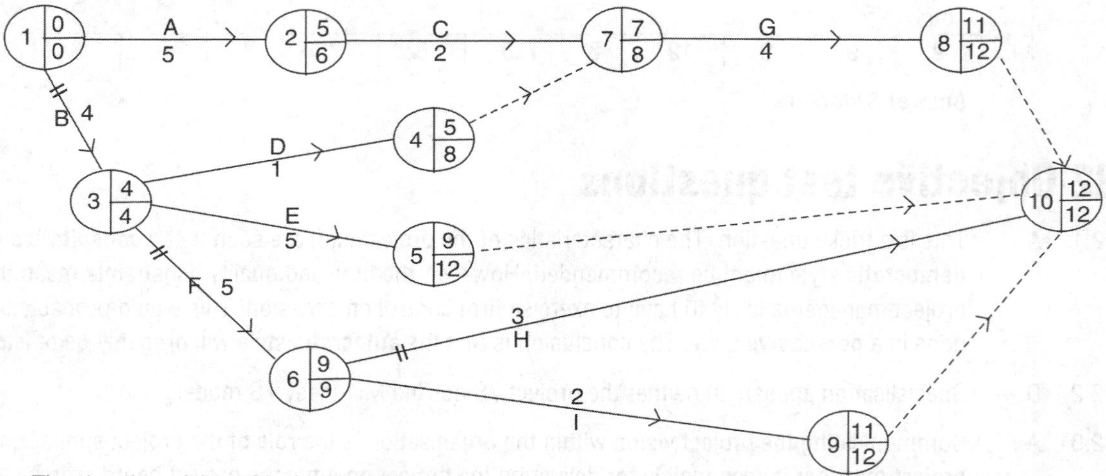

The duration of the critical path is 12 weeks.

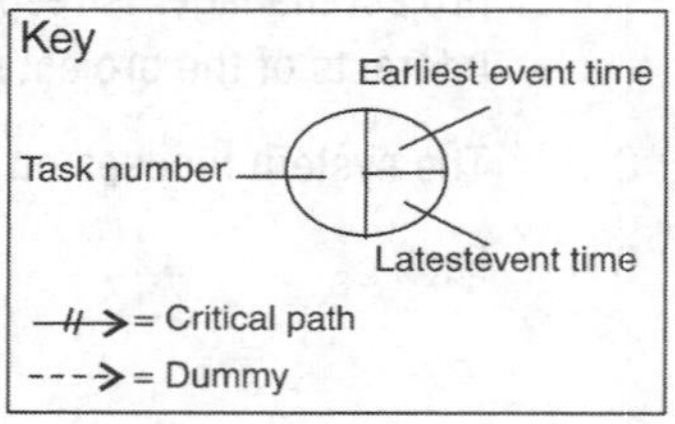

32.7 Total float is time available less duration. For D this is (8 – 4) – 1 = 3.

Free float is the delay possible assuming all preceding activities started as early as possible and all subsequent activities also start at the earliest time. **For D this is (7 – 4) – 1 = 2**.

Independent float is the delay possible if all preceding jobs have finished as late as possible and all succeeding jobs start as early as possible. For D this is the same as free float, since activity B is on the critical path and therefore cannot be delayed.

33 Project network

Text references. Chapter 8.

Top tips. We have shown both the activity-on-node style diagram and the activity-on-line style diagram but you only need to draw one of these. Choose the style with which you are most comfortable.

Easy marks. If you draw the diagram correctly, you already have the answers to parts (a) and (b).

(a) Either of the following diagrams.

Activity-on-node style

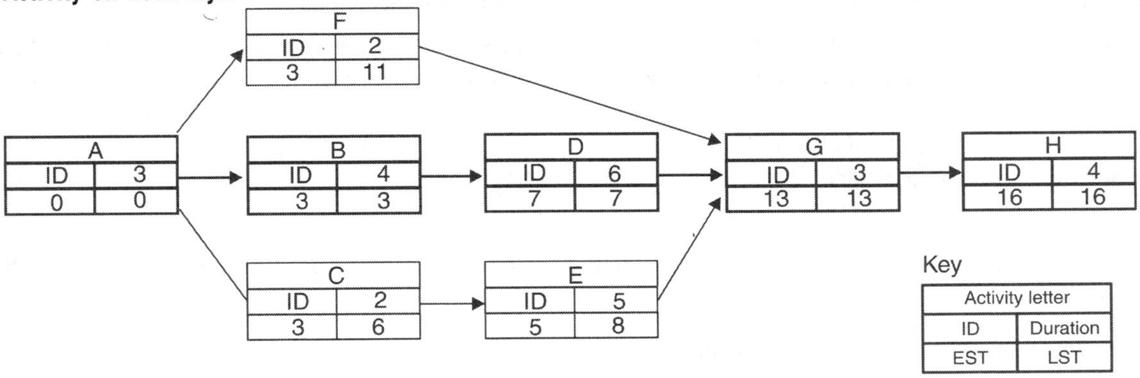

Activity-on-line style

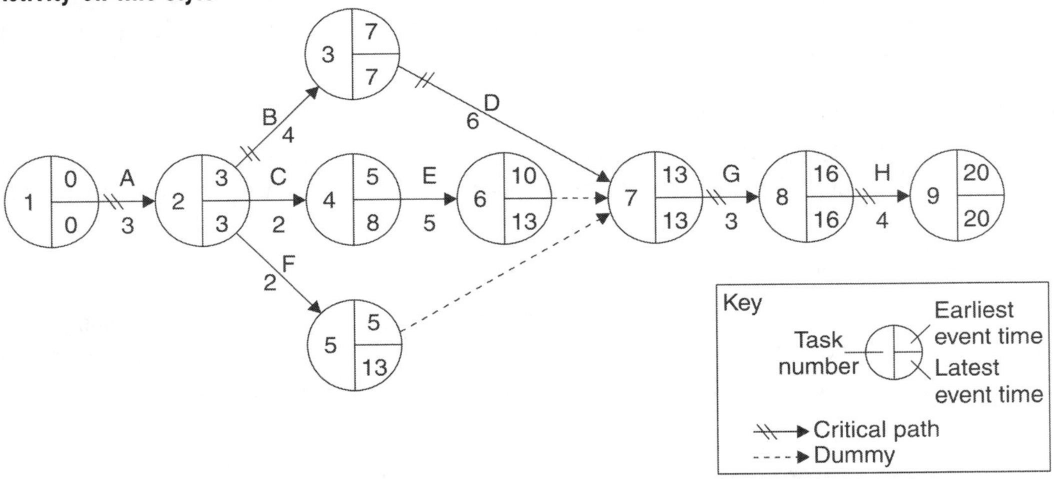

(b) Activities on the critical path are A, B, D, G, H.

(c) 20 days.

(d) Task C overrunning by two days would not change the elapsed duration.

(e) Task B overrunning by one day would increase the elapsed duration to 21 days.

34 FRS 1

Text references. Chapter 7.

Top tips. There are many ways to approach a question like this. You could for instance base an answer on the PRINCE2 methodology. **The important thing is to relate your answer to the detail of the setting**. This is a **key skill** and many candidates fail to show it according to the examiner!

A second point is to avoid obscure issues. Finally, think before setting pen to paper: your answer will be improved if you avoid a list of random notes.

Look at the advice we give in the front pages on how to approach discussion questions if you get stuck. Note how each paragraph should **make** a point, **explain** the point and **illustrate** the point.

Easy marks. You could use any standard list of project manager duties to help you with your answer here, but you will not score many marks if you do not address the situation given in the scenario.

To: Management team of FRS Co
From: Management Consultant
Date: 29 April 200X

The major issues to be considered in managing the project to implement the MRO Inc system at FRS are outlined below.

The project manager and the project team

It is important to establish who has overall responsibility for a successful implementation. The scope of the project needs to be established, and then a person with the required motivation and skills appointed as project manager. The composition of the project team is vital, particularly ensuring sufficient user representation. (Including actual 'hands-on' users, ie not only management.)

What the implementation hopes to achieve

The project team requires a focus. What the implementation is supposed to achieve should be spelt out clearly. The statement may seem like stating the obvious, but it provides a reference point for which all issues that arise should take into account.

How successful completion will be achieved

The project must be properly planned and controlled if it is to achieve completion on time, within budget and to required performance specifications. The availability of required resources must be established. Tasks need to be scheduled and allocated providing a framework for monitoring progress and exercising control.

Communication

Communication between developers and users is essential. The project team must establish line communication between team members (eg meeting, e-mail links) and between the team and all personnel affected. What the implementation hopes to achieve, from both users and an organisation-wide perspective, should be communicated to the personnel of FRS Co.

User training

The survival and prosperity of FRS Co is dependant on shop transactions. It is therefore essential staff are able to use the system before it 'goes live'. Training requirements should be planned as part of the overall implementation plan. 'Hands-on' sessions using the new system in a test environment are vital.

Method of implementation

How will the new system be implemented? Will a phased implementation be followed or is it practical to have a straight cut-off of the existing system. Will all shops change over at the same time?

Contingency plan

A contingency plan must be drawn up that enables business to continue in the event of system failure. This may involve utilising the old system or reverting to manual procedures.

35 FRS 2

Text references. Chapter 8.

Top tips. Concentrate on getting the logic of activities E, F, G and H right. Remember that you only need to draw one of the diagrams.

Easy marks. Activities A to D plot themselves!

[One of the following]

Activity-on-line style

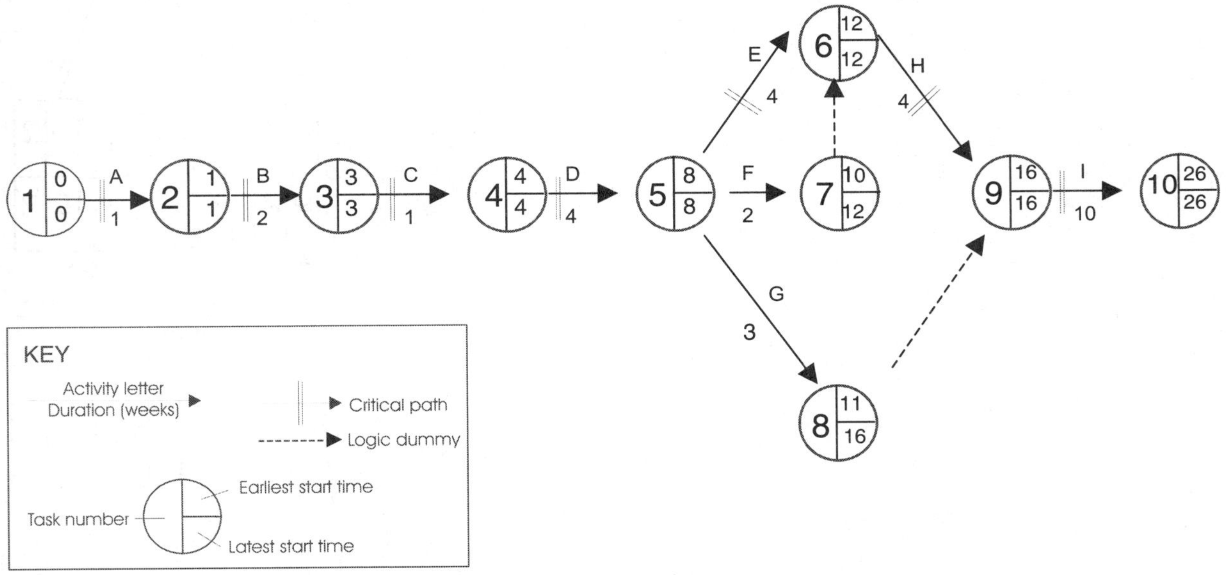

Activity-on-node style

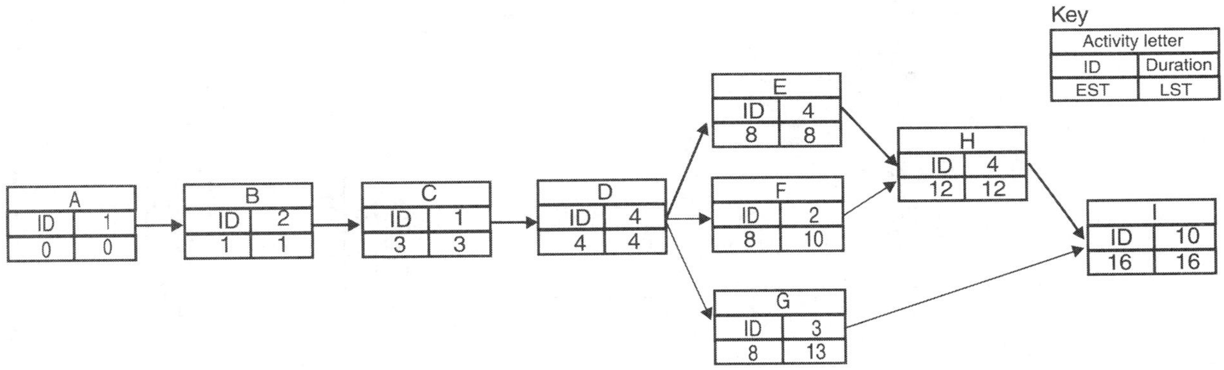

The critical path is A, B, C, D, E, H, I. The total elapsed time is 26 weeks.

36 Critical path analysis

Text references. Chapter 8.

Top tips. These diagrams illustrate how float time may be shown on a network. **This is for interest only: do not attempt this in the exam**. We have shown diagrams for both activity-on-line and node formats. You can use either approach.

Easy marks. This is quite a tricky network; you must recognise the logical requirements of activities G, H and I.

Helping hand. Most of us have to produce at least one preliminary sketch of a network in order to show the dependencies correctly. Try to allow yourself time to draw a fair copy as this will make the marker's job much easier. Try to draw your event circles neatly: you could draw around a coin or you could prepare a template from a piece of cardboard. Make a point of using a ruler for your straight lines.

Activity-on-line style

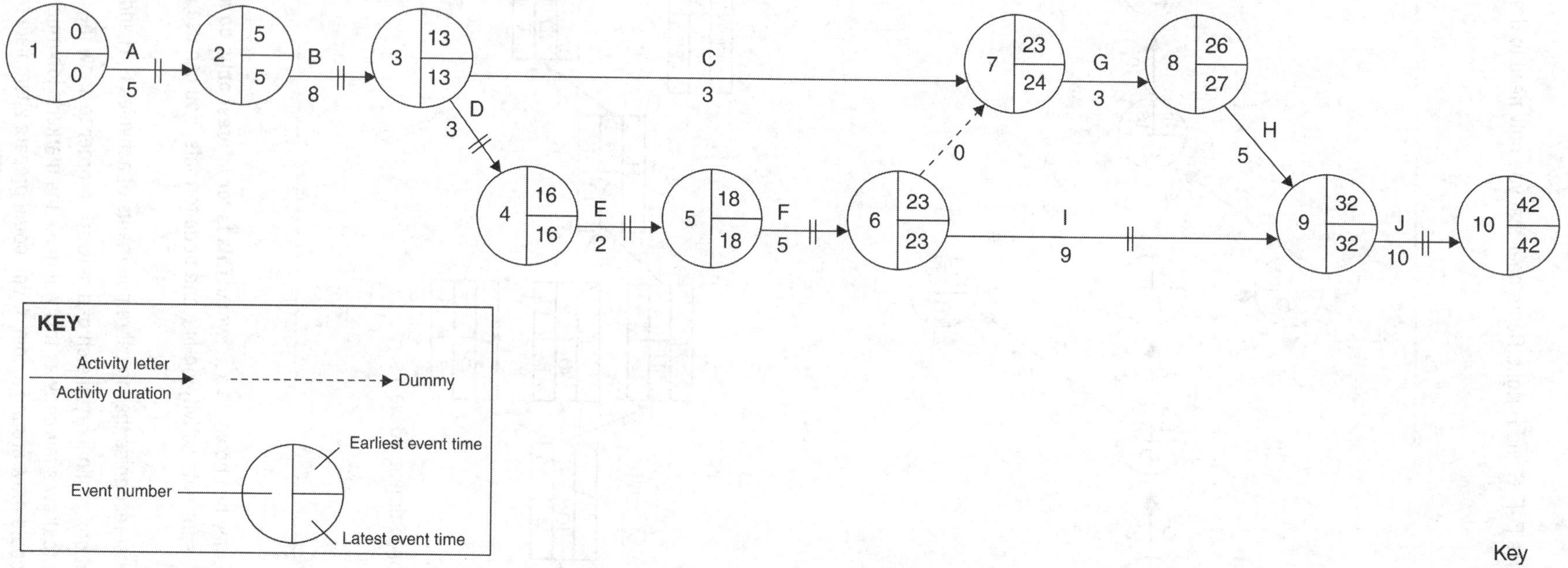

Activity-on-node style

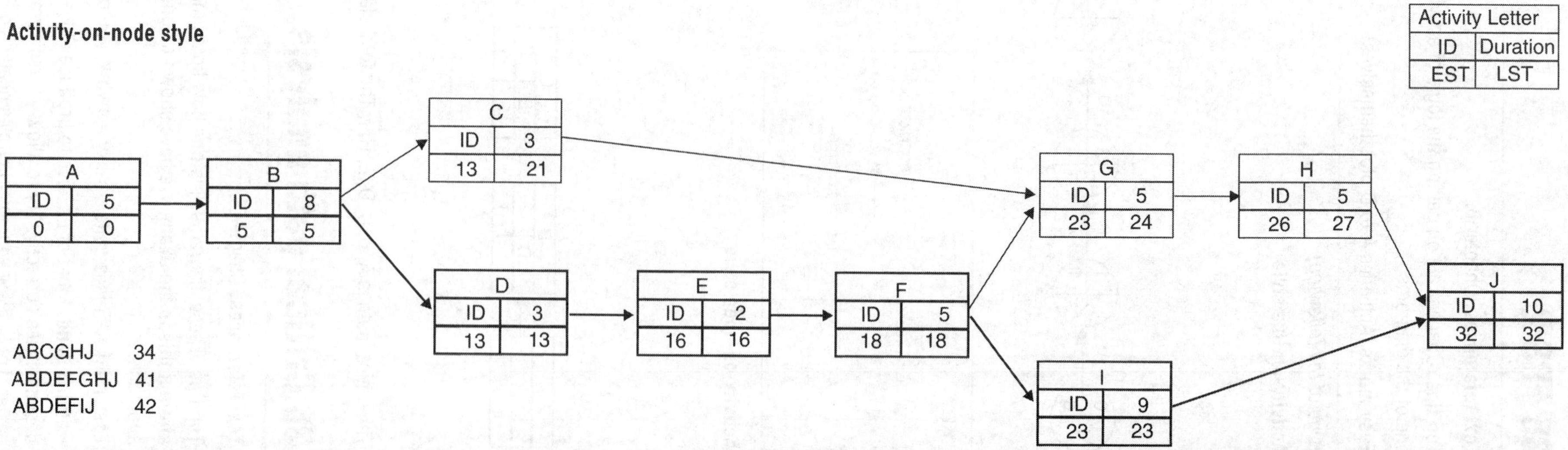

ABCGHJ	34
ABDEFGHJ	41
ABDEFIJ	42

37 R Company

Text references. Chapter 7.

Top tips. A number of bodies have designed project management methodologies, with perhaps the best known being the US Project Management Institute's Project Management Body of Knowledge and, in the UK, the PRINCE2 system. We have chosen to use PRINCE2 as the basis for our answer, but there is no reason why other approaches should not be used.

We have a single requirement worth ten marks here. Treat it in the same way you would a part of a Section C question. Make sure you follow the guidelines on how to develop your exam technique in the front pages. So read and analyse the question, jot down a plan and then answer the question.

Easy marks. Perhaps the aspect of PRINCE2 that is most relevant to the scenario is its **focus on results** rather than processes: this is clearly of great relevance to this question scenario.

Recommended project methodology

R Company would have benefited from the employment of the PRINCE2 project management method, which is now the *de facto* UK standard. PRINCE2 has three important design features that would have been particularly relevant to preventing the current problems.

(a) The system **focuses on delivering results** (called 'products') rather than on the technical processes of project management. This alone would have produced a bias towards the required outcomes.

(b) The system ensures that a project is driven by its **business case**: the continuing viability of the project is checked at regular intervals.

(c) A **clear management structure** of roles and responsibilities is defined.

Planning

One aspect of PRINCE2's focus on outputs rather than processes is the planning system it uses. Normal work breakdown structure is not used: instead, a **product breakdown structure** approach is used, thus providing an automatic focus on results. Products are initially divided into three groups.

(a) **Technical products** are the things the project has been set up to provide: in the case of R Company, these are the artefacts of a comprehensive logistic system.

(b) **Quality products** define both project quality standards and quality controls.

(c) **Management products** are the systems used to manage the project.

The second and third groups of products mentioned above were obviously largely missing from R Company's project.

Business case

R Company's project appears to have drifted along in an unorganised manner, with all concerned pursuing their own ideas of what it was about. Clear statement of the business case for the project would have helped to produce an equally clear statement of the **scope** of the project.

Organisation

R Company's project sounds as though it included both IT and physical system elements, which would have complicated the project aims, activities and priorities. Under such circumstances, an effective **management structure** is particularly necessary.

Under PRINCE2, the top level of management for an individual project is the **project board**. In the case of R Company's project, this would be chaired by a senior manager whose role would be to provide overall guidance and represent the business interests of the organisation. Two other constituencies would also be represented.

(a) The **senior user** represents the interests of those whom are affected by the introduction of the new system and is accountable for the quality of the specification. It would have been this person's job to ensure that the technical requirements of R Company's new system were clear and understood.

(b) The **senior supplier/technical person** represents those charged with implementing the project and would point out any unrealistic or excessively costly aspects of the specification as the work developed.

This is a comprehensive approach: regular meetings of this board would have gone a long way to prevent the un-co-ordinated work that has obviously taken place.

38 Conference network

Text references. Chapter 8.

Top tips. There are clearly two parts to this requirement:

- Construct a network diagram.
- Say why it is useful.

So, you need to show that you have **knowledge of the syllabus** and can produce an answer **tailored to the particular organisation** in the question.

However, they are not worth equal marks. The first part is worth six marks and the second is worth four. To score full marks for the first part you not only have to draw the network, you also have to identify the critical path and give the project duration. A properly drawn network will do both of these things, but you should remember in particular to mark the critical path by the use of hash mark or doubling the lines. To be on the safe side you may care to provide a small note of the kind we show in our solution. **We have shown the activity-on-line and the activity-on-node style. You only need to draw one**.

Don't forget to then comment on how the information from your network diagram could be useful to R!

Easy marks. The basic network is extremely easy to draw. However, do not fall into the trap of numbering the critical path events consecutively from start to finish and then numbering the remaining events on the other path: this would lead you to give a higher number to the last non-critical event than to the event that follows it, which is, of course, by convention not done and might cost you a mark.

Examiner's comments. The Examiner found that this question was generally done very well, but some candidates failed to say how the network information could be used.

[One of the following]

Activity-on-line style

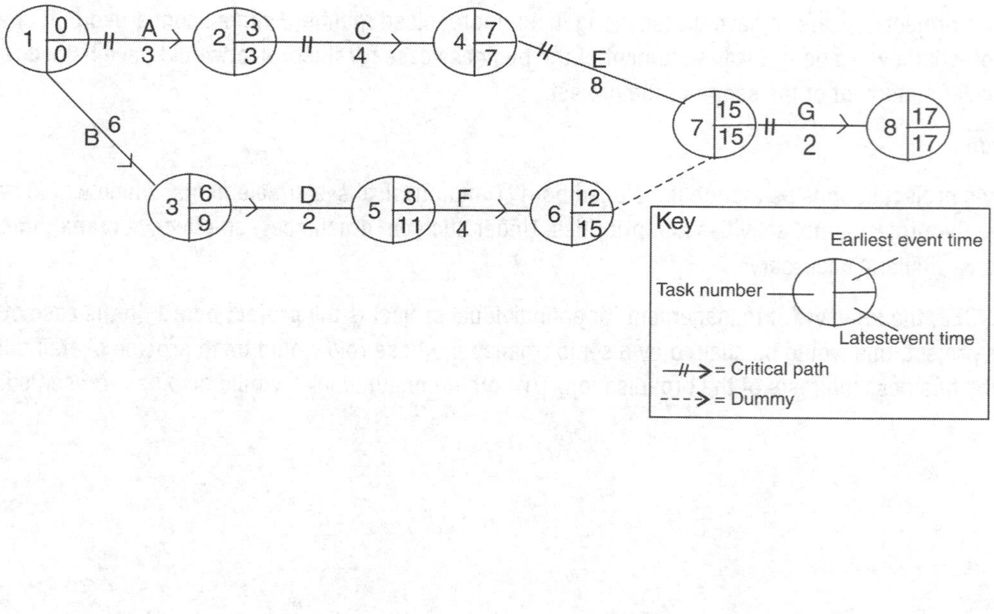

Activity-on-node style

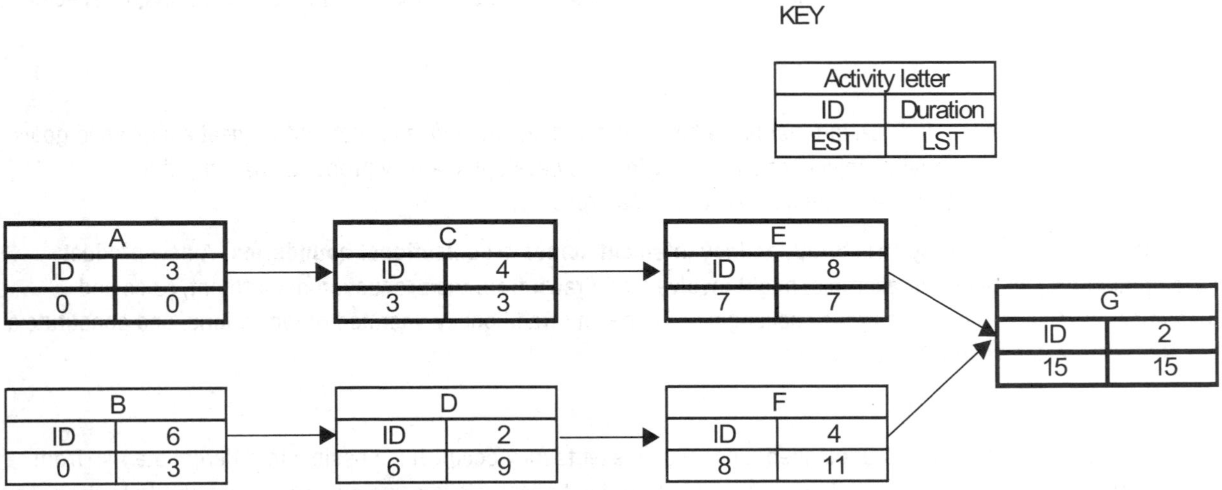

ACEG	17	Critical path
BDFG	14	

The critical path is activities A–C–E–G and last 17 days.

The network diagram provides several pieces of useful information.

(a) Knowledge of the **duration of the critical path** will provide R with a latest time by which she must have started work on her project.

(b) Knowledge of which **activities make up the critical** path will assist R in checking progress along it and in prioritising the work that has to be done on them.

(c) The two separate paths through the network show the activities that may be undertaken at more or less the same time, which will help with the **planning of resource utilisation**. This process would be further aided by the use of a **Gantt chart**.

(d) Awareness of the three weeks **float time** available on the non-critical path will allow R some flexibility in the management of her resources.

39 Risk

Text references. Chapter 7 covers project management and Chapter 8 covers risk management.

Top tips. This question brings together two topics – risk and project management. In your answer, try to make it clear that you understand how the two can be related. The linkage is specifically referred to in the question, but draw it out to demonstrate your understanding.

The examiners only awarded up to two marks for explaining risk. So the bulk of the marks were given for identifying the stages in risk management and strategies for managing risk. It is easy to forget the mark allocations in the 'heat of the battle'. Look back at the advice on **key skills** in the front pages on how to approach questions. This is **not an application question**, but **requires two key skills**. You need to **show your knowledge of the topic** and that **you understand** and **can apply the verbs in the question**.

Easy marks. A definition of both 'project' and 'risk' is a good starting point. An example of a typical project can also provide a framework upon which to hang your answer.

Examiner's comments. Answers should start with an explanation of what project risk is. They should then continue with a discussion of how risk can be managed and strategies for dealing with risk in projects. Weaker candidates failed to answer the specific question which asked for the ways in which risk can be managed in a project.

Organisational management involves making decisions about what needs to be done to further the strategy of the organisation. In general, the work which organisations undertake involves either day-to-day operations, or specific projects.

Projects

A **project** is defined as 'an undertaking that has a beginning and an end and is carried out to meet established goals within cost, schedule and quality objectives'. This may include developing a new product, changing the organisational structure, or implementing a new business process.

Projects need to be carefully structured, as they often cut across organisational boundaries. A new product development project team, for example, might involve staff drawn from the production department, sales and marketing and finance. This can prove challenging to large and traditionally operated organisations, and constitute a risk that the project will not be successful.

Risk

Risk exists in the possibility that unplanned, undesirable events may occur. It is possible to differentiate risk from **uncertainty**: in this strict sense, risk implies that it is possible to assign a specific numerical **probability** to the event in question; uncertainty implies that this cannot be done. In normal business contexts, including project management, risk analysis is about specifying and assessing **potential threats** to expected operations or progress.

Managing project risk

In the context of project management, identification of risks involves taking an overview of the project at the start, in order to establish what could go wrong, and the consequences. The project manager needs to consider whether the project involves an unacceptable amount of risk.

Dealing with project risk involves four possible strategies.

(a)	**Avoidance**	Factors giving rise to the risk are removed
(b)	**Reduction/mitigation**	Ways to mitigate the risk are found
(c)	**Transference**	Risk is passed on, such as via insurance
(d)	**Absorption**	Risk is accepted, and coped with if it occurs

Risk management may be viewed as a five stage process.

Stage 1 Identify the risks

Stage 2 Assess risk impacts and their likelihood (low, medium, high)

Stage 3 Plan and record responses to these risks. A contingency plan may be needed for risks that are regarded as high impact and high likelihood.

Stage 4 Carry out risk reduction activities

Stage 5 Review the risk management approach

The chief risk facing any project is, perhaps, the overall risk that the project itself is inappropriate for the organisation – for example, the new product being developed fails to find a ready market. Risk management here might include undertaking rigorous market research to estimate the likelihood that the new product under consideration will be adopted quickly by customers.

40 Project initiation stage

Text references. Chapter 7 covers project management.

Top tips. This question tests your understanding of one aspect of project management. Make sure you use the material in the question to illustrate the description asked for. Remember to **tailor your knowledge** to the circumstances in the question and don't write about theory without thinking of its practical application.

There were up to four marks for an explanation of the initiation stage and seven marks for the features of a project initiation document. Candidates would earn a maximum of four marks overall if they failed to mention either and answered in terms of general project management.

Easy marks. A definition of 'project initiation' is a good starting point.

Examiner's comments. There were some good answers to this question but many candidates failed to confine themselves to the specific stage being tested.

Initiating a project is usually the first stage in the project planning process. Initiation includes mission, goals and objectives and creating the **Project Initiation Document (PID)**. The PID sets out fundamental progress and success criteria. It establishes a benchmark against which progress is measured. The first productive stage of the project is planned during this process. So the PID defines the **terms of reference** for the project. It contains the statements of the project manager, team, stakeholders and sponsors about:

(a) **Overview of the project** including key dates
(b) The **scope of the project** so what it should and shouldn't cover
(c) The **objectives for the team** during and on completion of the project
(d) **Project team organisation**, **roles** and **responsibilities**

P needs to apply these four features to the project for rebuilding the school. An explanation of the main features in the PID follows.

Overview of the project and objectives for the team

This should set out the **objectives** of the project, which are its quantified goals. What does the project want to achieve? Clearly the intention is to have the school rebuilt and equipped in twelve months. Remember that objectives should be SMART. So the objectives need to state the time taken, the cost of the project and the quality of the output. Any constraints must be identified and factored into the planning process. Funding is clearly a major constraint so the project should include an estimate of the funding needed.

The project scope

This is all of the things that have to be achieved if the project is to succeed. So it is all of the work that has to be done. This is an essential stage of the project. As volunteers with charitable motives largely run the project, there is a danger of the project expanding to have too many aims. The scope also determines anything **not included** in the project. This also helps avoid the number of aims increasing too much.

There are a few approaches that can be used to work out what needs to be done for the project to succeed.

(a) **Gap analysis**. This looks at the gap between what is currently available and what is desired. This obviously includes funding but may also apply to personnel and expertise.

(b) **Reverse engineering** identifies the features of an existing product or system by taking it apart.

(c) **Functional decomposition** starts with the desired result and works out what must be done to achieve it. It starts with a broad approach and hones in on tasks and elements that must be achieved.

Project team

A project team made up of volunteers will need to have clear roles and responsibilities to ensure **accountability** and **responsibility** are maintained. Meetings and reporting deadlines should also be agreed upon.

41 Project feasibility

Text references. Chapter 7 explains what a project feasibility study is.

Top tips. This question wants you to **explain** what you know about project feasibility and **apply** this to the project. A feasibility study looks at whether a project is worth carrying out using a range of factors. There is plenty of information in the scenario to enable you to comment on technical, social and financial feasibility factors. Aim for two marks per factor identified.

Easy marks. Explaining the purpose of a project feasibility study in general should earn a couple of marks .

Examiner's comments. Some candidates didn't know what the various type of feasibility meant.

Purpose of a project feasibility study and the different types of feasibility that should be considered for the Snow Dome project

Project proposals must be assessed for their feasibility especially when the project is complex, innovative or difficult to achieve. Such projects are likely to be risky and expensive. The Snow Dome would be using the latest snow making technology for the first time. Therefore the project is certainly innovative for the company, likely to be costly, complex and there is a large element of the unknown involved in the project.

The purpose of a feasibility study is to establish whether a proposed **project can achieve its aim in a cost-effective manner.** It acts as a **filter** weeding out projects that cost too much, cause too much disruption, make excessive demands on resources or otherwise have disadvantages that outweigh their advantages.

There are three main areas where feasibility can be assessed for the Snow Dome project.

(a) **Technical feasibility**

This considers the technology required for the project. In the case of the Snow Dome this would be the **snow making technology that creates real snow**. The feasibility would consider issues such as:

(i) Does all the necessary technology exist or is significant **innovation** required?
(ii) Is the technology mature enough to use or is further **development** likely to be required?
(iii) How **specialised** is the required technology and is **the expertise** to make use of it available?

Technical feasibility also includes **technical matters that do not relate to technology**; that is to say, matters of technical expertise, such as marketing, financial strategy and human resource management. We might wish to know, for example, whether it is feasible to market the Snow Dome to customers who live outside the immediate area and who may be attracted by offering day passes.

In this category of technical feasibility assessment we would include **features analysis,** which is the process of identifying and prioritising those features of the project requirement that are critical to its success. This process can help to guide the allocation of project resources so that the importance of deliverable features is reflected in the resources expended on achieving them.

(b) **Social feasibility**

Any project is likely to have effects upon people, both those in the organisation concerned and those outside it. In the case of S Company this would be the employees and customers at the very least.

The social feasibility of a project depends on the nature and extent of the effects on people. There are obvious human resource management implications to most projects, in the area of forming, leading and motivating the project team. The progress and outcome of a project may also have important consequences for employees outside the team, such as increased demand for certain categories of staff, redundancies, training requirements and changed work patterns.

The opening of the Snow Dome could see activity moving away from other areas of the business with possible job losses or retraining and redeployment necessary. There would probably be a need for training of employees involved in the operation of the Snow Dome itself. The project team where it is made up of employees of S Company will be diverted from their existing duties which may have to be covered by co-workers.

Outside the organisation, the undertaking of the project and its outcomes may have **wider social consequences**. The hoped for outcome is a return of customers who have left to use other facilities. Building works may affect those in the local environment. Some customers may prefer the dry slope and so lose out from the conversion.

(c) **Financial feasibility**

It is appropriate to submit proposed projects to **cost-benefit analysis**, though this can be very difficult when the benefits are largely in intangible form. Part of the difficulty lies in **identifying** the benefits and part in **assigning monetary values** to them. S Company operates in the leisure industry and presumably aims to be profit-making. So the usual analysis of costs should be made.

(i) **Capital costs** are incurred in the purchase of equipment needed to manufacture the dome.
(ii) **Finance costs** are the charges made for the use of loan capital if this is needed.
(iii) **Revenue costs** are all other costs such as daily running costs of the facility.

The financial feasibility of a project is **assessed** using common techniques such as net present value, payback period and accounting rate of return.

42 Project completion

Text references. Chapter 7 explains well what is involved in project completion. Chapter 8 includes details of the completion report and post-completion audit.

Top tips. This question wants you to **explain why** project completion is important not just what you know about it. From the scenario it is clear that the project must be ready for a major hotel opening so this is one important reason for making sure that the new system is operational. There are other reasons too which you should be able to comment on from your studies. Don't forget to explain what is needed to be done on project completion too. We suggest up to five marks for a description of the completion report and up to four marks for describing what the post completion audit comprises. There would also be up to three marks for explaining why the final phase is important.

Easy marks. If you mention the importance of the project being completed by the opening of the hotel this should get you a mark. Referring to the scenario in your answer is important and will get you marks if it is relevant.

Examiner's comments. Weak answers explained the various stages of the project lifecycle rather than focusing on project completion.

The final phase of project management is completion and then review of the outcome of the project. This requires that work be finished, documentation completed, systems closed down and what has been agreed to be delivered has been handed over. A proper review must then be done to consider where improvements may be made in the future.

Project completion is important because a project has a defined beginning and end and agreed outcomes. **Completion determines if these outcomes have been met**. These outcomes reflect the expectations of the stakeholders when the project gets under way. So a project must come to an end once its goals have been met or it has been abandoned. The hotel chain requires that the new system be complete in time for the opening of its new flagship hotel. This is a clear deadline for the project and the project manager should be aiming to complete the IT project so that the new on-line booking system is ready for the launch in six months' time.

This stage of the project management lifecycle involves a number of activities.

(i) **Completion**. All activities must be properly and promptly finished. The project manager must ensure that contractors finish all the work they are contracted to do and don't draw out work if they are paid by time. The system is ready to 'go live' but the project manager must ensure in his rush to move on that he has checked off all activities necessary before the system can be formally handed over to the hotel chain.

(ii) **Documentation.** This must be completed especially any quality certificates that must be issued and operating documentation for users.

(iii) **Project systems.** These need to be closed down but only once all costs have been posted and transactions recorded.

(iv) **Handover.** As the project has been managed under a contract, S must obtain acceptance from X Hotel chain that the contract is complete and that it will take responsibility for any future action that may be required such as the operation and maintenance of the booking system.

(v) **Post completion report.** The project manager should produce a completion report for the client. This should include a summary of the objectives and subsequent outcomes of the project. It would also contain a final budget report with actual and expected expenditure and a brief outline of time taken compared with the original schedule.

(vi) **Immediate review of staff performance.** This is part of the tidying-up of the project and is useful for identifying staff training needs and feeding into the performance review process.

At a future date the project manager should also undertake a formal review of the project known as a **post-completion audit. This covers feedback on what went well and didn't. It also considers whether the project met client expectations and was it managed successfully. It contains recommendations for future projects. Thus the audit covers a balance of historical aspects of the project and forward-looking recommendations.**

43 Project planning and roles

Text references. Chapter 7.

Top tips. This is a very practical question, so avoid talking about the many interesting but rather theoretical aspects of project management, such as the project life cycle and project stakeholders. Stick very much to what the project manager has to do. So you are required to **identify** and **explain** in part (a) and **contrast** and **compare** in part (b). You must be clear what the examiner means in the verbs used in these questions. Look back at the advice on key skills in the front pages and refer to 'What the examiner means' if you have forgotten what the verbs mean.

Notice that we make an assumption in response to the ambiguous wording of the requirement. Should you find that you are not quite sure what is required, choose the simplest option and state the assumption you have made.

Easy marks. You have been given some clear indications of the matters the project manager has to deal with for part (a). Make sure you include these topics and the work related to them in your answer, if only as examples of work to be done.

Examiner's comments. Some candidates lost their way , going into too much detail on specific planning phases rather than giving an overview of the whole planning process

(a) **Activities in the planning phase**

(Note. We have assumed that the requirement for 'setting up a customer service contact team' means bringing the existing team to a state of operational readiness in the new premises rather than setting up a new team from scratch, with all that that implies in the way of recruitment, selection, training and development.)

Clarifying objectives

Very little planning can be done for any activity without a fairly clear idea of the **objectives** that are to be achieved. In this case, the overall objectives are indicated quite well and we might say that the aim is to prepare for and execute the move of S Company headquarters staff to their new premises. This overall aim will be supported by several **subsidiary or enabling objectives**.

(i) Ensure that all necessary and appropriate building services and facilities are in place and functioning properly.

(ii) Design, install, test and commission an upgraded office IT support system.

(iii) Close down the existing headquarters building.

(iv) Move portable equipment to the new building and install it.

(v) Brief and execute the transfer of existing staff to the new building.

(vi) Deal with any HRM problems arising from the move.

The subsidiary objectives listed above give a fair idea of the **scope** of the project; that is to say, the overall amount and type of work that has to be done to complete it. Establishing the project's scope in detail is the first step towards the **work breakdown structure** necessary for detailed project planning.

Stating roles and responsibilities

It is clear that the project has, effectively, already been authorised by the board of S Company and will be undertaken. Nevertheless, there will still be a need for a clear statement of roles and responsibilities in a **project authorisation document** (or project charter), so that all concerned know what is to be done and who is responsible for which parts. This will be particularly important in relation to the IT system, since its development must involve specialists who are likely to have their own ideas and priorities. If **external contractors** are involved, clear objectives and standards must be set for them from the outset.

Detailed planning

Once the objectives are in place and the scope of the work is agreed, detailed planning can commence. This will require the establishment of a **project team**, which should include an appropriate level of project dedicated staff and representatives from the various headquarters departments. For a project of this size, D will probably be able to manage with an assistant, so long as he or she can call upon departmental representatives for advice when required.

The detailed planning of the work to be done to enable the move to take place will revolve around three main areas of work: the IT system, the new building and the details of the move. **Network analysis** and **Gantt charts** will be useful for establishing time and resource requirements and constraints. The use of these methods also provides for detailed progress control by the project manager and the establishment of major review gates at which progress can be checked by P.

Budgeting

Other important aspects of planning are **risk** and **cost**. Costs must be estimated and a **budget** created so that expense can be monitored. Risk assessment leads to **risk management actions**, such as avoidance, minimisation and insurance.

(b) **The role of project sponsor and project manager**

Top tips. This is a rather easier question than part (a), dealing as it does with a much more specific and limited aspect of project management activity. Try to provide something more than two lists of bullet points by giving overall accounts of the two roles and, in particular, the ways in which their general natures differ.

Easy marks. Some of the project manager's tasks, such as monitoring progress and leading the project team, are fairly obvious.

Examiner's comments. Unsurprisingly, candidates tended to do quite well with this question.

P as project sponsor

The project sponsor is the person whose **overall authority** requires and permits the project to be undertaken. P will initiate the project, appoint the project manager and provide the resources used in the project.

P will exercise **general supervision** over the progress of the project without becoming involved in the detail of project management. This will involve giving **approval to plans, budgets and specifications**; receiving and approving **progress reports** and bids for changes; and ensuring that a clear focus is maintained on the project's **objectives and priorities**.

A further possible role for the project sponsor is that of '**project champion**', promoting and defending the project and providing moral support to the project manager D, particularly when delays occur and problems arise.

D as project manager

D, as project manager is responsible to the project sponsor for the **success of the project**. This means delivering the required results in accordance with planned requirements for **cost, time and quality**. To do this D must **manage and lead the project team** and may have a hand in its selection. He or she must also be responsible for the proper **planning** of the project; the **management of the resources** allocated to it; overall **progress management** and control; and reporting on progress to the project sponsor, P.

D will also have to **manage the expectations** of the various project stakeholders. These include P, the various headquarters groups that are involved in the move and any external contractors or consultants involved in the project. This is likely to involve extensive communication, negotiation and dispute resolution, especially when there are delays or changes of plan become necessary.

44 X Company

Text references. Chapters 1 and 7.

Top tips. It is important to read both requirements of this question before starting to answer part (a) so as not to confuse the two answers. Part (a) is about leadership, while part (b) is about everything else. As ever, **planning your answer** is essential to make sure you don't put down the same points in (a) and (b).

Part (a) is quite challenging since it demands **knowledge of both leadership style theory** and the **nature of project management**. The key to answering it is to understand that, in practice, managers rarely confine themselves to a single style in all circumstances: a contingent approach is more usual. This will tend to be especially true of project managers, who are likely to be faced with a greater variety of problems than normally occur in routine operations. You could base your answer on any of the well-known spectrum models, but you will need to include some kind of explanation of how contingencies will affect effectiveness.

Part (b) tests the nine project management knowledge areas but must be applied to the scenario to score well.

Easy marks. The easy marks in this question are for explaining the variable nature of leadership style. Explaining why this is relevant to managing projects will be the more difficult task.

(a) **Contribution of leadership style theory to project management**

The phrase 'leadership style' is commonly taken to mean the manager's beliefs and practices in relation to such things as degree of concern for the welfare and motivation of staff; degree of concern for achieving the task in hand; and extent of participation by subordinates in decision-making. Several models based on a **spectrum** running from autocracy to a *laissez-faire* approach have been suggested, as have more complex two dimensional descriptions and **contingency** models that have incorporated consideration of the work situation. **It is these contingency models that may be useful to Y in becoming more effective as a project manager, since it seems unlikely that a single style of management is appropriate to all circumstances**.

Contingency models of leadership style

Likert found that the most productive departments in an insurance company were managed in a participative or democratic style, while *Hertzberg* found strong evidence that motivation in professionals depended largely on such things as achievement, challenge and recognition. These ideas are highly relevant to an organisation such as X Company that must inevitably employ **intelligent and well-qualified staff**. An autocratic style would be unlikely to get the best out of such staff. The basic model for Y to adopt, therefore, would be towards the **participative-democratic end of the spectrum**.

However, this would not be appropriate for all occasions. A good manager will be able to make use of a variety of styles and will choose a style that is **appropriate to the prevailing circumstances**. Thus, it may be appropriate for a manager of a department to involve competent and experienced staff in the consideration of plans for a rearrangement of workflows, but equally appropriate for the same manager to issue unequivocal instructions on a matter of safety practice.

Application to project management

It is in the nature of projects and project management that circumstances change, things go wrong and crises occur. It is also likely that normal variation of professional opinion will become more pronounced on such occasions. A project manager must be prepared to deal **rapidly and firmly** with such untoward occurrences, imposing his or her will in order to restore the situation. Democratic and participative ideals become less attractive when this happens and a more autocratic style is appropriate.

The need for leadership style to reflect the various contingencies present in the work situation has been explored by *Fiedler* and by *Hersey and Blanchard*. Their models are quite complex and tend to be most appropriate for understanding a range of fairly stable work situations. *Adair's* functional or action-centred approach is perhaps more useful for understanding the more dynamic project management problem.

Adair suggests that the roles the leader or manager has to play fall into three main groups focussed respectively on the needs of the **individual**, the needs of the **work group** and the needs presented by the **task**. **Leaders shift the focus of their attention among these three sets of needs according to their assessment of circumstances.**

This approach would be particularly appropriate for the management of projects. Project managers often have a significant team-building role to discharge, since many project teams are newly assembled to deal with a given project. The team members are likely to be well-qualified and experienced staff with their own firm views about what should be done, but they must be brought together to work in harmony if the project is to achieve its aims. Any project manager must, in effect, apply *Adair's* theory, balancing the attention paid to task, individual and group needs.

(b) **Other skills of a project manager**

Top tips. There is a small trap waiting for the unwary candidate in this question: it would be very easy to confuse the Project Manager's **skills** with the **functions** of the Project Manager role, especially since words like *teambuilding*, *communication* and *problem solving* occur in both lists.

Notice that there are fifteen marks available for this part of the question. This is not unreasonable as we have to cover the whole range of project manager skills other than those relating to management style.

You will often find that the mark allocation for a question breaks down into roughly equal parts; this is not the case here. We discuss project management skills under seven headings, but the topics are not of equal size or complexity.

Easy marks. The requirement for project managers to be able to use project management tools, to solve problems and to be flexible are reasonably obvious.

The project manager (PM) must deploy a wide range of skills and personal qualities in addition to those associated with leadership and team building.

Organisational skills

By 'organisational skills' we denote the **tools and practices** that are specific to project management. These include the maintenance of appropriate **project documentation**, so that planning, progress and problems can be properly understood and dealt with; and the use of **project management tools** such as network analysis and Gantt charts.

Communication

The PM must be able to **speak, write and listen effectively**, deploying these skills when dealing with both members of the project team and with more senior managers. Effective presentation of progress reports at project review meetings will be particularly important, as will issuing clear instructions to direct project activity. **Negotiation**, particularly over proposed changes and to obtain resources, will be important.

Delegation

In all save the very smallest projects it will be essential for the project manager to delegate his authority to other team members in order that necessary tasks may be carried out.

As well as being essential to the running of the project, delegation also enables project team members to gain experience of handling problems and responsibility, which should promote feelings of empowerment and ownership of their part of the project.

Whilst the project manager delegates authority to team members, the project manager remains fully accountable for all aspects of the project. Responsibility and accountability cannot be abdicated by delegation.

Technical skills

Here we refer to skills that relate to the nature of the project work. It is not necessary that managers of IT projects, for example, should be skilled IT engineers, but they must know enough about the subject to understand what the experts are saying and to form broad opinions on technical issues.

Personal qualities

Some personal qualities are particularly desirable in the PM.

(i) **Flexibility** and **creativity** are needed to deal with changes in the project's aims, the plan and the resources available.

(ii) **Persistence** is essential to deal with a succession of major problems.

(iii) **Patience** enables the PM to be wary of quick fixes and seek sound solutions, even in the face of tight deadlines.

Problem solving

Uncertainty and **risk** are an inherent part of project work and problems can arise rapidly and without warning. The PM must be capable of **fast and effective reaction**. Solving significant problems will require the co-ordinated efforts of the whole project team. The PM should encourage team members to solve their own problems if they can, but to maintain good reporting in any case so that solutions to potentially major problems can be sought collectively, in a process led by the PM.

Change control and management

In this context, we are concerned with managing changes **to the project** rather than the wider problems of change management. Changes can arise from a range of sources and have the potential to cause severe disruption of progress. A particular problem is changes to the project's objectives and desired outcomes. Changes must be properly authorised, planned and resourced, and records must be kept of their source, impact and authorisation if the project is not to become unmanageable.

45 Z Company

Text references. Chapters 6 and 7.

Top tips. Part (a) is more about meetings than it is about project management, because, while project meetings may deal with matters peculiar to a given project, organising, chairing and participating in them is not different from doing the same things in some other kind of meeting. A good idea if you don't know how to start the answer is to look back at the advice given on key skills in the 'Passing P5' section in the front pages. This should help you **approach** answering the question.

Easy marks. You either have an idea of how to run meetings, or you don't. If you do, this is easy stuff.

(a) **Problems associated with project meetings and recommendations to resolve them**

Unnecessary meetings

The effectiveness of every hour the individual spends in a meeting has to be considered in terms of opportunity cost. **T needs to ensure that he gets value for money**. The first question about any proposed meeting should be whether or not it should be held at all. If the meeting will purely be a forum for disseminating information, a memo may be a more efficient means of communication.

Unsuitable participation in the meeting

Participants who have nothing to contribute, or to whom the meeting is irrelevant, are wasting time. Only those people with a genuine need to be at a meeting, and a genuine contribution to make, should be invited. This is an important consideration for project meetings, because of the need for stakeholder representation and communication.

Unclear objectives and remit

Unclear objectives will lead to irrelevancies being discussed. T should decide the objectives or desired outcomes of the meeting, and design the agenda (and conduct the discussion) accordingly. Project problem-solving meetings should have clear guidance on their decision-making authority.

Lack of planning and co-ordination

When involving a number of people, particularly when they do not work at the same location, **lack of planning can sabotage the meeting** (by preventing key stakeholders from attending), its tone (by creating frustration) and its effectiveness (eg by failing to include vital items on the agenda). T must give plenty of notice of the meeting, and send a formal notification of the meeting with either an agenda or a request for any further items for the agenda. (This is important to ensure that all stakeholder concerns and inputs have an opportunity to be aired.)

Poorly constructed agenda

Lack of a detailed pre-planned agenda causes problems by not allowing participants to prepare themselves for discussion and (even more crucially) not providing a framework for the meeting. It will be much harder for T to keep the meeting 'on track' if there is no 'track'! In order to minimise this problem, T should ensure that the agenda:

(i) **Follows a logical order**, with the most important and time-consuming matters in the middle (to focus quality attention)

(ii) **Gives sufficient detail about the purpose of each item** to guide preparation and discussion

(iii) **Shows the start and finish times of the meeting**, and also roughly how much time will be allocated to each item, in order to facilitate time-keeping

Poor chairing/leadership of the meeting

Whoever is leading the project meeting must be aware of the role of chair (leader or facilitator) and should have appropriate skills. Poor leadership can cause problems such as: the meeting getting off-agenda; uncontrolled conflict and 'power plays' by different participants; lack of equitable contribution (so that some stakeholders fail to get heard or give their input); lack of protocols for conduct and processes such as debate and decision-making; and failure to get to 'closure' (all discussion, no decision). These problems may have contributed to T's dissatisfaction with the earlier project meetings he attended.

A skilled and experienced chair or discussion facilitator should be appointed for the task. This may be T as project manager, or it may be a role that revolves among the project team over the period of the project. The leader should be supported by a secretary (or minutes taker) to record the discussion and decisions.

Lack of minutes and follow-up action

Lack of record of decision can create uncertainty and conflict about what was agreed and whose responsibility it was to take action. Lack of defined responsibilities for action can lead to inaction! All meetings should be minuted. After the meeting the person responsible for taking minutes needs to check with the chair that minutes and action points are a fair reflection of events. Action points should specify the action to be taken, by whom the action should be taken, and by when. There should be follow up and progress check on those with responsibilities before the next meeting.

(b) **Project closure and review**

Text references. Maylor's model is covered in Chapter 7.

Top tips. The Examiner uses the word 'contribution'. It is clear that she is not using it to mean revenue minus variable costs, but she does not tell us to what purpose she envisages this contribution being made. We must assume she means something like the contribution proper project closure makes to the organisation generally, rather than to the process of project management itself, which would be a rather smaller target.

Easy marks. The final D of *Maylor's* 4D model answers this question succinctly and accurately.

T is quite right to be concerned about failure to finish off a project properly. Because project management is episodic in nature, it is **difficult to improve**. The lack of continuous operation means that the skills and experience developed during a project are likely to fragment and atrophy after it is complete. The completion and review phase involves a number of important but often neglected activities that T should ensure are carried out at the conclusion of his new project.

(i) **Completion** itself is often neglected. All project deliverables must be, in fact, delivered and all activities properly and promptly finished; care must be taken that contractors do not either leave small things undone or, if paid by time, spin things out for as long as possible.

(ii) **Documentation** must be completed. This is important on any project but it is vital if there are quality certification issues or it is necessary to provide the user with operating documentation. Indeed, these two types of documentation should be specified as deliverables at the outset. Contracts, letters, accounting records and so on must be filed properly.

(iii) **Project systems** must be closed down, but in a proper fashion. In particular, the project accounts and any special accounting systems must remain in operation and under control until all costs have been posted but must then be closed down to avoid improper posting.

(iv) **Handover** must take place where the project has been managed for a client under contract. At some point the client must formally accept that the contract is complete and take responsibility for any future action that may be required, such as the operation and maintenance of a system.

(v) **Immediate review** is required to provide staff with immediate feedback on performance and to identify short-term needs such as staff training or remedial action for procedure failures.

The review process

A thorough review is the organisation's opportunity to make significant **improvements in how it manages its projects**. T should ensure that his review clear **terms of reference** and covers all aspects of the project, possibly organised on a functional basis. This cannot be done on the cheap: appropriate quantities of management time and attention must be allocated to the review process and to the assimilation of its results and recommendations.

Post Completion Audit

The post completion audit is the final stage of the review process. **It is a formal review of the project that examines the lessons that may be learned and used for the benefit of future projects**. Did the end result of the project meet the client's expectations: was it delivered on time and on budget? Was the management of the project as successful as it might have been, or were there bottlenecks or problems?

The audit helps to identify problems that might occur on future projects with similar characteristics, as well as to provide feedback for improvement of the performance of the project team. In other words any project is an opportunity to learn how to manage future projects more effectively. It should be clear that the audit has the potential to reduce the costs associated with future projects.

Longer-term review

Longer-term review is useful for the consideration of **lifetime costs**; which should be the eventual criterion for project success. It also allows individuals time to reflect on their experiences and to learn more thoroughly from them.

46 C Hospital

Text references. Chapter 7.

Top tips. Part (a) addressed the fundamental attributes of project work and, as such, was a straightforward question. However you need to **tailor** your answer to the circumstances found in C Hospital to gain good marks. Note that you only have to give two marks' worth of discussion for five attributes to earn your 10 marks. We have deliberately kept our answer concise, to demonstrate this. Part (b) was also straightforward, in that the four main stages follow a logical sequence and are easy to remember.

Easy marks. Easy marks were available in part (a) for identifying the characteristics of project work that distinguish it from 'business as usual' and only a modest amount of additional effort was required to relate these characteristics to the particular circumstances at C Hospital. In part (b), you needed to identify the four phases, with a brief description of each phase in the light of C Hospital's experience.

(a) **Attributes of project working**

In general the work which organisations undertake may be classified as either '**business as usual'** or **projects**. Whether an activity is classified as a project is important, as projects require management using specialised project management techniques.

A project has a number of attributes that distinguish it from 'business as usual'.

(i) **Projects have a defined beginning and end** – unlike operations which tend to be on-going. So, for example, the C Hospital project has a defined duration of 12 months to meet its deadline of May 20X7. This often allows them to be perceived in terms of a 'life cycle' of defined stages, from project definition and planning through implementation and control to closure and review.

(ii) **Projects have resources allocated specifically to them**, although often on a shared basis. This is reflected in the HR director's insistence on separating responsibility for the development of the new system, and staff involvement in it, from 'business as usual' working in the form of administering the system and dealing with staff enquiries. At the close of the development project, staff will return to their departments.

(iii) **Projects are often unique or 'one-off'**: intended to be done only once, in contrast to operations which involve recurring tasks. Thus the development of the new system is distinguished from its on-going operation.

(iv) **Projects follow a specific plan towards a clear intended end-result** (in this case, implementation of the new system), in contrast to operations for which goals and deadlines may be more general. There will be a specific schedule and resource plan for the system development project.

(v) **Projects often cut across organisational and functional lines**, while operations usually follow the organisation or functional structure. So, for example, the HR director argues that HR staff will only be one part of the project team, since a number of other stakeholders will need to be involved (including, say, payroll and accounts, IT, worker representatives and hospital management).

(b) **Outline stages for the systems design project**

The life cycle of the project to design and implement a new pay and reward system for C Hospital will include the following four main phases:

Identification of a need

Projects start when someone becomes aware of the **need** for one. This can occur at any level and in any context, though more formal business projects of management significance will normally be originated within the area of responsibility of the sponsoring manager.

At C Hospital the need has arisen as a result of the need to respond to government requirements to reform reward systems. A key first step is to **identify the goals and objectives** of the project – why we are doing it and what are we seeking to achieve. At this early stage one of the most important things to get under control is the **scope** of the project; that is, just what is included and what is not. A firm grasp of the agreed scope of the project must be maintained throughout its life. Government requirements in relation to reward systems will play a major role in shaping the scope of the project.

The **project team** will also be assembled at this stage and should include representatives from HR, Finance and those who can speak on behalf of each of the employee groups affected. The **project manager** will take ultimate **responsibility** for ensuring the desired result is achieved on time and within budget. A person should only take on the role of project manager if they have the time available to do the job effectively. Since that person is to be held responsible for the project, they must be given the **resources** and **authority** to complete project tasks.

Development of a solution

Planning is a key duty of the project manager and the initial outline planning will include:

(i) Developing project targets such as overall costs or timescales.
(ii) Dividing the project into activities and placing these activities into the right sequence.
(iii) Developing a framework for procedures and structures needed to manage the project – this could include weekly team meetings, performance reviews and so on.

Detailed planning may include use of techniques such as work breakdown structure and network analysis in order to produce a schedule of activities to be undertaken.

Implementation

This is the **operational** phase of the project. Planning will continue as required to in order to control agreed changes and to deal with unforeseen circumstances, but the main emphasis is on **getting the work done**.

There are several important aspects to this phase. **Management** and **leadership** assume a greater importance as the size of the project work force increases. **Time**, **cost** and **quality** must be kept under control, as must the tendency for **changes** to proliferate.

Problems are bound to arise and must be solved sensibly and expeditiously. At C Hospital the objective of the project, pay harmonisation, is potentially extremely contentious and it will be very important to resolve employee concerns quickly without imposing an ongoing insupportable financial burden upon the hospital.

Completion

The final phase of the project is **completion and review**. This phase involves a number of important but often neglected activities.

Completion itself is often neglected. All activities must be properly and promptly finished and **documentation** must be completed. This is particularly important on a payroll project where accuracy and timeliness of payment are of crucial importance.

At some point the HR department must formally **accept** that the project is **complete** and **take responsibility** for any future action that is required in relation to the new pay system, such as the maintenance of the system. The HR department will want to ensure that the project being handed over **conforms** to the latest **requirements definition** and **project specification**.

Completion will involve the **disbandment** of the project team. It is important for future projects that before the team members return to their previous roles there is a **formal process** that gathers the **lessons learned** so that they are available to future project teams and help those projects to avoid any mistakes or difficulties encountered whilst developing the payment system.

47 Project Management Software

Text references. Project management software is covered in Chapter 8 and Mendelow's matrix in Chapter 10.

Top tips. Project management software is a fairly specialised area of the syllabus but this scenario does not give enough detail to allow you to become totally bogged down in technicalities. By expressing the main principles and features of project management software, and relating these to the circumstances of M University in part (a), you will produce a good answer.

In part (b), analyse the scenario carefully to find all of the interested stakeholders. As a rule of thumb, look for at least five to be sure of satisfying the ten mark allocation. A good starting point is to consider the stakeholders in terms of *Mendelow's* matrix of power and interest. Make sure you refer to the factors in the matrix when commenting on each stakeholder. This shows how important it is to **tailor** your analysis to the particular scenario. The examiner suggests between two and three marks for each general heading in her marking guide.

Easy marks. You should be able to identify five stakeholders fairly easily.

Examiner's comments. In part (a), candidates need to explain where project management software can help in a project. A detailed discussion of how the software will help the finance team is also required. In part (b), answers need to explain who the stakeholders are in the context of the project. Then, candidates should explain why the finance director needs to consider the interests of the different stakeholders. Common errors included not explaining how the software could help in managing a project. Some candidates confused project management software with project management. In part (b) candidates needed to explain why the director should consider particular stakeholders.

(a) **How project management software may help make the project successful**

Software might be used for a number of purposes in helping the project manager with his job. Most packages involve a process of identifying the main steps in the project, and breaking these steps down into specific tasks. **Typically, a system requires the following inputs:**

(i) **The length of time required for each activity** – how much time does the project have?

(ii) **The logical relationships between each activity** (as an obvious example, building the student village cannot begin until the land has been acquired and architectural drawings have been produced)

(iii) **The resources available** – how much is likely to be invested by local businesses?

(iv) **When the resources will be available**

We can look at the role of software under the main general headings which are used when outlining the task of the project manager.

Planning

Network diagrams (showing the critical path, perhaps from the initial approach to the authority with the planning proposal for purchasing the land) and **Gantt charts** (showing resource use) can be produced automatically. Packages also allow some flexibility with variables such as start and finish dates, likely level of investment from local business, cost of the land, or available resources. This will allow **contingency plans** to be made following **'what if' analysis**.

The **complexity** of the M University project means that planning will also be complex and difficult to carry out accurately and quickly. The project software will help here with the scheduling of different activities.

Estimating

As the project progresses, actual data can be used to provide more accurate estimates of the likely duration or costs (for example) associated with the project. Estimates can be changed many times and new schedules produced almost instantly. This ability will enable the finance director to satisfy the project sponsors' need for reassurance that project costs are under control.

Monitoring

Actual data can be entered to monitor progress constantly, and automatically update the plan. **Budgeting** and **control** features of project software can help comparisons to be made between actual and budget costs during the project.

Reporting

Software packages allow both **standard** and **tailored progress reports** to be produced and circulated to interested parties at any time. This helps with keeping the stakeholders in the project informed, and with the co-ordination of activities.

The sponsors will require that monitoring and control of the project are undertaken in a competent fashion. They will also require regular, detailed progress reports: the features above will therefore assist the finance director to keep their needs satisfied.

(b) **Why the finance director should consider stakeholder interests**

Stakeholders are the individuals and organisations who are involved in, or may be affected by, project activities. The various stakeholders will differ in their attitudes and priorities concerning this building project. The following stakeholders can be identified from the scenario. All of their interests need to be considered as early in the project as possible.

Stakeholder mapping could be used to classify these stakeholders, so **Mendelow's matrix** of power and interest could help identify which stakeholders have power and the extent of their involvement in the project.

Regional authority

The **interests** of this stakeholder are clear, because it currently owns the land that the University wishes to acquire. It has considerable power of veto over this project. The authority needs to consider its own policies concerning development, as well as the interests of local residents (the electorate) who will be affected by the planned proposal. M University must make sure that its planning application is sound and addresses any concerns that the regional authority may have about the proposed development.

Residents

They are said to be unhappy about the proposal. The project manager needs to meet with their representatives to understand their concerns, as they will have a significant **influence** on the decision of the regional authority whether or not to sell the land to the university. Alternative plans that address the main queries of the residents may be able to be drafted.

Local business investors

These stakeholders are going to require an adequate return on their investment, and the project manager must be sure exactly what their expectations are, as part of the collaborative agreement. For example, if there are cost overruns there will need to be an agreement as to who will finance them.

Staff

Most members of staff are very unhappy about the extra travelling time that will be required. They may need to be compensated for this in the form of an additional allowance, which will add to the costs associated with the project. Some ways around this problem (free shuttle bus from the main campus, extra allowance for travel costs/time) may need to be made. Their interest is high but their influence is limited.

Students

The students will be **interested** in high quality accommodation, teaching rooms and other facilities. Their interests will need to be incorporated into the architect's plans. The prospect of high quality accommodation and other facilities could prompt some students to choose M University over another.

Corporate clients

As with students, these are the 'customers' of the project and so will expect the business and conference facilities to be top quality, or they will prefer to book conferences with other organisations.

48 Project planning

Text references. Projects and tools for managing them are explained in Chapters 7 and 8.

Top tips. In part(a) don't just fire off a list of potential problems without attempting to relate them to the scenario explained in the question. You must **tailor** them to the circumstances of the Shopping Centre project. Remember that you are thinking in particular about the **problems** that may occur when **planning** is neglected. The marking scheme awards one mark for each problem as it applies to the project. Answers that don't relate the problems to the specific project would earn a maximum of four marks.

Part (b) wants you to write about a variety of project management techniques. Once again don't just reel off lists of techniques without **applying** them to the Shopping Centre project. There were a maximum of four marks per technique awarded.

Make sure you keep to the time limits suggested by the mark allocation. Look back at the front pages for advice on **time management skills** and **answering discussion questions**.

Easy marks. You should be able to earn a few marks in part(b) explaining each technique.

Examiner's comments. In part(a) many students wrote about project planning rather than the problems where there is no planning. Part(b) was generally well answered but low scoring answers tended to simply discuss PRINCE2 methodology.

(a) **Potential problems faced by the Shopping Centre project without good project planning**

Projects are often seen as having a **lifecycle** and this idea helps when managing the project. Thus a project is broken down into manageable parts, which can be monitored as the project progresses.

Project **planning** takes place during the stage when the project is being **defined** and involves setting **objectives** and the time and resources needed to achieve these. If objectives aren't set clearly then they are open to changing specification by the client with likely knock-on effects on the project. It is possible that D will try to do this given her hands-on approach to managing the project.

The aim of planning at the **definition stage** should be to avoid the chaos of unplanned activity, provide a basis for accepting the project and identify problems in advance.

The Shopping Centre project could well end up with these problems if there is no planning. So activities would not be planned in sequence failing to take account of available manpower and funding, and unrealistic timetables end up in place. Resources are not planned for so budget overruns occur and delays may arise where resources aren't available.

Plans are refined further during the **design stage** of the project where they are fleshed out to include details of timings, costs, quality and risk and contingencies. At this stage **project management techniques** are used to plot out the **timetable** for the project. Resource plans are used to specify the types of resources needed and communication plans can be used to co-ordinate stakeholders in the project. If the Shopping Centre does not have a detailed timetable, it will be impossible to monitor progress. The project will not have contingency plans in place in case of slippage or unforeseen events.

Feasibility studies can be used to assess whether a project can achieve its objectives in a cost-effective manner. Technical feasibility can be used to assess whether the project can be completed with the available technology or whether further development is needed. This also includes technical expertise in other areas such as marketing and finance. Social feasibility applies to the effect a project has on people inside and outside the organisation. So will the project mean significantly increased workloads for employees or redundancies for instance? Financial feasibility includes a cost-benefit analysis and this may need the project team to look at intangible benefits. The Shopping Centre clearly has an effect on its local environment and local planning must be adhered to. Local residents should be consulted on the plans and the disturbance caused by building works.

In the early stages, the **roles and responsibilities** of project members are defined. Clearly if these are not agreed upon, members of the project team will find it difficult to work together as they will be confused about their roles.

Also **control systems** are set in place. Without an adequate control system, there is a good likelihood of lack of cost control and resultant overspend.

(b) **Contribution of project management, tools and techniques to planning the project**

G can use a variety of project management tools and techniques to help at the detailed planning stage of the project. Some of the most common are **Work Breakdown Structure, Gantt charts** and **Network analysis**.

Work Breakdown Structure (WBS)

This is the analysis of the work involved in a project into a structure of phases, activities and tasks. **Dependencies** determine the order in which tasks must be carried out, while **interactions** between tasks affect them without imposing order. The essence of WBS is analysing the work needed to complete a project into manageable components. WBS works backwards from the required outputs to plan what processes and components are then needed. **Responsibilities** are then assigned to these processes or tasks.

The Shopping Centre project could be broken down into manageable tasks by working back from the output, which is a shopping centre to the tasks and resources needed to achieve this. G can then develop a task list to assist in planning, control and monitoring the various stages of the project. These tasks can be analysed between dependencies and interactions. Individuals can then be given responsibility for certain tasks.

Gantt charts

The **Gantt chart** is a horizontal bar chart used to plan the time scale for a project and estimate the resources required. Once again the project is broken down into tasks, which are listed on the chart in order of commencement. Tasks are listed on the horizontal axis and weeks taken on the vertical axis. This is an easy visual tool for those involved in the Shopping Centre project to understand their responsibilities, resources required for the project and to monitor progress.

Network analysis

Network analysis is used to plan the sequence of the tasks making up the project scope and to determine the **critical path**. The project is broken down into tasks, which are arranged in a logical sequence. Each task then has an estimated duration. The analysis also reveals which tasks are **dependent** on others and that are known as **dependencies**. Dependencies are very important in project planning so that resources can be channeled into tasks on which others rely.

The project would be plotted on a **network diagram** showing all of the activities, their sequence, and **earliest event** and **latest event times** for each activity. The minimum possible duration of the project is found by plotting the **critical path**, which consists of critical activities. The critical path shows the elements which if delayed will delay the completion of the entire project. The analysis can also reveal where there is **slack** time, which is spare time.

The Shopping Centre project will find network analysis is a useful tool to work out what sequence activities must follow. So when the project is viewed overall, management can see what **activities are critical** and make these a priority. Where there is slack this can be used to cover unforeseen circumstances.

PERT

A variation on network analysis, which includes uncertainty, is known as the **Project evaluation and review technique** or **PERT**. Each activity has optimistic, most likely and pessimistic estimates of time calculated and these are used to calculate an expected time based on the mean value of these estimates. The technique also allows a standard deviation to be calculated for each activity.

G could use this technique to factor in uncertainty in the project. Times could be estimated for an ideal situation where everything goes well, the most likely 'normal' conditions and a pessimistic scenario where several problems may arise. The mean time could then be calculated along with the standard deviation, which allows a contingency time to be stated.

49 Project management

Text references. Chapter 7.

Top tips. In part(a), the question asks for the **responsibilities** of the project manager. It is a bit unclear whether these are also the **duties** of a project manager as responsibilities can include things required as part of a job and duties are the tasks required as part of a job. We have taken responsibilities to be obligations to others as this follows the general theme of the scenario: that the project manager has obligations to other departments, management and the project team, and have answered in this way. The question gives twelve marks for this part so you will need to write up to twelve separate points and illustrate these from the scenario.

As the requirement is slightly ambiguous, we also include a table listing duties but as an alternative answer rather than part of the main answer.

Note the verb used in part(b)(i). You need to **examine in detail** the purpose of project control and not just state what it is. Remember to make some reference to the situation found in the question to illustrate your answer.

For part(b)(ii) you could refer to any of a variety of project management methods to illustrate controls. We use PRINCE2 although you could use PMBOK too. You could expand your discussion to include a brief mention of some of the tools and techniques that are used to control progress such as Gantt charts and network analysis.

Easy marks. As is often the case, a little theoretical knowledge will earn you the easy marks in this question.

Examiner's comments. Candidates needed to focus on **responsibilities** rather than repeating the problems in the scenario. Some candidates relied too much on referring to the types of project management tool without explaining these in the context of project control.

(a) **The responsibilities of X in his role as project manager**

The project manager is the person who takes ultimate responsibility for ensuring the project is completed on time and within budget. 'X' will also have responsibilities to management, other business areas and the project team.

Responsibilities to management:

(i) **Ensure resources are used efficiently** and strike a balance between cost, time and results

(ii) **Keep management informed** with timely and accurate communications. Did "X" do this regularly as the project appears to be at a crisis point? The project steering committee is asking for answers.

(iii) **Manage the project to the best of his ability.** "X" appears to be having problems with the project in the form of poor team performance and pressure from the project sponsor to cut corners.

(iv) **Behave ethically**, and adhere to the organisation's policies. The sponsor is suggesting short cuts to ensure the project goes live. These may have ethical implications although this is not clear from the scenario.

(v) **Maintain a customer orientation**. This includes either internal or external customers as other departments depend on the database too. Customer satisfaction is a key indicator of project success.

Responsibilities to the project and the project team:

(i) **Take action to keep the project on target for successful completion**. It appears that members of the team don't know what they are supposed to be doing and are failing to perform their duties

(ii) **Ensure the project team has the resources required** to perform tasks assigned

(iii) **Help new team members integrate into the team**

(iv) **Provide any support required** when members leave the team either during the project or on completion

Alternative answer. The duties of a project manager are summarised below.

Duty	Comment
Outline planning	Project planning (eg targets, sequencing) • Developing project targets such as overall costs or timescale needed (eg project should take 20 weeks) • Dividing the project into activities and placing these activities into the right sequence, often a complicated task if overlapping • Developing a framework for procedures and structures needed to manage the project (e.g. decide, in principle, to have weekly team meetings, performance reviews and so on)
Detailed planning	Work breakdown structure, resource requirements, network analysis for scheduling.
Obtain necessary resources	Resources may already exist within the organisation or may have to be bought in. Resource requirements unforeseen at the planning stage will probably have to be authorised separately by the project board or project sponsor.
Teambuilding	Build cohesion and team spirit.
Communication	The project manager must let superiors know what is going on, and ensure that members of the project team are properly briefed.
Co-ordinating project activities	Between the project team and users, and other external parties (eg suppliers of hardware and software).
Monitoring and control	The project manager should estimate the causes for each departure from the standard, and take corrective measures.
Problem-resolution	Even with the best planning, unforeseen problems may arise.
Quality control	There is often a short-sighted trade-off between getting the project out on time and the project's quality.

(b) (i) **The purpose of project control**

Project control is an aspect of **project management**. This latter is the integration of the systems, techniques and people needed to **monitor and control** the activities undertaken in the project. The project is successful if it is completed **on time**, at the **required quality** and **within budget. This is effectively the purpose of project control**.

The project manager's role includes **responsibility** for **controlling** the resources needed to make the project successful. Frequent project review meetings are needed and these may result in corrective action being undertaken.

For "X" this means that he must control the project team and their progress on the project. He also needs to manage (or control) the expectations of the project sponsor who is making demands that could undermine the ultimate outcome of the project.

(ii) **Controls for the customer information database project to help X manage the stages of the project**

PRINCE2 operates **control** of a project **managing one stage at a time**. So the project board restricts authorisation to one stage at a time and manages by exception. Under the PRINCE2 methodology, project control includes a structure of reports and meetings.

This **formalisation** of the management of the project should benefit X who will be able to communicate effectively with his project team and get them to produce what they need to on time or get advance warning of slippage. It should also reassure the project steering committee that are being kept informed of progress on a major capital project. Hopefully it should persuade the project sponsor of that a reasonable approach is being taken and where short cuts are and aren't possible.

(1) A **project initiation** meeting agrees the scope and objectives of the project and gives approval for it to start. The project is already underway so it may be assumed that this has already been done.

(2) The completion of each project stage is marked by an **end stage assessment**, which includes reports from the project manager and the project assurance team. The next stage does not commence until its plans have been reviewed and approved. This would assist with the confusion felt by the team who are somewhat adrift and chase up those members who are late with their input.

(3) **Mid stage assessments** are optional and may arise if, for example, a stage runs for a particularly long time or it is necessary to start a new stage before the current one is complete. Once again this should help the team members if they are falling behind.

(4) **Highlight reports** are submitted regularly to the project board by "X" as project manager. These reports are the main overall **routine control mechanism** and their frequency (often monthly) is agreed at project initiation. They are essentially progress reports and should include brief summaries of project schedule and budget status.

(5) The **checkpoint** is the main control device used by the project team itself. Meetings are held more frequently than highlight reports are prepared (possibly weekly) and provide a basis for continuing progress review by team leaders and members. Once again this would help those in the team who are falling behind with their tasks and those who don't know what is going on.

There are several tools and techniques that "X" could use to help monitor and control the progress of the database project. These can be used to control different aspects of the project.

Thus **Gantt charts** show a list of tasks in a project and the timescale for each as well as the resources needed. This is illustrated graphically and the time allocated and actual time taken are shown together.

Network analysis extends the analysis of control in a project to the relationships between the stages of the project. The project is broken down into tasks, which are arranged in a logical sequence and estimated times given to each task. Then a **critical path** is determined which is the series of tasks or **critical activities**, which give the minimum time to complete the project. If these tasks are delayed then the project itself will be delayed.

50 Objective test questions

50.1 C Accounting software could conceivable offer a strategic advantage but it is much more likely to be a routine matter within the finance function.

50.2 C A is internal: a weakness. B is also an internal weakness, which interacts with the environment but is not part of it. D is a policy and therefore part of the mission.

50.3 B A and D relate to overall corporate strategy, while C is about functional or operational strategy.

50.4 C

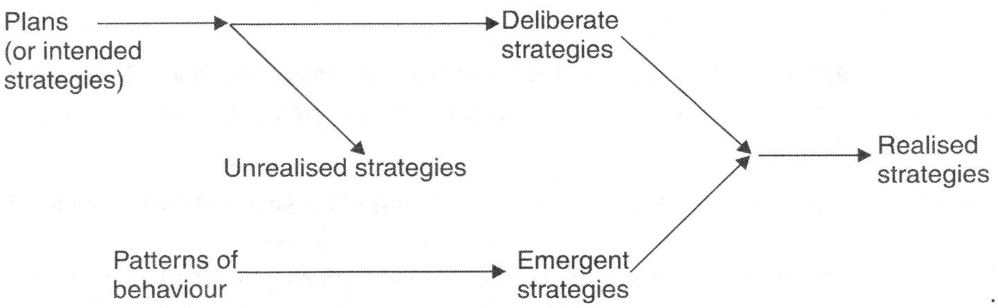

50.5 B A and D relate to the degree to which subordinate objectives support mission. C has much in common with *Kaplan and Norton's* internal business perspective but is not the phrase they use.

50.6 A This is *Daft's* analysis.

50.7 D A and C are internal stakeholders; B is an external stakeholder.

50.8 B 'Shared values' is one of the elements of the model.

50.9 B A is **corporate strategy**, C is **functional strategy** and D could be regarded as one aspect of corporate strategy.

50.10 A The groups in option B are all **internal stakeholders**; suppliers are regarded as **connected stakeholders** so options C and D contain mixed groups of stakeholders.

51 Objective test questions

51.1 C The name *Mintzberg* should immediately remind you of the idea of emergent strategies. This was part of his well-known attack on the rational model of strategy. Logical incrementalism is, purely on the face of it, an attractive answer to this question, but, of course, it is an idea based, like the rational model, on careful analysis. The term 'positioning' is used to contrast strategies that seek to fit the organisation to its environment with those that are based on the possession of some unique or valuable resource.

51.2 B Both approaches are built around deliberate decisions by managers. Neither emphasises the possession of core competences and, of the two approaches, only the rational model is dependent on detailed medium-term forecasting and deals with a wide range of strategic possibilities.

51.3 D Growth is identified by *Mintzberg* as 'the natural goal of the manager': managers benefit personally and directly from growth in terms of salaries and status and in reduced vulnerability to the environment.

51.4 Unless you were exempt from the Certificate stage, you should have been able to answer this question with knowledge brought forward from Paper C4, Fundamentals of Business Economics. Barriers to entry are of great practical importance in all industries and include those listed below.

Scale economies (perhaps the most important of all)	Switching costs
Capital requirements	Technical expertise
Strong brands	Access to distribution channels
Legal protection, such as patents	Access to input

51.5 True. Both display fluid structures in which expertise is more important than status, and commitment to the task more important than correct procedure, for example.

51.6 Market share and market growth.

51.7 Threat of new entrants; threat of substitute products; bargaining power of customers; bargaining power of suppliers.

51.8 Mendelow proposed classifying stakeholders in terms of their level of **interest** and **power**.

51.9 C The others are support activities.

52 Professional ethics

Text references. Chapter 10.

Top tips. This is a good question to test your knowledge of ethics and codes of conduct. Resist the temptation to write in general about business ethics. This question is as much about professional codes of conduct as it is about ethics.

Easy marks. It is fairly obvious that codes of conduct should be comprehensive, consistent and legally compliant.

Codes of conduct have become very popular in recent years in organisations concerned about ethical conduct. Where these contain specific clear rules they at least have the value of establishing what correct conduct is in the defined cases. This is both of benefit to the individual and useful at any subsequent disciplinary process. However, such codes have been criticised as tending to be **too legalistic** and encouraging a **compliance-based** rather than

principle (or integrity) -based approach. **Ethics is to some extent a matter of opinion** and highly specific codes tend to offer poor guidance in complex situations.

If professional bodies or other organisations have codes of conduct, **their first requirement is that they are carefully thought out**, with a minimum of loopholes and adequate coverage of the problems they are meant to address. The second requirement is that **they should be enforced by a proper system of discipline**. Among other characteristics, **such a system must conform with over-riding legal requirements**, such as, in common law jurisdictions, the rules of natural justice.

Such a system of discipline must be credible. Among other things, that means that it must be administered impartially. For a professional body, this may mean qualified legal input, possibly from a legally qualified president of the disciplinary forum. For a commercial organisation, it may be that non-executive directors can play a part.

The system should also be capable of detecting abuses. One method is a complaint system, to be impartially administered. Another feature would be a facility for 'whistleblowing' by insiders.

Another method of encouraging ethical behaviour would be a means of providing guidance when problems arise. The real difficulties with ethics arise when the rules or principles point in different directions. A telephone hotline to experienced advisers is invaluable in such circumstances.

53 Fast food culture

Text references. Chapter 11 (on culture) and 1 (on cross-cultural leadership)

Top tips. This is a very simple question based on culture in its widest sense, though management culture also rears its ugly head. Note the three problems mentioned in the question. How might these be analysed using *Hofstede's* model? Make sure you **tailor** your answer so that you address these particular problems. You would be equipped to produce a pretty good answer to this question if you merely read a decent newspaper regularly. Indeed, look at our advice in the front pages on how to develop business awareness.

Easy marks. Differences of national culture and *Hofstede's* model of management cultures are obvious bases to build an answer on. There is no need to go into great detail about the latter in particular, however.

The problems experienced by FFC reflect common points of difference between national (and organisational) cultures.

One of the key models used to categorise these points of difference is the **Hofstede model**, which identifies **four key 'dimensions'** on which national cultures (and the corporate cultures modelled on them) differ.

(i) **Power distance** describes the extent to which unequal distribution of power is accepted in a culture. **This may be a source of the complaints from country C employees about the style and practices of the country S managers**. It may be that country C is a low-PD culture, in which subordinates expect involvement and participation in decision-making, while country S is a high-PD culture, which favours top-down command and closer supervision: there will be an inevitable clash between managerial norms and assumptions, and the expectations of employees.

(ii) **Uncertainty avoidance** describes the extent to which security, order and control are preferred to ambiguity uncertainty and change. **This may also be causing stress and frustration for the country C employees**: either because (as a high-UA culture) they are given *insufficiently* clear task structure and rules by the country S managers, or because (as a low-UA culture) they feel restricted by excessive structure, rules and regulations. **Given the high degree of complaint by locals**, country C may be on the low-UA (dissent-tolerating) side of the scale.

(iii) **Individualism** describes the extent to which people prefer to live and work in individualist (focusing on 'I') rather than collectivist (focusing on 'we') ways. Again, we don't know where the two countries fall on the scale, but the **complaints about seating arrangements and music, for example, may be due to their interference with social interaction**, if country C is a collectivist culture.

(iv) **Masculinity** refers to the extent to which gender roles are distinct, and the extent to which masculine values (assertiveness, competition, material success etc) are dominant over feminine values (relationship, consensus, modesty etc). Again, we can only surmise that **there may be a clash of management styles**, in this respect, between **country S managers and country C employees**.

We might also note, more generally, that **two of the key elements of culture** (according to *Trompenaars*) are **rituals** and **artefacts**. There are **cultural differences in the values attached to food and rituals and customs around eating**, and these may account for some of country C's resistance to the food culture (and menus) introduced by the country S chain. There are, similarly, **cultural differences in 'taste' in artefacts such as music and architecture**: country C people may simply dislike country S's music, or have their sense of heritage outraged by incompatible architecture in their cities.

FFC's management have presumably decided to standardise as much of their operation as possible in order to enhance control and brand image and to achieve economies of scale. It seems likely that they will have to make some adjustments to this ethnocentric approach to their operation in country C if it is to be adapted more appropriately to the needs and wants of its new market.

54 T Venture

Text references. Chapter 10.

Top tips. The trick to part (a) is an understanding of the potential role of CSFs in strategy development and how the possession of core competences enables the CSFs to be achieved. **Unless you can distinguish between CSFs and core competences, you will not be able to answer this question**. The examiner noted that a significant number of candidates were unable to distinguish between CSFs and core competences and were unable to apply these concepts to the scenario.

Easy marks. A small number of easy marks will be available in part (a) for accurate definitions of CSFs and core competences. Linking CSFs and core competences in the context of strategy development will be more difficult and will generate the bulk of the marks. In part (b), full marks were available for simply stating, in bullet point format, four factors that would be critical to competitive success in relation to a business operation with which most students would be familiar.

(a) **Using Critical Success Factors**

Critical Success Factors (CSFs) are a **small number of areas in which (a) satisfactory results will enable successful competitive performance** and (b) an **organisation *must* excel in order to outperform competition**. *Johnson & Scholes* recommend six or fewer CSFs.

T must attempt to determine the CSFs for his new venture for a number of reasons.

(i) **It is the only way he can present potential investors with a sound business case for his venture**. He is convinced that he can succeed with his fast-food concept, but he needs to show that he can define what success is, and what is necessary to achieve it, within the business sector he has chosen.

(ii) **CSFs provide a basis for strategy formulation**, as they focus on the strategic goals that must be pursued in order to compete successfully: the features of T's product/service that will be most highly valued by customers, and which will be a potential source of competitive advantage. The fast food market is highly competitive, so outperforming competitors will be a helpful priority.

(iii) **CSFs offer an alternative to a more comprehensive goal structure or hierarchy of objectives, which may be too rigid for a small start-up venture** in a new market: they will enable T to focus on competitive essentials and remain flexible in how he (and individual outlets within his chain) will pursue them at the tactical and operational level. This will allow for variations in local markets, infrastructure, produce availability, outlet manager ability and so on.

(iv) **CSFs provide a useful framework for identifying the business processes and activities which will yield each CSF**; defining the Key Performance Indicators (KPIs) which will be used to evaluate performance in delivering them; and monitoring competitor activity for its effect on the CSF structure.

Distinguishing CSFs from core competences

Competences are 'the activities or processes through which the organisation deploys its resources effectively.' (*Johnson & Scholes).* Core competences are competences which both outperform competitors and are unique or difficult for competitors to imitate.

Core competences represent the distinctive abilities that T's venture must develop and display if its CSFs are to be achieved. The two concepts are related, in that CSFs should focus attention on whether the venture has or can develop the core competences to compete successfully: both concepts take a competitive view of strategy. However, the emphasis has shifted from what must be achieved (CSFs) to the special skills and processes that will enable the required achievement (core competences).

(b) **Possible CSFs for T's chain of fast food restaurants**

The CSFs for T's chain of fast food restaurants could include the following.

(i) **Right restaurant locations.** Proximity to significant centres of population, easy access and adequate parking facilities

(ii) **Distinctive brand identity.** Recognisable and distinctive brand with a good reputation for quality of service and diversity and freshness of produce

(iii) **Speed of service.** Must meet customer expectations based on benchmark standards set by competitors

(iv) **Child friendly facilities.** Needs of children and families must be catered for successfully

55 N Airline

Text references. Chapter 10.

Top tips. This is a simple question on a very basic topic in strategic management and should be easy for you to answer well. The terminology used here is widely standardised, so there should be no confusion in your mind. Look back at the advice given in the front pages on **key skills**. Remember to make a point using theory, explain that point and finally illustrate it using the example of N Airline.

Easy marks. A question like part (a) revolves around definitions: you do not have to quote *Mintzberg* verbatim, as we do, so long as you can produce a clear and succinct version of your own.

(a) **Mission and objectives**

Mintzberg says that **mission** 'defines the organisation's basic function in society, in terms of the products and services it produces for its clients'. A wider definition of mission would include reference to four elements.

(i) **Purpose** would differ among types of organisations, but would define why the organisation was created.

(ii) **Strategy** would define the nature of the organisation's activities and would therefore cover Mintzberg's definition quoted above.

(iii) **Policies and performance standards** as overall imperatives can be included in mission to emphasise their importance.

(iv) **Values** are the pervasive beliefs and attitudes that underpin the organisation's culture.

Mission is therefore the overall definition of what the organisation exists to do.

Objectives are specific, well, defined targets whose attainment will support progress towards achieving the mission. They translate the generalised aspirations of mission into more specific, measurable and concrete terms that can be used to organise the organisation's work and provide specific targets to measure its success against. They therefore flow from and support mission.

While an organisation generally has only one mission, it is likely to have many objectives. These will be arranged in a hierarchy, with a relatively small number of high level objectives directly derived from and supporting the mission, and each of these being broken down into a cascade of supporting departmental, functional and even individual supporting objectives.

(b) **Strategic objectives for the airline**

> **Top tips**. This question is unusual in its use of the instruction verb 'illustrate'. 'Illustrate' means 'use an example to describe or explain something'. The Examiner reminds you to use examples, so there is really no excuse for failing to link your answer to the setting in very concrete terms.
>
> Notice also the phrase 'strategic objectives'. **Try to focus on objectives that are truly strategic; that is, objectives that directly support N Airline's mission**. A good test of a possible objective would be to ask if it could be part of something with a wider scope. For example, 'minimise check-in delays' might be part of a wider objective to 'provide the best ground-based customer service'.
>
> This part of the question is worth six marks. The scenario is very short. You should therefore be aiming to find three, or possibly four, strategic objectives.
>
> Finally, do not forget the **SMART** mnemonic.
>
> **Easy marks**. The setting uses the word 'service' three times, which is an indication of a major priority for N Airline.

It is commonly considered that objectives should be specific, measurable, attainable, realistic and time bounded, **that is SMART**. The last quality in the list is probably inappropriate for many strategic objectives, since they will have continuing applicability.

Highest level of customer service

A **high level of customer service** is clearly a major part of N Airline's strategic vision and is intended to constitute its chief point of differentiation from its competitors. This might give rise to an objective such as the one below.

'To provide the highest level of customer service on the ground and in the air as measured by customer survey, unsolicited feedback and competitor benchmarking.'

The quality of customer service achieved will depend largely on **the people who deliver it**. HRM objectives might therefore be regarded as subordinate to the overall customer service objective. However, N Airline may wish to elevate its HRM objective to the strategic level in order to underscore its commitment to and dependence on its staff.

'To optimise recruitment, selection, training, development and remuneration practices so that all staff have the ability and motivation to deliver the highest level of customer service.'

Careful management of costs and revenues

N Airline's business model will inevitably involve a level of costs higher than those incurred by its rivals. This must imply higher revenues from higher ticket prices, which, in turn, will limit its market. **Careful management of costs and revenues** will be required if the company is to avoid cash flow crises. This is quantifiable in terms of gross and net margin, but the problem will be to set targets that are both adequate and attainable. An objective might be defined in terms such as those below.

'To manage the company's costs and revenues so as to facilitate the attainment of its objectives for customers and staff while generating a gross margin of X% and a net margin of Y%.'

56 Engines 1

Text references. Chapter 9.

Top tips. This is a simple question and revolves around knowledge of simple definitions of the three terms for which explanations are required.

Candidates often have difficulty **applying** their theoretical knowledge in papers that require written answers. This is a **key skill** in exams: knowing how and when to use theory in your answer. To help overcome this difficulty, we print the application points in this answer in *italic*. Note that we also continue to use italic for technical references and to indicate a particular emphasis on some words.

You need to mention the need for the three levels of strategy to be **linked**. An important aspect of the nature of the three levels of strategy is that they support one another: each higher level sets the context and basic premises of each lower one, while the strategies at the lower levels each amplify and implement some aspect of the higher ones.

Easy marks. As usual, the easy marks here are for providing simple definitions of the three terms used in the question.

Strategies at the corporate, business and functional levels form a hierarchy, each level having its specific function and relating up and down to the others.

Corporate strategy

Corporate strategy is decided at the strategic apex and 'is concerned with the overall purpose and scope of the organisation'. This is the level of strategy that directly addresses the **purpose** for which the organisation exists: in a business organisation, success at this level will be measured in terms of shareholder benefit. The **deployment of financial and other resources** within the organisation will form a major component of strategy at this level. A typical corporate strategy decision is which product-markets to compete in. In very large organisations, this may effectively become a **portfolio management** activity, with the organisation moving into and out of product-markets as seems advantageous from time to time. *The E company's corporate strategy appears to revolve around high quality engine design and production.*

Business strategy

Business strategy 'is about how to compete successfully in a particular market.' In a small business operating in a single market, this level of strategy will be very closely related to the overall corporate strategy. A bigger company might be made up of largely autonomous **strategic business units**, each responsible for developing and implementing a strategy to compete within a given market.

In the case of the E company, there are clearly three product-markets to consider: automobile engines, marine engines and aerospace engines. It would be possible to have a ***distinct strategy*** *for each. In fact, we are told that the company has emphasised design and quality; presumably that applies in all three major product groups. Other examples of business strategy that the E company could have pursued would include: concentrating on design and development in order to build a reputation for advanced engineering; and building market share in the automobile market by producing engines for less expensive cars.*

Business strategy is thus an amplification of corporate strategy: it lays down the general methods that will be used in the given product-market.

Functional strategy

Functional strategy (or operational strategy) flows from business strategy and supports it. This level of strategy is concerned with the optimum use and deployment of the **resources used within a given business strategy**. *For example, within the E company's marine engine operation, there might be separate functional strategies for R&D, sales and production. To take the example of production, strategies might range from in-house manufacture in a single integrated factory; through dispersed assembly plants, each intended to service one segment of the global market; to complete sub-contractorisation of production.*

Note, however, that functional strategy must **support** business strategy and, ultimately, corporate strategy. *For example, if the E company were determined to maintain its reputation for quality, it is unlikely that it would contract out much of its core manufacturing work as control is much easier to maintain over in-house activities.*

57 Engines 2

Text references. Chapter 9.

Top tips. We would repeat our advice given in the Top Tips for Engines 1. Remember to **apply** your **knowledge**. To help overcome this difficulty, we print the application points in this answer in *italic*. Note that we also continue to use italic for technical references and to indicate a particular emphasis on some words. If you are having difficulty in answering this question, refer back to our advice and seven-step plan on tackling questions found in the front pages.

Easy marks. It is not often the Examiner asks you to explain a piece of theory, so this question might have attracted the candidate who finds application difficult.

The strategic analysis phase of the **rational model** of strategy includes consideration of both environmental factors and those internal to the organisation. These two categories, internal and environmental are divided respectively into strengths and weaknesses; and opportunities and threats. The aim of strategy development is to take proper account of these four sets of factors, so that strategy exploits opportunities and strengths, evades or combats threats and minimises the effect of weaknesses.

There are **two schools of thought** about the strategic impact of the two main categories of factors to be taken into account.

The first approach seeks to achieve a **strategic fit** with the environment. The organisation that responds best to the pressures generated by its customers, its competitors and its wider environment is the one most likely to achieve a strategic advantage. Strategy here consists of developing the strengths needed to exploit opportunities and combat threats. This is sometimes known as the **positioning** approach.

A more recent development is the **resource based** or **core competence** approach. This proceeds from the view that strategic advantage is most robust when it is based on hard-to-imitate corporate capabilities. Exploitation of such capabilities gives the organisation a long term boost in the market place simply because rivals find it difficult to compete effectively.

*It is clear that manager C tends towards the **positioning view** of strategy, while manager D is more inclined to support the **core competence** approach. This may reflect their personal exposure to strategic considerations: manager C may be a marketing specialist and manager D an engineer, for instance. Alternatively, the difference may simply arise from their exposure to strategic theory, the core competence approach being more recent in origin than the positioning approach, as mentioned above.*

58 Screen

Text references. Chapter 10.

Top tips. This is a good question to practise **planning an answer**. Whatever stakeholders you choose, you will need to also think about their **power** and influence in terms of *Mendelow's* model.

We have identified four important stake-holder groups below. However, you might have chosen others. Local government perhaps has similar expectations to central government, but sees the Cinicentre as a major local employer and an attraction for people to visit the borough. Local residents are probably concerned about traffic noise and security.

We have answered this question in two parts by addressing expectations, and then power and influence separately for each stakeholder. You could also answer this by writing about all three issues under each stakeholder.

Easy marks. Our sentence about the ways *Mintzberg* says stakeholders exercise power is a simple piece of knowledge that is relevant to the question and probably worth a mark.

Expectations and interests of stakeholders

There are four key stakeholder groups. These are members of the society, its employees, the government (as a key funder) and the media.

(a) **Members**. People join such societies for a **variety** of reasons. Some **active members** may want put themselves up for election, providing a suitable number of secondments can be found. Other members may simply be pursuing a **vague interest** in films, and are chiefly interested in the publications and discounts that membership can bring. Members who feel that the Screen is becoming too commercial have protested – however the **deficit** should concern them too.

(b) **Employees and staff.** Their **interest** is in **continued employment** and the continued interest in the job. Obviously they must love film, particularly in the Film Archive Unit, where specialist expertise is highly valued. Staff in the museum must also enjoy and be skilled at dealing with the public, as expectations of quality rise.

(c) The **government** funds Screen as it is a public benefit and there would be a major protest, especially in the media, were the Cinicentre to close. It is a tourist attraction to London, it provides jobs, it is prestigious for Britain, and it supports education. Funding Screen is perhaps similar to funding museums, art galleries, orchestras the National Theatre and so forth. There are many calls on government spending, and the government will be concerned about financial efficiency.

(d) **The media.** Although this might seem surprising to list as a stakeholder, British media firms may see Screen as a resource for programming ideas. Certainly, the film industry will be keen to promote an interest in the cinema, both as art and as entertainment.

Power and influence

Mintzberg suggests that stakeholders can exercise power in three ways: loyalty, exit or voice (ie interfering with what is done so as to change it). The extent to which they can exercise power depends on the sort of relationship they have with the managers.

(a) **Members**. Members have **little power** as individuals, unless they are distinguished film-makers, producers, actors etc. Exit is relatively easy for them: they can simply resign or allow their subscriptions to lapse: in the long term this will threaten the existence of the organisation; in the short term, they do of course have the vote, and in theory are able to exercise voice through their representatives on the Board of Governors. This power is probably latent rather than active for the individual. Presumably, at elections, the Governors have to submit a manifesto as to what their main priorities are.

(b) **Employees**. In the **short term**, the **staff** can **disrupt totally the operations** of Screen even if in the long term this would be self-defeating. On the other hand the **staff at the FAU have little power in the short term** other than resignation but they could do long term damage to Screen's reputation and mission.

(c) **Central government's power is large**, as it provides most of Screen's revenue, covering most of its overheads. Its power of voice is significant.

(d) **Media**. The media have **no direct power**. They contribute no regular income, other than fees to use films from the archive. But they are powerful nonetheless in that they can mobilise the attention and interest of the public. They have the capacity for setting the agenda in terms of public policy. As Screen is a multi-stakeholder institution, such power is important.

59 Social responsibility

Text references. Chapter 10.

Top tips. There is no scenario here, so you are free to expound the theory you have learned. In essence, this question is asking what the proper purpose of business is. Is the traditional view correct, that the pursuit of personal interest automatically produces the best possible outcomes for society? Or is it more effective to pursue non-profit objectives directly? There are compelling arguments for both points of view. You will need to **plan** your answer carefully to ensure you bring out all of these points. So jot these down before you start writing and tick them off as they are covered. You can help yourself with this type of question by reading and developing your **business awareness** and the general knowledge useful for framing an answer where there is no scenario. See the front pages for advice on how to do this.

Easy marks. There are some fairly complex arguments to this debate, but don't overlook the simple things like the extra cost imposed by, for example, supporting community activities or the PR value gained by the same sort of thing. Some basic ideas from economics could be deployed, including, on the one hand, the view that free markets maximise output and minimise waste; and the existence of externalities on the other.

Examiner's comments. Some candidates neglected the arguments against the idea of socially responsible actions. Remember, this debate is still in progress.

Arguments against social responsibility

(a) The traditional view is that the legitimate responsibility and purpose of business is to increase the wealth of its owners by **generating profit**. Business undertaken on this basis, however, also **benefits society** by **providing goods and services**, by **creating employment**, by **funding tax revenues**.

(b) **Some economists argue that there is also a 'trickle down' effect,** whereby the creation of consumption, employment and investment encourages prosperity at lower levels of the economy.

(c) ***Milton Friedman*** **argued that businesses do not have social responsibilities: only people have them**. He asserted that managers who disburse corporate assets for social purposes were failing in their duty to their employers, usurping the role of government and furthering politically collectivist ideas.

(d) **It must also be acknowledged that socially responsible activities may in the short term directly disadvantage a business's owners** by incurring **extra costs**, or by **sacrificing profitable turnover**. Such activities must at the very least, have the potential to **reduce stakeholder value**, though it can be argued that compensating effects can make them worthwhile from this point of view, as we shall see.

It must also be made clear that this view does not envisage business being run in any way that is either illegal or unethical.

Arguments for social responsibility

The opposite view, that business should not simply pursue profit but should undertake socially responsible actions can be supported on both **practical** and **philosophical** grounds. Friedman advocated social responsibility on the grounds of 'enlightened self-interest' by corporations, and it can be argued that CSR is in an organisation's interests in a number of ways.

(a) **The modern marketing concept says that in order to compete successfully, organisations must satisfy the needs, wants and values of customers.** Communication and education have made people much more aware of issues such as environmental impacts, worker exploitation, product safety and human rights. CSR can generate good public relations, which can, in turn, enhance competitive advantage and shareholder value. A good example of this is found in *Fairtrade* coffee products that retail at premiums many times larger than the extra margin they provide to the growers concerned. On the other hand, bad publicity can cause severe damage to a business as *Shell* found when it took action to dispose of the *Brent Spar* oil production platform by sinking it in the North Atlantic.

(b) A business is a **social system**, not just an economic machine (*Mintzberg*). Organisations rely on the society and local community of which they are a part, for access to facilities, business relationships, media coverage, labour, suppliers and so on. Organisations which acknowledge their responsibilities may find that many areas of their operation are facilitated.

(c) Social responsibility recognises **genuine externalities**: costs imposed by businesses on other people (but not included in the costing of their products and activities), such as environmental degradation or health-damaging pollution.

(d) Employers must compete to attract and retain high quality employees, by developing a positive **employer brand**. If the organisation gets a reputation as a socially responsible employer, it will find this easier.

(e) There are **costs of non-compliance** with law, regulation and codes of practice which impose certain social responsibilities on organisations (in areas such as employment protection, equal opportunities, health and safety and so on).

60 Company J 1

Text references. Chapter 11 (culture) and 1 (cross-cultural leadership).

Top tips. This is a simple question. We use the list of factors that influence culture given in the BPP Study Text for *Managerial Paper 5*. The McKinsey 7S model could also form a basis for an answer, but if you have any knowledge of organisations you could almost invent your own list. You can help yourself here by having a good general knowledge and awareness of **business issues**. Make sure you relate your arguments to J Company's circumstances and refer back to these where possible. This shows you understand how to **apply** theoretical knowledge. In the absence of a mark allocation, allow equal marks for each of the two requirements.

Easy marks. The factors influencing culture should be straightforward. If 'Company J' reminded you of Ouchi's Theory J, you might have realised that you could use his Theory Z model to explain how a Japanese managed plant would differ culturally from other Western plants (as required).

Factors influencing the culture of an organisation

An organisation's culture is influenced by many factors.

(a) **The organisation's founder**. A strong set of values and assumptions is set up by the organisation's founder, and even after he or she has retired, these values have their own momentum.

(b) **The organisation's history**. *Johnson and Scholes* state that the way an organisation works reflects the era when it was founded. The effect of history is indicated by stories, rituals and symbolic behaviour, which legitimise behaviour and promote priorities.

(c) **Leadership and management style**. An organisation with a strong culture recruits managers who naturally conform to it.

(d) **Structure and systems** affect culture as well as strategy. *Handy's* description of an Apollonian role culture (bureaucracy) is an example (among others) where organisational form has cultural consequences.

(e) **The environment** from which management and staff are drawn, and within which the organisation operates. Nations, regions, occupations, industry sectors and business types may act as different 'spheres' of culture, with their own distinctive values, norms and artefacts.

Why Company J's Western plant may develop a different culture to other Western plants

It is clearly Company J's intention to 'transfer' Japanese cultural values, and resulting management styles and techniques, to the new Western car plant. We are told that the plant will initially be staffed with Japanese managers and supervisors, using Japanese working practices – despite the fact that other employees will be sourced locally.

Given that leadership and managerial style are a key determinant of organisational culture, it should be clear that the Western culture (whichever one it is) will be influenced by Japanese managerial culture, which will be strongly expressed and modelled, and reinforced through work practices such as quality circles, Total Quality management and so on.

Although there has been some debate as to how far cultures can be 'transferred', or adopted by another culture, clusters of Japanese managerial techniques (such as quality circles and the 'lean manufacturing' values of Taichi Ohno at Toyota) have been widely adopted.

One model to explain why a Japanised culture will be different from other Western plants is William *Ouchi's* 'Theory Z'. Profiling American management culture as 'Theory A' and Japanese management as 'Theory Z', Ouchi showed that Japanisation would introduce a number of key values, including: consensus decision-making; a more collectivist (family-based) interpretation of the employment relationship; and industrial relations characterised by trust, co-operation and mutual adjustment (rather than unionisation, demarcation and artificial status barriers).

61 Corporate appraisal

Text references. Corporate appraisal is covered in Chapter 12.

Top tips. You should be very familiar with the concept of the corporate appraisal, but **the key with this question is tailoring your knowledge to the S Company scenario**. The strengths, weaknesses and threats facing the company are very plainly laid out. Opportunities may be less obvious, but consider the strengths of the company and you should be able to suggest where opportunities could lie. The examiner suggests up to six marks each could be earned for comments made as an internal review and an external review.

Look at our guidance on **how to approach questions** included in the front pages. Use the seven-step plan to guide you when you answer written questions.

Easy marks. As usual the easy marks are for definitions. You should be able to define corporate appraisal and SWOT analysis and discuss internal and external appraisals.

Examiner's comments. Answers should begin by **discussing** what is involved in a corporate appraisal. They should then **discuss** what is required in conducting an internal review and how the results of this can help T. Answers need to include an analysis of the external environment and how this review can help T. A common weakness was the failure to **apply** the findings of the corporate appraisal to the scenario given.

A corporate appraisal is 'a critical assessment of the strengths and weaknesses, opportunities and threats in relation to the internal and environmental factors affecting an entity in order to establish its condition prior to the preparation of the long term plan' (CIMA). S Company is concerned with securing its long-term growth, and T is undertaking a corporate appraisal as a first step.

This environmental assessment, and the analysis of internal resources and capabilities are summarised in a **SWOT analysis**.

Strengths and weaknesses

A strengths and weaknesses analysis is an **internal appraisal** and will identify firstly those areas of the business that have **strengths** that should be exploited by suitable strategies. In the case of S Company its chief strength lies in its record for product innovation, which has historically enabled it to be the market leader, and to increase its market share. The company is likely to have a good reputation that can be built on in future strategies developed by T. Product innovation is a distinctive competence for the company, so it should use this strength to create new opportunities.

Secondly, a **strengths and weaknesses analysis** will identify those areas of the business that are **weak** and which need strategies to improve them. A potential problem area identified in the scenario is that of cost control. Investment in R&D has meant that costs have spiralled, and the increased costs have been passed on to customers in the form of increased prices. As part of his strategic review, T may decide that rigorous cost control is necessary to halt this trend. By controlling costs, prices can come down and market share may increase.

An **external appraisal** is required to identify profit-making **opportunities** that can be exploited by the company's strengths, and also to anticipate environmental threats against which the company must protect itself. The company could employ the **PESTEL** framework which analyses influences on the strategic development of a company including political, environmental and legal factors. Another useful tool which assesses competitors is Porter's Five Forces. This would enable T to assess the competitive forces influencing the hair and body care industry.

Opportunities and threats

For **opportunities**, T needs to ask in his review:

(a) What opportunities exist in the hair and body care market? It might be possible to start selling to supermarkets for their 'own brand' ranges.

(b) What are competitors up to? A competitor profile may show that they are not yet able to match S Company for product innovation, and this should be exploited for competitive advantage.

When considering **threats**, T needs to understand the following:

(a) **What threats are likely to arise?** There is a threat emerging in the form of sales of own brand products. S Company may be able to convert this threat into a chance to extend its product market opportunities with its strong record on product innovation.

(b) **How will S Company and its competitors be affected?** Given S Company's strength in innovation, it may be better placed than some of its competitors to counter the rise of the supermarkets.

62 Strategic planning

Text references. Approaches to strategy are covered in Chapter 9.

Top tips. Consider the features of T's business described in the question. You need to use these in your answer to explain where formal strategic planning is not suitable for T's business. So you need to list the features of a rational or formal strategy process and **explain using the scenario why these don't apply to T's business**. However don't forget that at this level you are expected to argue the **pros and cons** of models and so there may be reasons why the formal planning approach is useful. Remember to state these too.

As a general guide, up to two marks were available for explaining the process of formal strategic planning and one mark each for outlining the reasons why formal planning would not apply in T's business.

Easy marks. The easy marks come from stating the definition and components of formal strategic planning.

Examiner's comments. This question was answered poorly. Most candidates failed to explain the relevance of formal strategic planning to a small business.

Strategic plans are **formal statements** of direction. The **rational model** of strategic planning is a logical and comprehensive approach. It follows a sequence starting with an analysis of the environment and the organisation. Then strategies are generated, evaluated and the best alternative is chosen. This alternative is then implemented.

This formal planning process suits organisations that operate in a **stable environment** and which have the **resources** to undertake strategic planning. From the information given, T's business exists in a **dynamic environment and has few resources to devote to planning.**

T cannot afford to take time away from his business to attend the seminar so it is unlikely that he would have the resources to devote to drawing up formal plans for the direction of the business.

His business has experienced unplanned growth over the past year and he has won a significant contract so the environment is certainly not **stable**. A formal process may be too static to keep up with the dynamic environment of T's business. It may also feel **alien** and be unhelpful in a small, creative business.

A formal model considers the **mission and objectives** of the business. The expectations of stakeholders must be considered when setting strategy. T is an owner manager and has few shareholders or stakeholders to answer to. Any **mission or objectives** for the business are those he has developed from the time that the business grew out of a hobby. These are likely to be inseparable from his own goals.

T's view of strategy is **emergent** rather than rational. **Emergent strategies** arise from ad hoc or even uncontrolled responses to circumstances. If they work they may then become formal strategies. T's recent business success has been unplanned which reinforces his view on the usefulness of responding to events.

A planning approach that considers **new products and markets** is part of the formal planning process. T is likely to stick with the products that he knows and that are creating growth for his business. His success is built on his own talents as a hobbyist and he is effectively a 'one man band'. He has also just won a significant contract. He is therefore unlikely to have the inclination or resources to pursue new opportunities at present.

However, T can learn some useful lessons from the formal planning approach. Whilst T need not undertake a full strategic planning exercise, he can adopt some of the most useful features maybe using a 'back of the envelope' approach. Thus, he needs to consider his competitive environment and do a SWOT analysis. This should help him see where his strengths and weaknesses lie.

63 Corporate governance and ethics

Text references. Corporate governance and ethics are covered in Chapter 10.

Top tips. Pick out the main flaws or issues in the company as you read through the question. Note these down using them to **sketch a plan** for answering the question. Your answer will be framed in terms of how these represent **corporate governance** or **ethical issues**. Make sure that you are familiar with the **Combined Code,** as you will need to refer to its main features when answering the question.

From the examiner's marking scheme and as a rough guide, expect one mark for an explanation of Corporate Governance and up to eight marks for issues facing the company with one mark each per issue mentioned and discussed. Then up to three marks for discussing the ethical issues that apply to the company. With these shorter questions, make sure you develop time management skills and stick to the time suggested by the marks given. Look back at our advice in the 'Passing P5' section of the front pages if you are unclear.

Easy marks. As usual the easy marks are for definitions. You should be able to make at least a couple of clear points based on the flaws listed.

Examiner's comment. In general the question was well answered. However some candidates failed to apply their knowledge to the company and its circumstances.

Corporate governance is the system by which organisations are directed and controlled. It addresses the need to ensure that directors use their power in the interest of the owners and shareholders, as **agents** appointed to run the business on their behalf. **Ethics** are the moral principles by which people act or do business.

There were three significant corporate governance reports during the 1990s. These were reports by **Cadbury, Greenbury** and **Hampel.** The reports were merged into a **Combined Code** in 1998 and listed companies are expected to comply with the **Combined Code**.

Y Company is seeking a stock exchange listing and so the company will be expected to comply with the Combined Code.

Poor corporate government

The company shows signs of several poor **corporate governance** practices. These include the following:

Autocratic leadership. M is an autocratic leader. Many corporate governance failures have been as a result of a single board member dominating decision-making and other members merely agreeing to their actions.

Non-separation of the roles of Chairman and Managing Director. M holds both posts in the company. His dual roles, and the power that they hold, mean that it is difficult for others to challenge his decisions. The Combined Code recommends that the two roles are kept separate to ensure good control and a balance of power.

Lack of board involvement. The Combined Code states that all listed companies should be led by an **effective** board and also requires a board to meet regularly and have certain matters reserved for its decision. The board meets infrequently and irregularly. It is **ineffective** in its role as a board evidenced by its reluctance to challenge M's decisions. It is also unlikely to be involved in an overview of activities and risks which is crucial given the poor state of control systems and M's disregard for procedure.

Non-executive directors. Y Company has a board comprised wholly of employees. The Combined Code requires listed companies to include non- executive directors to ensure balance and so that no one group dominate.

Non-disclosure of directors' remuneration. The chairman has put pressure on the FD to cover up a remuneration package that he set for himself. The Combined Code states that directors should not be involved in setting their own remuneration. The annual report should contain a statement about the remuneration policy for directors and details of each director's remuneration.

Lack of appropriate control systems and accountability in the company. The poor quality of accounting information in the company will be a major problem if the markets are trying to make a fair assessment of the company's value. The Code requires that a good system of control should be maintained and its effectiveness reviewed annually by the directors. The board should present a balanced and understandable assessment for the company's position and prospects in the annual report. An audit committee should be set up consisting of non-executive directors. This committee should review the audit and the independence of the auditors.

Ethical issues

The company also has **ethical issues**. M has decided to close the local factories and move production to a country with poor employment legislation and human rights record. The decision may be legal and justifiable in cost terms. However, businesses must consider **ethical values** too when they make decisions.

It has been suggested that ethical values include **ordinary decency**, which is respect for property, fairness and legality, and **distributive justice,** which is that rewards should be proportionate to the contributions made to the organisation. So, if these principles are applied to the decision to move production, it may be argued that the new workers should be rewarded for their labour in proportion to the contribution that they make.

Other **ethical issues** to consider are the **acceptance of bribes** and **insider dealing**.

Nonetheless, ethics does not exist in a vacuum and must be developed in line with the mores of the host country. What can be said is that M must make these decisions using some sort of **ethical framework** developed for Y Company to cover such decisions.

Finally, D is aware of some of the ethical issues and has voiced her concerns to the board. She may choose to **adopt an ethical stance** and '**whistle blow**' on M's activities. This may result in her losing her job, as the board have not shown any concern or inclination to confront M on his practices.

64 Role culture

Text references. Role culture is explained in Chapter 11 which also discusses organisational culture in general.

Top tips. In part (a), you are being directed towards a discussion of **role culture**. This organisation type is one defined by *Harrison* and later, *Handy* in his classification of four types of organisation culture. You need to define this first and then set out why it would no longer suit the company using the information found in the scenario.

In part(b) you can use Harrison and Handy's classification to select a suitable culture. This would be consistent with part(a). There are other possible cultural types such as those defined by *Denison, Miles and Snow* or *Deal and Kennedy*. These all look at **culture and strategy**. However Handy's model also considers the **employee**, which is a key aspect of the scenario. These other models don't do this to quite the same extent.

Easy marks. You should earn a couple of handy marks by defining role culture.

Examiner's comments. In part (a), too much reliance was placed on repeating material without remarking on why a role culture was no longer appropriate. In part (b), weaker answers did not recommend an appropriate culture.

(a) **Role culture and why it may no longer be appropriate for the company**

A **role culture** is a bureaucratic culture shaped by rationality, rules and procedures. It is typically stable, slow-changing formalised, and impersonal. Authority is based on position and function. Role cultures can be very efficient in stable environments where workers have the opportunity to gain expertise. This is one of *Harrison* and *Handy's* four possible **cultural** types for organisations.

E Company has experienced a **shift in its environment** away from a comfortable monopoly position to competition and is experiencing severe difficulties.

The stable, slow moving role culture is no longer suitable for a competitive environment where E needs to be flexible and innovative, quickly responsive to changes in the environment and competitor initiatives.

Workers have expertise but they are unwilling to collaborate and work outside their specialism or function. This hinders innovation and the ability to develop new services.

In summary, the role culture worked well or at least was more suited to E's situation as a monopoly provider. Once competition destabilised its environment, E found itself unable to cope with the need for organisational flexibility.

(b) **The type of culture to which the company now needs to move**

Using *Harrison* and *Handy's* classification the 'best fit' type of culture would be a **task culture**. The task culture is one where management is directed at solving problems and completing projects. **The focus is very much on getting the job done.** The culture is team-based, horizontally-structured, flexible and values expertise.

Management in E Company clearly need to **direct their energies into solving any problems and getting projects completed.** This requires focusing on outputs ie products and on resolving staff problems especially 'work to rule' attitudes.

This would enable **new innovations** in services to be offered to customers **sooner** than at present.

Staff must learn to work in teams which cross functional boundaries and draw on specialisms as they are needed. They need to embrace a culture of problem solving and team working to get new products and services into the market place.

65 Levels of strategy

Text references. Chapter 9 is a good source of information on levels of strategy in organisations.

Top tips. This question gives you considerable discretion to write on levels of strategy as the scenario is brief. However do refer to the scenario as **application** is key at this level. So pick out the features of the organisation: a leisure and entertainment business with ventures operating as separate businesses across the globe.

We suggest that you start with a brief definition of strategy and follow this with an explanation of the different levels of strategy illustrating each from the scenario. Keep each key point separate by starting a new paragraph. This also helps to break up your answer and makes it easier to mark. Remember you only have eighteen minutes to answer this question so keep your answer brief.

Aim for three to four points (or marks) per level of strategy and two to three for an introduction to the topic.

Easy marks. You should earn a couple of handy marks by defining each level of strategy.

Examiner's comments. Weaker answers discussed how strategy is formed rather than the different levels at which strategy should exist.

Strategy is a course of action including the specification of resources required to achieve a specific objective.

Organisations draw up strategies which are embodied in corporate plans. These are **translated into more detailed operational plans** which are then **filtered down the organisation**. In this way high-level objectives become detailed operational activities. The **activities at the lowest level are guided by and constrained by activities at higher levels** so that strategy is consistent throughout the organisation.

However strategy can be made at any level of the organisation not just at the top.

Corporate strategy is the most general level of strategy in an organisation. **It covers what types of business the company as a whole should be in and is therefore concerned with decisions of scope. Decisions are made at the strategic apex.** Corporate strategy also considers how this would match the expectation of stakeholders and what investment it needs to make to get there. This will be set out in its mission and stated as decisions on future acquisitions, mergers, divestments and so on. V plc currently operates in the leisure and entertainment industry. As a corporate strategy it would consider whether to diversify into other activities such as food retail or maybe limit its activities or even cut these back.

Business strategy defines how a business operates in a particular market or the activity of a particular business unit within the overall corporate strategy. This refers to how a business should segment its market and specialise in profitable areas or compete by offering a wider range of products. **Responsibility for this level of strategy will lie in each strategic business unit which will then make decisions on what strategies to adopt in its own markets.**

V plc has a range of ventures across the globe which cover a diverse number of activities from cinemas to casinos. Each business unit operates as a separate business. As such they are responsible for decisions on activity within their market or activity. **Porter's Five Forces** is an useful tool to consider competition from new entrants, substitutes, and competitors, and relative power of its suppliers and customers.

Operational and functional strategies involve decisions of strategic importance which are made at operational levels. These decisions include product pricing, investment in personnel and in plant. These strategic decisions would be made within the individual businesses by the operational managers who may decide on the price of cinema tickets, opening hours for casinos and buying new equipment for the fitness centres. The contributions of these different functions determine the success of the strategy as effectively a strategy is only **implemented** at this level. **So the key point here is that strategy is ultimately implemented at the operational level.**

66 Key influences

Text references. Chapter 10.

Top tips. All the professional accounting bodies are concerned about the recent decline in ethical standards in commercial organisations. This decline undermines public confidence in both the profession and the wider world of business. Refer to the **CIMA active verbs guidance** in the front pages to make sure you are clear on the difference between 'describe' and 'explain'. Use the advice in the 'Passing P5' section in the front pages on the **depth of discussion** to help you construct an answer to this longer question.

Easy marks. Generally, in questions with an ethical theme, it is appropriate to take a high moral stance. Do not propose the utterly impractical, but emphasise the need for lawful conduct and to be fair to all stakeholder groups. Note that this does not necessarily involve an unquestioning acceptance of the 'social responsibility' case: hard decisions may have to be made.

(a) **Key influences on ethical conduct**

Organisations have ethical climates, heavily influenced by their **external cultural environment**. Notions of right and wrong tend to be conditioned by history, the behaviour of respected leaders and so on. This may have a *positive* effect (eg the enshrining of moral values in a constitution and educational systems) or a *negative* effect: it has been reported, for example, 'former communist states have been tainted by corruption since bribery and the black market became a means of survival in over-regulated, centrally planned economies.' (*The Times)*

Within organisations, **positive influences** on the ethical conduct of individual managers may be created by:

(i) The **behaviour and stated ethical values of more senior managers**, modelling what is acceptable and desirable to lower levels of management

(ii) **Corporate value statements and codes of conduct,** setting out the principles and parameters of ethical behaviour. These must be supported by **rewards, sanctions and controls** in order to be effective. Ethical standards should be included as selection, reward and promotion criteria; as key learning/development targets; and as the subject of disciplinary frameworks. This is the basis of a 'compliance-based' approach to ethics management. If it is not in place, lip service can be paid to ethical behaviour, without any enforcement in conduct terms. This was said to be a major problem for *Enron*, for example.

(iii) A more **'integrity-based approach',** using ethical principles (rather than rules), and discussion forums and hotlines, enabling managers with ethical dilemmas to bring them into the open. This helps encourage all managers to develop a principled approach to decision-making. It may also involve policy protection for whistle-blowers, guaranteeing a confidential and supportive hearing for ethical concerns.

Professional staff and auditors have their own codes of professional ethics, setting out the specific requirements for objectivity, impartiality, confidentiality, duty of care and so on made by their own professional bodies. These are similarly enforced by disciplinary procedures and reinforced by educational, qualification and membership systems. They are also reinforced by procedural safeguards and checks, in the form of internal controls.

Both of these systems are of course also underpinned by **legal and regulatory frameworks**, imposing sanctions for non-compliance.

Meanwhile, however, it is important to recognise that there may be **negative influences** on conduct.

(i) **Personal amorality** (or cultural values perceived as unethical by a different culture) can lead to unethical conduct by an individual or group.

(ii) **Financial pressures** may be a problem for those in charge of funds. They may lead to fraudulent behaviour at the individual level (eg inflated expense claims or theft) to the corporate level (eg external pressure from shareholders to improve profitability can lead to **bribery** to win contracts). It is a specific threat to auditors, since efforts may be made to undermine their impartiality and objectivity.

(iii) **Trickle-down** of lack of ethical values may occur through the bad example or expressed values of senior managers and influencers. Unprincipled demands for improved performance may also put pressure on successive levels of the organisation. CIMA's own code specifically identifies pressure from a superior as a potential cause of ethical conflict for professional staff, for example.

(b) **How business and professional bodies can promote ethical behaviour**

Coercion is the fallback position of all systems of behaviour control, including law and ethical codes. If organisations and professions want their people to behave in accordance with a particular set of rules, they must be prepared to **enforce** them. **Professional bodies**, such as CIMA have a set of law-based procedures for doing just that. You may occasionally find reports of CIMA's internal disciplinary proceedings in '*Financial Management*'.

Organisations, too, are capable of enforcing their ideas about ethics. An allegation of unethical behaviour at *Boeing* in late 2003 led to the dismissal of the head of finance and subsequently to the resignation of *Phil Condit,* Chairman and Chief Executive.

If **a willingness to enforce them exists, codes of ethics can have an effect**, both in organisations and in professions. If breaches of such codes are ignored or condoned, they will be treated with contempt and be worse than useless, since they will demonstrate that senior officers are hypocrites as well as unethical in their behaviour.

Ethics management has several tasks.

(i) To define and give life to an organisation's defining values.
(ii) To create an environment that supports ethically sound behaviour
(iii) To instil a sense of shared accountability amongst employees.

There are two approaches to the management of ethics, according to *Paine*, the **compliance-based** and the **integrity-based**.

Compliance-based approach

A **compliance-based** approach is primarily designed to ensure that the company **acts within the letter of the law**, and that violations are prevented, detected and punished. Some organisations, faced with the legal consequences of unethical behaviour take legal precautions such as those below.

(i) Compliance procedures to detect misconduct
(ii) Audits of contracts
(iii) Systems to protect and encourage 'whistleblowers'
(iv) Disciplinary procedures to deal with transgressions

Corporate compliance is limited in that it relates only to the law, but legal compliance is 'not an adequate means for addressing the full range of ethical issues that arise every day'. This is especially the case in the UK, where **voluntary** codes of conduct and self-regulation are perhaps more prevalent than in the US.

The compliance approach also overemphasises the threat of detection and punishment in order to channel appropriate behaviour. Furthermore, mere compliance with the law is no guide to **exemplary** behaviour.

Integrity-based approach

An **integrity-based** approach treats ethics as an issue of organisation culture. It combines a concern for the law with an **emphasis on managerial responsibility** for ethical behaviour. Integrity strategies strive to define companies' **guiding values**, **aspirations** and **patterns of thought and conduct**. When integrated into the day-to-day operations of an organisation, such strategies can help prevent damaging ethical lapses, while tapping into powerful human impulses for moral thought and action. Such approaches assume that people are social beings with values that can be supported and refined. They attempt to integrate ethical values into the organisation (or profession) by providing guidance and consultation and by identifying and resolving problems.

67 F Company

Text references. Chapter 9.

Top tips. This question is rather puzzlingly worded. The requirements of either part (a) or part (b), if taken in isolation, are clear enough. However, when they are combined it is difficult to see where one ends and the other begins: part (a) asks, effectively for the benefits and drawbacks of the policy suggested by G, while part (b) asks for a comparison of the views of G and P. The problem would appear to be avoiding in the answer to part (b) repetition of much that was said in the answer to part (a).

We think the best way to resolve this conundrum is to note carefully the last sentence of paragraph three of the scenario and to build an answer to part (b) around a comparison between the positioning and resource-based approaches to strategy. We can then relegate the formal, top-down model to a minor role as just one approach to a positioning-based strategy. **This confusion shows the importance of planning your answers carefully**. Read our advice on how to approach questions in the 'Passing P5' section in front pages to help you here.

You may care to note the way we have made reference to theorists in our answer: this sort of thing adds authority, but you have to get the names right! There were up to two marks for each benefit and each drawback in part (a). In part (b), there were a maximum of six marks each for key points on the positioning approach, and the resource based approach.

We have included more points in our answer than you need for a good answer. Extra material is identified as alternative answers which you can use for revision.

Easy marks. Candidates who have a basic knowledge of the rational model should find part (a) fairly easy to score a pass mark in.

(a) **Benefits and drawbacks of a top-down approach to strategy**

The most comprehensive kind of formal, top down strategic planning is described by the **rational model** of strategic analysis, strategic choice and strategy implementation (the ACI model).

This is a logical and comprehensive approach, which attempts to consider all relevant information and options. It is primarily top-down, because of the need for high-level information and decision making: strategic decisions then 'cascade down' to lower levels of the organisation for implementation at a tactical and operational level.

Benefits of top-down planning for F Company

F Company seems to be particularly concerned about **developments in its immediate market environment**, having lost market share and to new entrants and failed to respond to customer demand for new products. Proper, continuing **environmental analysis** should be one of the most important features, therefore, of any system of planning introduced by the company. This would be a fundamental aspect of the rational model.

The rational model could bring other advantages to F Company.

(i) It helps the organisation to take a **long view** and avoid short-termism while at the same time providing a sensible approach to the uncertainty of the future.

(ii) It guides the **allocation of resources**.

(iii) It **co-ordinates the activities** of the various parts of the organisation, ensuring the integration of operational management decisions into the higher strategy, the wider organisational context and longer term goals. This is another particular concern G has about F Company

Alternative answers

(iv) It sets a standard by which the actual performance of the organisation is **measured and controlled**.

(v) It comforts providers of finance in particular and encourages **suppliers and employees** to think in terms of a long-term relationship.

(vi) The process of forming strategy requires wide and complex input so it can have a beneficial effect on managers' **personal development** and awareness and can assist with management succession planning.

Drawbacks of top-down planning methods

The concept of formal processes for strategy generation and their limited success in practice has led to criticisms of both the rational model and the very idea of strategic planning as a separate business activity.

(i) The formal approach encourages a sense of **omniscience and control** among planners: this is dangerous because of the **inherent unpredictability of the business environment**, which F Company has already had experience of. In practice, strategic thinking tends to be iterative and even muddled, with the various processes and stages being undertaken on an *ad hoc* basis. Moreover, many developments of strategic significance, or information about them, occur at **operational** level. Environmental uncertainty also tends to lead managers to adopt an approach of **bounded rationality**, satisfying themselves with solutions that are acceptable rather than ideal.

(ii) There is an associated problem of **detachment**: planners' tendency to assume that strategy can be divorced from operations is inappropriate. Planners rarely have to implement the strategies they devise and feedback occurs too late or is badly filtered. Similarly, more junior managers, not directly involved in the planning process may misunderstand or resist the plans they are required to implement.

(iii) The idea of the **learning organisation** has been applied to strategy on the basis that an organisation's strengths and weaknesses can be in constant flux and strategy should reflect current developments as a kind of learning process itself.

Alternative answers

(iv) The formal approach is usually couched in terms of a **planning cycle** and this may extend for up to five years. Even a one year cycle is not responsive enough to changing circumstances.

(v) The **expense and complexity** of the formal approach are inappropriate for smaller businesses. Cost control is important for any organization and F Company, as an under-performing medium-sized business, must be particularly wary about spending on functions that do not have an immediate impact on the bottom line

(vi) There has been much comment on the place of **strategic objectives**. A sociological perspective, such as that of *Cyert and March*, views the emergence of strategic objectives as the result of a **political** or **bargaining process** involving a variety of priorities and interest groups. Here we may remark that today the capitalist, free market philosophy seems more strongly established than ever and most Western business organisations acknowledge the creation of shareholder value as their primary objective.

(vii) There is a view that great strategies should not really be rational at all, but should emerge from **inspiration and entrepreneurial talent**. *Brunsson* argues for the selection of a reasonable course of action from among a small number of choices, while *Ohmae* finds that good strategy is made by practical people who 'have an intuitive grasp of the basic elements of strategy'. The criticisms are directed less at planning in principle, than at the assumption that **planning can create strategies** as opposed to supporting strategic decisions, co-ordinating them and mobilising resources.

(b) **Alternative views of competitive advantage**

Positioning approach

The views of G and P represent opposite sides in a current debate about the best way to approach strategy. The rational model is only the most formal of several approaches to a strategic method that is based the process of **adapting the organisation to its environment**. This adaptive or **positioning-based strategy** approach, which pays great attention to markets, consumers and competitors, may be contrasted with the **resource-based approach**.

(i) In many modern industries, the **rate of environmental change is too great** for effective positioning strategies to be developed. F Company's experience seems to bear this out. The rate of economic and social change brought about by globalisation; shorter product lifecycles; rapid technological innovation; and changing consumer taste all make a measured response out of date before it can take effect.

(ii) **Positioning advantages cannot be sustained in the long term**. Advantageous product market positions are **too easy to copy** to last long and more rapid product lifecycles erode initial advantage. F Company is suffering from the efforts of agile new entrants to its industry.

(iii) It is more difficult to **adapt the organisation** than to **adopt a new environment**. The positioning approach may require significant change within the firm, which is difficult to achieve. It may be easier to move to a market environment that suits existing arrangements, skills, culture and capabilities.

Resource based approach

The resource based approach to strategy emphasises the **possession of scarce resources** and **core competences** by the organisation. Strategy, it is suggested, consists of exploiting such resources and core competences in order to gain competitive advantage. This approach lies behind the growing practice of **outsourcing**: the organisation concentrates its efforts on those parts of its operations that no other organisation can perform for it.

Resources may be obvious things such as favoured access to a particular **raw material** or a piece of legally protected **intellectual property**; they may also take less tangible forms, such as a well– known **brand**. F Company may be able to utilize these ideas by emphasizing **quality** or **innovation** in its future operations.

It is important to realise that it is possible to acquire or develop new competences, but this takes time. The possession of a particular advantage thus constitutes a competitive advantage but its validity may decline if other firms develop equivalent capabilities.

Competences must therefore be developed and kept up to date on a continuing basis. *Johnson and Scholes* define core competences as those that both **outperform competitors** and are **difficult to imitate**.

The resource-based approach is not without its difficulties.

(i) Core competences are **difficult to identify and assess**: a wrong appraisal could lead to the loss of wider competence or source of advantage by misdirected outsourcing.

(ii) Attempts to apply core competences (or other resources) widely across a range of markets and operations may make the firm **vulnerable to more focused, single market operations**.

(iii) The emphasis on unique resources is reminiscent of the 'product orientation' decried by marketing experts: competitors who are more in touch with **market requirements** may be more successful. On the other hand, a strategy based on a sequence of unique products, as in the pharmaceutical industry, can be successful.

(iv) **Investors** may or may not be convinced by the resource based view. Where there is a clear, identifiable and credible strategy, they may well maintain their support. However, a strategy based on exploiting existing markets may be more intuitively acceptable.

(v) The competence approach seems to support ideas such as cross-functional, activity based management, team working and the use of network structures both within the organization and in its relations with suppliers and customers. However, the need to safeguard core competence capability against erosion by staff turnover and direct sharing of know-how may lead to a **perceived need for close control of activities** and narrow limits on outsourcing.

68 X Company

(a) **Using the five forces model to assets industry competition in country Y**

Text references. Chapter 12 covers Porter's five forces and Chapter 1 covers *Hofstede's model.*

Top tips. *Michael Porter's* five competitive forces should be well known to students. It is very important to understand their purpose, to be able to apply them to a situation and to know how the results of any analysis should be interpreted. Look back at our guidance on the approach to questions included in the front pages. This should help you answer this question well. Aim for up to three marks for each force correctly described and **applied** to the scenario.

Easy marks. Easy marks could be gained by identifying the five forces. To gain the bulk of the marks however it was necessary to set out how, in general terms, they could be used to assess industry competition and then to set out in relation to each force the market circumstances which would tend to increase or reduce the strength of that force, with intelligent application to the drinks industry.

The level of competition which X Company and its joint venture partner will face in country Y will depend on the strength of the competitive forces at work in that country.

Michael Porter identified **five market factors**, or forces, that will drive the competitive position of a given supplier in a given market.

These five forces, taken together, will provide an overall assessment of X Company's competitive position in country Y. Entry into country Y would be suggested if, overall, the five forces were found to be weak and the prospective returns high.

Taking each force in turn:

Barriers to entry

X is considering **entry to the market** via a joint venture with a partner established in the drinks distribution business in country Y. This approach may facilitate its entry and enable it to overcome barriers to entry and commence operations relatively quickly.

Substitutes

Substitutes are products that differ from the product in question but provide similar satisfactions. In the case of soft drinks, substitutes might include some alcoholic drinks, such as beer; beverages such as tea and coffee; and small luxury or 'treat' items such as sweets and ice cream. X Company could use the experience of its partner to assess the importance of such substitutes.

Customers' bargaining power

Customers will be looking to achieve lower prices or to obtain a higher quality soft drink. If they have the power to get what they want they will force down the profitability of the firms in the drinks industry.

The strength of the threat from the **bargaining power of customers** will depend on a number of factors.

(i) **The level of differentiation amongst soft drink manufacturers** (including 'intangible' aspects such as brand strength).

(ii) **The cost to the customer of switching from one supplier to another** – X company's customers are likely to be retailers in which case they will exercise considerable power via their ability to switch easily between suppliers.

(iii) **Whether a customer's purchases from the industry represent a large or small proportion of the customer's total purchases.** In this case retailers could represent a material threat if – as in the UK – a small number of very large retailers account for a substantial proportion of soft drink sales and are in a position to drive a very hard bargain in relation to the prices paid to the manufacturers. X company could seek to counter such a threat by investment in their brands.

Suppliers' bargaining power

Suppliers can influence the profitability of a firm by exerting pressure for higher prices or by reducing the quality of the goods and services which they supply.

The **bargaining power of the supplier** depends on a number of factors.

(i) The number of suppliers in the industry
(ii) The importance of the supplier's product to the firm
(iii) The cost to the firm of switching from one supplier to another.

Given the widely available nature of the ingredients needed for soft drink manufacture it is unlikely that suppliers to X Company will be limited and hence the power of suppliers is likely to be modest.

Competitive rivalry

The intensity of **competitive rivalry** within the soft drinks industry will be driven by the number of companies operating in this sector, the anticipated industry growth rates and the profitability of the industry as a whole. If the market is dominated by multinationals with strong brands and there is modest growth and profitability levels this market will not be attractive to Company X. If at the other extreme a large number of small local suppliers dominate the market place, the margins being achieved are substantial and there are no well established brands the market opportunities for X Company could be significant.

(b) **Using the Hofstede model**

Top tips. *Hofstede's* work on national cultural differences is given prominence in the Study Text chapter on Management and students should not have found this question difficult. Students would have done well to adopt an approach that began with a **summary** of Hofstede's findings and their **significance** in terms of their impact on the behaviour of individuals at work and the way things are done in organisations. Of the ten marks available here, aim for two marks for each dimension and the remainder on an introduction explaining the model. This was a question in the May 2006 exam and the examiner said that many candidates seemed unprepared for it.

Easy marks. Easy marks could be gained by setting out the four dimensions of the Hofstede model in which national culture varies and explaining what each seeks to measure. More marks were available to those students able to explain how a country's position on the scale was likely to be reflected in that country's managerial style.

National cultures and **value systems** can be as distinctive as corporate cultures and value systems. It is potentially very important therefore for Company X to assess the compatibility of its strategy with the culture of country Y.

Hofstede sought to explain national differences by identifying key dimensions in the value systems of all countries. Each country is represented on a scale for each dimension so as to explain and understand values, attitudes and behaviour.

In particular, *Hofstede* pointed out that countries differ on the following dimensions.

(i) **Power distance**. This dimension measures how far superiors are expected to exercise power. In a high power-distance culture, the boss decides and people do not question. X Company needs to find out what organisations in Country Y fit into this continuum especially in relation to its current business model and possibly modify its local operation accordingly.

(ii) **Uncertainty avoidance**. Some cultures prefer clarity and order, whereas others are prepared to accept novelty. This affects the willingness of people to *change* rules, rather than simply obey them. X Company may need to tailor its current operations to suit the way the local workforce makes decisions.

(iii) **Individualism-collectivism**. In some countries individual achievement is what matters. In a collectivist culture people are supported and controlled by their in-group and put the interests of the group first. For X, this means the local organisation would need to think about how important individual achievement, relationships in the organisation and achievement of the task is.

(iv) **'Masculinity'.** In 'masculine' cultures assertiveness and acquisitiveness are valued. 'Masculine' cultures place greater emphasis on possessions, status, and display as opposed to quality of life and caring for others. X needs to understand how local norms would alter its management of the local business and educate its managers to expect possible differences.

Hofstede grouped countries into **eight clusters** using these dimensions. Countries in the 'Anglo group' (the UK, the USA) for example were found to be comfortable with less direction and order than their counterparts in the 'more developed Asian group' (ie Japan). This suggests that typical UK management styles may not work well in Japan and vice-versa.

Hofstede's work will be of particular relevance to X Company's intentions to joint venture with a company in country Y. Ideally, there should be minimal differences between the two cultures. Where differences are found to exist, plans should be made to overcome any problems that might result.

69 Imperial Traders plc

Text references. Chapter 12.

Top tips. It will be necessary to differentiate carefully between the topics that are relevant to part (a) and those that are relevant to part (b), since the effects of relocation and the benefits of thinking about it are clearly entwined. In essence the answer to part (a) is that a sensible decision can be taken, while that to part (b) is a discussion of the balance of considerations leading to the decision in part (a). This kind of complexity in the logic of a question is, unfortunately, not particularly unusual. You can help yourself here by **planning** your answer ahead of writing it out. This will help you separate the requirements for the two parts and ensure you have enough points to make in each part.

Easy marks. In part (a), some easy marks will be available simply for explaining the nature of a position audit.

(a) **Position audit**

A position audit is part of the strategic planning process which examines the current state of the entity in respect of:

(i) resources of tangible and intangible assets and finance;
(ii) products, brands and markets;
(iii) operating systems such as production and distribution;
(iv) internal organisation;
(v) current results;
(vi) returns to stockholders.

The question asked is **'Where are we now?'**. It is the beginning of the rational strategic planning process, on the assumption that in order to reach a desired objective you need to have a good idea as to where you are starting from and what resources, strengths and weaknesses you are dealing with. This will enable Imperial Traders plc to assess the extent to which continuing operations can contribute towards its goal, and to develop strategies to fill the gap between the goal and what is currently achievable.

Only after such a position audit is carried out, can management decide:

(i) **Whether to move at all**
(ii) **If a move is desirable, where to go to**
(iii) **How the move will be implemented successfully.**

Benefits of a position audit for IT plc

Benefits in carrying out a position audit in respect of this decision revolve around the role of Head Office.

(i) **Head office might simply set financial targets** and **let subsidiaries get on with meeting them**, avoiding interference with tactical or day to day decisions. In this case the role of Head Office will be to communicate with the investment community, to be a central location for financial reporting, and as a domicile for the company so that it can take advantage of a favourable tax regime. Thus it might be **better to keep it in the UK** for the benefit of the company's investors. Moreover, the City of London is a centre of world finance, and if the firm's activities require a great deal of financial sophistication, London might be the place to stay.

(ii) The **Head Office may take a hands-on approach** to the running of the company. If all its activities are heavily interrelated, Head Office coordination may be essential for the company's successful functioning. A position audit of the company as a whole would identify those **regions which are most critical to its long term success**. If that region is Japan, for example, this might be a good reason for relocating to that country.

(iii) The position audit should identify all the major costs and benefits of such a move, in a formal way, and so should result in a better decision.

(b) **Effects of relocating to a Pacific Rim country**

The proposed relocation will impact on each of the areas examined in the position audit.

(i) **Tangible assets.** For example, Imperial Traders will need to sell its London accommodation. The price it receives may be a major factor in the economic benefits of the relocation decision. It will also have to buy office space in its new location. The relative price of office space in each country will differ significantly. Japan, despite the current slump in land prices, is still extremely expensive. Perhaps an Australian location would be cheaper.

(ii) **Finance**. Imperial Traders will be moving from London, which has one of the world's most developed capital markets. It must ensure that its needs are as well satisfied in one of the Pacific Rim countries? A country with a relatively open financial system, such as Australia, might be a better than, say, Korea. The company will already deal with providers of trade finance, so this should not be any great problem.

(iii) **Products and brands.** We do not know which products are Imperial Traders plc's particular speciality. It might specialise in trading commodity products (like wool from Australia to textile factories elsewhere) or it might specialise in trading manufactured goods. It might not specialise at all.

(iv) **Markets.** If Imperial Traders plc is basically a transport and distribution company, active in several areas, then the domicile of its Head Office is unlikely to matter very much in terms of the goods it trades, nor in attracting business. However, moving Head Office closer to its main markets may enhance Head Office's market knowledge. If Head Office plays a coordinating role, it might be able to develop a better strategic vision as to where it wants to be if this function is located in its main market.

(v) **Operating systems**. The firm will have to arrange appropriate and secure telecommunications links, especially for the transfer of commercial documentation by fax or email. If most of its activities before the move were based in the region, changes should not be too drastic, but the firm will need to develop the right system for the Head Office function.

(vi) **Internal organisation**. This is where the difference will be greatest. Many of the London based staff may not wish to be relocated, and might leave the company. The company, moreover, might wish to avoid the expense of relocation, and prefer to recruit staff locally or transfer staff from the company's divisions in the regions to the new head office function. There are likely to be redundancy costs in the UK, and the cost of hiring and training staff in the area.

(vii) **Current results**. There will be a number of costs entailed in the move, and perhaps some loss of efficiency in the Head Office function. Careful planning should minimise this risk. It is possible that the firm might receive relocation subsidies from some countries, or it may be able to negotiate a tax holiday if the country wishes it to locate there.

(viii) **Returns to stockholders.** Initially, there might be an adverse effect, owing to the costs of the move. Later, if the move of Head Office significantly affects the firm's trading patterns or financial arrangements, the effect could be large. For example, the firm might have used Sterling more often than necessary as there was a London Head Office. As currency flows are likely to remain within the Pacific Rim region, the currency risk will be different. This might significantly affect the reported returns to stockholders, who are based in the UK. Furthermore, if the company can find capital at cheaper rates than in the UK this will reduce its interest charge, and might make certain activities appear more attractive.

(c) **Cultural differences in Pacific Rim countries**

A number of cultural differences may be experienced on relocation.

(i) **Language**. If the Head Office staff relocate to Australia, there will be no problem with language, as English is spoken there. English is used widely in Malaysia. In Korea or Japan, however, while English is taught, staff will find it hard to get by without a good working knowledge of Korean or Japanese.

(ii) **Business culture**. Different cultures have different ways of doing business, arranging deals and so forth. UK staff will have to get used to this in all of the countries mentioned.

(iii) **Different legal systems**. Australia's legal system is probably most like the UK's.

(iv) **Women**. The relative inequality of women in Japanese society is greater than that of the UK. Female executives may find it harder to be accepted by Japanese counterparts. (At the same time, this is an **opportunity** for the firm to recruit talented female employees who might be ignored by more chauvinist local managers.)

(v) **Personal problems**

(1) Newly expatriate staff will need to adjust to different climate, diet and working hours.

(2) Those with **families** will have to find education provision for their children, and perhaps employment for spouses. The firm might have to run a cultural adjustment program to help them cope. People might have initial difficulty in forming friendships if social mores are very different.

70 Bowland Carpets

Text references. Chapters 9 and 12.

Top tips. It is very important in a question like this not to generalise but to **relate the answer to the scenario**. Marks would be specifically awarded for Bowland's **competences**, **entry barriers** for Bowland and Bowland's **strategy**. Look back at the guidance in 'Approach to questions' if you get stuck when drafting your answer.

Easy marks. Competences and critical success factors are difficult and complex topics. However, a little background economic knowledge and clear thinking should enable you to come up with a few barriers to entry. Try using the value chain as a model of a business to focus your thoughts on how and where such barriers might arise.

(a) **Do Bowland's distinctive competences match the key success factors for change?**

Critical success factors are a small number of areas in which (a) satisfactory results will enable successful competitive performance and (b) an organisation *must* excel in order to outperform competitors. Having identified its CSFs, a business can identify the processes and activities which yield each CSF: that is, its core competences. **Distinctive competences** are the unique or hard-to-imitate skills and processes that give the organisation its competitive advantage.

Most organisations doing a SWOT analysis will find a mismatch between its CSFs and its core competences at any given stage. A company may be successful at establishing a strong position during the early stages of market development, only to lose ground later when the key success factors have changed. With **consumer products** marketing and distribution skills are dominant during the early phases but operations and manufacturing become more crucial as the product moves into the maturity and decline stage.

Bowland's distinctive competences

Bowland UK's competences are the ability to:

(i) Offer a wide range of high quality products at **competitive prices**.
(ii) Sustain **powerful brand names**, presence in different market segments.
(iii) Sustain **good relationships** with distributors.

Success factors for Bowland's new strategy

The proposed option of vertical integration into retailing raises a set of key success factors which will capitalise on some of these competences. However, there are gaps which are a cause for concern.

The **key success factors** for vertical integration into retail sales which have been developed in the US will not be totally transferable to the UK and the domestic company has no expertise in this field.

(i) **Distribution.** It is not clear whether the intention is to introduce this strategy as an addition to the current distribution network or instead of it. Both of these options would affect the **relationship with distributors** that has built up over a period and could be very **damaging to sales**. To compensate for this loss, Bowland Carpets would need to have a strong **geographical** presence either in High Street positions or in out of town developments. This could be **very costly** in both site selection and development.

(ii) **Expertise** in **retailing** and **distribution**. Staffing and servicing the retail outlets and training the staff in the skills required will be time consuming and expensive. When customers buy carpets they expect a measuring, fitting and laying service as well as after-sales support. It may be that the UK company can learn from the USA but the culture of marketing household durables is different in both countries.

(iii) The **ability to provide a choice of products and services for the customer**. If there is insufficient choice, Bowland Carpets will have to find competitive manufacturers to fill the gap. This action may defeat the strategy to raise the sales in the **domestic** carpet market.

The initial conclusion is that Bowland's distinctive competences are currently unlikely to support it in achieving its key success factors for the strategic change.

(b) **Entry barriers prevalent in the carpet retailing sector**

(i) The number of established carpet retailers in an already mature market
(ii) The variety of own brands available in dominant department stores
(iii) The cost, availability and maintenance of suitable retail sites
(iv) Suitable suppliers and reasonable terms
(v) The retailing skills which will need to be developed
(vi) Marketing investments (research, staffing)
(vii) The ability to offer a broad product line

(c) **Key external influences**

An external environmental analysis identifies emerging trends, **opportunities** and **threats** created by the forces outside the organisation. Firms must avoid major surprises by anticipating major changes in their business circumstances. They must also make daily responses to changes among their customers, suppliers and workforce. Those who discover the longer-term patterns can decide whether they pose a threat or an opportunity and can gain a head start on their competitors.

Specific influences may be identified through micro (competitive) and macro environmental analysis (eg using the PEST model).

(i) The **competitive** environment. Knowledge of the reactions of the other players in the market, both manufacturers and retailers, could be crucial to the success or otherwise of a new entrant's plan. Established businesses can adopt **retaliation strategies** to make it difficult for new companies to enter the market.

(ii) **Economic** factors include the **rate of growth** and the associated increase/decrease in **disposable income** the **rate of inflation**, the state of the domestic housing market (house moves are often associated with new refurbishments) unemployment, interest rates and the availability of credit, taxation levels and incentives.

(iii) **Political** factors include laws on the safety of the product, town planning, selling practices adopted and the way a firm treats its employees.

(iv) The **social, demographic and cultural** environment analysis would highlight issues such as: the growth or decline in population; changes in ages when people leave home and start their own household; trends in house refurbishments; trends towards car-centred shopping in superstores and out of town shopping 'cities'.

(v) The **technological** environment. Consumers expect modern carpets to have properties which keep stains and insects away. The manufacturing environment is undergoing rapid changes with the growth of advanced manufacturing technology. Retail outlets are using point of sale equipment which can be used for control of inventory and to analyse the customer trends. Some DIY stores allow customers access to large cutting machines to avoid expensive cutting and laying services.

71 Transaction cost theory

Text references. Transaction costs are covered in Chapter 9 and both the shamrock organisation and flexible firm models are covered in Chapter 2.

Top tips. What do people actually do in organisations? This question is all about the theory that organisation structure is determined by the relative costs of conducting activities either through the external market, or through the internal hierarchy. For example, A asks B to type up a letter. B provides this service (and others) for A in exchange for a monthly salary. In terms of what is achieved this is exactly the same as if A worked for one organisation and B worked for an independent typing bureau. A could engage in a transaction with the typing bureau to get the letter typed. The suggested marks in the examiner's marking guide give up to three marks each for explaining transaction cost theory, hierarchy solutions and market solutions. Analysing transaction costs by referring to N's restructure could earn up to seven marks.

In part (b) there were up to six marks available for different principles of flexibility and up to nine marks for applying one of the models. We have chosen the shamrock model made popular by *Handy*. You could equally use the flexible firm model.

The examiner's comments on this question show the importance of **knowing what you are writing about** and not using the wrong theory or information to answer a question.

Easy marks. Easy marks are for defining transaction costs and explaining the leaves of the shamrock.

Examiner's comments. In part (a), candidates need to explain transaction cost theory and then use this to analyse the restructuring strategy proposed by D.

Good answers will also identify the **benefits** and **limitations** of the restructure strategy.

In part (b) answers needed to start by explaining the types of flexibility in an organisation. Then an explanation of **either** the flexible firm model or the shamrock organisation was needed, and how that could help N achieve flexibility.

Common errors included, in part (a) discussing **outsourcing** rather than answering the question. In part (b) many candidates didn't read the question properly and explained **both** models thereby wasting time.

(a) **Transaction cost theory and restructure strategy**

Transaction cost theory

In its most fundamental form, all economic activity consists of the provision of goods and services in return for reward. These exchanges are called **transactions**. The great degree of specialisation in modern economies requires that many transactions take place in a highly co-ordinated manner. Generally, there are **two ways of achieving this** co-ordination: **through hierarchies (or organisations)** and **through market relationships**. Transaction cost analysis aims to establish which is the more cost-effective method for a given set of transactions. The costs are easy to determine in a market relationship. They are more difficult to establish when exchanges take place in an organisational setting, but they are just as real and just as relevant to decision-making.

Williamson described what he termed the 'M-form' organisation, which combines a **mixture of external markets** and **hierarchical organisation**. This allows the mixing of the formal hierarchy, which controls strategy, and the market, in which the day-to-day activities take place. **Thus at divisional level some competition takes place, not just between the divisions and their external competitors, but also between the divisions for internal allocations of resources.**

The modern impact of transaction cost analysis has been to show that many goods and services that organisations have traditionally provided for themselves from internal resources could be provided more cheaply by contracting with external suppliers. However, this process of outsourcing has to be used with care, since competitive advantage lies in the possession of resources and competences that competitors cannot obtain or imitate. It is not, therefore, good sense to attempt to outsource these resources and competences. **D must therefore decide which activities are crucial to N Company's success. These should be retained and nurtured; the rest may be outsourced.**

Restructure strategy

D is proposing a restructure of N that will see:

(i) **Manufacturing plants closed, and more bought-in products.** This is a recognition that the market may be able to provide cheaper components than N can make. The manufacturing plants may need to demonstrate that they can match the prices and quality being offered in the external market. With increased competition in the sector, N needs to make sure that its prices to customers are competitive. Reducing their cost is the obvious first step.

(ii) **A greater emphasis upon selling those components.** It may be that D considers marketing to be N Company's core strength; if so, this emphasis would work well with reduced manufacturing capacity. However, the 'off-shoring' of the customer call centre sounds like a risky move if this is the case, since this centre is one of the Company's main points of contact with its customers.

(iii) **The outsourcing of non-key functions such as cleaning and catering.** This would be the classic application of transaction cost analysis as outlined above. These are definitely not core activities and should be provided at the lowest price: if contractors can provide them more cheaply, they should be engaged.

(b) **Achieving flexibility using 'flexible firm' or 'shamrock organisation' models**

***Handy* defines the shamrock organisation as a 'core of essential executives and workers supported by outside contractors and part time help'**. Such a structure permits the buying in of services as needed, with consequent reductions in overhead costs. This structure also allows for a greater **flexibility** by cutting staff costs, being flexible with numbers of staff and finally with the skills available from core and drafted-in staff.

The first leaf of the shamrock is the **professional core**, consisting of the staff whose collective expertise defines the organisation's core competence and what its business is. They are essential for the ongoing growth of the organisation. For N Company in its new guise, this might consist of buyers to source cheaper components and a team of highly trained sales staff at the outlets to sell them. There would also be a key team of engineers and designers for the products that would still be manufactured in-house. All of the head office functions that are being retained rather than outsourced would also fall within this category.

The next leaf of the shamrock is made up of **self employed technicians** or **professionals** who are hired on contract on an ad-hoc basis as required. They are paid a fee rather than a salary, and do not receive benefits such as paid holidays. Staff in the newly outsourced functions (catering, cleaning, maintenance) would find themselves within this category. They would be providing support to the key business without attracting additional overhead costs, and could be called upon as business conditions demanded.

The third leaf comprises the **contingent workforce**, whose employment derives from external demand. These people perform routine work without a career track, and are usually employed on a temporary and part-time basis. Staff in the manufacturing plants, some of the staff in the retail outlets and perhaps some in head office could be employed on this basis. The overseas call centre staff would also be regarded as a contingent workforce.

72 Resource based view

Text references. Chapter 9 includes useful material to help answer part (a) of this question and Chapter 12 for part (b).

Top tips. In part (a) you will need to refer closely to the characteristics of the company to illustrate your explanation of the resource based view. **Explain** is a fairly low level verb so you just need to show you know what the resource based view is and illustrate it from the scenario. Make sure you do show the **extent to which** the company is adopting the resource based view however as this is asked for specifically. You can earn around four marks for explaining the basic principles of the resource based view. Aim for two marks per point of application of the model to C Company.

We have written a short preamble setting the resource based approach in the context of overall strategic planning and a short explanation of the positioning strategy to illustrate the differences between the two approaches. This is not needed in your answer and is for revision only.

Part (b) looks at how *Porter's* value chain can be used to analyse the company's **internal position**. You need to **show** how the nine elements in the value chain are reflected in the company. Once again we have included a short introductory explanation, this time of the value chain. We have not identified corresponding activities in the company for all nine of the activities in the value chain, only those we believe apply. Aim for a mark per point made on the application of the value chain to C Company. You should also be able to get a couple of marks for an introduction explaining the value chain framework.

Easy marks. Show your knowledge, in a couple of sentences, of the resource based view and the value chain.

Examiner's comments. Too many answers just reiterated the core competences mentioned in the scenario without explaining how the resource based view could deliver competitive advantage. In part (b) weaker answers described the value chain model but failed to apply it to the company.

(a) **The extent to which the company is adopting this strategic approach to gain competitive advantage, referring to the Resource based view**

A **strategy** is a course of action including the **specification of resources** required to achieve a specific objective. Organisations use **environmental analysis** as part of their strategic planning process. This information from environmental analysis can be used to take one of two possible strategic approaches. These are the **positioning** approach and the **resource based** approach.

Resource based view

C Company is using a deliberate strategic approach to achieve success and market leadership. This approach uses the **resources** the company has to achieve its objectives. This follows the **resource based** approach to strategy which suggests that the **main source of competitive advantage lies in how the organisation exploits its distinctive internal competences and resources**. Strategic objectives are set by reference to what the organisation is best able to do or do better than its competition.

Resources may be tangible, such as the quality of the company's recipes and cocoa beans. Less tangible resources can include a brand or reputation, and it is clear that the company has built up a strong brand. The research information that the company has built up can be seen as a resource to be drawn upon or even reflecting a competence shown by the company in acquiring and using market data.

Competences are abilities to do something well which would include the skills of staff involved in making the chocolates, the marketing capability of the company, its flexible and innovative approach to new product development and its successful use of IT. Competences reflect a real **competitive advantage** as it can take time to acquire or develop these in a company. Competences therefore need to be developed and kept up to date on a continuing basis to retain the relative advantage that a market leader possesses.

Positioning approach

This approach differs to the **positioning approach** which suggests that the main source of competitive advantage lies in how the organisation fits its strategy to its external environment. Strategic objectives are set by reference to market or product opportunities and threats and resources used to get the organisation to where it wants to be in the market by exploiting these opportunities and avoiding threats.

(b) **How the value chain framework would help the company to understand its internal position**

Value chain analysis considers how well an organisation is using its resources and how much value is added after those resources are acquired. It identifies the way in which the firm organises its activities. These activities are the actual work that is done not the functions which do it.

The value chain is a model of nine value activities which procure inputs, process them and add value to them to generate outputs for customers. The chain also shows the **relationships** between the nine activities. A value chain analysis of C Company would help it understand how its activities add value to the resources it uses. These are

(i) **Primary activities**

Primary activities are those directly related to production, sales, marketing, delivery and services. There are five primary activities.

(1) **Inbound logistics** are those activities involved with receiving, handling and storing inputs to the production system.

(2) **Operations** are those activities which convert resource inputs into a final product. For C Company these would be the skills of the staff making the hand made chocolates and using the recipes.

(3) **Outbound logistics** are those activities relating to storing the product and its distribution to customers.

(4) **Marketing** and sales are those activities that relate to informing customers about the product, persuading them to buy it, and enabling them to do so. C Company has a strong marketing capability which also allows it to track customer patterns and trends.

(5) **After sales service** includes activities such as installing products, repairing them and providing spare parts.

(ii) **Support activities**

Support activities are those which provide purchased inputs, human resources, technology and infrastructure functions to support the primary activities.

(1) **Procurement** consists of those activities which acquire the resource inputs for the primary activities (eg purchase of materials, subcomponents, and equipment). The company buys high quality cocoa beans to use in its recipes.

(2) **Technology development** (in the sense of apparatus, techniques and work organisation). These activities are related to both product design and to improving processes and/or resource utilisation. The company has developed a website that enables it to track trends and customer buying patterns. It also shows constant product innovation and a flexible approach to new product development. The company also has unique recipes.

(3) Human resource management is the activities of recruiting, training, developing and rewarding people. The company has a highly skilled work force who are essential to the manufacturing process.

(4) **Firm infrastructure**. The systems of planning, finance, quality control and management are activities which are crucially important to an organisation's strategic capability in all primary activities. The company's research information enables it to plan ahead and undertake constant product innovation.

73 Strategic models

Text references. Chapter 12 has good material to help you answer part (a) of this question. Part (b) refers to national culture which is explained in Chapter 1.

Top tips. The second paragraph in the question explains what you need to do in part (a). Whatever models you choose must provide data on the **external environment and competition** in L country. An obvious choice is PEST to analyse the environment and one of the models looking at competition such as Porter's Five Forces should cover that aspect of the question. You need to explain briefly why you have chosen the models to analyse W's strategy. There are lots of opportunities to earn marks here by explaining and applying the two models. As a rule of thumb, you should aim to earn two good points for each PEST factor and one or two for each of the Five forces. That means write a sentence or two but not a long paragraph on each! **Remember to explain and apply**.

Part (b) dwells on **cultural differences** which arise **between countries**. Thus this needs you to answer using theory that refers specifically to **national cultural differences** rather than theories of culture in organisations. A good model to use here is Hofstede's model of cultural differences between countries. Try to list each dimension of the model separately and explain why these may matter to W. Again there should up to two marks on offer for each dimension.

Easy marks. As is often the case, a little theoretical knowledge will earn you the easy marks in this question.

Examiner's comments. The main issue for a number of candidates was that they only used **one** strategic management framework rather than **two** as required. In part (b), common errors were to discuss culture in general terms without referring to *Hofstede* or applying it to the business. Some candidates wrote about organisational culture instead of international culture comparisons.

(a) **Evaluating strategy using models/frameworks to explain key external environmental and competitive factors**

PEST is a model for analysing the wider environment in which an organisation operates. PEST covers four headings: political-legal, economic, social and technological and is sometimes expanded to include legal, environmental and ethical matters. *[The examiner mentioned these latter matters briefly]*

W should use PEST to look at the wider environment in L country to consider factors such as the political environment, economy and available technology that would affect any investment before making a decision to invest. So W needs to ask what information should be collected as part of the PEST analysis.

Political-legal environment. This includes any laws in L such as contract law, employee law, customer protection legislation and regulation of industry via competition law. There may be **minimum wage laws** affecting the cost of labour relative to F country. **Competition regulation** may inhibit foreign investment or conversely positively encourage it. This heading also consists of the political environment of L country which includes internal stability, international relations and state involvement in the economy.

Economy. W needs to consider the rate of growth of the economy in L and internal demand for goods and services that would help or hinder its brand. If the economy is entering recession, W may still wish to invest but will have to keep an eye on margins and heightened competition. In times of boom, W must try to identify the level of demand and plan to meet this. **Inflation, unemployment, taxation** and the **availability of credit** are all factors W must consider carefully.

Social and cultural environment. Typical social and cultural trends that W may wish to consider include the number of women entering the workforce, rising standards of living, values and beliefs held and the population split between the sexes. These trends affect the type and availability of labour and the potential spending power of the customers for the clothing who are presumably women. **So there are two aspects to this analysis which are the composition of the workforce and the nature of consumers**. In turn these will be reflected in the attitude to working for foreign companies and buying from foreign companies.

Technological. W needs to find out what technology is available in L that would affect the manufacturing and sale of its clothing. If factories have suitable advanced manufacturing processes then W would be able to use these otherwise it would have to bring in its own technology and set up its own plant. Are sales done over the internet or would W have to sell the clothing through shops or catalogues? What transportation is needed and how would the clothes get to the point of sale?

Porter's Five Forces considers the specific market or industry for a business. The five forces are the threat of new entrants to the industry, the threat of substitute products or services, the bargaining power of customers, the bargaining power of suppliers and rivalry between current competitors in the industry. **W would use this analysis to review the clothing industry in L before it makes the decision to invest.** As W is seeking to escape a market with strong competition it would not wish to enter another market under the same conditions.

Threat of new entrants. If W looks at itself as a new entrant then it would consider how easy it is to break into the market. Factors to consider include the strength of competitive retaliation from existing firms and the technology it would need to compete in the market.

Threat of substitutes. Are there products which exist in another industry that would compete for disposable income with women's clothing in the industry W operates in? If there are strong threats from substitutes then W may wish to reconsider a decision to invest.

The bargaining power of customers. W needs to consider three main factors: how similar products are in its industry, the cost of customers going from one supplier to another and the proportion of total purchases by a customer that are spent on clothes. These all affect the bargaining power of customers relative to W.

The bargaining power of suppliers. Suppliers can influence the profitability of a firm by exerting pressure for higher prices or by reducing the quality of the goods and services they supply. W should investigate the number of suppliers in the industry, the importance of the products supplied to it and any costs of switching suppliers.

Current competitive rivalry in the industry. W needs to look at the number of competitors in L in the clothing market. Fierce competition will drive down profits if the market isn't growing and make it less of an attractive prospect especially if there are high costs of advertising and promotion and keen pricing.

(b) **Why W needs to take account of cultural differences when managing the new operation in L**

Country culture can have a significant impact on how operations are run in L. W needs to be aware at least of cultural norms regarding women, religion and status in L that will affect how employees relate to each other, management of the business and relations with its customers and suppliers. Language is a possible barrier requiring language training by W's managers. W also needs to consider the educational standards of the local workforce and adapt its training to accommodate this.

Hofstede devised a model of organisational culture which explains **work-related cultural differences**. He used five dimensions on which cultures differ. These are power distance, uncertainty avoidance, individuality/collectivity, masculinity/femininity and time orientation.

Power distance measures the extent to which the unequal distribution of power is accepted. So in a high power distance culture, the sharing of power is more unequal and subordinates accept greater control and less say over what they do. In low power distance cultures there is more participation in decision-making by all employees. W clearly needs to find out where organisations in L fit into this continuum especially in relation to its current business model and possibly modify its local operation accordingly.

Uncertainty avoidance denotes the extent to which security, order and control are preferred over ambiguity, uncertainty and change. Low uncertainty avoidance cultures welcome creativity and tolerate risk, dissent, conflict and deviation from norms more than high uncertainty avoidance cultures. W may need to tailor its current operations to suit the way the local workforce makes decisions.

Individuality/collectivity reflects the extent to which people prefer to live and work as individualists focussing on themselves primarily or as collectivists emphasising more the group or society. Where there is a high degree of individualism in the organisation, individual success in achieving the task is seen as more important than individual relationships. The organisation is largely impersonal.

For W this means the local organisation would need to think about how important individual achievement, relationships in the organisation and achievement of the task is. For instance, W needs to consider how staff are paid and whether it chooses to recognise unions.

Masculinity/femininity measures the extent to which social gender roles are distinct. High masculinity denotes cultures where roles are clearly differentiated and masculine qualities such as assertiveness, competition and decisiveness are dominant. Low masculinity cultures value feminine values of consensus and focus on relationships. Again W needs to understand how local norms would affect its management of the local business and educate its managers to expect possible differences.

Time orientation. This is the extent to which people expect rapid feedback on decisions, evaluation and promotion. Again, W need to look at how their existing ways of working would suit those in L country and modify them if necessary. For instance, time orientation may have an impact on the level of urgency expected from the management team.

In conclusion, Hofstede's model emphasises the importance of cultural and human factors. Many new developments fail because they fail to understand how cultures and organisations operate in a particular country.

74 Enterprise Associates 1

Text references. Chapter 8.

Top tips. This question is a good example of the level of complexity you can expect in this exam. It assumes you know *what* work breakdown structure is and *how* to do it and asks you *why* it is a good idea. *Why* questions tend to be more difficult than *how* questions, which, in turn are more difficult than *what* questions. This question illustrates the general principle that mere knowledge of facts and techniques is not enough: you must **understand** them as well.

Easy marks. Planning and control are the obvious benefits of the WBS approach. You should also have had no problem in coming up with budgeting: this is a management accounting exam, after all.

Benefit of using a WBS

A project work breakdown structure (WBS) is an analysis of the work involved in the project. It is used to establish a comprehensive list of the tasks that must be completed if the project is to succeed.

There are **four main areas of project management** that benefit from the use of WBS.

(a) **Budgeting**. WBS gives a clear statement of the **work** that is involved in a project. This is valuable in itself, since it prevents any misapprehension of the extent and complexity of the project. It is also the first step towards preparing a **budgeted cost**, since it is unlikely that the same levels of cost or cost techniques can be applied to all types of activity. In the case of E's house renovation, for example, where different trade specialities are involved, the tradesmen concerned will need a clear statement of what is required from each of them.

(b) **Planning**. Even the simplest project may display complex **interactions** and **dependencies** between activities. An example of a dependency in E's building project, for example, would be that all electrical wiring work would have to be complete before plastering could commence. Clear understanding of dependencies is obviously fundamental to any project planning, especially if time is short, as here, and a critical path method is to be used.

An example of an interaction arises in the implications of damp-proofing. If any kind of waterproofing barrier is applied to the walls, it is obviously vital that its integrity is not compromised by driving nails or screws through it; this will have a significant effect on the way that subsequent work is done.

Quality is another important aspect of planning, in that there may well be quality-related choices to be made about methods and materials. These too will have implications for time and cost.

(c) **Control**. E's house renovation is a fairly simple project, but it will have to be controlled like any other. WBS can be useful in deciding the structure and application of controls. While E takes **overall responsibility**, it will be useful to divide up the **operational responsibility** for individual activities and tasks to other people as far as possible. This division can be complicated when it becomes necessary to have input from the same person on more than one occasion, as when an electrician returns to the house to fit switch and socket accessories after plastering has been done. The responsibility for such dangling tasks must not be overlooked.

The other important aspect of control facilitated by having a WBS is that small but important factors and activities are less likely to be overlooked during the implementation phase.

(d) **Risk**. An awareness of the relative riskiness of different phases and activities is an important aspect of project management; it will usually be appropriate for the project manager to **direct extra attention and resources to the areas of highest risk** in order to give the best chance of success and take appropriate action if things start to go wrong. WBS allows particularly risky elements to be identified and managed separately from less risky but connected items. In a house renovation there is always a risk of tradesmen misinterpreting instructions, so, for example, if a wall is to be demolished, it might be a good idea to be on hand to ensure that the correct wall is dealt with.

75 Enterprise Associates 2

Text references. Chapter 6.

Top tips. As usual, this question requires a mix of principles (time management techniques) and application (E's particular situation). The requirement helps you by specifically asking you to identify relevant factors in the setting as well as asking for a time management plan for E. If you think about it, you will see that this is a logical approach. By understanding the things that will make demands on E's time you are better placed to plan the best use of it.

The Examiner's suggested solution was based on three factors: the nature of the work; the nature of the individual concerned and the nature of the other people involved. This is a logical approach; we have used a simpler division into two main areas, as you will see. This is an illustration of the general principle that most questions in the Paper 5 exam can be approached in more than one way.

You will notice that we have quoted from the question scenario in our answer. This is a perfectly reasonable thing to do when you wish to make reference to a particular point; if you decide to do this, make sure that the quote is as succinct as possible. CIMA examination questions are usually quite well written, with no superfluous wording, so this should be easy to do.

Easy marks. The scenario provides at least two easy points to mention. These are E's less than ideal use of time in 'business and social transactions' and the potential distractions of business and family obligations. These easy marks underline the need to read question scenarios very carefully.

Key factors in E's use of time

A simple analysis of the factors having a bearing on E's use of time might be to divide them into two: **internal** and **external**. The **internal** factors would be those personal matters affecting E's time management ability generally, whatever the circumstances she found herself in, while the **external** factors would be those present in the specific situation described in the setting.

As far as E herself is concerned, we are specifically told that her taste for human interaction often leads her to take 'more time than is necessary to conduct business and social transactions'. This is likely to be a significant hindrance to her. On the other hand, she seems to have been reasonably well-organised so far, having set up a company and obtained agreement from her partners to proceed with the house renovation project. Also, she is a management accountant, so it would probably be safe to assume that she is reasonably objective and organised in her daily work. However, we are not told very much about E's general management skills; she may have to develop her ability to organise other people, for example.

The situation E is taking on is complex. She has her normal work, she has her family obligations and she has the renovation. It is clear from the setting that E is, in fact, taking on the role of the **lead contractor**, as well as carrying out basic repairs and the decorating. This project management role is likely to present the most difficulties, partly because of her lack of experience and partly because it is likely to make unexpected demands upon her; she may not be able to totally compartmentalise her time and may find that urgent matters require her attention at times when she should be doing her normal work.

E should use a standard approach to time management.

First, she should identify her **objectives** and from them her **key tasks**. It is likely that continuing to do her normal job well will be an important objective, so she must establish boundaries to protect the time she needs to spend on this. Control of the telephone will be important: it will probably be necessary to deny knowledge of her work telephone number to her contractors and switch off her mobile phone when at work. She can then respond to messages at an appropriate opportunity.

She will also want to **protect her family relationships** and will have to set aside some time for this each day and at weekends.

Within both her normal job and the building project, E will find it necessary to **list**, **prioritise** and **schedule** her tasks so as to make best use of her time. We are not told what her part-time work pattern will be, but it would probably be useful if she could have a combination of whole days and part days available for the building project. When at work she will have to deal effectively with correspondence, limit the time she is prepared to give to other people for social purposes, and maintain an effective schedule for following up matters that cannot be completed in one go.

When managing the building project, the same ideas apply. In addition, a clear understanding of what is involved will be essential; a **work breakdown structure** approach will be invaluable. **Dependencies** and **interactions** must be understood so that contractors' time is not wasted and materials are available when required.

76 Enterprise Associates 3

Text references. Chapter 12.

Top tips. When answering this question, the first thing the well-prepared candidate must remember is that it is only worth 10 marks. Both of the requirements could give rise to lengthy and detailed answers; the skill here is to go into enough detail to get all the marks on offer, but no further. You need to **plan** how you will answer this question. Set out the key points which are a list of the five forces, a brief description of each and then how each relates to Enterprise Associates. Also make sure you cover the SWOT analysis asked for.

At first sight, the changes in the competitive environment do not look as though they are particularly susceptible to five forces analysis. However, the model works pretty well and fits quite neatly with the marks available: two marks per force. You will have to work quite hard to get these marks, because five forces analysis is not simple to do. It is very easy to confuse the effects of the various factors.

Easy marks. The question asks for a report from a management consultant. It is worth dressing up your answer in an appropriate format, as there may be an easy half-mark for doing that, but do not spend more than a few moments on doing this.

Note the way we discuss opportunities and threats under the five forces analysis: considering them separately would lead to some repetition and unnecessary complexity.

Sharp and Keen Chartered Management Accountants

To: Chief Executive Officer, Enterprise Associates
Date: 1 July 200X

Enterprise Associates – Business environment

1 Scope of this report

You asked us to prepare a report for you on the recent changes in the business environment and how they affect your company.

Michael Porter suggests that the task environment can be analysed under five headings, which he calls the **five competitive forces**; we will use this model to assist us in our discussion.

2 Threat of new entrants

New businesses entering an industry in competition with established suppliers bring extra capacity. This will tend to **drive prices down** and may lead to the **loss of economies of scale** if market share is significantly eroded. In your market you have seen a significant increase in the buy-to-let property sector and we would expect this to have had the effect of depressing market rents. However, the current upward trend in interest rates is likely to create something of a barrier to entry and reduce the rate at which new suppliers emerge in the near future.

3 Threat of substitute products

A substitute product is a product that does the same job in a different way. In your case, the only real substitute for renting a house is to buy one. The current movement in interest rates is also significant here, since it will reduce the finance available for builders of new houses. However, the decision by the government to **release more land for building** is probably more significant in determining the potential supply of this substitute product and its effect on your competitive position.

4 Bargaining power of customers

Customers want more for their money of everything: volume, quality and service. They are better able to obtain this when competition between suppliers increases. This can come about when demand is low relative to supply, when products are not differentiated, when the cost to the customer of switching suppliers is low and when customers buy in bulk.

In your market, the **rise in interest rates** and consequent increase in mortgage costs is likely to reduce demand for new houses and may increase demand for rented property. At the same time, demolition of older properties to allow road construction is likely to increase demand for houses for both purchase and rent. Your products are highly differentiated, your customers have no bulk purchasing power and switching costs really only apply to repeat purchases. It seems likely, therefore, that customers' bargaining power is likely to decline in the near future.

A related factor is the apparent emergence of a **preference for new homes**. This does not really affect customers' bargaining power, however, merely their inclinations.

5 Bargaining power of suppliers

Suppliers want more money for what they supply. Their ability to obtain it depends on the availability of supply, the purchasers' switching costs and the importance of the individual supply to the purchaser. You should not have to worry about switching costs, but both **availability and choice of tradespeople** are likely to be affected by the current increase in general building activity caused by the release of extra land for construction.

6 Rivalry among competitors

The number of competitors has increased over the last four years, and this has doubtless had an effect on margins by increasing supply. Taken together with the likely future increase in the availability of new houses, this effect is unlikely to abate and may worsen.

7 Summary

The picture is complex, with forces pulling in opposite directions, and in the absence of hard econometric data, it is difficult to say what the overall effect is likely to be.

77 WAM Organisation 1

Text references. SWOT analysis is covered in Chapter 12 and stakeholders are covered in Chapter 10.

Top tips. This is quite a simple question and is unusual in that there is really only one way to answer it: the WAM Organisation is making strategy in a fairly deliberate way.

You will notice that we have quoted from the question scenario in our answer. This is very much what the examiner wants to see: an answer **tailored** to the scenario given.

Easy marks. This is quite a difficult question, requiring the ability to analyse and conduct abstract thinking. Perhaps the only easy marks is the use of the *Ansoff* matrix to classify the company's policy of overseas expansion.

(a) **WAM's approach to strategy**

The WAM Organisation's strategic approach is clearly **deliberate and considered**; it displays the major characteristics of the well-known rational model of strategy. This is an iterative process, often undertaken on an annual cycle

A useful starting point for discussion is the establishment of **aims and objectives**. At the highest level of corporate strategy, this may take the form of a mission statement: this must then be interpreted into business and functional objectives so that detailed planning can take place.

Deliberate strategy is based on a thorough knowledge of the **threats and opportunities** presented by the business environment and the **strengths and weaknesses** of the organisation itself. This information is then assessed in the process of corporate appraisal. Potential strategies are generated from this process and appraised in detail. A strategy emerges and is developed into detailed **business and functional plans and budgets**. The outcomes of the activity undertaken may then be fed back to the corporate appraisal stage (and, indeed, to the mission stage) to begin the next iteration.

Content of WAM's strategy

The WAM Organisation has undertaken this process in some detail. It is apparent that **continued growth** is a major strategic objective. After 'a careful process of internal and external analysis', the company has decided on a strategy of overseas expansion. In terms of *Ansoff's* product market vector analysis, this is a strategy of **market development**: new markets for existing products. (The company has already undertaken significant **product development** with its launch of personal finance and telecom services and has expanded the **place** component of its marketing mix with the introduction of Internet shopping.)

The chosen location for the new outlet matches a significant WAM Organisation **strength** with a clear **opportunity**. The WAM Organisation's single outlet will offer the enhanced convenience of **one-stop shopping** to customers who at present have to visit a number of small stores for their shopping. This advantage will be enhanced by the WAM Organisation's size; its **bulk purchasing power** will enable it to offer **reduced prices** that small operators cannot match, or, as an alternative, will allow it to achieve **higher margins**. It is likely that the existing small retailers will only survive if they can achieve an effective differentiation of their market offerings.

(b) **Secondary stakeholders in the supermarket project**

> **Top tips.** The setting for this question includes a lot of detail that you must deal with in your answer, so a quick audit when you think you have finished in order to check that you have covered all the salient points will be a good idea. Apart from that, this is a fairly simple question, especially if you have studied and understood *Mendelow's* stakeholder mapping concept.
>
> **Easy marks.** *Mendelow's* matrix is a sufficiently complex idea that it is probably worth a couple of marks to explain it in brief. If you do this in an appropriate fashion you will find you have gone a long way to satisfying the second part of the requirement.

Stakeholders may be divided into primary and secondary groups according to whether or not they have a **contractual relationship** with the organisation in question. **Internal stakeholders are dealt with under the terms of their contracts in the normal commercial fashion. Secondary stakeholders, however, have less well-defined status and their interests and influence are less clear-cut**. They must be approached with care because they may, in fact, wield considerable power *via* lobbying, public campaigning or the provisions of statute law, for instance.

In the case of the WAM Organisation's new venture, several important groups of external stakeholders may be identified. These include the state and local governments, the Civic Society, local shopkeepers, local residents, the staff and governing body of the local school, potential customers, potential employees and all the interested mass communications media. No doubt these groups will have overlapping membership, with many individuals having more than one interest.

Mendelow classifies stakeholders on a matrix whose axes are **power held** and the **likelihood of showing an interest** in the organisation's activities.

Level of interest

Power	Low	High
Low	A	B
High	C	D

This analysis could be usefully employed by the WAM Organisation when considering how to deal with its secondary stakeholders.

Key players are found in segment D: **strategy must be acceptable** to them, at least. In the worst case, the local and state governments will fall into this category, since they probably have the power to hamper operations severely and even to rescind the hard-won planning consent for the new store. In the best case, they will fall into segment C, but even then, they might be moved into segment D by vigorous protest activity. Local custom and practice in dealing with government and officialdom must be followed here and it would be a good idea to engage the services of locally based advisers and lobbyists. These would have the job of reassuring officials and politicians that the WAM Organisation was behaving in a proper manner and of presenting and emphasising the benefits to local employment and living standards that the new store would bring.

As a general principle, stakeholders in segment C must be treated with care. While often passive, they are capable of moving to segment D, as discussed above, and they should, therefore be **kept satisfied**. The mass communications media may well fall into this segment. Their power to influence both public opinion and the attitude of government is very high, but, being largely devoid of moral principles, their interest is generally restricted to obtaining a good story. They can be managed by retaining the services of good PR agents, who would also emphasise the positive aspects of the project.

Stakeholders in segment B do not have great ability to influence strategy, but their views can be important in **influencing more powerful stakeholders**, perhaps by lobbying. Most of the remaining groups identified earlier will probably fall into this segment. An important part of dealing with these groups is to keep them informed, since a great deal of their interest may well be based on inaccurate or even deliberately distorted information. There should be a two-way communication process so that stakeholders have proper information and the organisation can make a careful assessment of specific problems.

Minimal effort is expended on segment A, but those identified as falling into it should be monitored in case they move into another segment for any reason.

In dealing with all aspects of its foreign venture, the WAM Organisation should be prepared to adjust its plans in the light of changing circumstances, including the activities of the groups opposed to the building of the new store. In order to do this it must have a clear view of its overall aims and of what is essential to them; and what is negotiable.

78 WAM Organisation 2

Text references. Resource-based strategy can be found in Chapter 9 and Hofstede's model is covered in Chapter 1.

Top tips. Why does this question call for your answer to be in the form of a report to a major investment bank? The question would have been just as valid had it started 'Explain the resource-based approach ...'. We can only conclude that using some kind of formal heading features in the marking scheme, though surely it cannot be worth more than one mark. However, make sure you get that mark!

Also be sure that you understand the difference between resource-based strategy and the transaction cost approach to the firm. They both have implications for outsourcing, but approach it from very different directions.

Easy marks. As is so often the case in this paper, the easy marks are available for explaining the basic theory: here you are specifically asked for an explanation of resource-based strategy, so there will be a substantial number of marks available for doing so: perhaps as many as half of the total.

(a) **Resource and competences**

To: The Directors, A Major Investment Bank plc
Date: 1 July 200X

The WAM Organisation and resource-based strategy

1 **Resource based strategy**

Much strategic thinking is based upon adapting the organisation's characteristics to match the demands of its environment; that is, to the exploitation of opportunities and the avoidance of threats. The resource-based approach shifts the emphasis towards the organisation's strengths and weaknesses and proceeds on the basis that competitive advantage comes from the possession of **scarce resources** and the exploitation of **unique competences**.

This approach is therefore equally applicable to organisations that have **favoured access** to material resources such as, for instance, vital raw materials; those that possess a specific but intangible protected **intellectual property** such as a patent on a drug; and those whose advantage consists of the **experience and expertise of its staff and the capabilities of its systems**. The advantage of firms in the last category is based on what are now known as **core competences**. A good example is the way *Enron* exploited deregulation and created a new field of business activity when it established itself as a specialist broker in energy resources.

Johnson and Scholes define core competences as those that both **outperform competitors** and are **difficult to imitate**. Organisations must achieve an acceptable or **threshold** level of competence in all of their activities, but it is core competences that give a lasting competitive edge. Indeed, the exploitation of such core competences is potentially a more durable source of competitive advantage than more specific assets such as raw materials and intellectual property. Raw material sites become exhausted and patents expire, but good management can maintain a technical lead almost indefinitely, by paying proper attention to innovation and the nurturing of what the firm does well.

2 The WAM Organisation: resources and core competences

We do not have a great deal of information on the WAM Organisation other than that it is a very successful supermarket chain with the largest share of its domestic market. We know that it is customer focused; provides value for money; is operationally efficient; and uses the latest technology. It is also innovative and has launched successful personal finance, telecom and Internet shopping services.

We might, if we were pushed, make some tentative suggestions about the firm's resources and core competences based on this rather sketchy account.

2.1 Costs

The WAM Organisation's size should give it extensive purchasing power and enable it to achieve significant **economies of scale**. This, taken together with its operational efficiency should make a policy of cost leadership attainable.

2.2 Customer focus

Customer focus is valuable in any business, but it is essential in a retailer; the example of *Marks & Spencer* in the early millennium illustrated what happens when a previously successful retailer loses touch with its customers. If the WAM Organisation has really achieved more extensive customer focus than its rivals it should show in such areas as continuing successful new product development, a high degree of customer satisfaction and differentiated product offerings in geographical areas that vary in socio-demographic makeup.

2.3 Technology

The WAM Organisation uses the latest technology. This does not just have the potential to cut costs, as in *Wal-Mart's* introduction of radio frequency identification tags; it has the potential to achieve important improvements in customer focus through the use of **loyalty cards**. Effective use of this technology is very difficult, simply because of the volume of data involved, but *Tesco* has used it with great success in such areas as targeted price cuts, response to emerging preferences and effective promotions.

2.4 Innovation

The WAM Organisation's customer focus has no doubt helped it in its introduction of new products that challenge traditional notions of what the grocery business is about. Introduction of more new products and new product categories is an obvious route to continued turnover growth. We may assess the ability to make regular and successful product launches to be a core competence of the organisation and one that it should sustain and exploit.

(b) **Problems of cross-cultural management**

Top tips. This question really requires a discussion of culture at two levels: overall **national culture** and the more specific idea of **corporate or management culture**. *Hofstede's* model is obviously an essential component of the material to be covered.

As we have been given no details of the prevailing cultural norms in either the WAM Organisation's home country or in country Y, it will not be possible to give any real illustrations of how cultural interactions might affect the new venture.

Easy marks. A perfectly acceptable answer to this question can be prepared with minimal reference to the scenario as it revolves around theory. We discuss both *Ouchi's* model and Hofstede's for completeness. You could probably score up to five marks for explaining either.

General cultural differences

Culture is an important determinant of behaviour. It is about beliefs, values, attitudes, customs, rituals and artefacts. The nature of culture varies between countries and, indeed, within them. Typically, different regions, social classes, religious denominations, industries and professions will all have their own variations on the generally prevailing cultural norms.

There can be wide cultural differences between neighbouring countries that are part of the same basic society. If country Y's national culture is significantly different from that of the WAM Organisation, it is likely that there will be problems. This is particularly so as customs and taboos associated with food are particularly strong. These problems will be exacerbated by the current tendency to decry 'globalisation' as an evil and to denounce cultural insensitivity and even cultural imperialism whenever there is the slightest excuse.

Management culture

A factor which has an impact on the culture of transnational organisations, or organisations competing in global markets, is **management culture**. This consists of the views about managing held by managers, their shared educational experiences, and the 'way business is done'. Obviously, this reflects wider cultural differences between countries, but national cultures can sometimes be subordinated to the corporate culture of the organisation.

Ouchi and Theory Z

Ouchi identified important differences between a typically US management approach and a typically Japanese one. This work was done at a time when Japanese methods appeared to be far more successful than Western ones and there was great concern to adopt them. This process is now largely complete, and the failure of the Japanese economy in recent years has tempered any further move towards Japanese methods. It is perhaps mostly in the field of organisation culture that the Japanese approach has had least influence.

Theory Z. Ouchi called the US approach **Theory A** and the Japanese approach **Theory J**. He then proposed that US firms should adopt a compromise between the two, which he called **Theory Z**.

The Hofstede model

The **Hofstede model** was developed in 1980 by Professor Geert Hofstede in order to explain national differences by identifying **key dimensions** in the value systems of all countries. Each country is represented on a scale for each dimension so as to explain and understand values, attitudes and behaviour. Global businesses have to be sensitive to these issues.

In particular, Hofstede pointed out that countries differ on the following dimensions.

Power distance. This dimension measures how far superiors are expected to exercise power. In a high power-distance culture, the boss decides and people do not question.

Uncertainty avoidance. Some cultures prefer clarity and order, whereas others are prepared to accept novelty. This affects the willingness of people to change rules, rather than simply obey them.

Individualism-collectivism. In some countries individual achievement is what matters. In a collectivist culture people are supported and controlled by their in-group and put the interests of the group first.

'**Masculinity**'. In 'masculine' cultures assertiveness and acquisitiveness are valued. 'Masculine' cultures place greater emphasis on possessions, status, and display as opposed to quality of life and caring for others.

Clearly, there is potential for misunderstanding and conflict between managers and their subordinates when their native societies make different assumptions on these matters. The WAM Organisation's managers must be alert to any potential problems.

79 WAM Organisation 3

Text references. Chapters 8 (project risk) and 6 (negotiation).

Top tips. 'Identify' (in part (a)) is a low-level instruction, corresponding to 'comprehension' in the CIMA table of learning objectives, so it should not be too difficult to satisfy the requirements of this question. A simple list would seem to provide an appropriate answer. Even giving a detailed description of each risk would not be too challenging. However, the question is worth 15 marks, which seems quite a lot for such a simple task. We thus have a problem of interpretation.

Unfortunately, it is not unusual for the Examiner to present such dilemmas. If you come across a problem like this, it is better to err on the side of overkill than to take the question requirement too literally. You must provide an answer that is worth the marks on offer rather than one that is restricted to the minimum requirement implied by the wording of the question. In this question, for example, you might choose to proceed as though the requirement said 'Discuss the nature of ...' rather than 'Identify ...', 'discuss' being a higher level requirement corresponding to 'analysis.'

However, do not be tempted to waffle! Merely increasing the length of your answer will not increase its value.

The Examiner's own suggested solution bears out the value of our suggestion above: it discusses success criteria in order to be able identify risks as things that might prejudice such criteria; goes on to mention the categorisation of risks according to their potential impact and where control of them should lie; and mentions some of the ideas associated with risk management.

Easy marks. The easy marks come from the process of identification mentioned above.

(a) **Identifying project risks**

WAM's exposure

The WAM Organisation has chosen to enter its new market in a risky way. It has decided to create a completely new supermarket operation from nothing. This will require the commitment of considerable funds and extensive management time and effort. We may assume the organisation took this path because it wanted to install its own business model complete, wholly owned and controlled by itself. Compare this with *Wal-Mart's* entry into Europe and Japan, where it has bought controlling interests in existing supermarket chains and is gradually remodelling to conform more closely to its own ideas. The WAM Organisation has total control and risks total failure; Wal-Mart's control is less extensive, but its worst outcome is a poorly performing local chain that could be sold if necessary. Generally, increased control requires an increase in the resources committed, which in turn brings increased risk.

Project risk

This requires a clear definition of success or project deliverables. For example, if the WAM Organisation defined success for its project as opening a properly completed and stocked store by a certain date without including any mention of a turnover targets, the possibility of an organised customer boycott would not be recognised as a risk factor. If we work on the assumption that success is defined in terms of **achieving commercial viability in a reasonable time**, then we might identify a number of risks.

Technical risks

These would include risks such as misdelivery of supplies; poor quality of work and materials; accidents; design inadequacies; and co-ordination failures. Some of these problems might be exacerbated by local conditions; after all, this is the WAM Organisation's first foreign venture and it is not expert in the way things are done in country Y. Indeed, there may be completely new threats that arise from this unfamiliarity, particularly in matters affected by local law, custom and practice. For example, activity duration estimates may be compromised by the extent of public holidays, local working practices and working time regulations.

Business risk

This is very wide ranging and includes factors in the immediate task environment and in the wider PEST environment as well. Obvious simple examples include the possibility of a change in national economic conditions leading to a reduction in potential demand; the appearance of a competitor from another country; difficulty in recruiting or training local staff; and, if some element of local finance is being used (as would be sound financial management), a rise in the cost of capital.

More specific risk factors revolve around the strong body of opinion that is opposed to the WAM Organisation's plans. It is not impossible that this opposition might achieve some success, perhaps constraining the new store's opening hours, for example, even if it did not succeed in having the construction permit revoked.

Risk reduction and mitigation

Once risks have been identified and assessed, a proper programme of risk reduction may be undertaken. The technical and cultural risks associated with the building programme might be reduced by engaging the services of local architects and building project managers who should be familiar with local conditions and can advise accordingly. A similar approach might be used with the business risk category, making use of the services of local consultants. Certainly local lobbying and PR specialists should be employed to manage the threat from the campaign of opposition to the new venture.

(b) **Negotiating strategy and principles**

Top tips. Your ability to answer this question really depends on your knowledge of the way negotiations are carried on. You have very little opportunity to apply principle to the scenario here, other than by couching your remarks in terms of what the WAM Organisation should and should not do.

Easy marks. An outline of a basic negotiation process and its implications for the negotiators should provide up to five marks here.

Negotiation is a process whereby two parties come together to confer with a view to concluding a jointly acceptable agreement. This is conducted through a process of both **purposeful persuasion** (persuading the other party of the merits of one's case or position) and **constructive compromise** (being willing to move closer toward the other party's position).

This is a particularly helpful process for the implementation of any strategy, as it:

(i) Recognises that stakeholders in decision (in this case, state and local government officials, protesters, media, local shopkeepers and so on) will have differing and potentially conflicting interests in the situation

(ii) Recognises that the interests of powerful stakeholders (in this case, the local and state government officials who represent the 'opposing' party in the negotiation) must be **taken into account** in developing strategies and solutions, especially if (as in WAM's case) there is to be an on-going working relationship.

(iii) Recognises that there may genuinely be **common ground** which can be built on, and other view points which can be taken into account, in order to develop **better solutions** which genuinely benefit both parties: a 'win win' solution. In this case, for example, WAM can offer employment opportunities and perhaps also investment in the local community, in return for the permissions it seeks.

In order to secure the authorities' commitment and genuine (hopefully on-going) co-operation, WAM should specifically pursue an **integrative**, rather than distributive or 'zero-sum', approach to negotiation, aiming to work constructively towards mutually acceptable solutions – and recognising the balance of power in the negotiating situation.

If the parties are realistic, they will have established in their own minds not only their **ideal** outcomes, but also a minimum **acceptable outcome**. If the acceptable outcomes overlap, it should be relatively easy to reach a **mutually acceptable** result. If they do not, the task becomes much harder. It is clearly very useful for a negotiator to have a good idea of what the other side's minimum position really is, and, equally, to conceal his or her own.

In the case of obtaining permission for the WAM Organisation's new supermarket, there would probably be **much common ground**, in that a successful venture would have the potential to increase the local level of economic activity, providing increased employment opportunities and greater consumer utility. However, differences of emphasis would arise: the WAM Organisation would be more concerned about its costs and commercial prospects, while the government would be more concerned about local amenity and environmental effects and the way established local retailers would be affected. However, it should be possible to reach an agreement that is **acceptable to both sides**.

At the start of the negotiation, the WAM Organisation should state its **opening position** clearly and realistically. The opposing position should be **challenged on its merits**; it is important to leave the opponent with room for manoeuvre. It is desirable to say as little as possible at this stage and to concentrate on assessing the other side's strengths and weaknesses. A bargaining phase may then ensue.

The bargaining phase is a process of argument and persuasion. There are some important tactics.

(i) The WAM Organisation should not allow elements of the dispute to be settled **piecemeal**. This limits room for subsequent manoeuvre.

(ii) Any concession should be **matched** by a concession from the other side.

(iii) To avoid one-sided concessions, the WAM Organisation should make proposals that are conditional on the other side moving too: 'If you do this I will agree to that'.

Closing a negotiation is similar to closing a sale; it means attempting to bring the process to a conclusion. There are several techniques the WAM Organisation could use.

(i) Offer to trade a concession for an agreement to settle.

(ii) When there is a single outstanding issue, offer to split the difference.

(iii) Offer a choice between two courses of action.

(iv) Summarise the arguments, emphasise the concessions that have been made and state a final position. However, a bluff runs the risk of being called.

80 Pilot paper

80.1	B	This is a definition.
80.2	C	This is a definition.
80.3	C	Flatter structure implies wider span of control and thence the acceptance of greater responsibility by work people.
80.4	B	This is a reference to *Belbin's* work on the roles played by team members. Note, in relation to option D, that while more than one role may be played by a single member of the group, it is not necessary for group effectiveness for all the roles to be played by a few people.
80.5	B	Organisation structure is an aspect of strategic implementation and should support the strategic objectives and general strategic approach.

Network diagram for questions 80.6 and 80.7

The critical path is A – B – C – E – F – G – J – K

Activity-on-line style

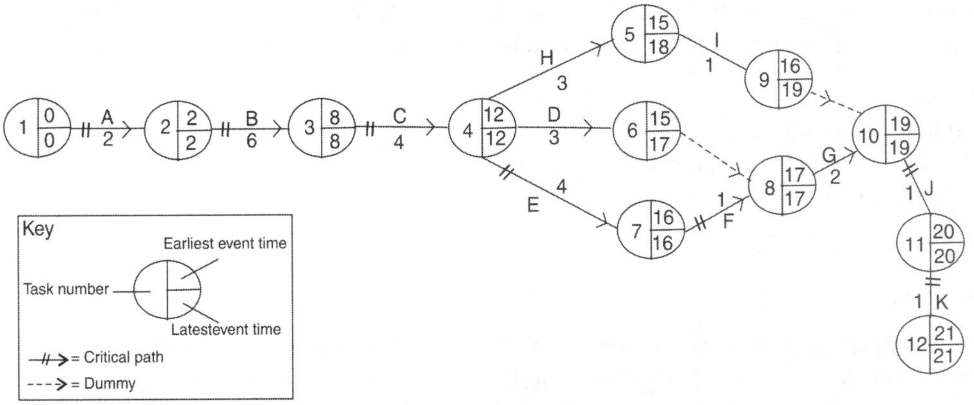

Total project elapse time is 21 weeks.

Activity-on-node style

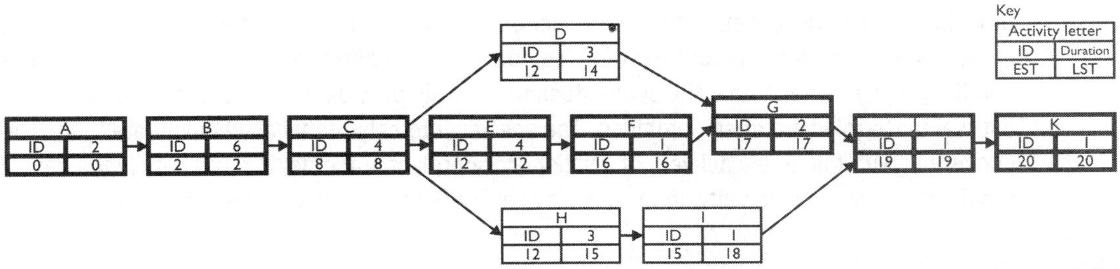

ABCDGJK 19

ABCEFGJK 21 Critical path

ABCHIJK 18

80.6 C 21 weeks

80.7 B Activity A is complete. Annie Li is commencing activity B, which is scheduled to last 6 weeks. Activities C to K will take 13 weeks. Annie must thus reduce the duration of activity B to no more than 3 weeks in order to achieve a delivery date 16 weeks from now.

80.8 AAA

Blake plc
AGAI

81 November 2005 examination

81.1 C This question is based on *Mendelow's* stakeholder model. By coincidence, the letter C is also used by Mendelow for the quadrant occupied by these stakeholders. Such stakeholders must be treated with care: while often passive, they are capable of developing a higher degree of interest and starting to use their power.

81.2 A High regard for individual self-sufficiency and achievement contrasts with a more supportive and controlling approach: these two attitudes form the extremes of the individualism–collectivism dimension of *Hofstede's* cultural analysis.

81.3 B The phrase 'markets or hierarchies' was originated by *Williamson* who suggested that in the longer term and with increasing complexity, the organisation of production through a network of contracts would become unsatisfactory. Larger, hierarchically structured organisations would have to be developed.

81.4 D This is a reference to one particular model of the project life cycle: the project initiation document would effectively conclude the first phase, known in this model, as 'identification of need'.

81.5 The benefits of mentoring are said to include improved staff motivation; lower staff turnover; faster career progress; and fewer and more quickly resolved disputes. To these we might add improved work performance and increased job satisfaction for both mentor and protégé.

81.6 A Environmental analysis
B Corporate appraisal
C Evaluation and choice of options
D Strategic control

81.7 (2) Development of a solution

(4) Completion

This question is based on the same model as that used for question 81.4, which seems like overkill. *Maylor's* model would use 'Design the project' and 'Develop the process' for stages two and four of the project life cycle, while the US project Management Institute Body of Knowledge would use 'planning' and 'controlling' for the equivalent stages.

81.8 'Project owner' is one of a number of terms used to designate the head of the department or organisation that will benefit from the project output. Other terms used for this person are 'business owner', 'customer' and, under PRINCE2, 'senior user'. The difference between the project sponsor and the project owner is that the owner does not usually provide the resources needed, though, of course, these roles are often combined. The specific interests of this stakeholder are therefore concerned with the timely delivery of a satisfactory project outcome; this will satisfy the design requirements for functionality and will achieve everything defined by the scope of the project.

82 May 2006 examination

82.1 C Corporate appraisal centres on a consideration of internal **strengths** and **weaknesses** and external **opportunities** and **threats**. This is known, unsurprisingly, as **SWOT analysis.**

82.2 B Kerzner's project management maturity model is a five level maturity framework aimed at identifying areas where an organisation's processes may need improvement.

82.3 D There are certain constraints involved in working with others. Irving Janis likens Groupthink to a situation where a team becomes dangerously blinkered to what is going on around them and confidently forges ahead in completely the wrong direction. The cosy consensus of the group prevents consideration of alternatives, constructive criticism or conflict.

82.4 A The project sponsor provides and is accountable for the resources invested into a project and is responsible for the achievement of the project's business objectives.

82.5 The benefits of good corporate governance include:

(a) **Risk reduction.** Clearly, the ultimate risk is of the organisation making such large losses that bankruptcy becomes inevitable. The organisation may also be closed down as a result of serious regulatory breaches, for example misapplying investors' monies. Proper corporate governance reduces such risks by aligning directors' interests with the company's strategic objectives and by providing for measures to reduce fraud.

(b) **Performance enhancement**. Performance should improve if accountabilities are made clear and directors' motivation is enhanced by performance – related remuneration. Also, the extra breadth of experience brought by non-executive directors and measures to prevent domination by a single powerful figure should improve the quality of decision-making at board level.

(c) **External support**. External perceptions of the company should be enhanced. This can have wide-ranging benefits such as improved ability to raise finance, improved corporate image with public and government and improved relations with stakeholders such as customers and employees.

(d) **Enhanced marketability of goods and services**. Confidence is engendered among other stakeholders including employees, customers, suppliers and shareholders.

82.6 Work breakdown structure aids the management of project work by analysing it into manageable components and establishing any dependencies and interactions that may exist between the components.

82.7 Thomas' framework for classifying different ways of handling conflict.

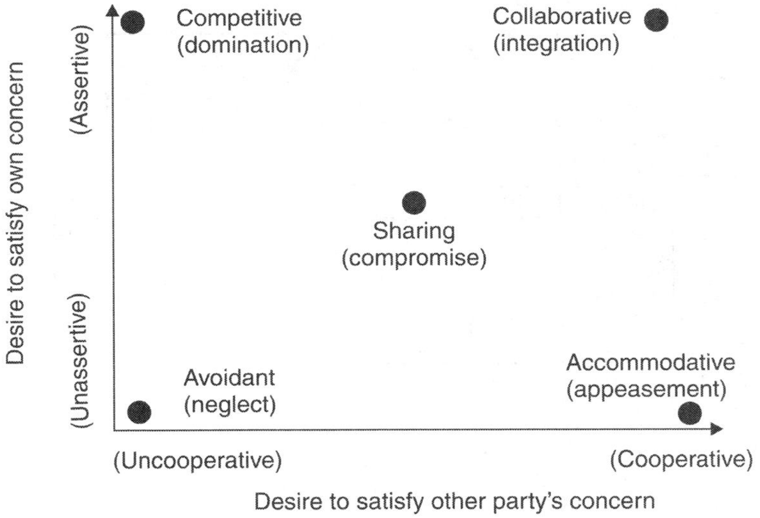

Behaviourial modes of tackling conflict with (in brackets) the outcome sought in each mode.

82.8 Project risk can be classified as follows.

(a) Quantifiable risks. These are risks where the probability of an event occurring can be established by statistical analysis of past occurrences.

(b) Unquantifiable risks. These are risks which cannot be quantified which makes them difficult to manage.

(c) Socially constructed risks. These risks arise from human perceptions which may not be justified.

83 November 2006 examination

83.1 D

83.2 B

83.3 B

83.4 C

83.5 The resource-based approach to strategy emphasises the importance of the possession and utilisation of unique assets or resources, along with core competences, in securing competitive advantage.

83.6 An important aspect of Fiedler's theory is that of 'situational favourableness', which is defined as the degree to which a situation enables a leader to exert influence over a group. There are three of these situational factors.

(a) **Leader-member relations:** the degree to which the employees accept the leader.

(b) **Position power:** the amount of formal authority the leader possesses by virtue of his or her position in the organisation.

(c) **Task structure:** clear, well-defined tasks make work easier to organise. Vague and unstructured tasks make it difficult to control, the quality of performance.

Diagram for answers 83.7, 83.8 & 83.9

Activity-on-node style

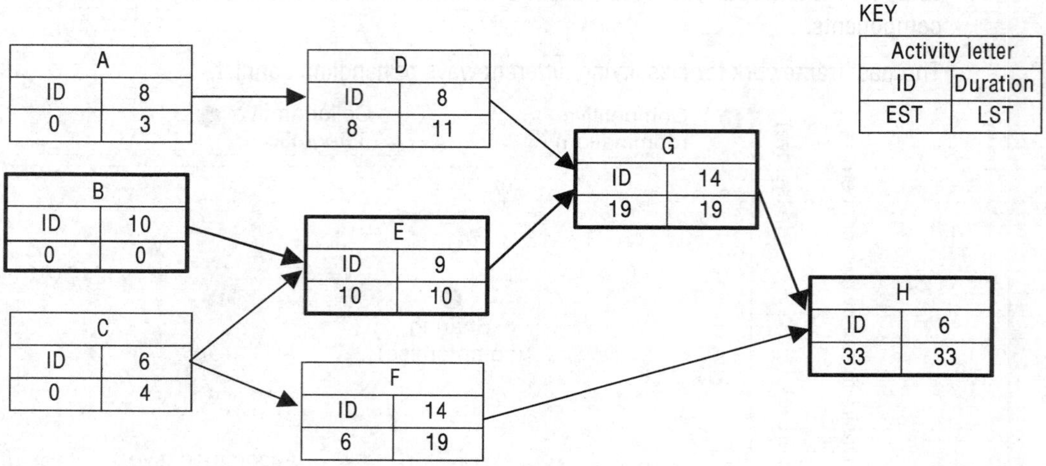

Paths

ADGH 36
BEGH 39 critical path
CEGH 35
CFH 26

Activity-on-line style

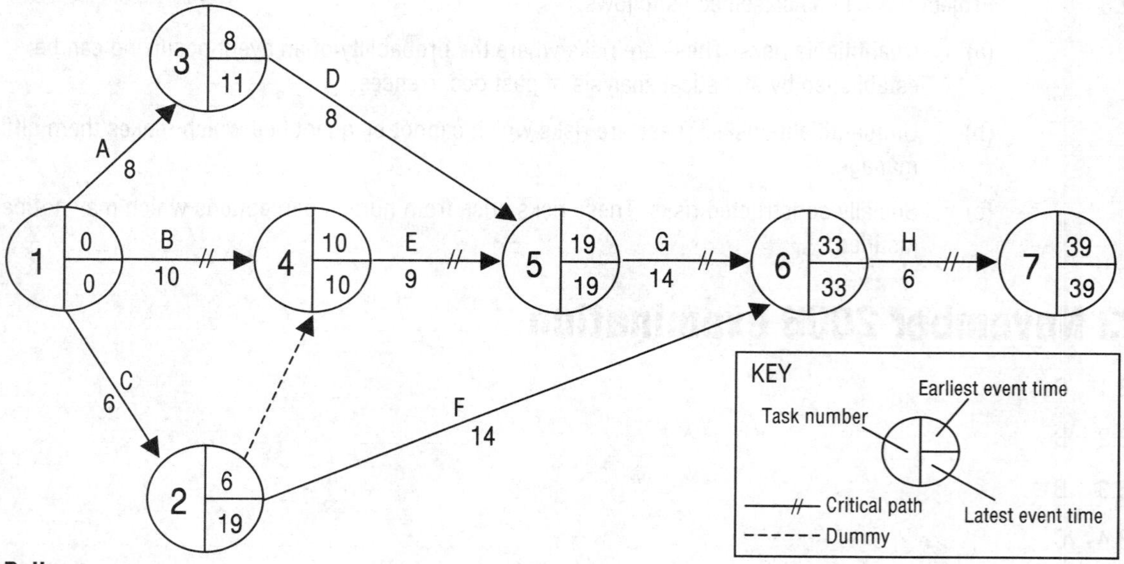

Paths

ADGH = 8+8+14+6= 36 weeks
BEGH= 10+9+14+6= 39 weeks
CEGH= 6+9+14+6= 35 weeks
CFH = 6+14+6 = 26 weeks

83.7 The critical path is BEGH

83.8 The overall expected duration of the project is 39 weeks

83.9 The earliest time that the sales campaign (event G) can start is week 19.

84 May 2007 examination

Top tips. If you need a bit of help, refer back to the guidance on answering MCQs and OTs in the front pages.

84.1 D. **Authority** is the right to do something, or to ask someone else to do it and expect it to be done. It is therefore another word for position or legitimate power.

84.2 C. A **project scope** states what is included and what is not in a project.

84.3 B. **Low switching costs** allow buyers to switch between products and services cheaply. This means that buyers have more power than in markets where switching costs are higher.

84.4 A. **Feasibility analysis** looks at whether a proposed project can achieve its objectives in a cost-effective manner.

84.5 Firms undertake corporate appraisal to establish their condition prior to preparation of the long-term plan. This takes the form of a SWOT analysis looking at internal and external factors that affect the firm. The SWOT analysis can be used to establish a **positioning strategy**, which considers product market opportunities. So firms must look at what opportunities exist and align their resources with environmental conditions.

The firm obtains **competitive advantage** from its position in relation to its environment. Finally, the firm should **adapt its strategy** to fit with its external environment.

84.6 The conflict outlined in the question would be **vertical conflict**. This is caused by a power imbalance between different levels in the hierarchy.

84.7 Project evaluation and review technique or **PERT** is a modified form of network analysis designed to account for **uncertainty**.

84.8 In critical path analysis the spare time for an activity is called **float.** This is also known as **slack** or **buffer**

84.9 (i) Plant
(ii) Completer- finisher
(iii) Team worker

85 November 2007 examination

85.1 D **Functional flexibility** is the requirement or expectation that workers will perform tasks beyond those strictly specified as their main role or function. This is achieved through giving workers new or additional skills and training and redeploying them flexibly within core tasks.

85.2 C **Norming** is the team stage during which norms are established and procedures evolve. The team agrees on work sharing, individual requirements and expectations of output. This is based on Tuckman's stages of group development.

85.3 B **Project scope** is all the things that have to be achieved if the project is to succeed. This should be done at the beginning of the project lifecycle when the project is being **initiated.**

85.4 B These decisions are **strategic** and therefore would ordinarily occur at the highest level. In this case, the corporate level is the highest level listed.

85.5 The **critical path** is those parts of the project which, if delayed beyond the allotted time, would delay the completion of the project as a whole.

85.6 These are **skills, staff and shared values.** You need to learn these!

85.7 Technostructure, Support Staff and Middle Line. Once again you should know these.

85.8 Preparation, opening, bargaining and closing.

86 May 2008 examination

86.1 C **Primary objective**. A primary objective of a business must be **financial**. Financial objectives would include profitability, return on capital employed and earnings per share. Secondary objectives support the primary goal and include market position and technology. Tactical objectives are stated as implementation targets for business units and functions and focus on the medium term (1 to 2 years). Operational objectives are set as action targets for departments and units and focus on detailed activity and resources over the short term (up to one year).

86.2 B **Referent power**. Referent power is based on the force of personality or charisma that can attract, influence or inspire other people. Power is the ability to get things done. The types of power listed in the question are all classifications made by *French and Raven.*

86.3 D **Logical incrementalism.** Logical incrementalism makes strategy in a series of incremental changes rather than big leaps. **Ecological strategy** suggests that as an organisation's environment changes it will only survive if it adapts and evolves. **Bounded rationality** refers to decision making by managers where they take quick and expedient decisions and follow courses of action that are good enough but not ideal. **Positioning** suggests that the main source of competitive advantage lies in how the organisation fits its strategy to its external environment.

86.4 D **Reduction** is the means by which measures are taken to reduce the likelihood of the risk event. **Absorption** is where the risk is accepted in the hope that the consequences can be coped with. **Transference** is where the risk is passed on or shared.

86.5 **Scalar chain is** the number of levels by which authority passes vertically down a clear chain of command from top to bottom. That is, from the strategic apex to the operating core. **Span of control** is the number of people who report to one manager in a hierarchy.

86.6 Projects have a defined beginning and end, have resources specifically allocated to them, are unique or one-off and follow a plan toward a clear intended end-result. A fifth characteristic is that projects often cut across organisational and functional lines.

86.7 (i) **Loops are not allowed in network analysis** so an activity cannot lead back to an earlier event. By convention, events are numbered from left to right and the event at an end of any activity has a higher number than the one at its start.

(ii) A **dummy activity** should be used here instead of a **dangler** since all activities must contribute toward the progression of the network.

Mock Exams

CIMA – Managerial Level

Paper P5

Integrated Management

Mock Examination 1

Instructions to candidates:

You are allowed three hours to answer this question paper.
In the real exam, you are allowed 20 minutes reading time before the examination begins during which you should read the question paper, and if you wish, make annotations on the question paper. However, you will **not** be allowed, **under any circumstances**, to open the answer book and start writing or use your calculator during this reading time.
You are strongly advised to carefully read the question requirement before attempting the question concerned.
Answer the ONE compulsory question in Section A. This is comprised of sub-questions.
Answer ALL THREE compulsory questions in Section B.
Answer TWO of the three questions in Section C.

DO NOT OPEN THIS PAPER UNTIL YOU ARE READY TO START UNDER EXAMINATION CONDITIONS

SECTION A – 20 marks

Answer ALL EIGHT sub-questions in this section

1.1 Which researcher is associated with work on the roles necessary for an effective team?

A *Tuckman*
B *Belbin*
C *Sherif*
D *Likert* **(2 marks)**

1.2 *Mintzberg* identifies several political games played within organisations. Which of the following is not one of the games he described?

A Games to defeat rivals
B Games to resist authority
C Games to confuse stakeholders
D Games to build power bases **(2 marks)**

1.3 Company J is considering an adjustment to its strategy based on a newly patented technology to which it has exclusive rights. Should this strategy be evaluated in terms of

A Suitability
B Feasibility
C Both of the above
D Neither of the above **(2 marks)**

1.4 Projects are subject to major constraints that must be satisfied if they are to be considered successful. Which of the following is not such a constraint?

A Cost
B Time
C Risk
D Quality **(2 marks)**

1.5 *Harrison* identified four organisational types, each with its own culture. Which of the following is not one of those types?

A Role
B Machine
C Power
D Task **(2 marks)**

The following data is to be used to answer questions 1.6, 1.7 and 1.8

FOODAID is a UK-based charity that delivers food to communities in need because of war or natural disaster. Its overall management is in the hands of the Director-General, Sally Porter, who reports to the Board of Trustees. This Board sets overall priorities for aid distribution in line with the charity's constitution. FOODAID currently operates in Africa, Asia and the Americas. Sally Porter is assisted by three Directors: Sam Mbube, Director of Transport and Distribution, Jack Staff, Director of Fundraising and Isobel Brammer, Director of Administration. The Directors are supported by their departmental staffs.

As well as raising liquid funds, FOODAID also runs regular campaigns in which it collects, stores and distributes tinned foodstuffs donated by individuals in the UK. To do this the charity has entered into a leasing arrangement with Whiteknuckle Airlines to use a transport aircraft for 200 hours each year. The movement of foodstuffs from the UK to its destination is planned in detail by Sam Mbube's planning cell, headed by Alex Boyle, a very experienced transport operations manager.

Jack Staff, Director of Fundraising, has recently authorised a press advertising campaign at a cost of £500,000. His media buyer, Lucy Chen, has advised him that rising costs mean that this campaign is unlikely to be as effective as that mounted one year previously.

1.6 List four areas of project management skill that Sally Porter, Sam Mbube, Jack Staff and Isobel Brammer should be skilled in.

(4 marks)

1.7 Using the terminology of Porter's value chain, identify the value activity most closely associated with Lucy Chen and Alex Boyle

Give the name of the person most closely associated with 'human resource management'.

(3 marks)

1.8 Identify two primary stakeholders (other than trustees and staff) and one secondary stakeholder mentioned in the narrative. **(3 marks)**

(Total for Section A = 20 marks)

SECTION B – 30 marks

Answer ALL THREE questions – 10 marks each

Note to candidates:

The scenario for the three questions in this section is divided into two parts. Read Part 1 to answer questions two and three and then read Part 2 before answering question four.

Spiral of decline – Part 1

Because of its failure to serve a sufficient number of clients and/or to provide a service of the required quality, Company J, a state-owned business has had its funding cut for three consecutive years. This is putting pressure on people throughout the organisation. Departments and individuals have been set more demanding targets and large-scale redundancies have recently been announced. This has resulted in considerable conflict. The service professionals are convinced that the marketing and sales department is responsible for the troubles of the organisation. This view is not shared by the marketing and sales people. They believe that the poor quality of service offered is the real reason for the decline in demand for services and for the resulting cuts in government funding. The effect of these differences between departments is one of declining co-operation between the direct service providers and the personnel in marketing and sales.

Of the more immediate concern to senior management, however, is the threat of industrial action by the trades unions determined to protect their members' jobs. Even individuals like the management accountant are finding themselves in conflict with departmental managers with whom they have previously enjoyed good relations. Requests for information on the costs of providing services are being met with hostility and the management accountant's job becomes more difficult by the day.

Question 2

Required

Discuss the potential consequences arising from the conflict between the various departments and groups within SOB. **(10 marks)**

Question 3

Required

Describe how senior management can best manage the conflicts between the various parties. **(10 marks)**

Spiral of decline – Part 2

Two years later, Company J has overcome its immediate problems but is still not working efficiently. The Board have decided that a new information system is required and have entered discussions with contractors. The management accountant has been appointed project manager. She is concerned about several problems that she can foresee arising during the lifetime of the project.

First, she is worried about the CEO's habit of vagueness and lack of precision in speech and writing. She fears that her responsibilities will be confused and the aims of the project unclear. She is also concerned about her personal working relationships, in that neither the Finance Director nor the Operations Director appears to be taking much interest in the project. She is not sure who she should report to, with what frequency and about what. Finally, she worries that proper control over the external contractors will not be exercised since she has had no contact with them: all discussions have been at Board level.

Question 4

Required

Explain how the PRINCE2 system of project management could help the management accountant solve these specific problems. **(10 marks)**

(Total for Section B = 30 marks)

SECTION C – 50 marks

Read the following scenario and answer TWO questions ONLY – 25 marks each

Gensup plc has been formed from the acquisition by a major distributor – Universal Sales plc (Unisal) – of three manufacturing businesses – A, B and C. This occurred following discussions among the shareholders of A, B and C regarding the problems and opportunities facing their companies. An approach was made to Unisal, as a result of which it has acquired all three businesses.

As part of the reorganisation which followed the acquisition, Gensup has established a joint research and development centre for the manufacturing units. Corporate planning, management services, finance functions and group purchasing of common raw materials have been centralised at the Head Office of Gensup.

Universal Sales plc (Unisal)

This was an internationally-established distribution company specialising in the worldwide distribution of products and components to the engineering industry. Its customers included those of A, B and C.

Unisal had a number of distribution centres in countries where demand was strong. The distribution managers liaised directly with contract customers. The distribution centres were also a base for the sales force. Sales persons focused on particular types of customer, such as manufacturers of cars or power plant, to which they sold a wide range of products. Marketing was co-ordinated at Head Office.

The shares of Universal Sales plc were traded on various stock exchanges. The acquisition leaves the former owners of A, B and C as minority shareholders in the quoted company, Gensup plc.

Manufacturing

A, B and C were all private limited companies. A manufactured aluminium rods and wire. B manufactured copper rods and wire. C manufactured plastic rods and thread.

The manufacturers all produced their products using continuous processes with a relatively small number of production workers, most of whom were unskilled. These continuous processes required large, expensive manufacturing plants. Packaging of the output, and distribution were on a batch basis. Their main raw materials were ores, raw chemicals, water and electric power. These raw materials represented a large part of the finished product cost. Many new sources of ore and chemicals have become available from Eastern Europe.

Maintenance, purchasing, quality control and research and development were important functions, with skilled and professional staff. These functions were managed by directors who were not shareholders.

The market

There were numerous competing companies in the industry, operating either in a similar way or as part of larger groups. The market of A, B and C was exclusively in the United Kingdom. It consisted of a large number of engineering companies which used the products in their own conversion processes.

During the last few years, amalgamations and takeovers have reduced the number of customers, but changing economic conditions have also opened considerable export potential for A, B and C. Unfortunately, the companies did not have the staff or expertise to take advantage of the opportunities.

Total quality control policies among the customers have meant that quality specifications and ordering procedures have become much more sophisticated, requiring substantial expenditure to meet customers' demands.

Question 5

Required

(a) Identify and explain the structural forms that might be appropriate for Gensup. **(7 marks)**

(b) Explain, with reference to the information provided in the scenario, the advantages and disadvantages of each structural form identified. **(18 marks)**

(Total = 25 marks)

Question 6

Required

(a) Suggest a mission statement which might be applicable for Gensup. Explain the significance of **each** component of this mission statement. **(10 marks)**

(b) Suggest suitable **operational goals** for **four** primary tasks of Gensup. **(11 marks)**

(c) Explain which generic strategy is currently being used by Gensup. **(4 marks)**

(Total = 25 marks)

Question 7

Required

(a) Contrast the task environments of the manufacturing plants and of Gensup. **(7 marks)**

(b) Describe **four** sectors of the task environment of the manufacturing plants. **(8 marks)**

(c) Contrast the task environment of Gensup with that of the original manufacturers. **(10 marks)**

(Total = 25 marks)

(Total for Section C = 50 marks)

Answers

DO NOT TURN THIS PAGE UNTIL YOU HAVE COMPLETED THE MOCK EXAM

A plan of attack

First things first

You should spend the 20 minutes reading time doing the Section A questions. These are compulsory so it's worth getting stuck into these. If you have any spare reading time you should plan your answers to longer Section B questions and select your Section C questions. You mustn't spend more than 36 minutes doing the Section A questions. If you get stuck on a question, move on and come back to it later if you have time.

The next step

Section B is compulsory as well so these questions should be next. It is worth reading both questions 2 and 3 before diving into an answer as they are both on the subject of conflict. Be careful not to fall into the trap of answering question 3 in your answer to question 2. Question 4 requires knowledge of PRINCE2 which you should be familiar with. Once again, make sure that you stick to the allocated time of 18 minutes on each Section B question. The first five marks of any question are usually the easiest and you must get all the easy marks! Don't lose out on these by spending too much time finishing off a question.

Section C

Make sure that you look at the requirements first and decide which questions you think you can answer. Then read through the scenario to make sure that you can answer your preferred questions based on the scenario given.

If you choose **Question 5** you must make sure that you write about *appropriate* structural forms as per the requirement. Part (b) specifically asks for reference to the information in the scenario so it may be useful to circle or underline relevant information in the scenario. Notice that the majority of marks are for part (b) so don't spend too long on part (a).

All three questions relate to the scenario so there is no getting away from having to *apply* your knowledge.

Question 6 is possibly the trickiest of the three questions. Part (a) requires an explanation of the components of your mission statement, so make sure it is long enough to enable you to do this. For part (b) it may be helpful to think about what you appreciate when you buy a good or service and what disappoints you.

Question 7 needs some planning as each requirement is about task environment. You need to plan what you're going to say in each part to avoid repeating yourself or making your point under the wrong requirement.

No matter how many times we remind you...

Always, always **allocate your time** according to the marks for the question in total and for the parts of the questions. And always, always **follow the requirements exactly**.

You've got free time at the end of the exam.....?

If you have allocated your time properly then you **shouldn't have time on your hands** at the end of the exam. If you find yourself with five or ten minutes spare, however, go back to **any parts of questions that you didn't finish** because you ran out of time.

Forget about it!

And don't worry if you found the paper difficult. More then likely other students would too. If this were the real thing you would need to forget the exam the minute you leave the exam hall and think about the next one. Or, if it's the last one, celebrate!

SECTION A

Question 1

1.1 B *Belbin* described the effective team's roles. *Tuckman* is known for his work on the development of team cohesion and effectiveness. *Sherif* and *Likert* worked in other areas of management research.

1.2 C Attempts to spread confusion might be part of several of the games *Mintzberg* describes, but he does not describe a game in these specific terms.

1.3 C A new strategy based on proprietary technology is **suitable** since it exploits a distinctive competence and **feasible** to the extent that the company has access to the technology in question.

1.4 C Risk is a factor that must be managed if the three main constraints of time, cost and quality are to be satisfied.

1.5 B The fourth of *Harrison's* types was labelled 'people'.

1.6 (Four of) Leadership, team building, organisational, communication, technical, personal.

1.7

Lucy Chen	**Marketing and sales**
Alex Boyle	**Outbound logistics**
Isobel Brammer	**Human resource management**

1.8 Primary: Whiteknuckle Airlines and the publications used in the advertising campaign.
Secondary: the donors of tinned food.

SECTION B

Question 2

Text references. Chapter 5

Top tips. Clearly, this question is not based on any simple or well-known model. A satisfactory answer requires you to think around the **topic of conflict**. You will not be able to produce a pass mark by misapplying a model such as one of the many change management processes. However, you may be able to use one or more simple models to assist your thought processes. The value chain is often very useful for this sort of exercise and here would prompt you to think about consequences involving suppliers and customers. It is important to **plan** your answer here especially if you are going to apply a specific model as otherwise you may miss important points or run out of things to write about.

Easy marks. Many problems in management revolve around human behaviour: in this question there are fairly easy implications on such topics as communication, morale, staff attitudes and culture.

Consequences of conflict

There is clearly a vicious circle in operation within the organisation. Its **funding** has been cut because of poor service; this must make it even more difficult to improve its service. Also, as **morale** has fallen, **conflict** has arisen and the consequent **deterioration of communication and co-operation** must inevitably further erode **performance standards**. The process is likely to continue, with undesirable consequences.

Within the organisation, **conflict will increase and morale will continue to fall**. This will produce its own undesirable symptoms such as **increased staff turnover**, **absenteeism** and **trade union hostility**. These problems in turn bring their own costs.

Service to customers is likely to decline even further, with **loss of goodwill and orders** where substitutes are available. Competitors will exploit the business's weakness where they can and attempt to poach the best staff.

As the business declines, **suppliers will also lose business**.

As the business is state owned, the Government will take a close interest in developments and are likely to impose further **sanctions, restrictions and conditions**. These will inevitably hamper progress. If there is an independent regulatory office, it will make its own unwelcome inputs.

The business's problems will attract **extensive media coverage** and much adverse publicity is likely to be generated. This will further hamper attempts at recovery, **deterring potential customers and recruits**.

Eventually, if nothing is done, management will expend all its efforts dealing with crises and **overall direction will disappear**. This tendency will be exacerbated by the declining timeliness and quality of management information.

Question 3

Text references. Chapter 6

Top tips. Company J's status as a state-owned business is important since any plan must be politically acceptable. It is not necessary to make extensive assumptions about government policy in order to make this point.

Easy marks. You should be able to score a few marks very easily with appropriate references to mechanisms for consultation, communication and negotiation, since these are obvious requirements for sensible management of conflict.

Managing the conflict

The organisation clearly has a **major problem separate from the present disruptive conflicts**: its continuing failure to provide a satisfactory level and quality of service to its customers. Any attempt to improve matters must start by **diagnosing the reasons for this failure** and **deciding what is to be done about it**. Another over-arching consideration is that **leadership of a very high quality will be required** from top management throughout the process of recovery.

It may be that **interdisciplinary working parties** could contribute to the process of diagnosis. The establishment of such groups would also be a good first step to reducing conflict, since members could air their grievances and would be forced to work together.

When a **coherent and convincing plan for recovery** has been drafted, government must be approached with the aim of obtaining the **necessary finance**. A particularly important aspect will be the negotiated settlement of the trades unions' concerns. Improving future operations may, in fact, require redundancy or it may require increased numbers, but **manpower planning** must start from a consideration of ends rather than means. Simply cutting numbers to save cost may be entirely **inappropriate** if it prejudices the company's ability to achieve its mission.

Assuming that the plan is accepted by government, it will then be top management's role to put it into effect. This will require a combination of techniques. The plan is effectively a **programme of change** and ideas of **change management** may help.

Enhanced, continuing and effective communication of goals, plans and progress to all staff will be required. There should be scope for upwards communication of individuals' concerns and these should be dealt with as sympathetically as possible. The aim should be to convince all staff that there is a rational programme underway to tackle the organisation's problems and remove the causes of friction. This should help to create a **culture of co-operation in a common cause**.

Resistance to change may be weakened by a changed system of rewards; the cost implications of this must be built into the plan.

At the same time, **top management must be prepared to dominate** the organisation and impose its will if necessary. It may impose **super-ordinate goals** on the various departments. These are goals which can only be reached through effective co-operation. Foot-dragging and adversarial behaviour must not be tolerated.

Question 4

Text references. Chapter 7.

Top tips. We are told that the Examiner regards PRINCE2 as a *de facto* standard for project management , so it is important that you understand how the system works. In particular, you must be able to explain the system's emphasis on outputs rather than processes. This principle is carried forward into the analysis of project scope in terms of what is to be achieved rather than what is to be done. Don't just describe the components of PRINCE2 but explain **how** it can help the specific situation in the question. If you are unclear on precisely what 'explain' means, refer to 'What the examiner means' in the front pages. At this stage you should be fairly confident in answering questions. Make sure you stick to the time given and develop time management skills. Advice on these issues can be found in the *Passing P5* section of the introductory pages if you need a reminder.

Easy marks. There are no easy marks here unless you are familiar with PRINCE2.

PRINCE2 is a widely accepted, standard method of project management. It offers clear management structures and planning and control methods and is noteworthy for its focus on **outputs** rather than processes.

The methodology is built up mainly from eight **components** and eight **processes**. Three of the components and two of the processes are likely to be of particular interest to the management accountant.

Business case

A business case is not something that is confined to commercial organisations; the term may be understood as meaning a reasoned account of what is to be achieved and why it will be of benefit. It is fundamental to the **PRINCE2** system that a project is driven by its business case. The business case may require updating as the project progresses. The need to agree a clear and comprehensive business case may assist the management accountant in her dealings with the CEO.

Organisation

Management implies a structure of authority and accountability. PRINCE2 recognises four layers of management responsibility, though levels may be combined or eliminated if appropriate. Company J's project has been initiated at Board level; it may be appropriate for the Board to appoint one of its number to guide policy on the project. The management accountant's concerns about her reporting responsibilities would be solved by the appointment of a **project board** to provide overall guidance and represent the business interests of the organisation.

Two other constituencies would also be represented.

(a) The **senior user** represents the interests of those who are affected by the introduction of the new system and is accountable for the quality of the specification. This role would seem appropriate for the Director of Operations.

(b) The **senior supplier/senior technical** person represents those charged with implementing the project. This role could be filled by the senior representative of the external prime contractor.

In PRINCE2, the project manager reports to the project board.

Configuration management

A **configuration** is a technical description, a complete specification of everything that is needed to bring a project to a successful conclusion. With complex projects, it is likely that frequent technical changes will be made and all of these changes must be approved and documented. Configuration management controls the processes by which projects develop.

A proper system of configuration management would assist the management accountant in dealing with any confusion that might arise over just what the new system was supposed to do

Controlling a stage

Controlling a stage is the process undertaken by the project manager to ensure that any given stage of the project remains on course. A project might consist of just one stage, of course.

PRINCE2 project control includes a comprehensive structure of reports and meetings that will give structure to the management accountant's discharge of her responsibilities.

A **project initiation** meeting agrees the scope and objectives of the project and gives approval for it to start.

The completion of each project stage is marked by an **end stage assessment**, which includes reports from the project manager and the project assurance team. The next stage does not commence until its plans have been reviewed and approved.

Highlight reports are submitted regularly to the project board by the project manager. These reports are the main overall routine control mechanism and their frequency (often monthly) is agreed at project initiation. They are essentially progress reports and should include brief summaries of project schedule and budget status.

Managing product delivery

Managing product delivery is the process that controls work done by specialist teams by agreeing what work is to be done and ensuring that it is carried out to the proper standard. The management accountant would use this process to define and implement her relationship with the external contractors.

SECTION C

Question 5

Text references. Chapter 2

Top tips. There is an explicit requirement to relate ideas about structure to the nature of Gensup as an organisation. A theoretical discussion will not be adequate. For example, we do not mention the matrix since it does not seem appropriate to any of Gensup's activities. There is plenty of evidence of how Gensup might choose to develop its structure in the precedents given in the scenario. In a question like part (a), worth only seven marks but with plenty of ground to cover, you must be reasonably brief. Do not try to be exhaustive. When you **plan your answer** to this question, make sure you don't duplicate what you have said in part (a) in part (b). Use part (a) to briefly introduce the different structural forms and part (b) to then comment on the advantages and disadvantages of each form found in part (a).

In part (b) the marking scheme might be expected to be based on the handful of possible structural forms, with up to five marks available for the discussion of each, to the stated overall maximum of eighteen marks.

It is also possible to use Mintzberg's structural configurations model to answer this question so we have provided an alternative answer to part (b) using the five types.

Easy marks. As is often the case, a little theoretical knowledge will earn you the easy marks in this question.

(a) **Classical approaches to organisation structure**

(i) **Functional structure**. The organisation hierarchy is drawn up according to the type of work that people do. Marketing staff are managed in one department; finance staff are managed in another and so on. Functional departments existed within A, B and C. In Gensup as a whole, **purchasing** is an example of a central business function.

(ii) **Geographical structure. Unisal** appears to have been organised on a geographical basis, as it was a distribution and logistics firm.

(iii) **Product organisation**. Gensup seems to have adopted this approach for A, B and C. All the activities involved in producing and selling a product are brought under one roof.

(iv) **Customer/market**. The organisation structure reflects the customer base. Unisal had aspects of this, with specialised sales forces for different industries.

In practice, Unisal has a hybrid structure, combining these approaches.

(i) Some activities as we have seen are run on a functional basis

(ii) A, B, and C are to a degree run as product divisions

(b) **Advantages and disadvantages of each structural form**

(i) **Functional departments**

Advantages

(1) They enable **specialist expertise to be concentrated** in one place, and a more **effective division of labour** within the function. For Gensup, this is seen in the centralised R & D function, which can probably do better as one than if it remained split into three.

(2) Functional organisation is **simple and logical**. Gensup has exploited this to obtain **economies of scale** – the larger purchasing function should be able to achieve bulk discounts on orders, and hopefully reduced administration costs.

Disadvantages

(1) **Functions** reflect the way the business works internally, but not **products or markets it makes and serves**.

(2) It is **hard to identify profits/losses on individual products**, unless something like activity based costing is used.

(3) They **inhibit organisational learning**, in that systems thinking (seeing the wood for the trees) and multi-disciplinary teams are not encouraged.

(4) **Horizontal communication is limited** so decisions related to more than one department are only taken at the highest levels.

(ii) As for **geographical organisation**, there is an obvious logic for Unisal's distribution operations, especially dealing with export markets over a wide area.

(1) **Better decision making** at the point of contact with the customer.

(2) The **goods are closer to the customer**, so delivery is quick and cheap – important in just-in-time applications.

(3) There is potentially a **duplication of management effort**.

In such a set-up, **each warehouse needs to operate as an independent** unit, with its own local customers. Whereas the output of each warehouse is locally managed, the **inputs are managed by the central purchasing department**.

(1) To work, the centralised purchasing operation must be in **regular and close contact with the warehouses** to see they have the right supplies in stock; the firm needs **excellent internal communications**.

(2) Gensup will have to work hard to ensure **consistency of performance** in all its export markets, especially if it sells to multinational firms.

(iii) **Product divisions. Gensup is effectively in two businesses now**: manufacturing and distribution.

Advantages of a product division structure

(1) It **enhances accountability for a product range**. Gensup's reorganisation has in fact clouded this issue, as purchases for the manufacturing firms and the old Unisal have been combined.

(2) **Gensup must decide how far A B and C remain independent of the distribution centres**. Unisal was not a manufacturer, and the scenario does not make clear how A, B and C's products are to be distributed. If A, B and C retain their own sales forces, or deal with the old Unisal distribution centre at an arm's length basis, function as divisions. But none of this is particularly clear from the data.

The **disadvantage** of **product division** is the **increased complexity** of the firm. A B and C could be integrated into one production organisation. This would enhance the transfer of manufacturing know-how (eg TQM techniques) and personnel between them. They produce similar products for similar markets. Retaining them as separate divisions would seem to undermine some potential; economies of scale that a unified functional management structure would bring them.

(iv) As for **customer or market segment**, this form of departmentation has not been adopted, other than at a fairly low level for the sales force. Marketing is to be a central function of the business.

Gensup's **hybrid structure** seems sensible the light of its diverse activities but it is not perfect. The **manufacturing divisions are imperfectly integrated** into the structure as a whole: no indication is given of the precise nature of the relationship with the distribution centres, who have traditionally purchased from a range of suppliers. We do not know if the purchasing function will treat A, B and C at an arms length, thus injecting market control into the process.

To summarise, the current hybrid structure proposed has not gone far enough in addressing some of the important structural issues raised by the acquisition.

Top tips. Alternative answer to part (b) based on Mintzberg's structural configurations model

The **pros and cons of each structural configuration**

(i) Simple structure. This is not appropriate for Gensup. Gensup is too big and complex. Whilst Gensup must innovate, much of its production output is standardised. Individual departments, however, might be arranged in a fairly informal manner (eg R & D).

(ii) **Machine bureaucracy**. Such bureaucracies exist to perform standardised work according to a set routine, and are **appropriate in stable simple environments**. At the moment, there appears to be **environmental instability**, with the consolidation of the customer base into larger firms, new markets and sources of supply opening up. The firm is positioned on a fairly long value chain, **so a machine bureaucracy is not really suitable if flexibility is required**. The manufacturing plants require standardisation, however, to ensure consistent quality, and some sort of functional specialisation is, therefore, inevitable.

(iii) **Divisional form**. Given that the manufacturing firms and the distribution firm are very different, some degree of divisionalisation will be necessary although some synergies (eg central R&D and purchasing) can be expected. The firm might therefore contain:

(1) a distribution division, formerly Unisal, to service customers;
(2) a manufacturing division, featuring A, B and C.

The **two divisions should be kept at arms length**, to ensure the customer still benefits from Unisal's purchasing expertise. Unisal may be able to obtain some products cheaper from the manufacturing division. However the existence of many common functions means that full divisionalisation will not be practised.

(iv) Unisal has some of the features of a **professional bureaucracy**, in that **sales staff are 'experts'** on particular types of customer, and that the firm was essentially involved in services. This is still appropriate for the **distribution operation**, but not suitable for the whole of Gensup.

(v) There may be some scope for developing features of an **operating or administrative adhocracy**. This will depend on the degree to which the firm can mobilise the expertise of its various personnel in: sales, research and development and purchasing.

The **shared expertise** gives the firm the opportunity to innovate more. As the **'operating core' of the manufacturing plants has effectively been automated**, a configuration encouraging project teams across the firm may be the best way of ensuring competitive advantage and customer benefits. Sales staff can communicate customer requirements to staff in R & D.

Question 6

Text references. Chapter 10 covers mission and Chapter 12 covers strategies.

Top tips. Fairly obviously, part (a) is best answered with a fairly lengthy mission statement perhaps based on the common four part model.

- Purpose
- Strategy
- Policies and standards
- Values

A snappy one-liner, such as Komatsu's 'Beat Caterpillar', will not give you much to write about.

(a) **Mission statement for Gensup**

> Mission statements range from brief sentences to long paragraphs.
>
> 'Gensup is a materials manufacturing and components sourcing and distribution group, which services selected niches in the engineering market on a global basis.
>
> Our continuing central aim is the continuing optimisation of shareholders' investment through earnings per share and increase in capital value. Our activities are in raw materials manufacture and the provision of specialist expertise to our dealings with customers.
>
> To this end we seek to:
>
> - operate in markets where we have comprehensive expertise and knowledge;
> - continually ensure that we identify and anticipate our customers' needs;
> - develop new materials and processes through the application of technological development programmes.
>
> We aim to be the best in our chosen fields, and thereby to increase the wealth of our shareholders and enhance the prosperity and well-being of our customers, employees and the communities of which we are a part.'

Importance of the different components of the mission statement

(i) The statement **defines what business the firm is in**, and the customers it serves. This **communicates basic facts** about the company to an outsider. In the materials business, the mission suggests extension into other materials markets.

(ii) Shareholders are addressed in the statement's **'central aim'**. Unisal was quoted on several stockmarkets world-wide, so the overall commitment to enhance **shareholder value** would seem appropriate.

(iii) The firm **competes** in a number of different ways, but it seems to be highlighting quality of service and manufacturing innovation.

(iv) Connected stakeholders are mentioned: the mission refers to the well-being of **customers, employees and the community**. The statement is perhaps deficient in that it does not state how this is to be achieved. Interestingly, it **excludes suppliers**, which are resource rich countries, but which may be poor in terms of economic development.

(v) There is no mention of **social responsibility**, other than vague waffle about the community. Gensup does not trumpet its desire to be a 'good corporate citizen' nor is any mention made of the **environment**, even though many firms in extractive industries make such a point. Given Gensup's manufacturing capability, some mention of these issues could have been expected.

(b) **Operational goals**

> **Top tips.** The word 'primary' should prompt you to think of the value chain model. Identifying four of the primary value activities should be worth at least two marks, and possibly four if you provided a brief explanation of each. We have referred to more than four primary tasks and the extra answers are in a box for information only.
>
> **Easy marks.** Further easy marks are going to be difficult to find. Making sensible suggestions about goals and critical success factors is difficult to do without good experience of the industry in question. The best most candidates will be able to do will be to pick reasonably obvious ideas such as speed of delivery. Ask yourself what you appreciate when you buy a good or service and what disappoints you.

Operational goals can cover a wide variety of organisational activities, including overall performance measurement, production, maintenance, boundary-spanning (eg purchasing, marketing) and so forth. The examples offered below are activities selected from *Porter's* value chain analysis. (In this model, primary activities are those directly related with production, sales, marketing, delivery and services.)

(i) **Inbound logistics** deal with receiving, handling and storing inputs to the production system. They cover warehousing, transport, stock control and so forth. **Operational goals** could include the following.

(1) Lead times from suppliers
(2) Incidence of stock-outs
(3) Quality of purchased inputs (eg through quality assurance)
(4) Warehousing costs

The goal would be to make **efficient use of warehouse to support the production function** at lower cost. A related 'support activity' (procurement) would be concerned with issues such as price per unit purchased and supplies.

(ii) **Operations** convert resource inputs into a final product. In a manufacturing firm, this is relatively easy to identify as the factory. In a service company, operations include those activities which make up the basic service. Operations include the entire management of the production function. With Gensup's strategy of customer service, and the customers' espousal of TQM, something such as BS EN ISO 9000 certification may be required. **Goals can include** those below.

(1) Quality targets
(2) Throughput speed
(3) Targets for reducing waste

(iii) **Outbound logistics** relate to storing the product and its distribution to customers. They include packaging, warehousing, testing and so forth. **Goals will include** the following.

(1) Speed of processing
(2) Response times
(3) Error-free deliveries

(iv) **Marketing and sales** are those activities that relate to informing customers about the product, persuading them to buy it, and enabling them to do so. This includes advertising, promotion and so forth. Some **performance measures** can include the following.

(1) Raising customers' awareness (measured by survey) of the firm
(2) The incidence of repeat business
(3) Market share

Additional answer

(v) **After sales service**. For many companies, there are activities such as installing products, repairing them, upgrading them, providing spare parts and so forth. This is at the **heart of Unisal's business**. Suitable goals could include the use of aftersales service visits as a means of generating new orders or finding more about the customer.

In short, **the firm will be driven by goals relating both to product quality and service quality**. Suppliers who are on contractual relationships are perhaps less worried about price, in the short term at least, than about reliability.

(c) **Generic strategies**

Top tips. Remember *Porter's* conclusion that both cost leadership and differentiation are expensive strategies and that most businesses will have to settle for some kind of focus strategy.

Easy marks. At managerial level there may well be some credit available for a brief summary of relevant theory such as we provide. However, it could not be worth more than two marks.

(i) **Cost leadership**: be the lowest cost producer in the industry as a whole.

(ii) **Differentiation**: offer a unique product or service to the market as a whole.

(iii) **Focus**: restrict activities to only part of the market (a segment).

(1) Provide goods and/or services at lower cost to that segment (cost-focus).
(2) Provide a differentiated product/service for that segment (differentiation-focus).

What strategy is Gensup pursuing?

(i) **Unisal probably pursued a differentiation-focus strategy** in that it concentrated on servicing the needs of customers in identified market segments.

(ii) On the other hand, the **manufacturing plants produced commodity items**. In such a case, especially where raw materials are an important part of cost, cost leadership is important. As there are so many suppliers, these firms **probably pursued a cost-focus strategy**, based on the UK market.

(iii) The new developments offer new opportunities and so **Gensup's strategy of differentiation-focus in the global market will probably predominate** especially if the manufacturing plants are to be exploited to extend Gensup's product range.

Question 7

Text references. Chapter 12

Top tips. Make sure you read all the requirements carefully and **plan** what you are going to put into the answer to each part. It would be very easy to produce a poor answer by making good points in the wrong place.

Easy marks. All three parts of this question revolve around task environment, so spend a few moments making sure you are aware of all the factors that go into the various task environments discussed. This will take you a long way towards a pass mark, though you will have to provide some discussion to reach it.

(a) **The task environments of the manufacturing plants and Gensup**

The environment is 'all elements that exist outside the boundary of the organisation' which have the potential to affect all or part of the organisation.

The task environment of the **manufacturing plants** is fairly restricted.

(i) **Investors**. All the firms were privately owned, without the need to communicate with a large number of investors or potential investors on a stock exchange.

(ii) **Resources**. Each of the manufacturing firms depends on raw materials. In this respect, the firms might be vulnerable to:

(1) interruptions in supply, as metals, in particular, are not found everywhere. Aluminium and copper, or ores at least, have to be imported;

(2) changes in price levels from their major suppliers. As far as plastics are concerned, the main supply would appear to be the oil and chemicals industries. There is a developed international market.

(iii) Other common inputs are **water** and **electric power** in the UK. Normally, there should be no problem (but beware droughts!)

(iv) The firms are **not affected by social trends or changes in consumer tastes**.

(v) **Technology** is a crucial area to keep costs down and to attain, through innovation, a significant advantage.

Gensup's task environment is much wider. Effectively, Unisal has engaged in a degree of **backwards vertical integration**.

Gensup is vulnerable to the same international trade and political issues relating to acquiring its resources as the former manufacturing companies. Furthermore, it is able to take advantage of export opportunities more effectively, so its chosen domain has shifted towards an **international** orientation, and it will therefore be **more exposed to international political influences** than the three firms before.

Gensup's **value chain** is more extensive than that of the manufacturing firms or indeed of Unisal. The firm combines both a manufacturing and distribution capacity, so the domain in which it operates is large.

(b) **Sectors of the task environment**

Top tips. We have described more than four sections, as you had a choice.

Some sectors of the task environment of manufacturing plants

(i) **Financial resources**. Management of cash and other **working capital** items is an essential part of the day to day management of any business; a firm which runs out of cash goes under. Obviously, **long-term finance** is less of a day to day issue. Purchasing raw materials exposes the firm to exchange risk: they might operate on the futures market.

(ii) **Human resources**. Even in times of unemployment, many companies complain of 'skills shortages' implying that they cannot obtain the right staff. This is obviously affected by demography and government policy on education and training policies.

(1) No problem with recruiting unskilled production workers.
(2) Skilled staff are needed in R&D and maintenance.

(iii) **Market**. The 'market' is a firm's current and potential customers. The manufacturing firm's markets were fairly small. Unisal's markets are extensive.

(1) **Customer needs change over time**: the marketing department should identify these needs, and to suggest how they can be met most effectively.
(2) The market is changing to one where size is important and where the customer base is becoming concentrated. See (iv) below. Unisal is taking over marketing activities.

(iv) **Industry and competition.**

Unisal and the manufacturing plants merged because of the **evident concentration among the customer base** and the potential increase in customer bargaining power *(Porter)*.

Additional answer

(v) **Raw materials**. The manufacturing plants need raw materials (and energy) to make their products. Is there competition for raw materials, effectively bidding up the price? Are they easily obtainable, or is there a restricted supply? Are prices volatile?

(1) New supplies in eastern Europe should reduce the dependency on one source.
(2) Unisal is a sourcing and distribution firm, so some expertise already exists. Gensup will perhaps be able to take advantage of bulk discounts.

(c) **Contrasts between the task environment of Gensup and that of the original manufacturers**

(i) **Financial resources**. Gensup is a plc. In theory, long-term financial resources should be easier to obtain, but that the **share price will determine the cost of capital** and the **returns** expected. In this, Gensup differs from the original manufacturing firms, which were not quoted companies (although Unisal was quoted).

(ii) **Human resources**. Gensup results from a merger of manufacturers and a distribution firm.

(1) Unisal had developed a large sales force, who will now have to liaise directly with the plants. Whereas **the plants** dealt with external customers or the market directly, **they will now do so through the former Unisal's sales force**.
(2) There might have to be **changes in corporate culture** to accommodate the specialists now working in corporate R & D.

(3) Gensup probably has a **larger pool from which to recruit** than A, B and C, as it is an international firm.

(iii) **Market**. This relates to (ii) (human resources) above. From dealing with customers directly, the **manufacturing plants will become internal suppliers** of a sales force already used to dealing with a large number of suppliers. **For the manufacturing plants, their environment will be simpler**.

(iv) **Industry**. The **plants will be more secure** as part of a larger firm, dealing with customers whose **increasing size** effectively increases their bargaining power and competitive ability.

(v) **Raw materials**. This situation has not changed significantly, other than in east Europe. Gensup might be able to force price decreases in electricity or even water. The firm's total demand for ores and chemicals is not increased by virtue of the merger alone. Increased activity levels might lead to more purchases. However, centralisation of some purchasing functions should enable greater expertise in purchasing to be developed.

(vi) **International**. The firm is now dealing in a global market, which offers more threats but more opportunities.

(vii) **Complexity**

Gensup's task environment is inevitably more complex than the environment of its predecessor companies, because the **value chain of a vertically integrated conglomerate is longer and more complex** than that of a firm focused on one area.

(1) The **variety of influences**. The greater the number of markets the organisation operates in, the greater the number of influences to which it is subject.

Gensup faces an increased variety of influences, as it tackles new markets. The complexity is probably at a medium level. Although Gensup is effectively a new company, Unisal, its predecessor, was a plc already listed on a number of stock exchanges.

(2) The amount of **knowledge** necessary. Some environments, to be handled successfully, require knowledge. Gensup needs some specialist knowledge in a fairly restricted area. However, this required knowledge and expertise is likely to increase, as customers require more sophisticated materials.

(3) The **interconnectedness** of environmental influences. Importing and exporting companies are sensitive to exchange rates, which in turn are sensitive to interest rates. Interest rates then influence a company's borrowing costs.

Many of the **environmental factors are interconnected. Commodity prices are perhaps very susceptible to changes in exchange rates**. These might be volatility in raw materials prices.

CIMA – Managerial Level

Paper P5

Integrated Management

Mock Examination 2

Instructions to candidates:

You are allowed three hours to answer this question paper.
In the real exam, you are allowed 20 minutes reading time before the examination begins during which you should read the question paper, and if you wish, make annotations on the question paper. However, you will **not** be allowed, **under any circumstances**, to open the answer book and start writing or use your calculator during this reading time.
You are strongly advised to carefully read the question requirement before attempting the question concerned.
Answer the ONE compulsory question in Section A. This is comprised of sub-questions.
Answer ALL THREE compulsory questions in Section B.
Answer TWO of the three questions in Section C.

DO NOT OPEN THIS PAPER UNTIL YOU ARE READY TO START UNDER EXAMINATION CONDITIONS

SECTION A – 20 marks

Answer ALL TEN sub-questions in this section

Question 1

1.1 Which of the following is not one of the categories of needs identified by John Adair as crucial to the leadership process?

A Individual
B Group
C Task
D Control **(2 marks)**

1.2 Which of the following is not a feature of a good disciplinary procedure as defined by the UK ACAS code?

A Disciplinary matters are dealt with without delay
B Except for a first offence, workers are dismissed for gross misconduct
C Disciplinary action is not taken until the case has been carefully investigated
D There is a right of appeal **(2 marks)**

1.3 'Business Process Re-engineering' can be said to be lineally descended from the work of which management thinker?

A Henry Mintzberg
B Henri Fayol
C Charles Handy
D Frederick W Taylor **(2 marks)**

1.4 Which one of the following is not one of the four perspectives of Kaplan and Norton's balanced scorecard

A Financial perspective
B Customer perspective
C Internal business perspective
D Environmental perspective **(2 marks)**

1.5 The concept of asset specificity generally supports a strategy of:

A Horizontal integration
B Vertical integration
C Cost leadership
D Market development **(2 marks)**

1.6 The logical incrementalist approach to strategy resembles the rational model in that it

A Is similarly dependent on detailed medium-term forecasting
B Depends on managerial activity
C Emphasises the possession of core competences
D Can deal with a wide range of strategic possibilities **(2 marks)**

1.7 Which one of the following is not one of the five stages in the process of project management

A Initiation
B Planning
C Management
D Controlling
E Completing **(2 marks)**

1.8 Michael Porter identifies five competitive forces in the task environment. State four of them other than current competitor rivalry **(2 marks)**

1.9 Say whether the statement below is true or false

'Conflict between goals will inevitably lead to a policy of accepting merely adequate performance in a number of areas' **(2 marks)**

1.10 Say whether the statement below is true or false

'The organismic (or organic) organisation described by Burns and Stalker appears to have much in common with the task-oriented organisation described by Harrison **(2 marks)**

(Total for Section A = 20 marks)

SECTION B – 30 marks

Answer ALL THREE questions – 10 marks each

Question 2

Sam is the Chief Executive Officer (CEO) of T Inc, a tobacco company. He has traditional views about the purpose of business in general and his own organisation in particular. Though he is frequently pressured by a variety of groups and organisations that think he should run his organisation differently, he sticks firmly to the view that the overriding purpose of business is to make money for the shareholders. His son, Frank, who is being coached to take over the CEO role, takes a very different perspective. In his view, T Inc has a responsibility to a wide range of stakeholders.

Required

Explain how

(a) Sam would justify his view that the overriding purpose of the business is to make money for the shareholders

(b) Frank would justify his view that T Inc has a responsibility to a wide range of stakeholders. **(10 marks)**

Question 3

The CityGo Bus Company, formerly a regional operating division of a public corporation, has been acquired through a management buy out led by the general manger, Jim Ryan.

Competition will be intense as soon as the routes become fully competitive in January 20X3. The company has a number of weaknesses that have to be attended to immediately.

The most important of these is that its computing systems are totally integrated into the previous owner's systems. Internal management accounts are almost non-existent and most management reports were directed at the corporation's management team not at CityGo's management. It had never been possible to devolve budget responsibility down to key line managers in operations and maintenance.

The privatisation timetable means that CityGo has only a few months to set up new computer based systems.

The requirement will be for a project management process that can deal with tight timescales involving a complicated set of interrelated decisions and actions. CityGo management must realise that effective project planning and control need different management skills than those required to run operational processes.

This is the immediate requirement but in the longer term CityGo must put in place a strategy for managing information resources in ways which enable it to achieve a competitive advantage or at least competitive parity with other bus operators.

Required

Examine the attributes of a project management process and assess the range of project management tools and techniques which are available to CityGo to help achieve an efficient changeover to new financial systems.

(10 marks)

Question 4

NYO.com was established in February 2000. Since then, the company, which provides on-line financial advice, has experienced rapid growth and the management has not really had the time to get all management systems and procedures into place.

The company has asked you to look at the way in which the company deals with its disciplinary problems and procedures.

Required

Explain why NYO.com should have a formal disciplinary procedure. **(10 marks)**

(Total for Section B = 30 marks)

SECTION C – 50 marks

Answer any TWO questions from this section – 25 marks each

Question 5

Thurnon plc are to initiate a project to study the feasibility of a new product. The end result of the feasibility project will be a report recommending the action to be taken for the new product. The activities to be carried out to complete the feasibility project are given below.

Activity	*Description*	*Immediate predecessors*	*Expected time Weeks*	*Number of staff required*
A	preliminary design	–	5	3
B	market research	–	3	2
C	obtain engineering quotes	A	2	2
D	construct prototype	A	5	5
E	prepare marketing material	A	3	3
F	costing	C	2	2
G	product testing	D	4	5
H	pilot survey	B, E	6	4
I	pricing estimates	H	2	1
J	final report	F, G, I	6	2

(a) Prepare a network for the scheme of activities set out above. Determine the critical path and the shortest duration of the project. **(10 marks)**

(b) Assuming the project starts at time zero and that each activity commences at the earliest start date, construct a chart showing the number of staff required at any one time for this project. **(10 marks)**

(c) Explain what is meant by the term 'project life cycle'. **(5 marks)**

(Total = 25 marks)

Question 6

The Supreme Football Club (SFC), a profit-making company with directors and shareholders, has received a take-over bid from one of the satellite-broadcasting corporations. The club is currently assessing whether to accept the bid.

SFC is a multi-million dollar business. Its income consists of gate receipts, fees for TV rights, merchandising, sponsorship, conferencing and catering. The club is very successful; the team's performance on the pitch has made it a very popular club and this success has been reflected in growth in turnover and profits in recent years. The advent of satellite TV has made football a worldwide spectator sport and the club has fans throughout the world.

The success of the club has not, however, prevented it from receiving some criticism. One of the issues causing continuing concern has been the constantly-changing replica shirts as worn by the club's football team. Parents of young fans have felt pressurised into spending large sums of money every year or so because the club has changed its shirt style six times in as many years.

Another issue has been the increase in ticket prices over the past few years. These have risen far faster than inflation, and the fan club has made several representations to the board of SFC in protest at these increases.

The income from TV rights is much welcomed by the club, but matches have been rescheduled at short notice to suit satellite stations and their exclusive audiences. It is perhaps not surprising therefore that the bid to take over the club by the satellite-broadcasting corporation has been met with hostility by the fans and others who see the club they have supported and the game they love as being treated like any other profit-making organisation.

Required

(a) Identify the stakeholder groups of the SFC. Describe the particular interest of each stakeholder group in the club. **(15 marks)**

(b) Explain which stakeholder groups are likely to exert the most influence on the decision to accept/reject the takeover bid, indicating their power and influence. **(10 marks)**

(Total = 25 marks)

Question 7

Project background

Southern Regional Health Authority (SRHA)

The SRHA manages the provision of medical care to the public within its local area. It is responsible for 50 medical centres and 10 hospitals.

You are a senior management accountant working for one of the southern region hospitals.

The 'Healthweb' national information network is a central government-led initiative which aims to provide a secure and dedicated network environment for all medical practitioners and managers, to share and access healthcare information. Other regions within the country have already connected to the network, with 95% of medical centres and hospitals within these regions utilising the facilities.

The SRHA has been sent a target by the central government to have 80% of all medical centres and 90% of all hospitals within the region connected to the Healthweb one year from now. Prior to the project commencement, most information within the hospitals and medical centres was kept by a manual, paper-based system, and all data exchange was done by means of telephone or by post. The senior management team of the SRHA set a project board in January 2002 to oversee the progress of the project and so specify the project objectives.

Project management

The central government has contracted a large telecommunications company, T, to manage and control the network and to project-manage the regional connection projects. T was contracted to provide all hardware and software systems support, training and maintenance.

The SRHA project team was mainly made up of managers and technicians from T, but also included three doctors and three senior managers.

Project progress

Each medical centre and hospital within the southern region was allowed to discuss terms of usage, (that is, the hardware and software requirements, which aspects of the Healthweb to utilise and the timing of the implementation) separately with the GPC project team.

Financing within the SRHA

Many doctors and senior managers were concerned about the limited resources of the hospitals and medical centres being spent on unnecessary technology and that the disruption of the project might affect the quality of service to patients. Other regions had reported large costs in computer upgrades and facilities, which could have been better spent on direct patient care.

Although the central government has set up a 'Technology Fund', some of which has been set aside for this project, obtaining the funds has proved difficult in other regions. In addition, there has been no previous consistency in financing connection to the network, with some regional health authorities paying all of the costs. Other regions have invested only in the initial technology, with all on-going operational costs being paid by the individual hospitals and medical centres.

The hospital executives at the hospital in which you are a senior management accountant are concerned that the senior managers not involved directly in the GPC project are unaware of its nature and importance.

Required

You have been asked by the executives of your own hospital to prepare a memorandum to the other senior managers in the hospital which should:

(a) Discuss the relationship of the project manager to:

(i) The project sponsor (that is, the central government).
(ii) The project board.
(iii) The medical and administrative users (in medical centres and hospitals).

Include in your answer a discussion of the potential conflicting project objectives of the above stakeholders.

(15 marks)

(b) Explain the potential project management problems which might arise from allowing each hospital and medical centre to discuss individual terms of usage of the Healthweb separately with the GPC project team.

(10 marks)

(Total = 25 marks)

(Total for Section C = 50 marks)

Answers

DO NOT TURN THIS PAGE UNTIL YOU HAVE COMPLETED THE MOCK EXAM

A plan of attack

First things first

You should spend the 20 minutes reading time doing the Section A questions. These are compulsory so it's worth getting stuck into these. If you have any spare reading time you should plan your answers to longer Section B questions and select your Section C questions. You mustn't spend more than 36 minutes doing the Section A questions. If you get stuck on a question, move on and come back to it later if you have time.

The next step

Section B is compulsory as well so these questions should be next. There shouldn't be anything you are unfamiliar with on these particular questions. (If there is, go back to the study text and revise.) Make sure you read the requirements carefully, particularly on Question 4. Be careful not to write everything you know on disciplinary procedures. The requirement asks why they should have a procedure. Once again, make sure that you stick to the allocated time of 18 minutes on each Section B question. The first five marks of any question are usually the easiest and you must get all the easy marks! Don't lose out on these by spending too much time finishing off a question.

Section C

Make sure that you look at the requirements first and decide which questions you think you can answer. Then read through the scenario to make sure that you can answer your preferred questions based on the scenario given.

If you have revised network diagrams, Gantt charts and project lifecycles then **Question 5** should be fairly straight forward. Your network diagram can be in activity-on-node style or activity-on-line style. Remember to draw a key.

Question 6 shouldn't cause you too many problems, although you may feel you are not sure who exerts the most influence. This does not matter. If you pick one particular group and give reasons for your choices you will score well.

You need to have a good knowledge of project management to answer **Question 7** so consider how you will answer the question before plunging in to it; sometimes planning an answer will reveal that you actually have very little to say and would be better of trying something else.

No matter how many times we remind you...

Always, always **allocate your time** according to the marks for the question in total and for the parts of the questions. And always, always **follow the requirements exactly**.

You've got free time at the end of the exam.....?

If you have allocated your time properly then you **shouldn't have time on your hands** at the end of the exam. If you find yourself with five or ten minutes spare, however, go back to **any parts of questions that you didn't finish** because you ran out of time.

Forget about it!

And don't worry if you found the paper difficult. More then likely other students would too. If this were the real thing you would need to forget the exam the minute you leave the exam hall and think about the next one. Or, if it's the last one, celebrate!

SECTION A

Question 1

1.1 D Control might be seen as one of the task needs

1.2 B The relevant provision actually says that, except for gross misconduct, workers should not be dismissed for a first breach of discipline.

1.3 D Taylor pioneered the scientific management movement and his aim of increased productivity is still a major preoccupation for management at all levels.

1.4 D The missing perspective is the innovation and learning perspective, or ' can we continue to improve and create value'?

1.5 B **Vertical integration**. Some assets have little or no value outside a given contractual relationship that requires their use. Firms may therefore be reluctant to invest in such assets, making it necessary for firms at a different stage in the value system to extend their operations upstream (or even downstream) in order to secure access to such assets.

1.6 B Both approaches are built around deliberate decisions by managers. Neither emphasises the possession of core competences and, of the two approaches, only the rational model is dependent on detailed medium– term forecasting and deals with a wide range of strategic possibilities

1.7 C Leadership is the third stage in the process of project management. The first, second, fourth and fifth of these stages correspond closely to the phases of the project life cycle.

1.8 Threat of new entrants; threat of substitute products; bargaining power of customers; bargaining power of suppliers.

1.9 False. Satisficing is one possible response to goal conflict. Daft also identifies bargaining, priority setting, and sequential attention.

1.10 True. Both display fluid structures in which expertise is more important than status, and commitment to the task more important than correct procedure, for example.

SECTION B

Question 2

Text references. Chapter 10.

Top tips. Make sure your answer refers to the information given in the question. You need to comment on Sam's beliefs and Frank's beliefs when explaining their opposing stances. Interestingly, the Examiner's answer to this question makes no reference at all to the contentious nature of T Inc's product. Many people would consider that the addictive nature of tobacco and its proven threat to the health of its consumers would be important considerations in any discussion of T Inc's goals and responsibilities.

Easy marks. The Friedmanite or ownership interest approach is quite easy to describe and is a good way of starting your answer.

(a) **Sam's view of the business**

Sam could support his view that the purpose of T Inc is to make money for the shareholders to the exclusion of any other interests, by using the arguments below.

(i) A business is **owned** by its shareholders. Property rights are fundamental to a free society and an efficient economy and should not be infringed without very good reason. Such infringements must be sanctioned by law. If the aim of maximising shareholder value is subordinated to any other goal, the shareholders' assets are being misused.

(ii) Even if it is accepted that groups other than shareholders are intimately affected by a company's behaviour, many of those groups' **legitimate concerns** are satisfied by their contractual relationships with the company. Staff are paid salaries. Suppliers are paid for their supplies. Customers are provided with the products they require and pay for. Taxes are paid to central and local government.

(iii) Other groups may feel that they have an interest in what companies do. In the case of a tobacco company, which may source its raw material from poorer countries, **exploiting cheap labour** in the process; which may cause **pollution** in its manufacturing operations; and which may be accused of **marketing dangerous substances** without proper controls, there is likely to be a large, vocal, well-organised and powerful body of opinion about its activities. The **anti-smoking lobby** will do what it can to hamper T Inc's activities. The correct response to such action is to point out the legal position. It is for government, not pressure groups, to decide what is legal and what is not and the extent to which companies have responsibilities to society at large.

(b) **Frank's view of the business**

The stakeholder view of organisations' social responsibility is based on the idea that people have inalienable natural rights in addition to any granted by the law as it exists from time to time. Frank might argue along the lines below.

(i) Employees' relationship with their employment is such that **they establish greater rights** than simply the right to remuneration. They **invest a great deal of their lives and personal consequence** in their work and deserve to be treated with care and consideration.

(ii) Large companies, in particular, control so much in the way of resources that their conduct has **wider implications** for society than just its commercial effects. They also do not bear the total cost of their activities, since many **externalities** exist This should be recognised by the companies themselves and they should acknowledge their duty to society.

(iii) Corporations' relationship with government through the mechanism of tax is subject to **manipulation**. Many companies do not pay a fair amount of tax. An acceptance of social responsibility can go some way to compensate for this.

Question 3

Text references. Chapter 8.

Top tips. Scenario detail is sparse in this question, so most marks will be awarded for a sensible discussion of project management in the context of IT and financial systems. You will not need to draw a diagram. We have only done one to illustrate our answer but you are unlikely to have the time to do so in the exam.

Easy marks. Our answer is fuller than necessary to score a good mark on this question. Essential points are the nature of the project management and how projects are organised; the trade offs available between time, cost and quality; the basic planning and scheduling techniques; and a mention of risk management.

Project management process

The implementation of its own financial systems will require the management at CityGo to set up a **project management process** which can deal with tight timescales involving a complicated set of interrelated decisions and actions.

(a) **Project management** differs from the management of resources which is attempting to achieve specific objectives within set **timescales** and **budgets** – a one-off activity.

(b) **Functional management**, on the other hand, is concerned with providing an on-going service.

A project has boundaries and it is one of the activities of the project management team to set and keep the project within those boundaries. The set of attributes that are needed to achieve the project's objectives are shown in the diagram below.

For illustration only

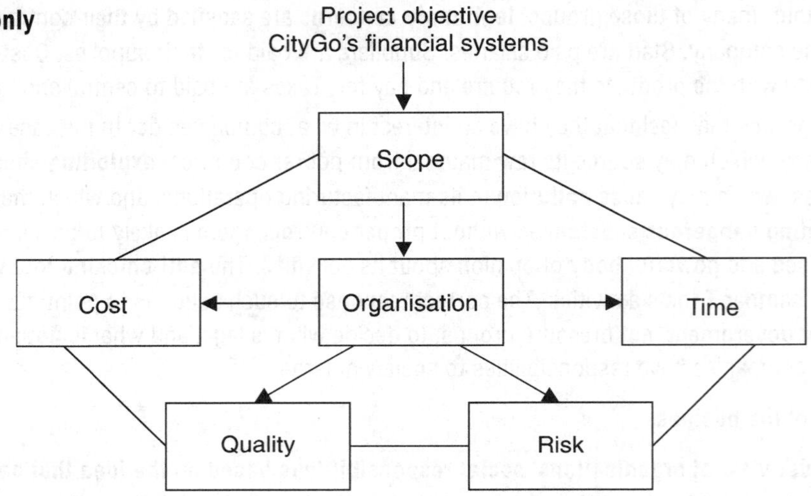

The **scope** of the project is to ensure that the project's purpose is achieved by specifying the work that must be done and excluding superfluous or otherwise unnecessary work.

The project **organisation** assembles the appropriate resources required to undertake the project.

Cost, time and **quality** can be juggled to produce the optimum result. For example, decreasing the cost to deliver the optimum result without compromising the quality objective might mean allowing more time for the project. In the case of CityGo the time element is crucial. They only have a few months to set up these new computer based systems.

Risk. The project manager can then determine how the risks can be lessened, deflected or avoided and draw up a risk management plan, including contingency plans.

Using project management techniques

Project techniques can be managed under suitable project management software, which incorporates most of the techniques familiar to project management.

(a) **Scope**

  (i) **Project definition**. A precise definition as to what is expected of the project is required.

  (ii) **Work breakdown structure (WBS)** defines the scope of the project in detail by breaking it up into smaller parts. This is the best way of discovering the work that must be done, as well determining the resources required.

(b) **Organisation**. The roles and responsibilities between the parties at the different levels must be identified, as well as the level and competence of the resource to be used.

(c) **Cost**. The WBS can be used to analyse direct and indirect costs of each activity. This structure can then be used for estimating or tendering for the project.

(d) **Time**. Tasks need to be scheduled and planned in order to make the most effective use of the resources available. **Scheduling techniques** use the work breakdown structure to plan the time required to complete each task. **Network analysis** identifies the dependence of one task on another. A **critical path** will exist throughout the project.

(e) **Quality**. CityGo management should state their precise requirement for the financial systems so that the standards against which the quality is measured are clear.

(f) **Risk**. The team can attempt to reduce the risk through good work practices, quality specifications and standards, backup systems and contingency plans. The remaining risk may be an **insurable risk**.

Question 4

Text references. Chapter 5.

Top tips. This is a fairly easy question to score a pass mark on if you have a reasonable idea of what discipline is and some knowledge of modern disciplinary procedures.

However, note carefully the use of the word 'why' in the question .You are **not** being asked what discipline is, you are being asked **why** discipline is a good idea. **This shows the importance of reading the question carefully**. If you need reminding of how to approach answering questions, refer back to the advice in the opening pages.

Easy marks. Speed, consistency and fairness are obvious requirements of any disciplinary system.

Discipline promotes order and good behaviour in an organisation by enforcing acceptable standards of conduct. It can be enforced by sanctions, encouraged by example or created by individuals' own sense of what is fitting and proper.

The purpose of disciplinary action is not punishment or retribution. It should have as its goal the **improvement of the future behaviour** of the employee and other members of the organisation. The purpose obviously is the avoidance of similar occurrences in the future.

Disciplinary action tends to generate **resentment** because it is an unpleasant experience. The challenge is to apply the necessary disciplinary action so that it will be least resented. A formal, written disciplinary procedure can enhance and support the maintenance of workplace discipline by ensuring consistency, speed, transparency and fairness of application.

(a) Discipline must be **consistent** in application. Inconsistency is bad for morale and brings the whole system into disrepute. Those responsible for administering discipline must know in detail what is expected of them so that the system runs satisfactorily.

(b) Disciplinary action should be taken as **speedily** as possible, subject to the need to investigate thoroughly while at the same time avoiding haste.

(c) **Transparency** is an important contributor to fairness; people subject to disciplinary rules must not only know what those rules are, but also how they are to be administered and enforced. This is so important that many national legal systems include rules with which the procedures of individual organisations must comply.

(d) **Fairness** is provided for by incorporating legal principles such as proper rules of evidence and natural justice into the organisation's procedures.

There is no doubt that NYO needs a comprehensive and workable disciplinary system. Its business of providing financial advice makes it subject to specific rules relating to investment markets and professional conduct. NYO's employees will be subject to considerable temptation to infringe such rules, especially if they are paid by commission. The continuing investigations and reforms relating to the mis-selling of financial products in the UK illustrate this. It will be essential for NYO to be able to demonstrate to regulators and customers that they have in place an effective and robust system for dealing with transgressions.

A statutory disciplinary procedure exists within the UK. This includes a requirement for careful investigation of any disciplinary incident and gives any work person the right to be accompanied by an advisor at any disciplinary meeting.

SECTION C

Question 5

Text references. Chapter 8 covers network analysis and Chapter 7 covers *Maylor's* model.

Top tips. *Maylor's* model is fairly memorable, but not essential here: you could discuss the typical project life cycle without using these headings at all. We have shown both activity-on-line and activity-on-node styles for the diagram. You need only do one in the exam! In part (c) we have written far more than you would need to for five marks. Use the material in the additional answer box for revision.

Easy marks. One of the essential features of project management is **control**. There will be marks available for simple ideas such as initial project authorisation and tidying up loose ends at the completion stage as well as for the obvious specialised techniques used in the execution phase.

(a) **Activity-on-line style**

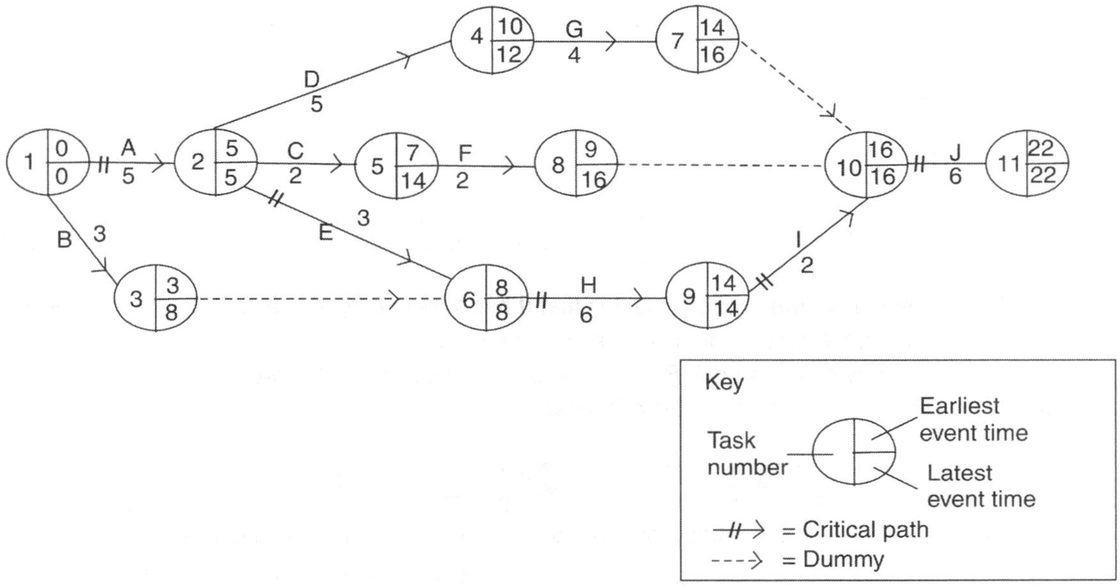

The critical path is AEHIJ, and the minimum total duration is 22 weeks.

Activity-on-node style

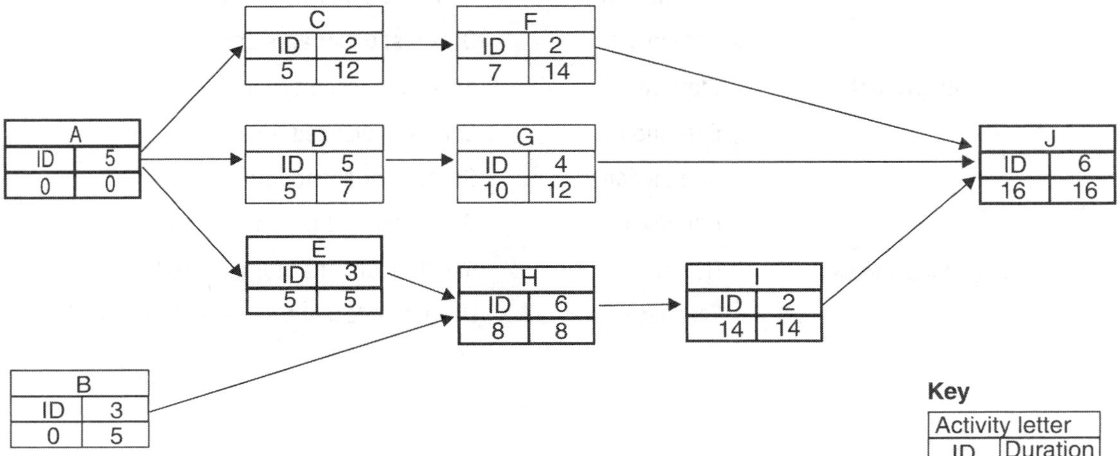

ACFJ	15
ADGJ	20
AEHIJ	22
BHIJ	17

(b) To construct a Gantt chart we need to list all possible paths through the network.

A E H I J
A D G J
A C F J
B H I J

Then using the critical path as the basis, we can construct the Gantt chart as follows.

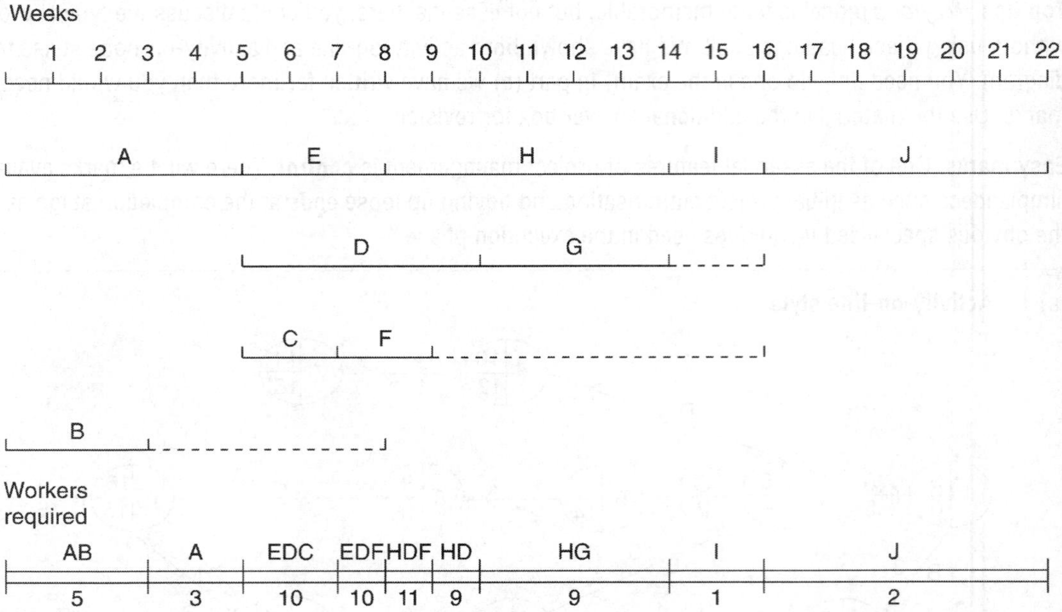

(c) **Part of the accepted definition of a project is that it has a beginning and an end**; the term 'project life cycle' simply means the succession of stages or processes the project moves through on its progress from one to the other. *Maylor*, in his book *Project Management*, tells us that the projects can be thought of as having four phases or stages: this is the **4-D model**.

Stage in project life cycle	Component	Activities
Define the project	Conceptualisation	Produce a clear and definitive statement of needs
	Analysis	Identify what has to be done and check its feasibility
Design the project	Planning	Show how the needs will be met
	Justification	Compute costs and benefits
	Agreement	Obtain sponsor agreement
Deliver the project	Start up	Assemble resources and people
(Do it!)	Execution	Carry out planned project activities
	Completion	Success or abandonment
	Handover	Output passed to sponsor/user
Develop the process	Review	Identify outcomes for all stakeholders
	Feedback	Document lessons and improvements for future use

Additional answer

Define the project

Projects start when someone becomes aware of the need for one. Larger projects are likely to involve the creation of a **project brief** or **terms of reference** for discussion. A **project initiation document** may be prepared.

Design the project

There are several aspects to detailed project planning. *Maylor* categorises the various techniques used for scheduling, such as network analysis and Gantt charts as **time planning**. He also deals with the need to plan for **cost**, **quality** and **risk**.

Deliver the project

This is the operational phase of the project. Planning will continue as required in order to control agreed changes and to deal with unforeseen circumstances, but the main emphasis is on getting the work done.

There are several important themes.

(a) **Management and leadership**: people management assumes a greater importance as the size of the project work force increases.

(b) **Control**: time, cost and quality must be kept under control , as must the tendency for changes to proliferate.

(c) **Supply chain**: all the aspects of logistic management must be implemented, especially with projects involving significant physical output.

(d) **Problems and decisions**: problems are bound to arise and must be solved sensibly and expeditiously. Complex problems will require careful analysis using the scientific tools of decision theory.

Develop the process

Because project management is episodic in nature, it is difficult to improve. The lack of continuous operation means that the skills and experience developed during a project are likely to fragment and atrophy after it is complete. This is especially true of organisations that do not have many projects or manage them on an *ad hoc* basis. The completion and review phase involves a number of important but often neglected activities.

(a) **Completion**. All activities must be properly and promptly finished.

(b) **Documentation** must be completed.

(c) **Project systems** must be closed down. In particular, the project accounts and any special accounting systems must remain in operation and under control until all costs have been posted but must then be closed down to avoid improper posting.

(d) **Immediate review** is required to provide staff with immediate feedback on performance.

A thorough review is the organisation's opportunity to make significant improvements in how it manages its projects: appropriate quantities of management time and attention must be allocated to the review process and to the assimilation of its results and recommendations. Longer-term review is useful for the consideration of **lifetime costs**; which should be the eventual criterion for project success.

Question 6

Text references. Chapter 10.

Top tips. The examiner has been quite careful in his choice of organisation for this question. Clearly, the fans of the club will expect that their interest and loyalty will be reciprocated. They are more than customers but their continuing adherence to the club cannot be taken for granted. Spend some time before you launch into the answer on jotting down the classes of stakeholder and where the parties in the scenario fall into these classes. In part (b), there is not necessarily a correct answer. It will be possible for you to sit on the fence or choose one particular group. However, you *must* substantiate your position.

Easy marks. This question is a good example of the very common type in which part (a) is simple and part (b) requires a little more judgement. However, even in part (b), identifying the most important stakeholders should be quite easy.

(a) **Stakeholder groups of SFC and their interests in the club**

Any organisation has many stakeholders and all have their own views on what they are entitled to expect from the organisation. *Freeman* defines stakeholders as 'any group or individual who can affect, or is affected by, the performance of an organisation'.

Stakeholders may be classified as falling into one of three categories. These include:

(i) **internal stakeholders** such as employees and managers
(ii) **external stakeholders** which include pressure groups, government and the community
(iii) **connected stakeholders** like shareholders, providers of finance, customers and suppliers.

Internal stakeholders of the Supreme Football Club (SFC) include the club's directors, the club manager, the players, the ground staff and other employees such as those employed in sales, marketing, finance and administration.

For internal stakeholders the relationship with the club is likely to be strong and long term. Both management and employees look to the club for their livelihood, for career development, for the opportunity to achieve something, for status and to associate with others.

(i) As well as guiding the affairs of the club, the **directors are often major shareholders** with a financial interest in its success.

(ii) The **players are key stakeholders because** the club provides both their incomes and their careers.

(iii) **Managers and other employees will have a financial interest in the club** and also have individual interests and goals such as:

(1) Security and increases of income
(2) A safe and comfortable working environment
(3) A sense of community
(4) Career development
(5) A sense of doing something worthwhile

Connected stakeholders include **shareholders, sponsors, bankers, fans and their parents and suppliers**. Like internal stakeholders, the relationship with the organisation may also be long term and strong but it is different. Shareholders, bankers, fans and other customers and suppliers do not work directly for the club – although some may do as in the case of employees who hold shares – and so their concern is not with the day-to-day operations of the club as it is for the managers and employees.

(i) For the **shareholders** a major interest in the club is a return on their investment, but they are almost certainly also emotionally involved as fans.

(ii) **Sponsors** provide funds for football clubs as a way of showing their interest and also as a means of advertising. They are interested in the club because of the media interest when the team is successful.

(iii) **Bankers** who have provided loan finance will be interested in the club for both security on any loans granted and the interest they will receive.

(iv) **Fans** are customers and are interested in the club as a source of leisure interest and pleasure. Parents of younger fans are stakeholders as a result of their children's interest. As customers they buy the club's merchandise and have an interest in good quality products at reasonable prices.

(v) **Suppliers** are interested in additional orders from the club and payment for what they supply.

(vi) **The mass communication media** such as TV and radio companies, newspapers and magazines have a financial interest because football is a game of worldwide interest and attracts millions of viewers, listeners and readers. For satellite-broadcasting corporations with specific rights to film the games, this provides direct income from pay-to-view charges and indirect income from the advertising income attracted by a wider TV audience.

External stakeholder groups interested in the club **include the government, local authorities, the community at large and the governing bodies in football**.

(i) The **government and local authorities** have an interest because they tax receipts from the games and the club's merchandise. The government has a duty to see the club complies with various aspects of legislation including health and safety.

(ii) The **community at large** and especially those near the stadium are interested from the point of view of parking, pollution, crime and crowd problems.

(iii) The **football governing bodies are required** by their constitutions to regulate the game and see that it is not brought into disrepute.

(b) **Stakeholder influence**

All of the stakeholders will have an interest in the outcome of the bid for the club but **the ones that are likely to influence the outcome will be those directly involved in the negotiations**. These are the directors, the representatives of the satellite-broadcasting corporation and the football authority.

The **directors are the legal representatives of the shareholders of the club**. In many circumstances they will also be shareholders themselves. They have significant influence because they must recommend whether or not to accept a bid. The shareholders will determine whether or not the bid is accepted by voting in a ballot, but they are likely to follow the directors' advice.

The **representatives of the satellite-broadcasting corporation are able to exert influence by how much they are prepared to offer for the club**. As is often the case, the satellite company making the bid may not be the only interested party wanting to take over the club. There may be other companies waiting until negotiations start to find out how much is at stake; once this is known better offers might be placed before the directors. Until this happens they are not key stakeholders in the situation.

The football authorities that regulate competition in the industry will also influence the decision. They will wish to promote competition in the industry and avoid over-concentration of ownership.

Although they are not party to the negotiations, other stakeholders will have influence. The sponsors of the team may be direct competitors of the satellite broadcasting corporation or may not agree with the principles involved and decide not to continue with their contract when it comes up for renewal. The supporters may try to influence the decision by exploiting media interest.

Question 7

Text references. Chapter 7.

Top tips. This question wants you to write on project management, conflict, objectives and closely refer to the issues in the question. You will need to **plan** your answer carefully making sure you answer the specific requirements asked of you in (a)(i)-(iii) and (b).

Easy marks. The relationships the project manager must establish and maintain are basic aspects of your syllabus and you should have a good idea of the sort of interests that have to be dealt with. As ever, a mark is available for using the correct reporting format so don't waste it!

(a) **Memorandum**

MEMORANDUM

To: Senior Management Team
From: Management Accountant
Subject: The GPConnect (GPC) project

This memo outlines the nature of the GPC project in relation to two areas; the relationship of the project manager to key stakeholders and potential project management problems.

1 Project manager relationships

1.1 Project manager and project sponsor

Central government provides the funding for the GPC project, and is therefore the project sponsor. The project manager is employed by T, the company responsible for carrying out the GPC project.

Central government will be concerned with how the project impacts upon the achievement of long-term strategic objectives. They will be keen to ensure that the project is not seen to waste public resources, so the project manager will need to work with the sponsor to resolve potential conflict over project costs. The role of the central government in this project as a fund provider may also cause conflict between central government and the SRHA.

With regard to the day-today running of the project, it is unlikely that the project manager would have significant direct contact with central government, as project progress will be reported mainly to the project board.

1.2 Project manager and the project board

The project board is responsible for the overall running of the project and will be concerned with the achievement of management/business level objectives, in particular that the project improves business efficiency and effectiveness. The board is ultimately responsible for the achievement of the sponsors' targets. The board delegates authority to the project manager who is responsible for achieving objectives set by the board.

Regular, direct communication between the project manager and the project board is necessary, for example regular project milestone review meetings.

1.3 Project manager and medical and administrative users

The project manager is responsible for delivering a system that meets user requirements. User objectives in the GPC project would be for the system to facilitate effective patient care whilst minimising staff workload. Administrative and medical staff will be use the completed system to help them perform their day-to-day duties. Good communication between users and the project manager is essential to ensure user needs are understood – and to prevent unrealistic expectations.

The project manager should 'sell' the benefits of the new system to users, as, without user backing, the project is unlikely to succeed. The project manager is responsible for ensuring the system is designed to meet the needs of all users, as far as is practically possible within the project budget and schedule, and for planning user training.

1.4 Possibility of conflicting objectives

User/staff objectives will centre around the need to provide good quality patient care whilst minimising their workload. This may conflict with the objectives of the sponsor, whose primary concern is to achieve an improvement in the standard of service provided to patients – within budgeted cost levels. Central government and the project board are likely to be concerned with minimising costs, which could cause conflict with end users as this may impact upon the quality of system produced.

There is the potential for conflict between the sponsor and the project board over funding. Although a technology fund has been set up by the central government, this funding has not been easy to obtain, causing financial concerns for hospitals, medical centres and the SRHA. Some doctors have already expressed concern over resources being spent on the new system, rather than being committed directly to patient care.

The potential for conflict is further increased by central government allowing individual hospitals and medical centres to decide how they operate, rather than implementing a consistent policy.

(b) **Potential problems**

2 Project management problems

Allowing individual medical centres and hospitals to discuss individual terms of usage of the Healthweb is likely to cause problems for the project manager.

2.1 Aspects of the Healthweb utilised

Each site will have different connection preferences and needs, which could lead to a wide variety of different terms, options and patterns of usage. These options all need to be documented and implemented, which will consume project resources. Sites may wish to constantly amend their connection options, causing much time to be spent administering changes.

A consistent core approach across all sites would reduce the administration requirements of the Healthweb and allow control to be maintained more easily. A single consistent approach should also keep costs to a minimum. Allowing individual terms is also likely to lead to a less unified approach to the overall project, as sites concentrate on their own agendas.

2.2 Timing of connection

If hospitals and medical centres are able to negotiate their own terms this will prevent the project team controlling the timing of connection of sites. The project manager and team need the freedom to plan for a gradual phasing in of the Healthweb across sites. Allowing the timing of this process to be subject to the whims of individual hospitals/centres is likely to lead to excessive demands being placed upon the project team at certain times – and under utilisation of the team at other times.

2.3 Hardware and software costs/management

Allowing individual terms of connection is likely to prevent hardware and software being purchased centrally, causing the loss of any discounts available for large purchases. This will add significantly to project costs and is also likely to cause delays – and require greater co-ordination and monitoring to ensure no compatibility problems occur.

CIMA – Managerial Level

Paper P5

Integrated Management

Mock Examination 3 (November 2008)

Instructions to candidates:

You are allowed three hours to answer this question paper.
In the real exam, you are allowed 20 minutes reading time before the examination begins during which you should read the question paper, and if you wish, make annotations on the question paper. However, you will **not** be allowed, **under any circumstances**, to open the answer book and start writing or use your calculator during this reading time.
You are strongly advised to carefully read the question requirement before attempting the question concerned.
Answer the ONE compulsory question in Section A. This is comprised of sub-questions.
Answer ALL THREE compulsory questions in Section B.
Answer TWO of the three questions in Section C.

DO NOT OPEN THIS PAPER UNTIL YOU ARE READY TO START UNDER EXAMINATION CONDITIONS

SECTION A – 20 marks

Answer ALL NINE sub-questions

1.1 Which ONE of the following is an example of an 'intervening factor' that can encourage group effectiveness?

A Productivity of the group
B Motivation of the group
C Satisfaction of the group
D Task of the group **(2 marks)**

1.2 An organisation that seeks to maintain or increase share of an existing market with an existing product is following which ONE of the following strategies?

A Market development
B Diversification
C Market penetration
D Product development **(2 marks)**

1.3 The difference between the latest event time and the earliest event time in a project network analysis is referred to as:

A Critical activity
B Float
C Milestone
D Critical path **(2 marks)**

1.4 Which ONE of the nine Project Management Body of Knowledge areas involves project plan development, project plan execution and change control?

A Scope management
B Quality management
C Integration management
D Time management **(2 marks)**

1.5 Identify the analytical framework that is used in the process of strategic management to summarise the key issues arising from an assessment of the internal and external environments of an organisation.

(2 marks)

1.6 Describe briefly what is meant by the contingency approach to effective leadership.

(2 marks)

1.7 Kerzner describes a five level model of continuous organisational improvement in the methodology of project management. The final level is continuous improvement. Identify any TWO of the other levels.

(2 marks)

1.8 Identify THREE types of cost that need to be considered when undertaking the financial feasibility of a project.

(3 marks)

1.9 Explain briefly the concept of clan/cultural control. **(3 marks)**

(Total for Section A = 20 marks)

Section B – 30 marks

Answer All THREE questions – 10 marks each

Question 2

M Call Centre takes on outsourced work from a number of different organisations including financial service and telecommunication companies. Whilst the number of companies using M Call Centre is growing, it is facing some internal difficulties in coping with the new business due to high levels of labour turnover and staff absenteeism. Despite performance bonuses being paid, M Call Centre is finding it difficult to retain staff and labour turnover is much higher than the industry norm. A consultant has been brought in to investigate and help diagnose the problems facing M Call Centre.

The consultant has observed that the call centre operates within a system of tight controls and targets. Incoming calls are routed depending on the nature of the query. This means that a telephone operative answers only a narrow rage of queries. If a query is made that is outside an operative's area of responsibility, they have to re-route the call, since they have only been trained on answering specific queries related to their role. Those making outbound sales calls have a script that they must not deviate from.

Discussions the consultant has had with employees revealed that they feel that the working conditions in M Call Centre compare to those of a traditional factory assembly line. Telephone operatives feel that they are used as robots. They report that they are under pressure to keep call length with customers to a minimum time and that their conversations are listened to by their supervisors. Management has measured the time different calls should take to answer or make and imposes these times on staff.

The consultant's overall conclusion is that the scientific management approach to managing the call centre is unsuitable. She recommends that a more human relations approach should be adopted.

Required

With reference to M Call Centre, distinguish between the scientific management approach currently being used and the human relations approach being proposed by the management consultant.

(10 marks)

Question 3

P works for Z Co, whose business is commercial interior design. She is managing her first project which involves the refurbishment of a prime site office building. P is due to make her first report to Q, the project sponsor, but things are not going well, causing her to have sleepless nights worrying about the project. The refurbishment is overrunning on both time and budget and P cannot understand how the project has slipped so seriously without her realising. Keen to overcome the problems, P checks a recommended internet site on project management and finds the section on monitoring and control very helpful, particularly the section on progress reports.

Required

(a) Describe how the use of progress reports could help P. **(6 marks)**

(b) Identify the corrective action P could take to overcome the project slippage on time and budget. **(4 marks)**

(Total = 10 marks)

Question 4

Required

(a) Describe the role of each of the five basic building blocks which Mintzberg gives as the basis of his organisational structural configurations. **(5 marks)**

R is the owner/manager of X Company, which he set up just over 12 months ago. The company's main business is the development of computer based training packages and it currently employs 12 people.

(b) Recommend which of Mintzberg's structural configurations would be most appropriate for X Company, giving reasons for your choice. **(5 marks)**

(Total = 10 marks)

(Total for Section B = 30 marks)

SECTION C – 50 marks

Answer ANY TWO questions from this section – 25 marks each

Question 5

The Chief Executive of C Company, a chemical manufacturing company, has put a number of proposals to the Board on what the company can do to become more socially and environmentally responsible than simply complying with legislation. He wants to introduce a number of social and environmental objectives linked to reducing carbon emissions in production, improving on waste treatment, using more environmentally-friendly methods of waste disposal and recycling. He also wants to support the local community through financial donations and by seconding staff to provide help to local charities.

The proposals will require some investment in clean production technologies, buying environmentally friendly raw materials where possible, and reducing the use of business transport. The Chief Executive is also suggesting the company should have an eco-balance sheet which includes financial data on environmental costs.

The Chief Executive's interest in socially and environmentally responsible strategies is partly motivated by the media attention on the carbon footprint of companies such as C but is also driven by his personal beliefs. His view is that sustainability should be at the centre of all C Company's activities since it makes good business sense. He sees his proposals as 'win-win', but is facing strong opposition from the Finance Director, who is concerned about the costs and potential negative impact on financial performance and hence shareholder value.

Required

(a) Discuss the different viewpoints of the Chief Executive and the Finance Director on C Company becoming more socially and environmentally responsible. **(15 marks)**

(b) Explain the different research methods that could be used to collect information from staff to gain their ideas on the ways in which C Company could become more socially and environmentally responsible. **(10 marks)**

(Total = 25 marks)

Question 6

B Bakery is a family owned form with around 250 employees. It has been in business for over 50 years and supplies bread and confectionary products to a number of different businesses, including supermarkets and pub-chains. The firm has experienced mixed fortunes over the years in terms of business performance, but in the last few years has experienced a growth in orders for some of its new healthy product ranges. These products have been developed as a result of the Managing Director's wife's interest in healthy eating. However, the Bakery has recently lost some key accounts as a result of being unable to produce some of its products at a competitive price.

Six months ago, the first non-family Board member, CT, joined the company as Operations Director. CT is surprised to find that the firm does not have a mission statement or any formal planning process in place. He is even more concerned that the Bakery does not have any clear objectives or key performance indicators. In a recent conversation with the Managing Director, CT suggested that the Board should be more proactive and that adopting a more formal approach to planning would help better inform the future development and direction of the Bakery. He suggests that the Board should consider using the rational approach to strategic management.

He was rather surprised by the response from the Managing Director, who said that in his 30 years with the firm, it had grown and been successful despite the absence of formal plans. He commented that planning creates lots of analysis that does not result in action and he prefers strategies to emerge. His view is that planned and intended strategies often turn out to be invalid.

Required

(a) Distinguish between the views of the Managing Director and the Operations Director on how strategy occurs. **(17 marks)**

(b) State the arguments that the Operations Director could use to persuade the Managing Director of the benefits of having a formal strategic plan. **(8 marks)**

(Total = 25 marks)

Question 7

Currently, each department of S Company has its own IT support team but a decision has recently been taken to centralise IT support. The Head of IT has stated that the new IT centralised support centre will lead to an improvement in service. However, staff in the different departments are unconvinced of this, rather they see it as a cost cutting exercise and feel that the individual requirements for IT support will be compromised.

A project has been set up and resourced by the Head of IT, who has appointed F as Project Manager. F's brief is to implement the new IT centralised support service. Her project team is made up of both IT staff and staff representatives from the departments which will use the IT centralised support service.

A key part of the project is the development of a standardised set of working practices, but F is already facing resistance from members of the project team and from department heads. At a recent project meeting there was clearly tension and conflict between the IT staff from the different departments in agreeing new working practices. This appears to be due to the fact that currently each IT support team has its own way of doing things to meet the needs of different departments and each sees its approach as best practice. Departmental heads are also concerned that they have very different needs and through the standardisation process, these needs may not be met.

In addition, there is hostility since the centralisation project will result in the IT staff having to take on different roles with different working practices, and some may lose their jobs.

F is glad that she has recently been on a training course on managing conflict. She had not realised how soon she would need to make use of the skills she has learned.

Required

(a) Explain why F, as Project Manager, needs to be aware of the interests of stakeholders. Your answer should make reference to the different stakeholder groups for the IT centralised support service project. **(13 marks)**

(b) Advise F on the different strategies that can be used to handle conflict between the different stakeholders in the IT centralised support service project. **(12 marks)**

(Total = 25 marks)

(Total for Section C = 50 marks)

Answers

DO NOT TURN THIS PAGE UNTIL YOU HAVE COMPLETED THE MOCK EXAM

A plan of attack

First things first

You should spend the 20 minutes reading time doing the Section A questions. These are compulsory so it's worth getting stuck into these. If you have any spare reading time you should plan your answers to longer Section B questions and select your Section C questions. You mustn't spend more than 36 minutes doing the Section A questions. If you get stuck on a question, move on and come back to it later if you have time.

The next step

Section B is compulsory as well so these questions should be next. Question 2 deals with scientific management and contrasts this with the human relations approach.. Question 3 tests progress reports and project progress and Question 4 wants you to write about Mintzberg's structural configurations. These are all quite different areas of the syllabus, so there should be no confusion though you will need to switch quickly from topic to topic in the time given. Once again, make sure that you stick to the allocated time of 18 minutes on each Section B question. The first five marks of any question are usually the easiest and you must get all the easy marks! Don't lose out on these by spending too much time finishing off a question.

Section C

Make sure that you look at the requirements first and decide which questions you think you can answer. Then read through the scenario to make sure that you can answer your preferred questions based on the scenario given.

If you choose **Question 5** you must make sure that you write about the different viewpoints expressed in some detail. Also think about how information and views can be gleaned from the employees.

Question 6 tests two quite different views on strategy. Use the clues in the question to illustrate your answer.

Question 7 examines stakeholders and conflict. There is a lot to cover in this question and you could write a good couple of pages. So keep to the point or else you will run out of time.

No matter how many times we remind you...

Always, always **allocate your time** according to the marks for the question in total and for the parts of the questions. And always, always **follow the requirements exactly**.

You've got free time at the end of the exam.....?

If you have allocated your time properly then you **shouldn't have time on your hands** at the end of the exam. If you find yourself with five or ten minutes spare, however, go back to **any parts of questions that you didn't finish** because you ran out of time.

Forget about it!

And don't worry if you found the paper difficult. More then likely other students would too. If this were the real thing you would need to forget the exam the minute you leave the exam hall and think about the next one. Or, if it's the last one, celebrate!

SECTION A

Question 1

1.1 B This is a term used by *Charles Handy* to describe dimensions of group effectiveness.

1.2 C This is one of *Ansoff's* product-market strategies.

1.3 B Float time is the time available for unforeseen circumstances.

1.4 C

1.5 **SWOT** analysis is an analytical framework used to review the internal and external organisation environment given its mission and objectives. SWOT stands for strengths, weaknesses (both internal factors), opportunities and threats (external factors).

1.6 **Contingency theory** is based on the belief that there is no one best way of leading. Leaders need to interact with their teams in different ways in different situations. Effective leaders adapt their style to suit the task, team, culture and so on.

1.7 Common knowledge, common processes, singular methodology, benchmarking *[two only asked for]*.

1.8 Capital costs, finance costs and revenue costs.

1.9 **Clan control** is based on corporate culture. It depends on shared values and standards of behaviour within the organisation, and assumes that employees 'buy in' to the purpose, goals and expectations of the organisation.

SECTION B

Question 2

Text references. Chapter 1.

Top tips. The main points to bring out are the control and micromanagement inherent in scientific management which emphasises the **design of the job** and compare this with the human relations approach which considers the **social aspects** of work. You should mention Herzberg as it is clear in the question that hygiene factors and motivator factors are involved.

Easy marks. There is plenty of information in the question to refer to in illustrating your answer.

Scientific management

This is an approach to management based on principles which include the **scientific selection and progressive development of workers**, application **of techniques to measure and plan and control work** and **co-operation between management and workers**. A number of the key elements in the approach are evident at the Call Centre.

- The use of **work study techniques** to analyse tasks and establish the most efficient work methods. In the call centre, management has measured the length of time different calls should take and requires staff to go by these as guidelines.
- Jobs are **micro-designed**. Jobs are divided into single, simple tasks which are then combined to make a job for an individual worker. The worker cannot perform outside these task areas. At the call centre, workers can only answer calls within their area of responsibility and where they have been trained.
- Workers' **pay** is their only incentive. Pay is assumed to be the only important motivating force. The call centre has paid bonuses based on performance but, despite this, staff still leave and labour turnover is much higher than the industry norm.
- **Planning work is separate from doing work**. Individual workers are not in control of planning their workload: this is done by the manager. Again the evidence for this is in the narrowness of the individual roles, with no discretion to act outside the role, a standard call length, pressure to keep calls to a minimum length of time and in fact supervisors oversee their work by listening in to their calls.

Comments made by the workers convey their unhappiness: being treated as robots, and feeling like they are working on a traditional factory assembly line. This is typical of the problems created by the scientific management approach to organising work.

Human relations approach

The human relations approach emphasises **employee motivation and task commitment.**

A study of production line workers and their output (the Hawthorne study) led *Elton Mayo* to conclude that **worker attitudes and group relationships** had a greater impact on productivity than technical and workplace environmental factors.

In fact groups were very influential and could impose their behavioural norms on members so that these affected behaviour including productivity.

Mayo also concluded that **workers were motivated by social needs** as much as financial. The call centre workers' remarks about being used as robots and feeling that they are on a traditional assembly line hint at alienation and a longing for social interaction.

Herzberg developed the human relations approach and identified the **need for workers to feel challenge, responsibility and personal development in their job**.

The call centre workers **are challenged but in the wrong way**: their jobs are stressful because they are constantly monitored and not because they have discretion to take on responsibility.

Herzberg identified factors in the job that caused satisfaction or dissatisfaction. He called these factors **hygiene factors and motivator factors**.

Hygiene factors enable workers to avoid unpleasantness and these include salary and job security. There is a system of bonus payments at the call centre which would be a hygiene factor as it would go some way toward lessening dissatisfaction. However it is clear that it isn't entirely successful in this as there is still a high level of turnover in staff.

Motivators create job satisfaction and motivate a worker to superior performance. These include challenging work and gaining recognition. The roles of individuals could be redesigned to allow them more scope and discretion in their response to customers. They could be set targets based partly on using their own initiative and rewarded by recognition as much as pay. Promotion could be offered if it is possible to build this into the staff structure or at least some degree of responsibility could be designed into jobs.

Question 3

Text references. Chapter 8.

Top tips. In part (a) refer to how progress reports can aid monitoring both **time and cost**. In (b), we suggest writing about four options as there are four marks. The other possibilities mentioned in the Study Text are **to do nothing** – decide to leave things as they are and hope to improve anyway; **replan** where the project plan has become invalid; **reschedule** certain milestones or deliverables without changing the entire plan.

Easy marks. Part (b) can be answered using your knowledge of project slippage from the Study text. Just remember to refer to examples in the question to get extra marks.

(a) **Progress report**

A progress report shows **the current status of a project,** usually in relation to the planned status. The report is **a control tool** intended to highlight the discrepancies between where the project is and where the plan says it should be. A common form of progress report shows the planned time and expenditure alongside the actual time and expenditure.

P could **draft a progress report** to show the planned timetable for the refurbishment and alongside this, the actual progress at each stage by way of comparison. So weekly or monthly resource reports would show where the project was over-running on budget. P could also understand the reasons for overruns and assess any risks arising out of the project running late and over budget. The report could also have a budget for the refurbishment project broken down into stages and the actual monies spent so far at each stage.

A **milestone slip chart** may be included in a progress report to compare the actual and planned progress toward project milestones. A milestone is an event which is clearly identifiable as a measure of how far a project has progressed and how far it has to run.

P would need to decide what the milestones are for the project and use the slip chart as a means of breaking the project down into manageable stages.

Using a **progress report** will aid P in managing the project by alerting her to deadlines and the risk of cost overruns on a regular and timely basis before the project becomes unmanageable. It will allow her to take corrective action eg allocate more resources to something running behind schedule.

(b) **Overcoming project slippage**

P has a choice of what to do to overcome the slippage on time and budget.

She could add resources to the project. If there is a shortage of staff or resources, P could request that staff be drafted in to help make up lost time. Subcontractors could be used if in-house staff are unavailable. This would mean that costs would increase so would the budget be revised to reflect this?

Another option is to work smarter. It may be possible to use current resources more effectively and source cheaper but suitable materials. P may need to negotiate new work patterns and new supplier contracts if she chooses to do this. She may also have to pay to come out of existing contracts or **decide to remain in these if overall it works out cheaper**.

Staff incentives such as bonuses could be offered if P believes the team on the project could work quicker and more effectively to deadlines.

The project specification could be changed if P believes the original objectives of the project were unrealistic given the time and budget for the project. This option depends on how successfully P could renegotiate the original objectives of the project.

Question 4

Text references. Chapter 2.

Top tips. Part (a). This is a straight descriptive part-question. Use the material straight out of the Study Text. We call them components but they are also known as building blocks.

Part (b). Apply the information in the Study Text Chapter 2 to the five organisational configurations in the scenario. There is not a lot to go on but use the information given so: a young company, owner managed, in the software business and only 12 staff.

Easy marks. Part (a) is just writing down what you know about the building blocks.

(a) **Mintzberg's five building blocks**

Mintzberg suggests that all organisation structures have five **components** or **building blocks**. These are the strategic apex, middle line, operating core, technostructure and support staff.

The **strategic apex** ensures the organisation follows its mission and serves the needs of its key stakeholders. It acts as a force for direction in ensuring a shared vision and goals. It also manages the organisation's relationship with the environment.

The **middle line** conveys the goals set by the strategic apex down the organisation and plans and controls the work of the operating core toward these goals. So, the middle line is middle management.

The **operating core** is the people directly involved in the process of obtaining inputs and converting them into goods and services. These would be operations and production staff.

The **technostructure** is that part of the organisation which analyses, determines and standardises work processes, techniques, skills and outputs. The technostructure includes strategic planners and quality controllers.

The **support staff** are the ancillary and administrative services in the organisation. They are separate to operations and production.

(b) **Appropriate structural configuration for X Company**

X Company is a small company with twelve staff, and only a year old. It is run by an owner-manager and in the business of developing computer based training packages.

The **simple or entrepreneurial structure** is usually appropriate in small companies run by a single leader and is noted for a coherent sense of direction.

This organisational type has **informal relationships**, **flexibility** in relationships and **control comes from the strategic apex**. As the company is still **small** with **little need for layers of management** and closely associated with its founder this configuration would seem to suit it well. Its business is in computer development and this is a **fast-developing marketplace** which would benefit from **flexible** and **informal workplace communications** where decisions need to be made quickly. Any strategic decisions would need to be nimble and this too would suggest that a simple configuration with its strong sense of direction and clear leadership would be a good model.

SECTION C

Question 5

Text references. Chapters 6 and 10.

Top tips. In part (a) the question is asking you to contrast the two views. You do need to flesh this out with examples and state arguments for social and environmental responsibility to support the Chief Executive's stance. Remember to state any disadvantages of his approach too and any advantages of the Finance Director's view. This is not black and white so try to balance your discussion of each viewpoint.

In part (b) you can use material from Chapter 6 on information-gathering to answer the question.

Easy marks. Part (b) can be taken directly from the Study text and fleshed out with examples from the question.

(a) **Social and environmental responsibility**

The stakeholder view of organisations emphasises that many parties as well as the organisation have an interest in the performance and practices of an organisation.

Chief Executive

The Chief Executive (CEO) is **promoting social and environmental responsibility**. Modern business has increasingly adopted social responsibility goals which are non-financial objectives for the business. This partly reflects political and consumer pressure from certain stakeholders. There are good reasons why C Company should strive to be socially and environmentally responsible. The CEO could also be seen as taking a long-term view of the business.

The CEO also believes in the centrality of **sustainability** in the business. A **sustainable enterprise** is one whose competitive strategy does not fundamentally conflict with the long term needs and values of society.

Arguments in support of the CEO's viewpoint and for social and environmental responsibility:

(i) **Legal requirements on health and safety and environmental care** require organisations to comply with minimum standards or risk fines. C Company is a chemical manufacturing company which is likely to produce toxic or environmentally-harmful by-products. The Chief Executive wants to reduce carbon emissions, and improve waste treatment both of which should reduce the risk of non-compliance with standards.

(ii) **Recognising externalities** or the costs imposed on outsiders by the business, typically pollution by production processes affecting health and the environment. The Chief Executive recognises that there are externalities arising from his business **and wants to try to reduce them**. Hence he has implemented emissions reduction and improvements in waste treatment.

(iii) **Promoting the business as a good employer** which is aided by being seen as a socially responsible employer. The initiatives undertaken by way of improving the environmental impact of the business such as the environmentally friendly methods of waste disposal and recycling should make the business **more attractive to environmentally-conscious potential employees**. Similarly, the plans to support the local community can only be looked on positively by many of those looking at employment in the Company.

(iv) **The business is a social system** which depends on its society and community for access to resources. Where an organisation acknowledges its responsibility as part of the community it may find these resources come to it more easily as the community responds to it more positively. The initiatives to support local community activities may make the community see C Company more positively.

(v) **Many consumers** or purchases of C Company's chemicals nowadays are aware of and concerned about the environmental impact of business, the exploitation of workers, product safety and consumer rights. The Chief Executive is aware that the media pays attention to the carbon footprint of C Company and his proposals to lessen the negative environmental aspects of the business will be seen positively by those consumers who pay heed to the media.

(vi) **Investor relations**. He also intends to publish an eco-balance sheet which should bring the initiatives to the attention of a large investment audience who may choose to invest based on **the 'green' credentials of the business.**

However there are costs entailed in these plans. The Chief Executive is willing to invest in clean technologies, buy environmentally friendly materials where possible and reduce business transport. He is also proposing to make financial donations and second staff to local charities. These will have direct cost and opportunity cost effects. These may have a cost above that of the existing technologies and materials although the cost of 'green' materials may not necessarily be more than that of current materials. Employees may consider the company a less attractive employer if they can no longer use business transport and leave or use other means of transport with an environmental or cost impact.

Employees may **resist the withdrawal of business transport** as this will have a direct effect on them whereas they might be more positive about other measures that have little or no direct impact on them.

Finance Director (FD)

The FD's view is that while social and environmental responsibility are noble goals, **these goals must be congruent with all stakeholder needs and interests** where possible and certainly satisfy shareholder return on investment. The FD could be viewed as taking a short-term view of the business.

The Finance Director is right to be concerned about the costs of these initiatives. Adopting the initiatives will **cost the organisation more** than not adopting them **in the short term, especially the investment in clean production technologies**. However, he also needs to consider the **long term positive effects** of the organisation being seen as a 'green' organisation and one involved in its local community.

These positive effects are financial ones if buyers, retailers and end consumers are more willing to **buy the chemical products because of their green credentials**.

His job is a difficult one: he will need to persuade shareholders who expect a return on their investment that **the initiatives will bring benefits over time.** He could look at promoting sustainability as a measure of performance but how would he value the benefit the company brings toward the long term needs and values of society? Another possibility is adopting the eco-balance sheet as a positive measure of performance: yes these initiatives cost the business more but they also have non-financial benefits.

(b) **Research methods for staff attitudes**

There are a variety of techniques C Company could use to get staff ideas. These include surveys, questionnaires and interviews. The method chosen depends on a number of factors: cost of the survey, whether a range of views is wanted, the open-endedness of the responses wanted and the timescale for reporting the results. Consultants could be brought in to administer and design these research methods.

Surveys

Attitude surveys can be carried by interviewing staff individually or in groups or by using a questionnaire to get their views or attitudes. These can get an in-depth response and can be open ended if a range of ideas is wanted. They should also seek to extract information on attitudes so questions should be framed so that attitudes can be assessed. They can also be focused on particular issues so a series of statements could be presented and the respondent's agreement or disagreement asked for as in a Likert scale. The use of scales is quicker for collating responses than using interviews.

Questionnaires

These could be sent out to staff to be completed. These have advantages in that there is less bias than in an interview and they can be analysed quickly as they are uniform. They are also quite cheap to draw up and administer compared with interviews. However the questionnaire needs to be designed carefully to capture the required information and by its nature is not open ended so will not capture all possible responses. The response rate can be low for questionnaires so maybe an incentive such as a prize draw may encourage more responses from staff.

Interviews

These are intended to obtain in-depth information but can be time consuming, and so potentially costly. They need to be planned with the objectives of the interview in mind before the interview is conducted. During the interview, the interviewer must ask open questions designed to extract useful answers and listen carefully to the interviewee's responses. The interviewee must be allowed to speak freely and feel at ease. The key feature of interviews is their interactivity which means a better quality of information. Therefore the sample size could be smaller than using the survey or questionnaire format.

Question 6

Text references. Chapter 9 covers strategy and the approaches to making strategy.

Top tips. In part (a) use the clues in the question to pick up what you should be putting down for each Director's views. Words and phrases such as 'emerge' and 'more formal approach to planning' should be clear hints here! The action verb 'distinguish' is a lower level verb than the requirement in question 5 to 'discuss' and only asks you to **highlight differences** rather **than examine in detail by argument** which the latter verb requires you to do.

In part (b) you can answer using material straight out of the Study text and adding comments from the scenario.

Easy marks. Part (b) asks for arguments for formal planning which you can answer straight out of the Study Text.

(a) **Views on strategy**

Managing Director

The Managing Director prefers strategies that 'emerge' to those that are planned. **Emergent strategies develop out of patterns of behaviour**. They are unconscious patterns which eventually have long-tem strategic effects. However they do need to be grasped by management and used for the benefit of the organisation. So adhoc responses can be turned into strategies in time if they are successful. They are also **flexible** and **reactive** rather than **proactive**.

Mintzberg refers to **crafting strategies**. If an emergent strategy works, it is developed into a successful strategy by a gradual process of acting on and refinement of the strategy.

The growth of the healthy eating ranges developed as a result of the interest in healthy eating by the MD's wife is a good example of an **emergent strategy**. The move into healthy eating products was not planned ahead but just happened or emerged as B Bakery moved into this market and was then 'grasped' upon as a good move and **crafted** into a product range.

The bakery has also lost business from expensive products and had mixed fortunes over time. This failure can happen with rational strategies too as no amount of planning can entirely predict what is going to happen in a business. However it does hint at a lack of planning and control over what happens as the bakery must have had forewarning about the potential loss of contracts.

Operations Director

The operations Director clearly prefers the **rational planning approach**. The rational planning approach has three stages: strategic analysis, strategic choice and strategic implementation. The model represents a planned approach to strategy development. This approach is typically rigid, strategies feed down in a top-down approach and can be too **linear**.

Strategic analysis involves a review of the environment, and internal resources and then the firm draws up its mission and sets goals. The reviews come together as a corporate appraisal taking into account the mission and goals of the organisation. **Strategic choice** then takes place and a variety of strategies are tested for feasibility, suitability and acceptability to stakeholders.

A **suitable strategy is chosen** which is then embodied in a corporate plan and **implemented** by being cascaded down the levels of the organisation as corporate, business and operational strategies.

The Operations Director clearly adheres to this approach as he is surprised that there is no mission statement or formal planning process in the bakery. He believes by adopting the rational approach to strategy the bakery will be able to plan ahead and this will benefit the future development and direction of the bakery. He also expresses concern that there are no clear objectives or key performance indicators in place.

The bakery **may well benefit from planning** if this would avoid the mixed fortunes and loss of business that it has experienced in recent years.

However **the business environment is unpredictable** so that even a detailed plan may come unstuck if an unpredictable occurrence occurs. The failure of world wheat harvests, say, could lead to large price increases in the cost of flour.

The bakery is a relatively small business and may not be able to justify the cost and time needed for detailed strategic planning anyway.

(b) **Arguments for having a formal strategic plan**

There are some advantages in having a formal strategic plan:

(i) It helps the **organisation adopt a long-term view** and thus avoid staying focused on the short-term. This would help the bakery, particularly where it has recently lost business, to make some plans to replace the lost business.

(ii) It also allows **the organisation to focus on future uncertainty** and make some attempt to provide for this in its planning process.

(iii) It **guides the allocation of resources**. The success of the healthy eating products should mean that resources are allocated here but the Board should also think about how to redeploy resources affected by the recent loss of the key accounts.

(iv) It **co-ordinates the activities of the parts of the organisation** so operational goals are integrated with those higher up and the need for successful strategy lower down the organisation is recognised.

(v) The bakery might then recognise **the importance of employees** in the success of its business as it is possible that it has tended to rely on the bright ideas emerging from the Board and emergent strategies.

(vi) It **sets a benchmark for measuring success** in the organisation. There is a need for the bakery to assess performance in some way although it has clearly grown over time. How it does this at present is unclear.

(vii) It **reassures banks and other lenders that there is a plan in place** for the organisation. The bakery would benefit from showing evidence of planning as it has recently lost business which may concern any lenders to the business.

(viii) It **also reassures other stakeholders** including employees who may be comforted by seeing long-term plans for their employer.

Question 7

Text references. Chapters 5, 7 and 10.

Top tips. Read the question carefully as there is a lot of information that needs to be referred to in your answer.

In part(a) remember to include all stakeholders in your discussion: there are at least three main stakeholders interested in the project. Be clear about why their interests are important: what can happen if they are unhappy with the project aims?

In part (b) you can range fairly widely on strategies for handling conflict. There are examples in Chapter 5 but you can think of some others to suit the circumstances of the project. Can conflict be a good thing? Are the stakeholders entirely justified in their response to the project plans?

Easy marks. A few marks should be available for suggesting strategies for handling conflict.

(a) **Stakeholder interests**

Stakeholders are the individuals or organisations who are involved in or may be affected by project activities. **The success of the project depends on their commitment toward a common goal: the project aim.**

The IT staff and the IT user departments are two groups of stakeholders represented on the project team. **The project has a direct and significant impact on their roles and working conditions.**

A third stakeholder will be the Head of IT and possibly the Board, represented by F as the project manager. **They will be keen to see the project completed successfully.**

So all of these stakeholders have an interest in the outcome of the project but it affects them in different ways. They have different roles, points of view and conflicting objectives.

The IT staff are unhappy about the plans to centralise their function and standardise their working practices. The see the plans as a cost cutting exercise which ignores local expertise or 'best practice' and the individual IT needs of their user departments. Some IT staff may also lose their jobs and their roles will change. They have already argued about new working practices and are probably not committed to the project because of the insecurity that it brings to their roles and jobs.

The users of IT are concerned that the standardisation of the IT service will not cater for their individual IT needs. F needs to listen to their concerns to ensure any that are valid are addressed.

The impact of the project on stakeholders has already led to tension and conflict at an earlier project meeting where IT staff clashed over agreeing new working practices. So F will need to manage this conflict.

Therefore F needs to manage stakeholder expectations and perceptions. The existing conflict must be dealt with before it endangers the success of the project. It is possible that more disagreements may arise and F must be ready to deal with these too.

(b) **Handling stakeholder conflict**

F needs to deal with the disagreements already aired before they escalate. She may also uncover new disagreements that have developed since the last project meeting.

There are a range of strategies that may be used to handle conflict between stakeholders.

However, F needs to decide how much of the conflict expressed is a bad thing for the project. Some conflict is constructive as it airs views and emotions that need to be brought out and dealt with. Conflict can also lead to better ideas as it questions established practices. So **F needs to ensure that the conflict isn't buried or ignored** but allowed to be expressed in a constructive manner at the next project meeting.

Perhaps the standardisation and centralisation of the IT function is a bad idea. The IT staff and their users are unhappy with the proposals for standardising the way IT services are delivered. By **listening to the project group's objections**, a superior structure for delivering the IT service can be developed especially as both provider and user are involved in the project process.

However, F still needs to ensure the views of the Head of IT and the organisation are taken into account and they clearly want a standardised and centralised IT function.

So F can look **at negotiation** as a way of settling the disagreements. The IT staff, users and F or a representative of the Head of IT would discuss their disagreements with a view to finding a mutually acceptable compromise. A neutral **arbitrator** could be brought in to intervene in the discussion and get the stakeholders to come to an agreement.

Stakeholders **should be encouraged to be honest about their reasons for being unhappy with the project** and express these at the next project meeting.

The IT staff would have to consider honestly how much of their objections lie in having to give up the entrenched power that they hold at present in their decentralised structure. How much of their objection to standardisation is fear of change, genuine concern over a 'one size fits all' solution or exposure of less than ideal working practices.

Concerns over redundancies must be directly addressed with up front **communication** between management and the staff involved. It is important that F is able to explain the need for the change and the benefits it will bring.

The users need to state their requirements as users exactly so that these are included in the project specification for the new IT service. They must think about how far they are willing to concede non-essential services and whether it is realistic to expect a 'bespoke' service from a dedicated IT department.

IT staff could also consider **trying out roles in other IT departments** so that they get to know how other IT staff work and barriers are broken down. This would help break down some of the preconceptions about work practices. Management could also **consult** with the IT staff in their restructuring plans when they come to draw up the new IT roles so that their views are represented and also when they start to make decisions on redundancies.

Review Form & Free Prize Draw - Paper P5 Integrated Management (1/09)

All original review forms from the entire BPP range, completed with genuine comments, will be entered into one of two draws on 31 July 2009 and 31 January 2010. The names on the first four forms picked out on each occasion will be sent a cheque for £50.

Name: ______________________ **Address:** ______________________

____

____

How have you used this Kit?
(Tick one box only)

☐ Home study (book only)
☐ On a course: college ______________
☐ With 'correspondence' package
☐ Other ______________

Why did you decide to purchase this Kit?
(Tick one box only)

☐ Have used the complementary Study text
☐ Have used other BPP products in the past
☐ Recommendation by friend/colleague
☐ Recommendation by a lecturer at college
☐ Saw advertising
☐ Other ______________

During the past six months do you recall seeing/receiving any of the following?
(Tick as many boxes as are relevant)

☐ Our advertisement in *Financial Management*
☐ Our advertisement in *Pass*
☐ Our advertisement in *PQ*
☐ Our brochure with a letter through the post
☐ Our website www.bpp.com

Which (if any) aspects of our advertising do you find useful?
(Tick as many boxes as are relevant)

☐ Prices and publication dates of new editions
☐ Information on product content
☐ Facility to order books off-the-page
☐ None of the above

Which BPP products have you used?

Text	☐	*Success CD*	☐	*Learn Online*	☐
Kit	☑	*i-Learn*	☐	*Home Study Package*	☐
Passcard	☐	*i-Pass*	☐	*Home Study PLUS*	☐

Your ratings, comments and suggestions would be appreciated on the following areas.

	Very useful	*Useful*	*Not useful*
Passing CIMA exams	☐	☐	☐
Passing P9	☐	☐	☐
Planning your question practice	☐	☐	☐
Questions	☐	☐	☐
Top Tips etc in answers	☐	☐	☐
Content and structure of answers	☐	☐	☐
'Plan of attack' in mock exams	☐	☐	☐
Mock exam answers	☐	☐	☐

Overall opinion of this Kit *Excellent* ☐ *Good* ☐ *Adequate* ☐ *Poor* ☐

Do you intend to continue using BPP products? *Yes* ☐ *No* ☐

The BPP author of this edition can be e-mailed at: helendarch@bpp.com

Please return this form to: Nick Weller, CIMA Publishing Manager, BPP Learning Media Ltd, FREEPOST, London, W12 8BR

Review Form & Free Prize Draw (continued)

TELL US WHAT YOU THINK

Please note any further comments and suggestions/errors below.

Free Prize Draw Rules

1 Closing date for 31 July 2009 draw is 30 June 2009. Closing date for 31 January 2010 draw is 31 December 2009.

2 Restricted to entries with UK and Eire addresses only. BPP employees, their families and business associates are excluded.

3 No purchase necessary. Entry forms are available upon request from BPP Learning Media Ltd. No more than one entry per title, per person. Draw restricted to persons aged 16 and over.

4 Winners will be notified by post and receive their cheques not later than 6 weeks after the relevant draw date.

5 The decision of the promoter in all matters is final and binding. No correspondence will be entered into.